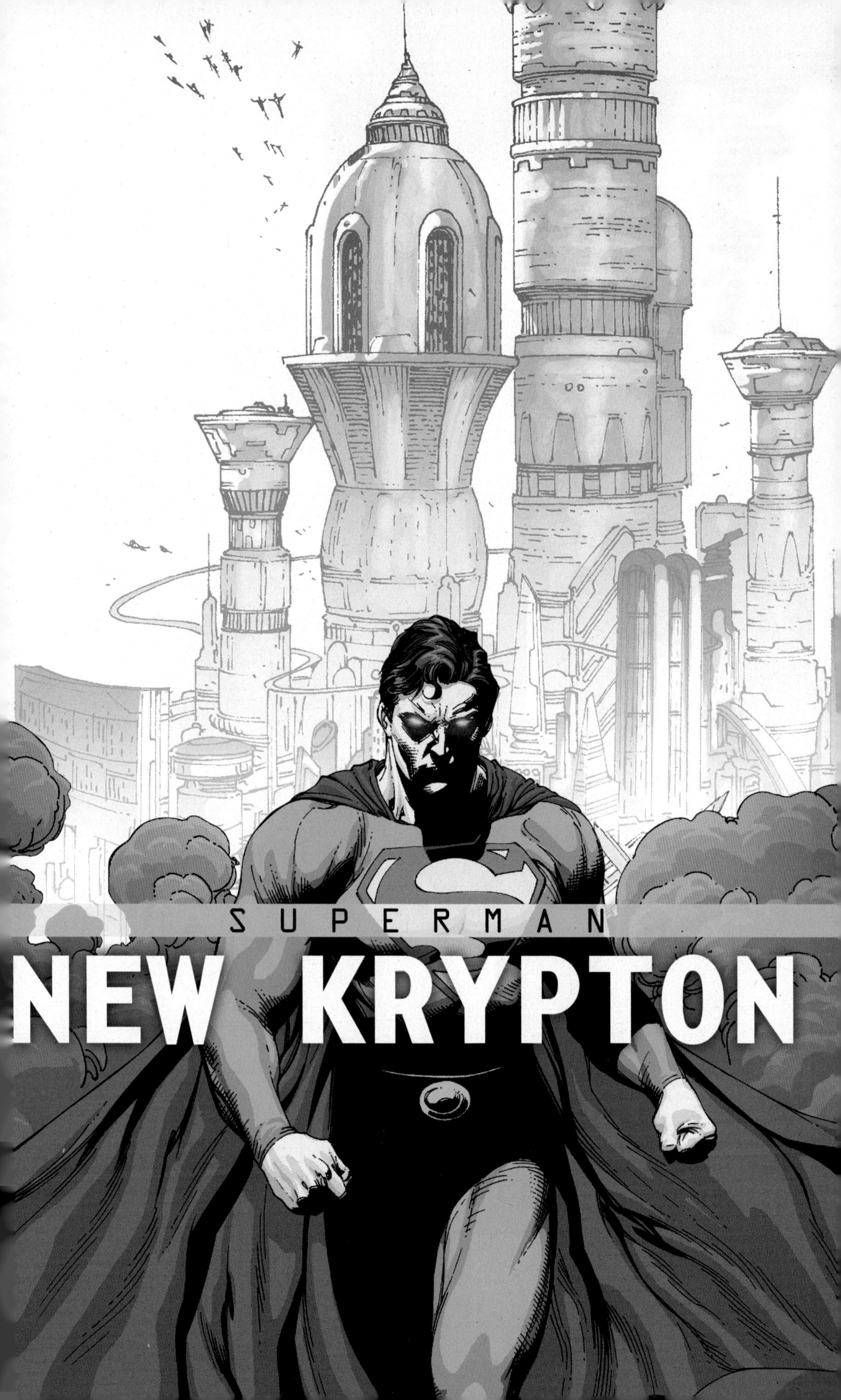
SUPERMAN
NEW KRYPTON

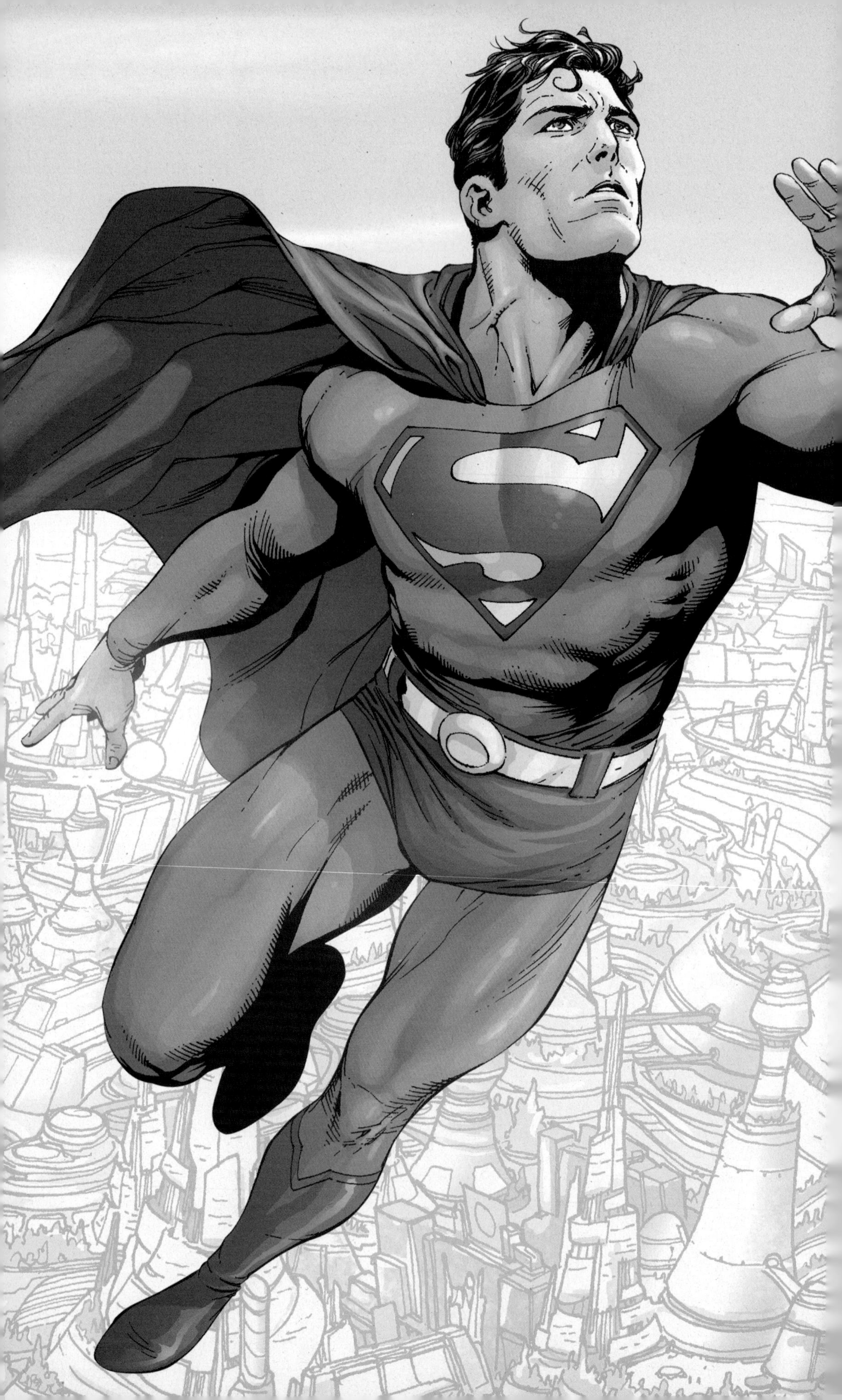

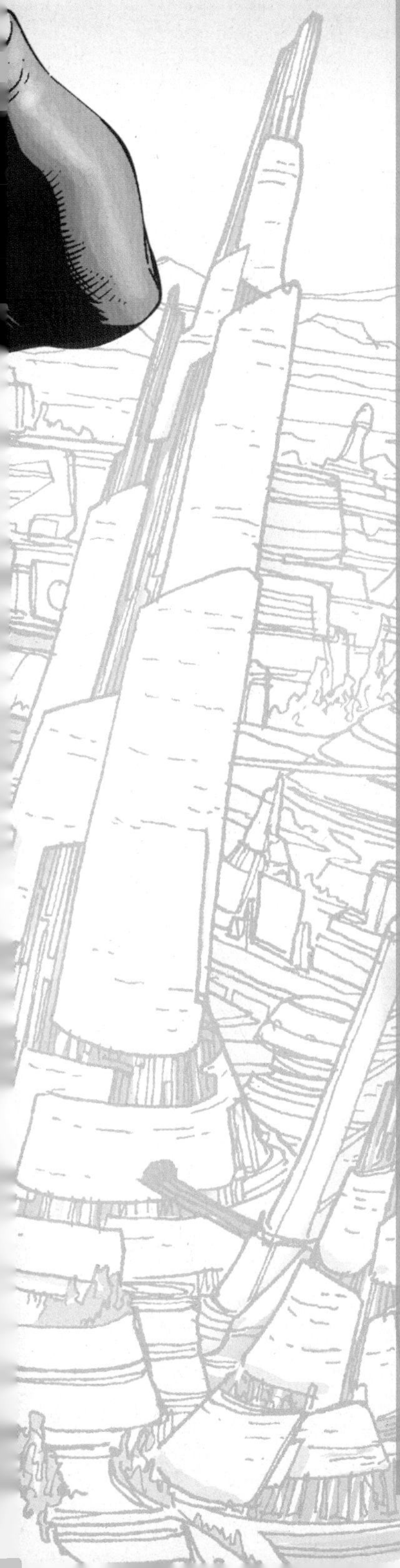

SUPERMAN

NEW KRYPTON

VOLUME **ONE**

//FROM A CUB TO A WOLF

JAMES ROBINSON<WRITER>
JESUS MERINO//LENO CARVALHO//STEVE SCOTT
<PENCILLERS>
JESUS MERINO//NELSON PEREIRA//KEVIN STOKES
<INKERS>
LEE LOUGHRIDGE<COLORIST>
SAL CIPRIANO<LETTERER>

//THE WORST NIGHT OF HIS LIFE

JAMES ROBINSON<WRITER>
PERE PÉREZ<ARTIST>
DAVID BARON<COLORIST>
JOHN J. HILL<LETTERER>

//NEW KRYPTON

GEOFF JOHNS//JAMES ROBINSON//STERLING GATES
<WRITERS>
PETE WOODS//GARY FRANK//RENATO GUEDES
<PENCILLERS>
PETE WOODS//JON SIBAL//JOSÉ WILSON MAGALHÃES
<INKERS>
HI-FI<COLORIST>
STEVE WANDS<LETTERER>

//STRANGE MEETINGS AND CHANCE ENCOUNTERS

JAMES ROBINSON<WRITER>
RENATO GUEDES<PENCILLER>
JOSÉ WILSON MAGALHÃES<INKER>
DAVID CURIEL<COLORIST>
JOHN J. HILL<LETTERER>

//BEYOND DOOMSDAY

GEOFF JOHNS<WRITER>
PETE WOODS<ARTIST>
BRAD ANDERSON<COLORIST>
ROB LEIGH<LETTERER>

<SUPERMAN>**CREATED BY JERRY SIEGEL AND JOE SHUSTER**

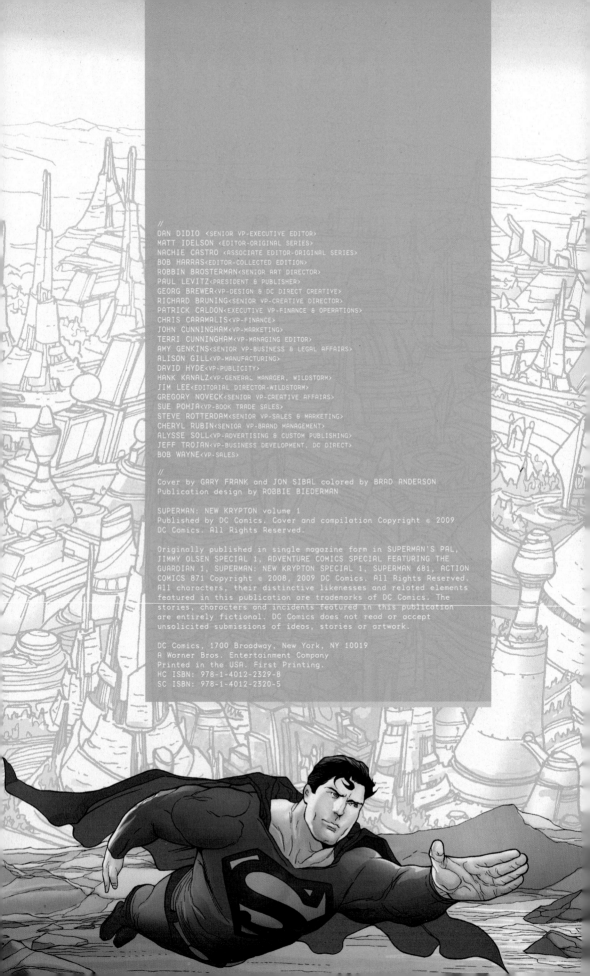

//
DAN DIDIO <SENIOR VP-EXECUTIVE EDITOR>
MATT IDELSON <EDITOR-ORIGINAL SERIES>
NACHIE CASTRO <ASSOCIATE EDITOR-ORIGINAL SERIES>
BOB HARRAS<EDITOR-COLLECTED EDITION>
ROBBIN BROSTERMAN<SENIOR ART DIRECTOR>
PAUL LEVITZ<PRESIDENT & PUBLISHER>
GEORG BREWER<VP-DESIGN & DC DIRECT CREATIVE>
RICHARD BRUNING<SENIOR VP-CREATIVE DIRECTOR>
PATRICK CALDON<EXECUTIVE VP-FINANCE & OPERATIONS>
CHRIS CARAMALIS <VP-FINANCE>
JOHN CUNNINGHAM<VP-MARKETING>
TERRI CUNNINGHAM<VP-MANAGING EDITOR>
AMY GENKINS<SENIOR VP-BUSINESS & LEGAL AFFAIRS>
ALISON GILL <VP-MANUFACTURING>
DAVID HYDE<VP-PUBLICITY>
HANK KANALZ<VP-GENERAL MANAGER, WILDSTORM>
JIM LEE<EDITORIAL DIRECTOR-WILDSTORM>
GREGORY NOVECK<SENIOR VP-CREATIVE AFFAIRS>
SUE POHJA<VP-BOOK TRADE SALES>
STEVE ROTTERDAM<SENIOR VP-SALES & MARKETING>
CHERYL RUBIN<SENIOR VP-BRAND MANAGEMENT>
ALYSSE SOLL<VP-ADVERTISING & CUSTOM PUBLISHING>
JEFF TROJAN<VP-BUSINESS DEVELOPMENT, DC DIRECT>
BOB WAYNE<VP-SALES>

//
Cover by GARY FRANK and JON SIBAL colored by BRAD ANDERSON
Publication design by ROBBIE BIEDERMAN

SUPERMAN: NEW KRYPTON volume 1
Published by DC Comics. Cover and compilation Copyright © 2009
DC Comics. All Rights Reserved.

Originally published in single magazine form in SUPERMAN'S PAL,
JIMMY OLSEN SPECIAL 1, ADVENTURE COMICS SPECIAL FEATURING THE
GUARDIAN 1, SUPERMAN: NEW KRYPTON SPECIAL 1, SUPERMAN 681, ACTION
COMICS 871 Copyright © 2008, 2009 DC Comics. All Rights Reserved.
All characters, their distinctive likenesses and related elements
featured in this publication are trademarks of DC Comics. The
stories, characters and incidents featured in this publication
are entirely fictional. DC Comics does not read or accept
unsolicited submissions of ideas, stories or artwork.

DC Comics, 1700 Broadway, New York, NY 10019
A Warner Bros. Entertainment Company
Printed in the USA. First Printing.
HC ISBN: 978-1-4012-2329-8
SC ISBN: 978-1-4012-2320-5

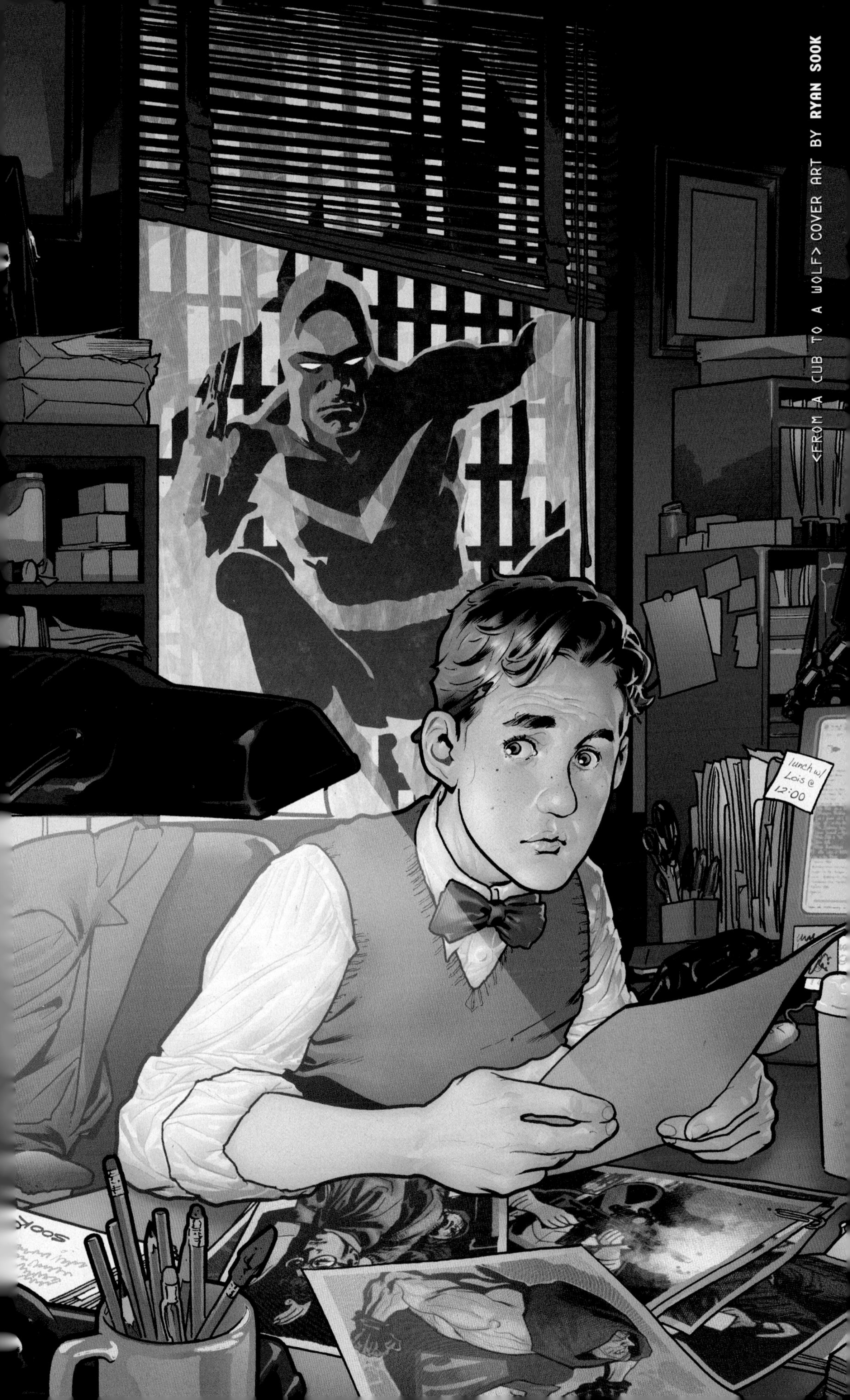
lunch w/
Lois @
12:00

<FROM A CUB TO A WOLF> COVER ART BY **RYAN SOOK**

<VARIANT> COVER ART BY **KEVIN NOWLAN** COLORED BY **DAVE STEWAR**

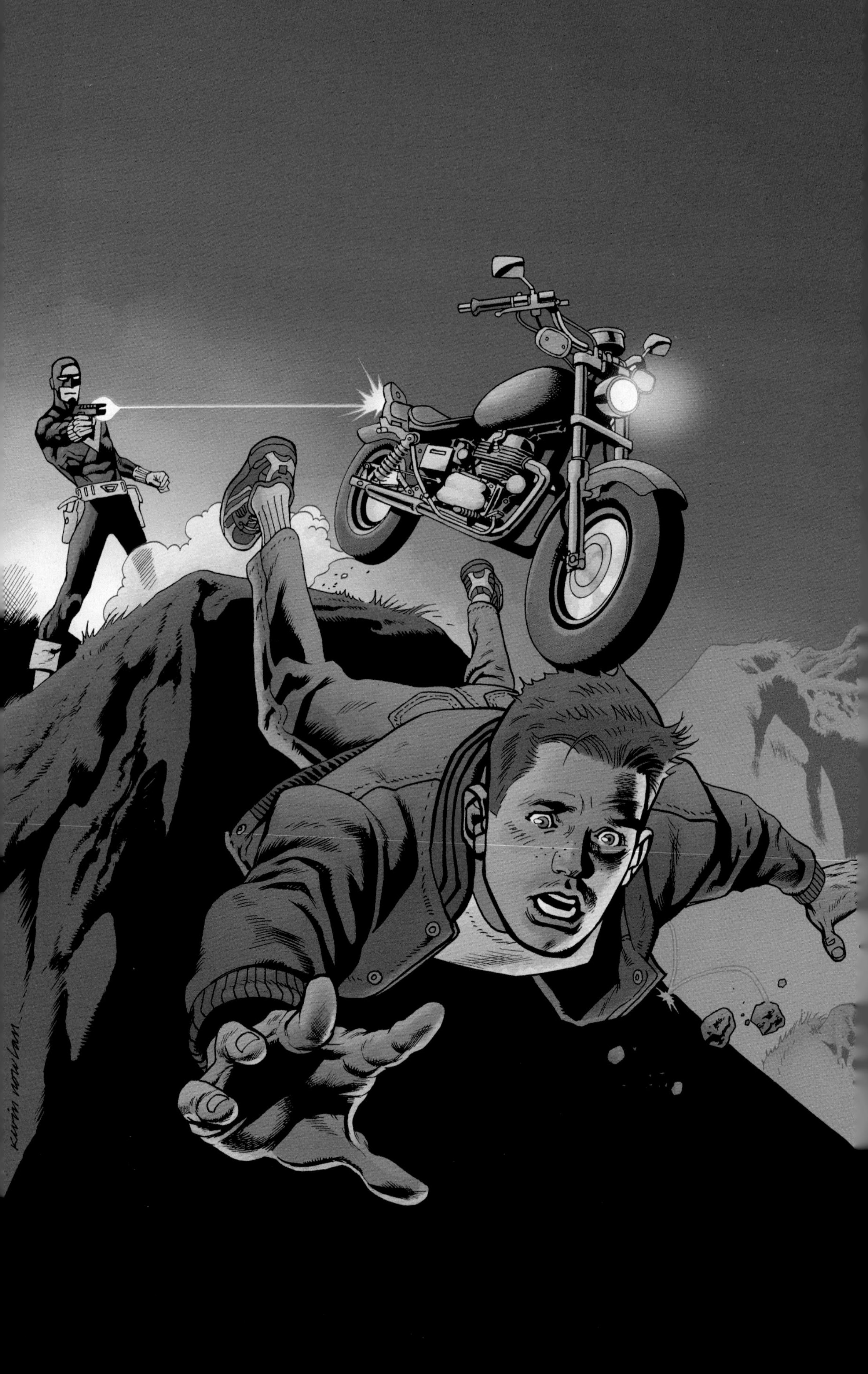

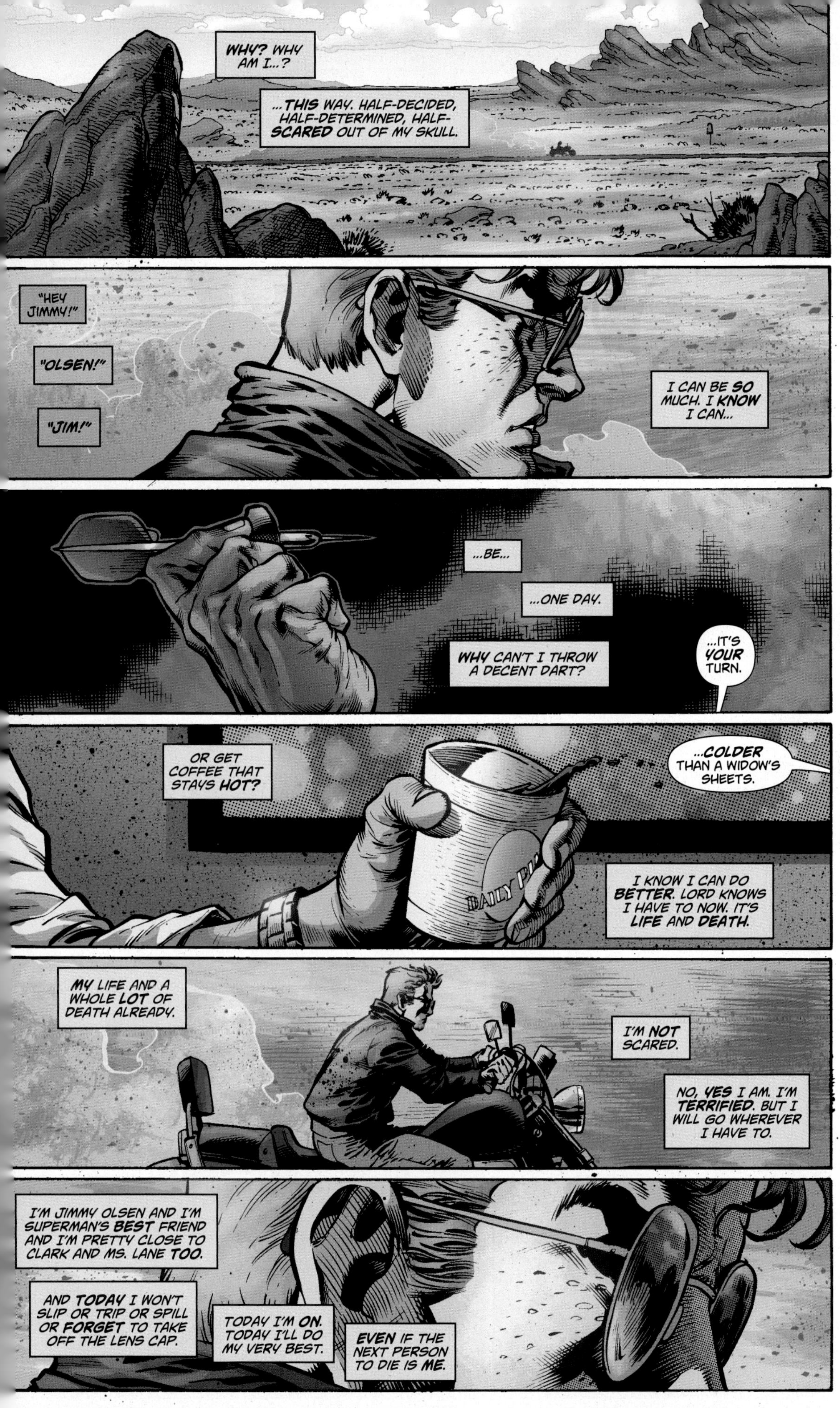

WHY? WHY AM I...?
...THIS WAY. HALF-DECIDED, HALF-DETERMINED, HALF-SCARED OUT OF MY SKULL.
"HEY JIMMY!"
"OLSEN!"
"JIM!"
I CAN BE SO MUCH. I KNOW I CAN...
...BE...
...ONE DAY.
WHY CAN'T I THROW A DECENT DART?
...IT'S YOUR TURN.
OR GET COFFEE THAT STAYS HOT?
...COLDER THAN A WIDOW'S SHEETS.
I KNOW I CAN DO BETTER. LORD KNOWS I HAVE TO NOW. IT'S LIFE AND DEATH.
MY LIFE AND A WHOLE LOT OF DEATH ALREADY.
I'M NOT SCARED.
NO, YES I AM. I'M TERRIFIED. BUT I WILL GO WHEREVER I HAVE TO.
I'M JIMMY OLSEN AND I'M SUPERMAN'S BEST FRIEND AND I'M PRETTY CLOSE TO CLARK AND MS. LANE TOO.
AND TODAY I WON'T SLIP OR TRIP OR SPILL OR FORGET TO TAKE OFF THE LENS CAP.
TODAY I'M ON. TODAY I'LL DO MY VERY BEST.
EVEN IF THE NEXT PERSON TO DIE IS ME.

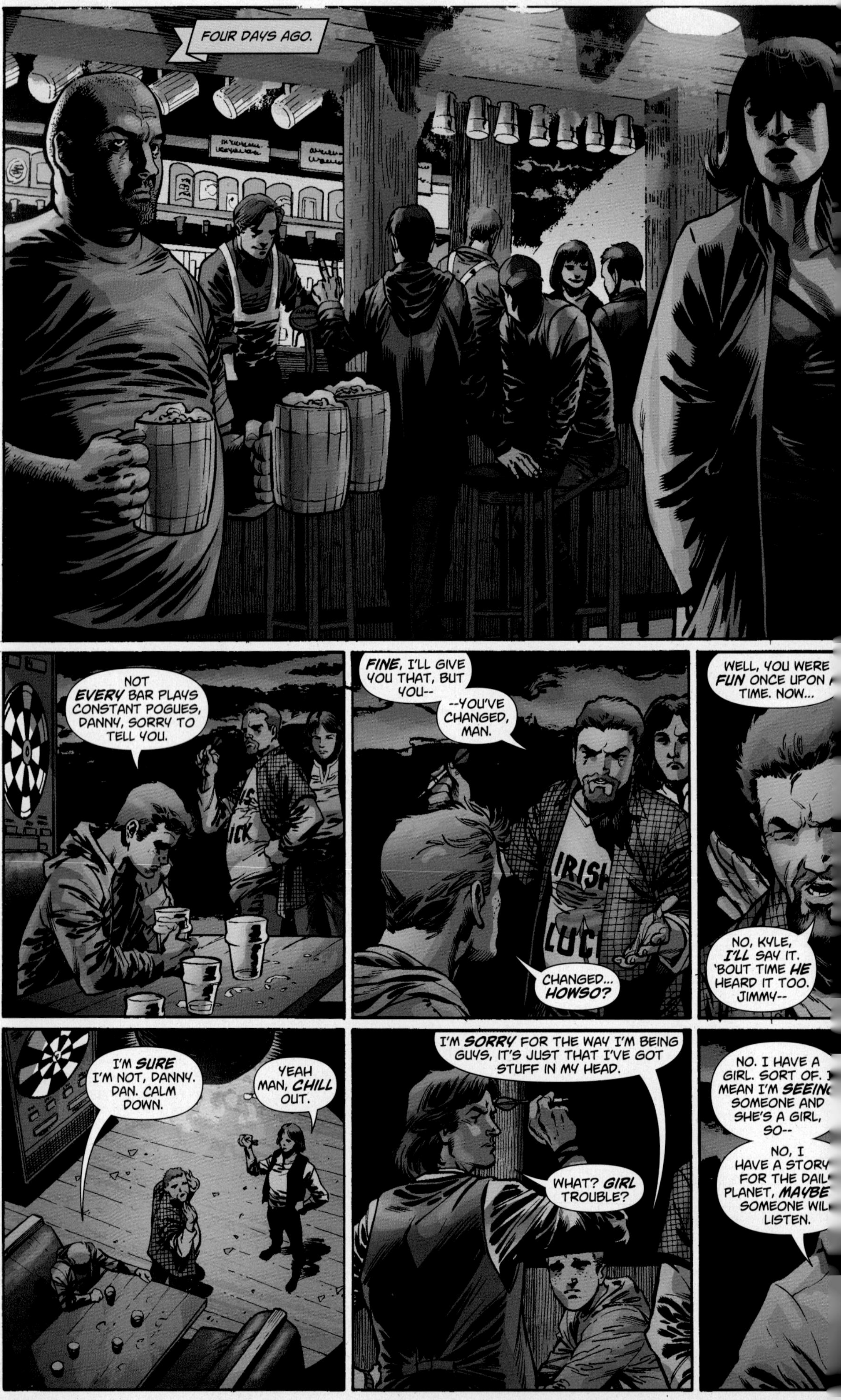
FOUR DAYS AGO.
NOT EVERY BAR PLAYS CONSTANT POGUES, DANNY, SORRY TO TELL YOU.
FINE, I'LL GIVE YOU THAT, BUT YOU--
--YOU'VE CHANGED, MAN.
CHANGED... HOWSO?
WELL, YOU WERE FUN ONCE UPON TIME. NOW...
NO, KYLE, I'LL SAY IT. 'BOUT TIME HE HEARD IT TOO. JIMMY--
I'M SURE I'M NOT, DANNY. DAN. CALM DOWN.
YEAH MAN, CHILL OUT.
I'M SORRY FOR THE WAY I'M BEING GUYS, IT'S JUST THAT I'VE GOT STUFF IN MY HEAD.
WHAT? GIRL TROUBLE?
NO. I HAVE A GIRL. SORT OF. MEAN I'M SEEIN SOMEONE AND SHE'S A GIRL, SO--
NO, I HAVE A STORY FOR THE DAIL PLANET, MAYBE SOMEONE WIL LISTEN.

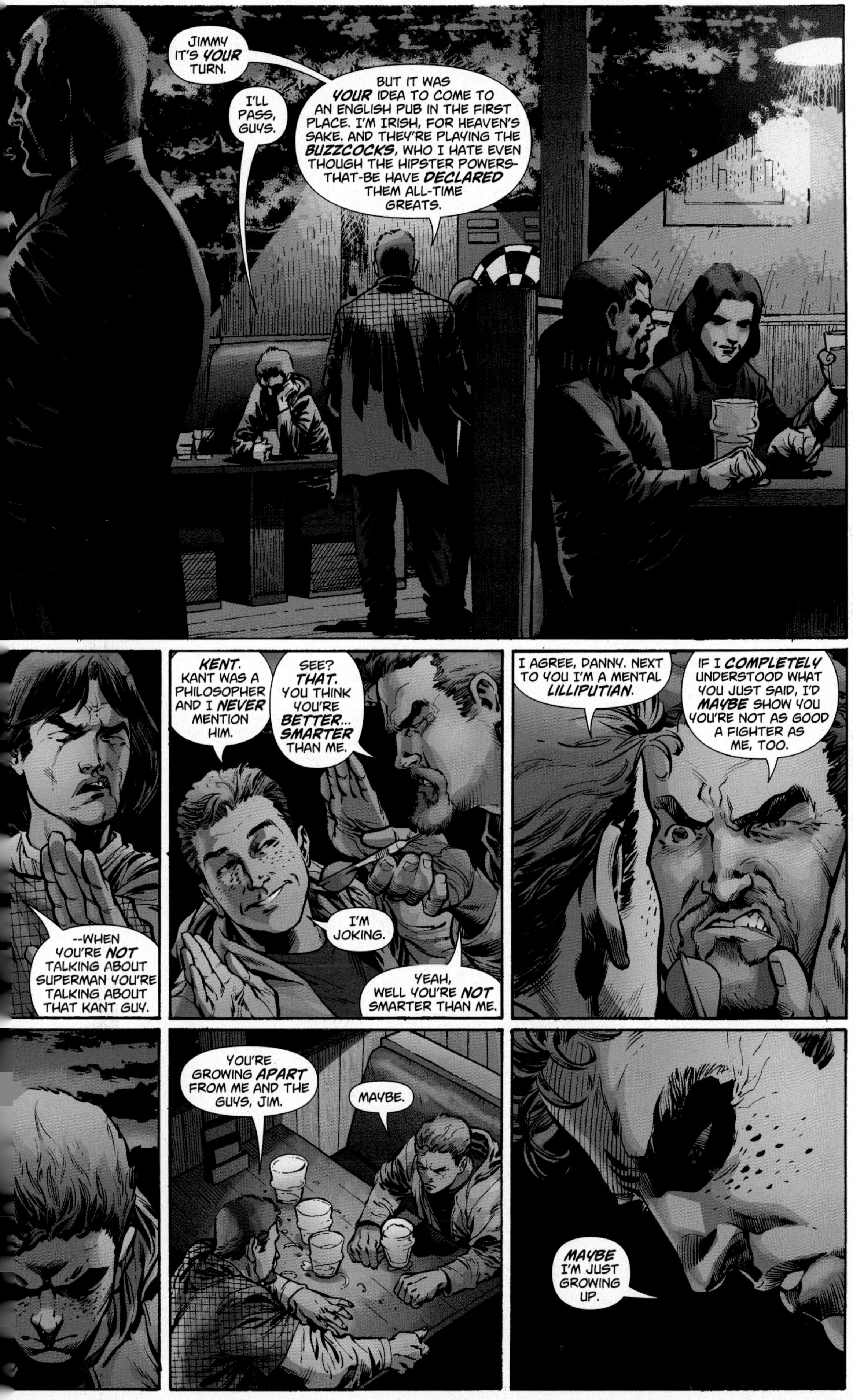
JIMMY IT'S YOUR TURN.
I'LL PASS, GUYS.
BUT IT WAS YOUR IDEA TO COME TO AN ENGLISH PUB IN THE FIRST PLACE. I'M IRISH, FOR HEAVEN'S SAKE. AND THEY'RE PLAYING THE BUZZCOCKS, WHO I HATE EVEN THOUGH THE HIPSTER POWERS-THAT-BE HAVE DECLARED THEM ALL-TIME GREATS.
--WHEN YOU'RE NOT TALKING ABOUT SUPERMAN YOU'RE TALKING ABOUT THAT KANT GUY.
KENT. KANT WAS A PHILOSOPHER AND I NEVER MENTION HIM.
SEE? THAT. YOU THINK YOU'RE BETTER... SMARTER THAN ME.
I'M JOKING.
YEAH, WELL YOU'RE NOT SMARTER THAN ME.
I AGREE, DANNY. NEXT TO YOU I'M A MENTAL LILLIPUTIAN.
IF I COMPLETELY UNDERSTOOD WHAT YOU JUST SAID, I'D MAYBE SHOW YOU YOU'RE NOT AS GOOD A FIGHTER AS ME, TOO.
YOU'RE GROWING APART FROM ME AND THE GUYS, JIM.
MAYBE.
MAYBE I'M JUST GROWING UP.

MAYBE IT'S JUST THAT I'M GROWING UP, JIMMY. BUT I CAN'T HANG AROUND ANYMORE WAITING FOR YOU TO STEP UP.

AS IN WHAT? MARRIAGE? WE'VE BEEN TOGETHER FOR LIKE NO TIME AT ALL AND WE'RE YOUNG...WAY TOO YOUNG FOR WALKING DOWN THE AISLE.

I DIDN'T MEAN THAT.

I MEANT...JUST...YOU SEE ME, WE HOOK UP, YOU GO OR I DO.

I KNOW YOU DON'T LOVE ME, BUT DO YOU EVEN LIKE ME?

SURE I DO. YOU'RE COOL.

IT'S JUST I HAVE STUFF IN MY HEAD.

LET ME GUESS. SUPERMAN... "YOUR BEST BUDD CLARK KENT "YO NEXT BEST BUDD THEN "MISS" LO LANE," THEN "PEF WHITE," THEN, THEN, THEN.

OH.

THAT IT? NOT "NO"? NOT "BABY, NO"?

I GUESS NOT.

GOOD LUCK WITH YOUR CRAZY WORLD, JIMMY.

I'LL THINK OF YOU WHILE I'M LIVING IN M SAFE ONE.

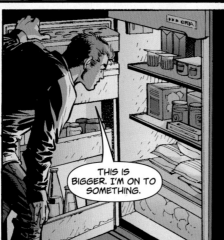

THIS IS BIGGER. I'M ON TO SOMETHING.

ME TOO. I'M ON TO A NEW JOB IN MIDWAY CITY. SALON... REALLY COOL UP-AND-COMING SALON THERE, NEEDS A COLORIST. THEY OFFERED ME THE JOB AND I'M GOING.

OLSEN!

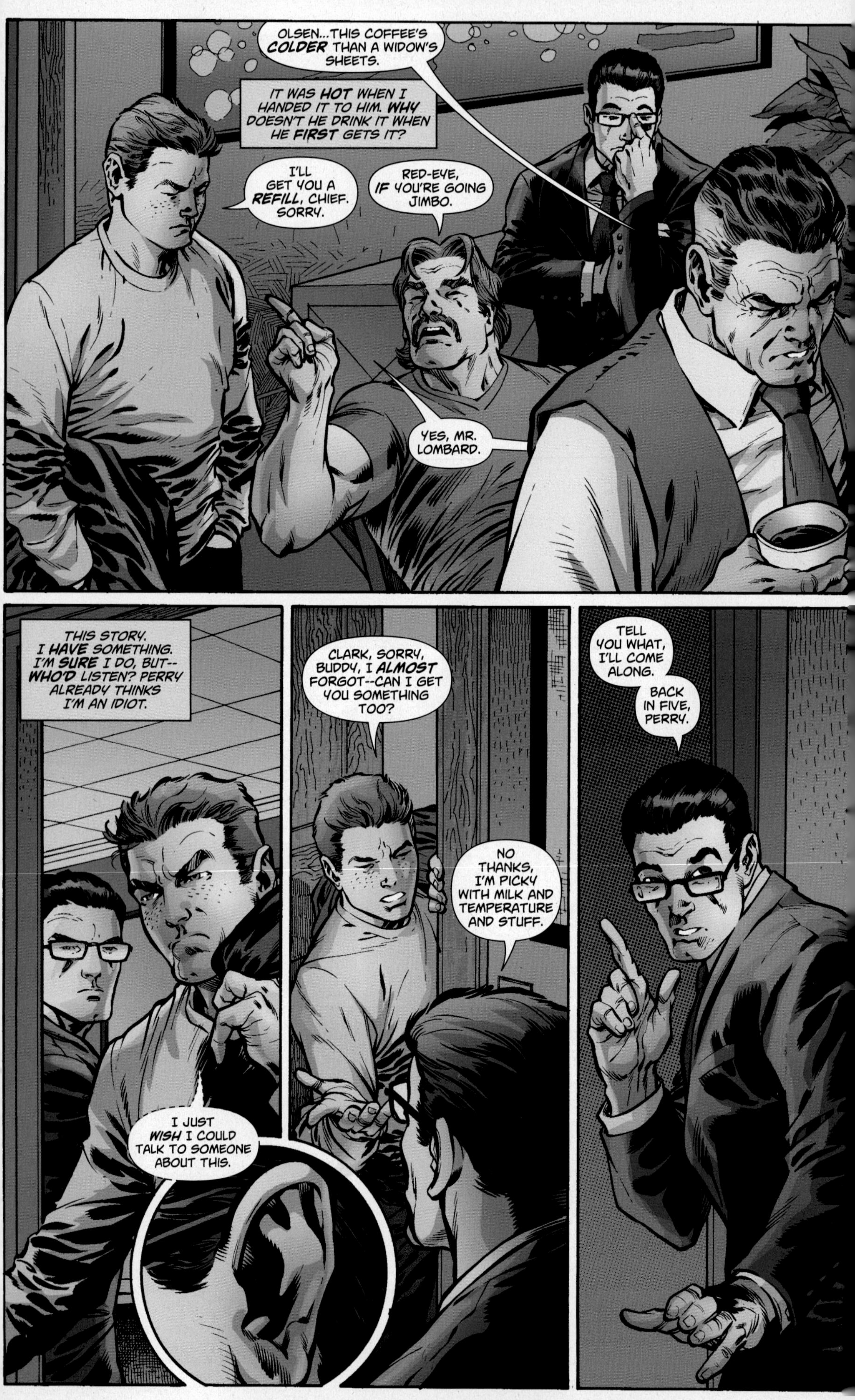
OLSEN...THIS COFFEE'S COLDER THAN A WIDOW'S SHEETS.
IT WAS HOT WHEN I HANDED IT TO HIM. WHY DOESN'T HE DRINK IT WHEN HE FIRST GETS IT?
I'LL GET YOU A REFILL, CHIEF. SORRY.
RED-EYE, IF YOU'RE GOING JIMBO.
YES, MR. LOMBARD.
THIS STORY. I HAVE SOMETHING. I'M SURE I DO, BUT-- WHO'D LISTEN? PERRY ALREADY THINKS I'M AN IDIOT.
I JUST WISH I COULD TALK TO SOMEONE ABOUT THIS.
CLARK, SORRY, BUDDY, I ALMOST FORGOT--CAN I GET YOU SOMETHING TOO?
NO THANKS, I'M PICKY WITH MILK AND TEMPERATURE AND STUFF.
TELL YOU WHAT, I'LL COME ALONG.
BACK IN FIVE, PERRY.

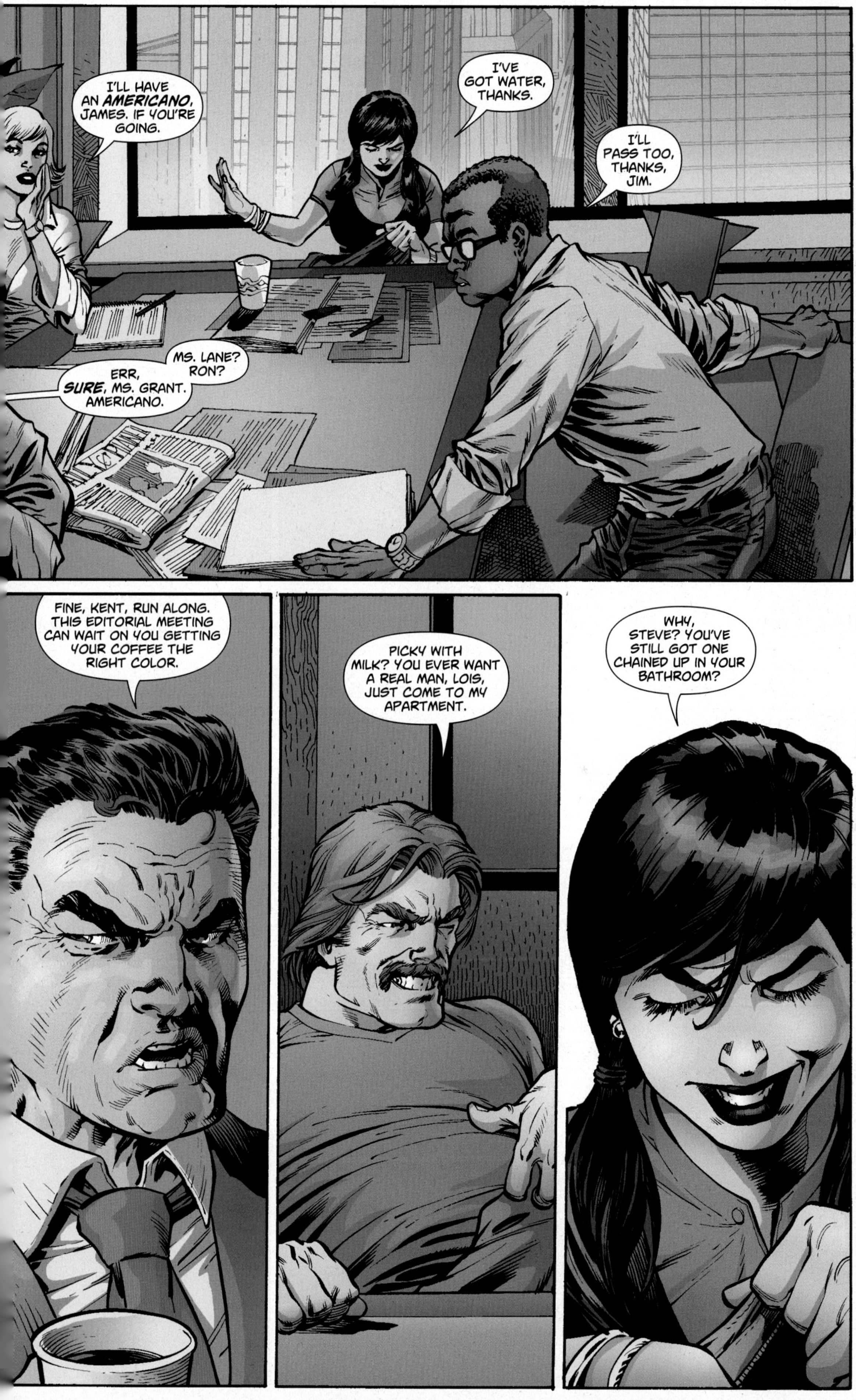
I'LL HAVE AN AMERICANO, JAMES. IF YOU'RE GOING.
I'VE GOT WATER, THANKS.
I'LL PASS TOO, THANKS, JIM.
MS. LANE? RON?
ERR, SURE, MS. GRANT. AMERICANO.
FINE, KENT, RUN ALONG. THIS EDITORIAL MEETING CAN WAIT ON YOU GETTING YOUR COFFEE THE RIGHT COLOR.
PICKY WITH MILK? YOU EVER WANT A REAL MAN, LOIS, JUST COME TO MY APARTMENT.
WHY, STEVE? YOU'VE STILL GOT ONE CHAINED UP IN YOUR BATHROOM?

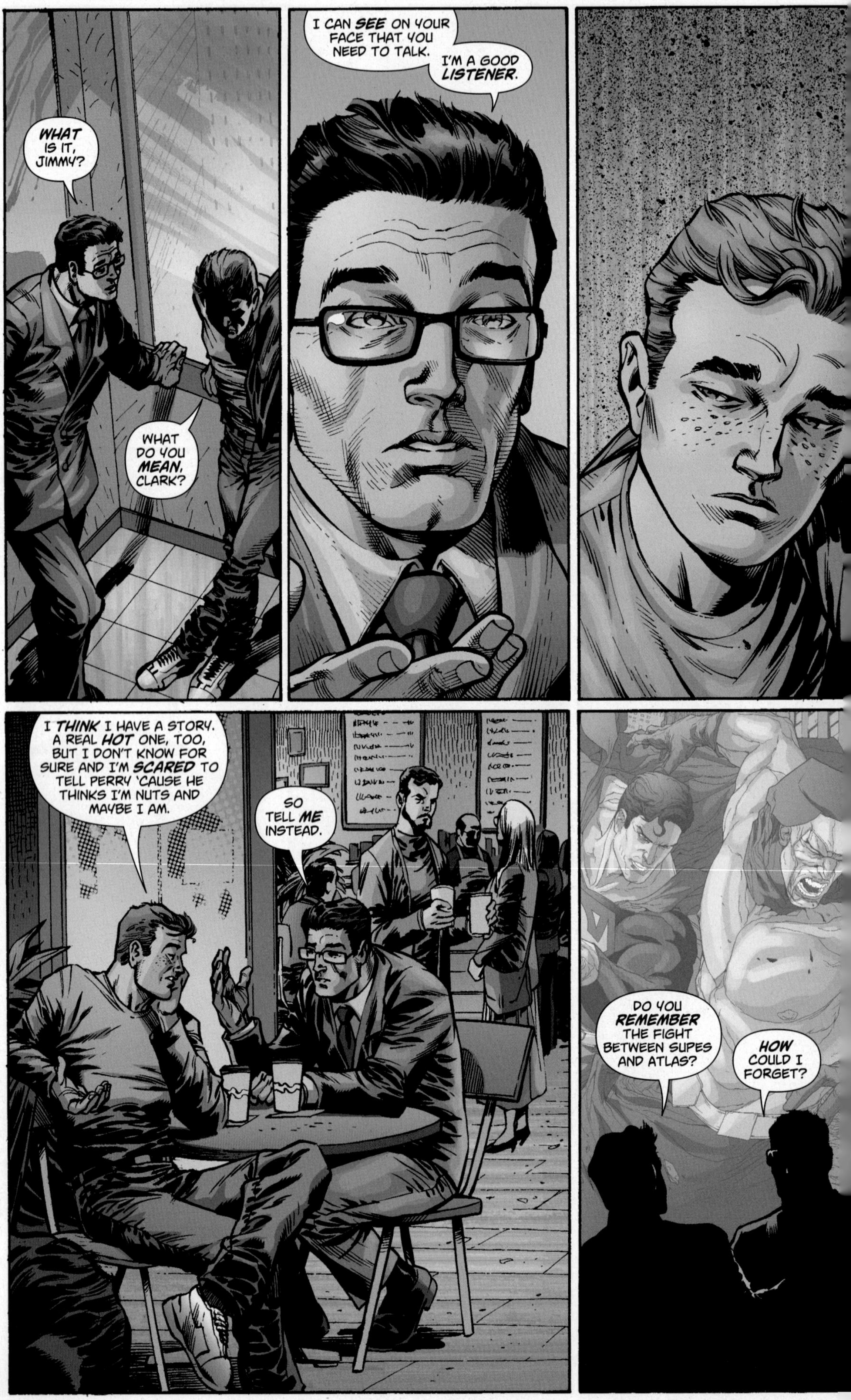
WHAT IS IT, JIMMY?
WHAT DO YOU MEAN, CLARK?
I CAN SEE ON YOUR FACE THAT YOU NEED TO TALK.
I'M A GOOD LISTENER.
I THINK I HAVE A STORY. A REAL HOT ONE, TOO, BUT I DON'T KNOW FOR SURE AND I'M SCARED TO TELL PERRY 'CAUSE HE THINKS I'M NUTS AND MAYBE I AM.
SO TELL ME INSTEAD.
DO YOU REMEMBER THE FIGHT BETWEEN SUPES AND ATLAS?
HOW COULD I FORGET?

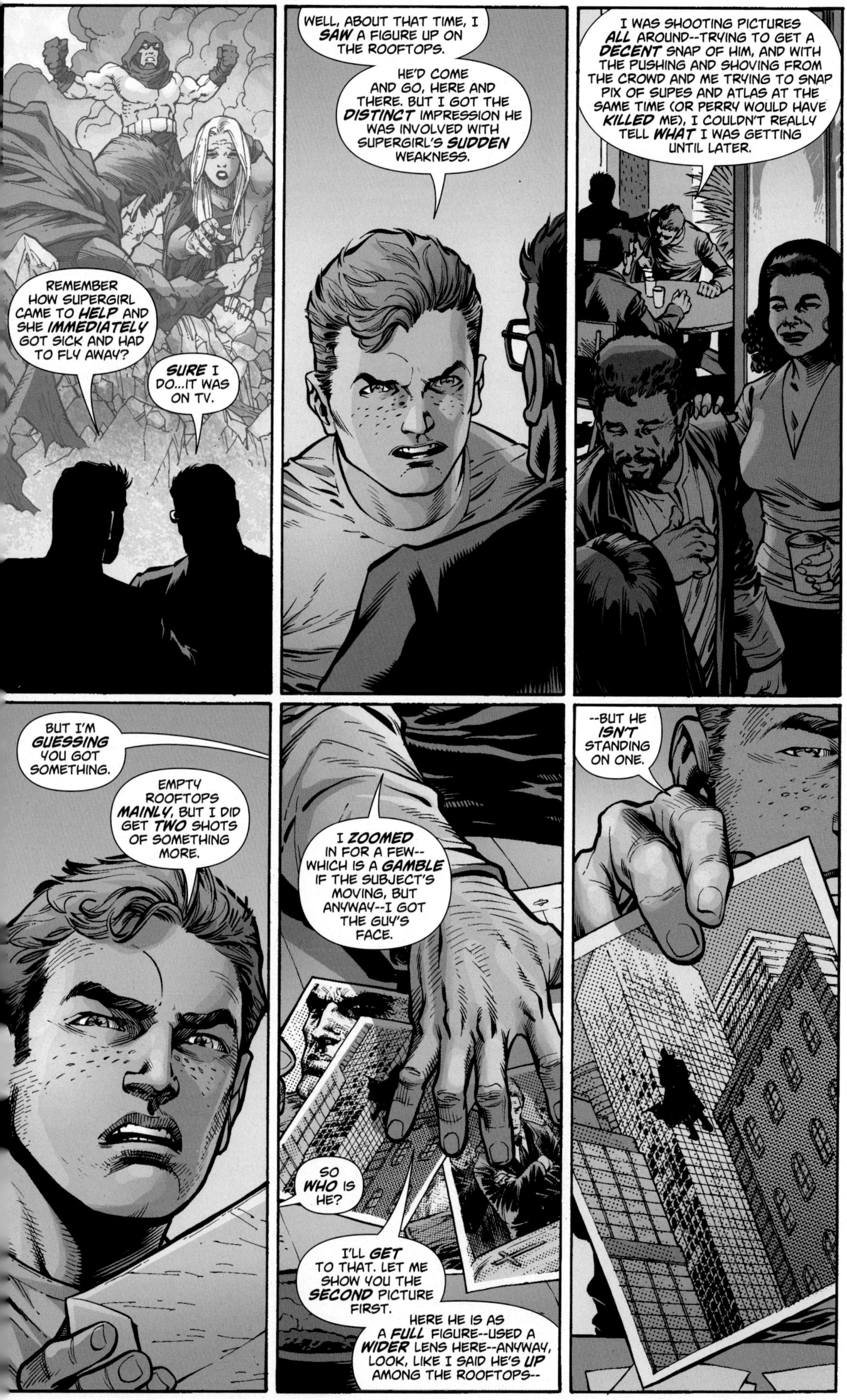
REMEMBER HOW SUPERGIRL CAME TO HELP AND SHE IMMEDIATELY GOT SICK AND HAD TO FLY AWAY?
SURE I DO...IT WAS ON TV.
WELL, ABOUT THAT TIME, I SAW A FIGURE UP ON THE ROOFTOPS.
HE'D COME AND GO, HERE AND THERE. BUT I GOT THE DISTINCT IMPRESSION HE WAS INVOLVED WITH SUPERGIRL'S SUDDEN WEAKNESS.
I WAS SHOOTING PICTURES ALL AROUND--TRYING TO GET A DECENT SNAP OF HIM, AND WITH THE PUSHING AND SHOVING FROM THE CROWD AND ME TRYING TO SNAP PIX OF SUPES AND ATLAS AT THE SAME TIME (OR PERRY WOULD HAVE KILLED ME), I COULDN'T REALLY TELL WHAT I WAS GETTING UNTIL LATER.
BUT I'M GUESSING YOU GOT SOMETHING.
EMPTY ROOFTOPS MAINLY, BUT I DID GET TWO SHOTS OF SOMETHING MORE.
I ZOOMED IN FOR A FEW--WHICH IS A GAMBLE IF THE SUBJECT'S MOVING, BUT ANYWAY--I GOT THE GUY'S FACE.
SO WHO IS HE?
I'LL GET TO THAT. LET ME SHOW YOU THE SECOND PICTURE FIRST.
HERE HE IS AS A FULL FIGURE--USED A WIDER LENS HERE--ANYWAY, LOOK, LIKE I SAID HE'S UP AMONG THE ROOFTOPS--
--BUT HE ISN'T STANDING ON ONE.

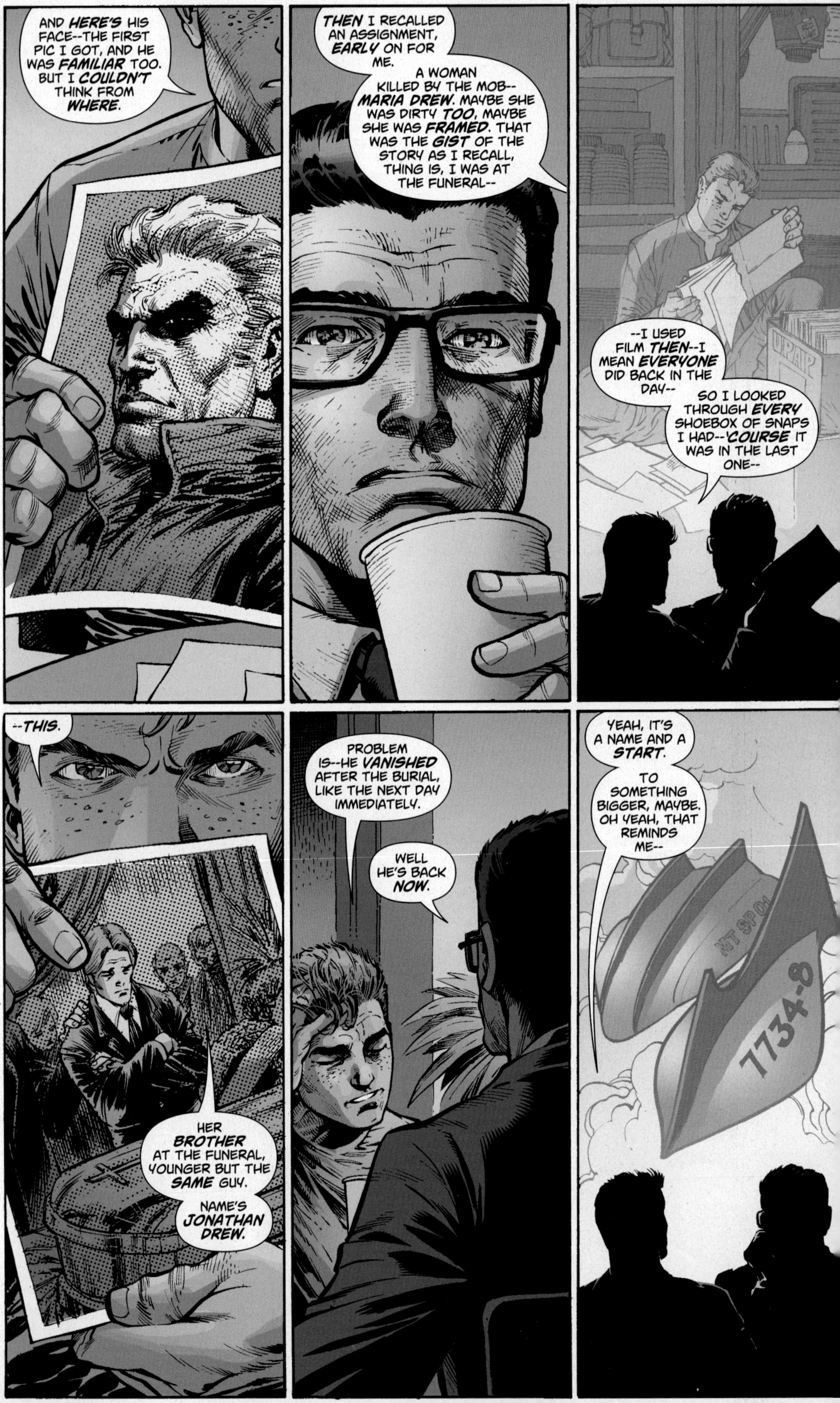
AND HERE'S HIS FACE--THE FIRST PIC I GOT, AND HE WAS FAMILIAR TOO. BUT I COULDN'T THINK FROM WHERE.
THEN I RECALLED AN ASSIGNMENT, EARLY ON FOR ME.
A WOMAN KILLED BY THE MOB-- MARIA DREW. MAYBE SHE WAS DIRTY TOO, MAYBE SHE WAS FRAMED. THAT WAS THE GIST OF THE STORY AS I RECALL, THING IS, I WAS AT THE FUNERAL--
--I USED FILM THEN--I MEAN EVERYONE DID BACK IN THE DAY--
SO I LOOKED THROUGH EVERY SHOEBOX OF SNAPS I HAD--'COURSE IT WAS IN THE LAST ONE--
--THIS.
HER BROTHER AT THE FUNERAL, YOUNGER BUT THE SAME GUY.
NAME'S JONATHAN DREW.
PROBLEM IS--HE VANISHED AFTER THE BURIAL, LIKE THE NEXT DAY IMMEDIATELY.
WELL HE'S BACK NOW.
YEAH, IT'S A NAME AND A START.
TO SOMETHING BIGGER, MAYBE. OH YEAH, THAT REMINDS ME--
NT SP 01
7734-8

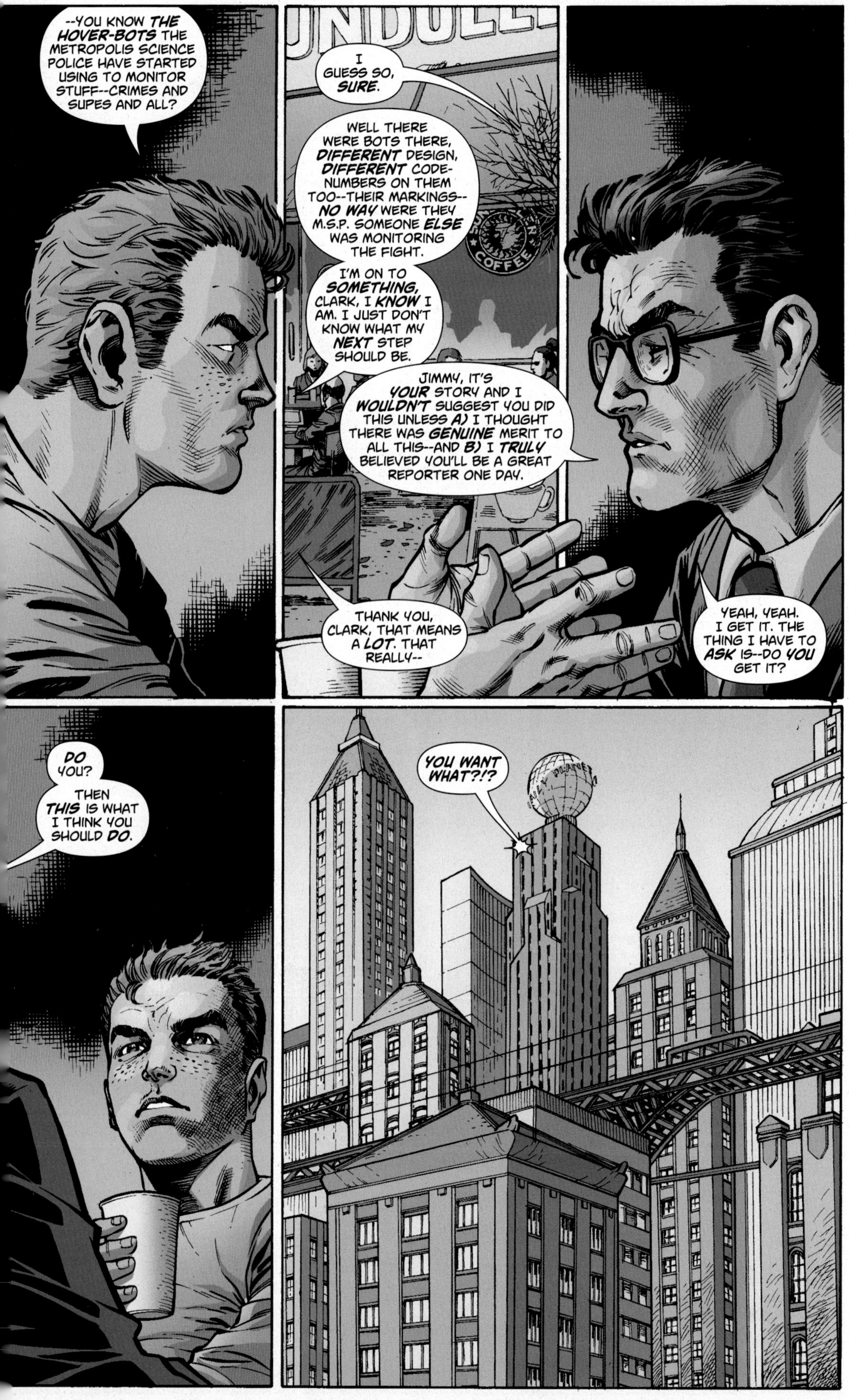
--YOU KNOW THE HOVER-BOTS THE METROPOLIS SCIENCE POLICE HAVE STARTED USING TO MONITOR STUFF--CRIMES AND SUPES AND ALL?
I GUESS SO, SURE.
WELL THERE WERE BOTS THERE, DIFFERENT DESIGN, DIFFERENT CODE-NUMBERS ON THEM TOO--THEIR MARKINGS--NO WAY WERE THEY M.S.P. SOMEONE ELSE WAS MONITORING THE FIGHT.
I'M ON TO SOMETHING, CLARK, I KNOW I AM. I JUST DON'T KNOW WHAT MY NEXT STEP SHOULD BE.
JIMMY, IT'S YOUR STORY AND I WOULDN'T SUGGEST YOU DID THIS UNLESS A) I THOUGHT THERE WAS GENUINE MERIT TO ALL THIS--AND B) I TRULY BELIEVED YOU'LL BE A GREAT REPORTER ONE DAY.
THANK YOU, CLARK, THAT MEANS A LOT. THAT REALLY--
YEAH, YEAH. I GET IT. THE THING I HAVE TO ASK IS--DO YOU GET IT?
DO YOU?
THEN THIS IS WHAT I THINK YOU SHOULD DO.
YOU WANT WHAT?!?

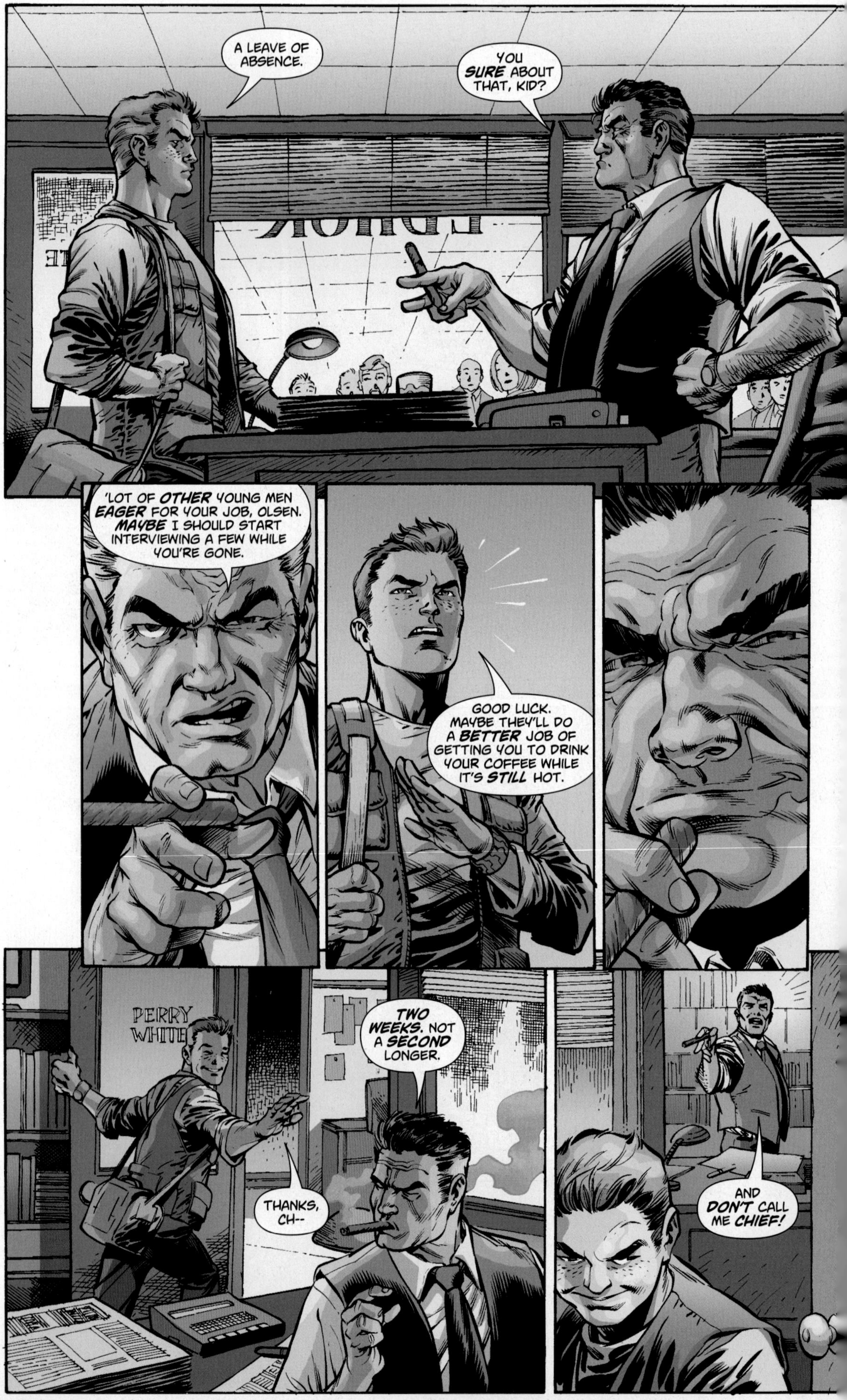
A LEAVE OF ABSENCE.
YOU SURE ABOUT THAT, KID?
'LOT OF OTHER YOUNG MEN EAGER FOR YOUR JOB, OLSEN. MAYBE I SHOULD START INTERVIEWING A FEW WHILE YOU'RE GONE.
GOOD LUCK. MAYBE THEY'LL DO A BETTER JOB OF GETTING YOU TO DRINK YOUR COFFEE WHILE IT'S STILL HOT.
PERRY WHITE
TWO WEEKS. NOT A SECOND LONGER.
THANKS, CH--
AND DON'T CALL ME CHIEF!

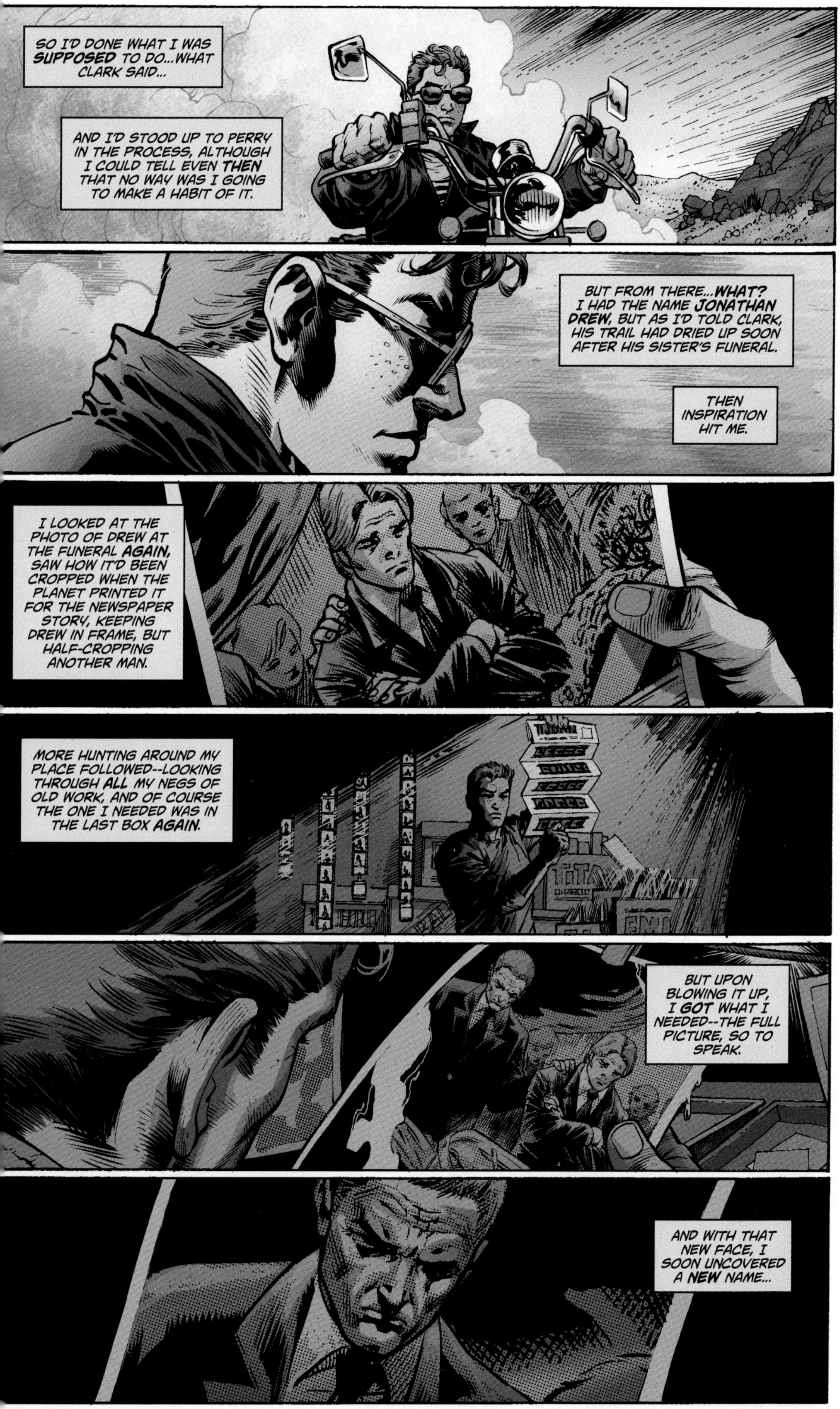

SO I'D DONE WHAT I WAS SUPPOSED TO DO...WHAT CLARK SAID...
AND I'D STOOD UP TO PERRY IN THE PROCESS, ALTHOUGH I COULD TELL EVEN THEN THAT NO WAY WAS I GOING TO MAKE A HABIT OF IT.
BUT FROM THERE...WHAT? I HAD THE NAME JONATHAN DREW, BUT AS I'D TOLD CLARK, HIS TRAIL HAD DRIED UP SOON AFTER HIS SISTER'S FUNERAL.
THEN INSPIRATION HIT ME.
I LOOKED AT THE PHOTO OF DREW AT THE FUNERAL AGAIN, SAW HOW IT'D BEEN CROPPED WHEN THE PLANET PRINTED IT FOR THE NEWSPAPER STORY, KEEPING DREW IN FRAME, BUT HALF-CROPPING ANOTHER MAN.
MORE HUNTING AROUND MY PLACE FOLLOWED--LOOKING THROUGH ALL MY NEGS OF OLD WORK, AND OF COURSE THE ONE I NEEDED WAS IN THE LAST BOX AGAIN.
BUT UPON BLOWING IT UP, I GOT WHAT I NEEDED--THE FULL PICTURE, SO TO SPEAK.
AND WITH THAT NEW FACE, I SOON UNCOVERED A NEW NAME...

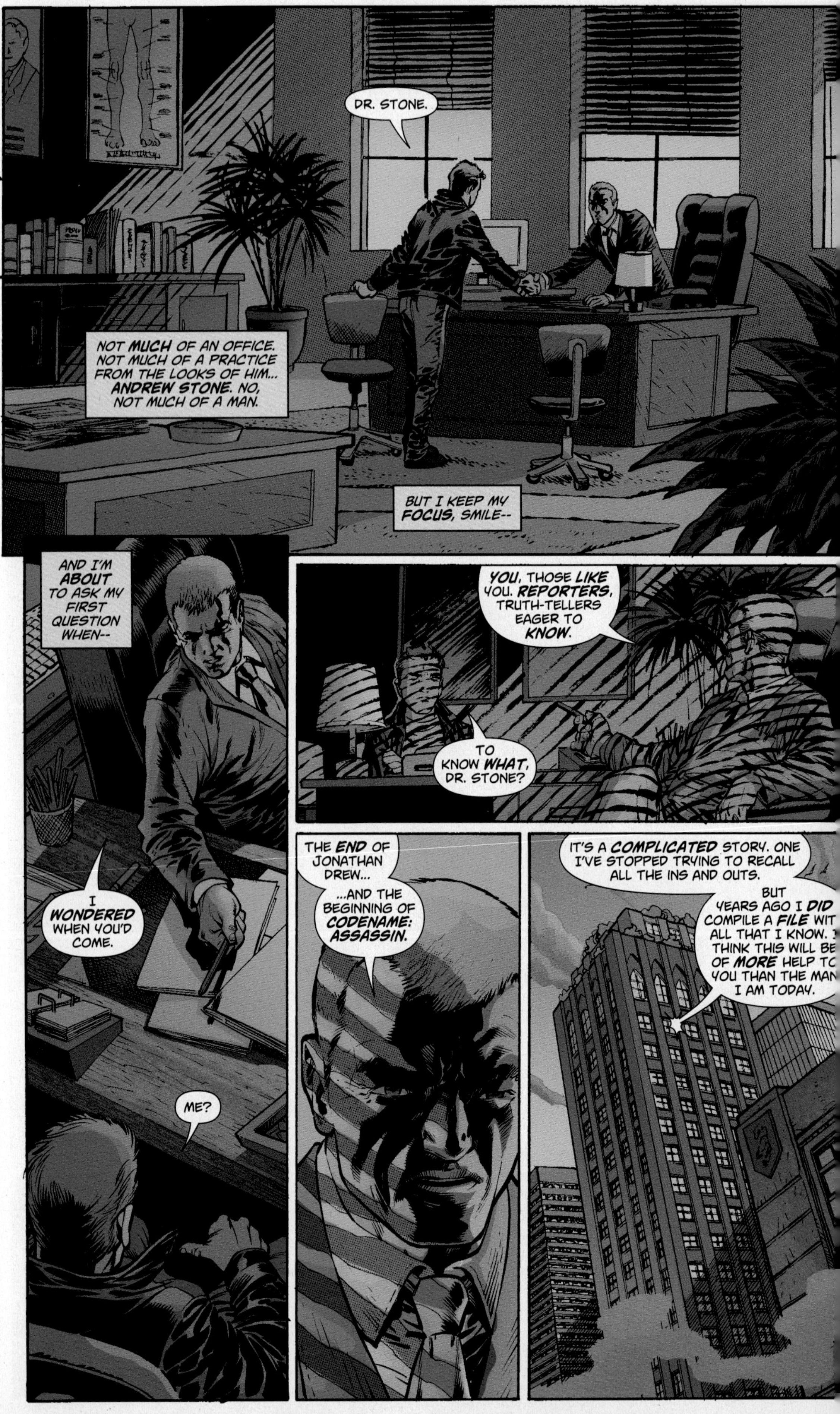
DR. STONE.
NOT MUCH OF AN OFFICE. NOT MUCH OF A PRACTICE FROM THE LOOKS OF HIM... ANDREW STONE. NO, NOT MUCH OF A MAN.
BUT I KEEP MY FOCUS, SMILE--
AND I'M ABOUT TO ASK MY FIRST QUESTION WHEN--
I WONDERED WHEN YOU'D COME.
ME?
YOU, THOSE LIKE YOU. REPORTERS, TRUTH-TELLERS EAGER TO KNOW.
TO KNOW WHAT, DR. STONE?
THE END OF JONATHAN DREW...
...AND THE BEGINNING OF CODENAME: ASSASSIN.
IT'S A COMPLICATED STORY. ONE I'VE STOPPED TRYING TO RECALL ALL THE INS AND OUTS.
BUT YEARS AGO I DID COMPILE A FILE WIT ALL THAT I KNOW. I THINK THIS WILL BE OF MORE HELP TO YOU THAN THE MAN I AM TODAY.

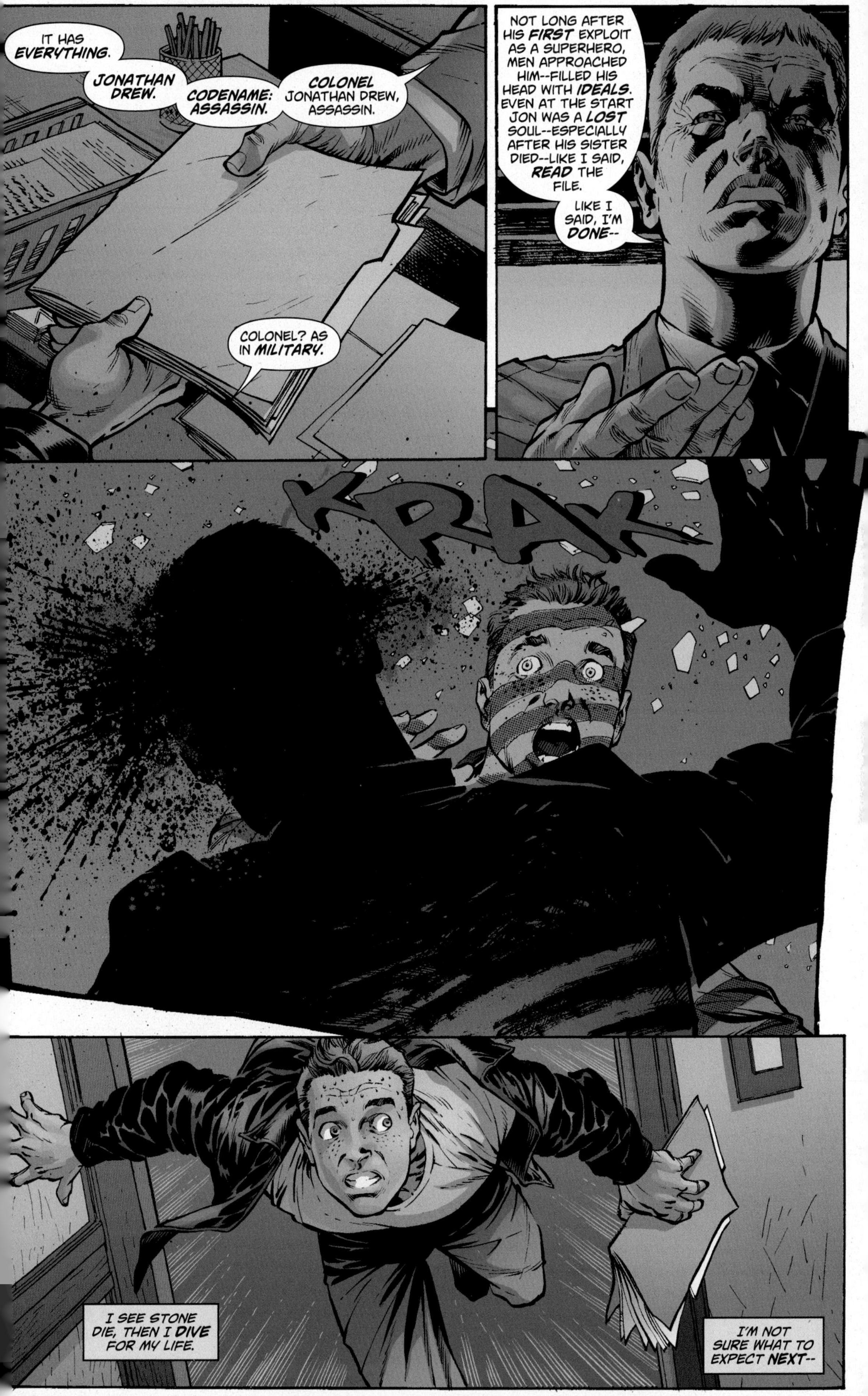
IT HAS EVERYTHING.
JONATHAN DREW.
CODENAME: ASSASSIN.
COLONEL JONATHAN DREW, ASSASSIN.
COLONEL? AS IN MILITARY.
NOT LONG AFTER HIS FIRST EXPLOIT AS A SUPERHERO, MEN APPROACHED HIM--FILLED HIS HEAD WITH IDEALS. EVEN AT THE START JON WAS A LOST SOUL--ESPECIALLY AFTER HIS SISTER DIED--LIKE I SAID, READ THE FILE.
LIKE I SAID, I'M DONE--
KRAK
I SEE STONE DIE, THEN I DIVE FOR MY LIFE.
I'M NOT SURE WHAT TO EXPECT NEXT--

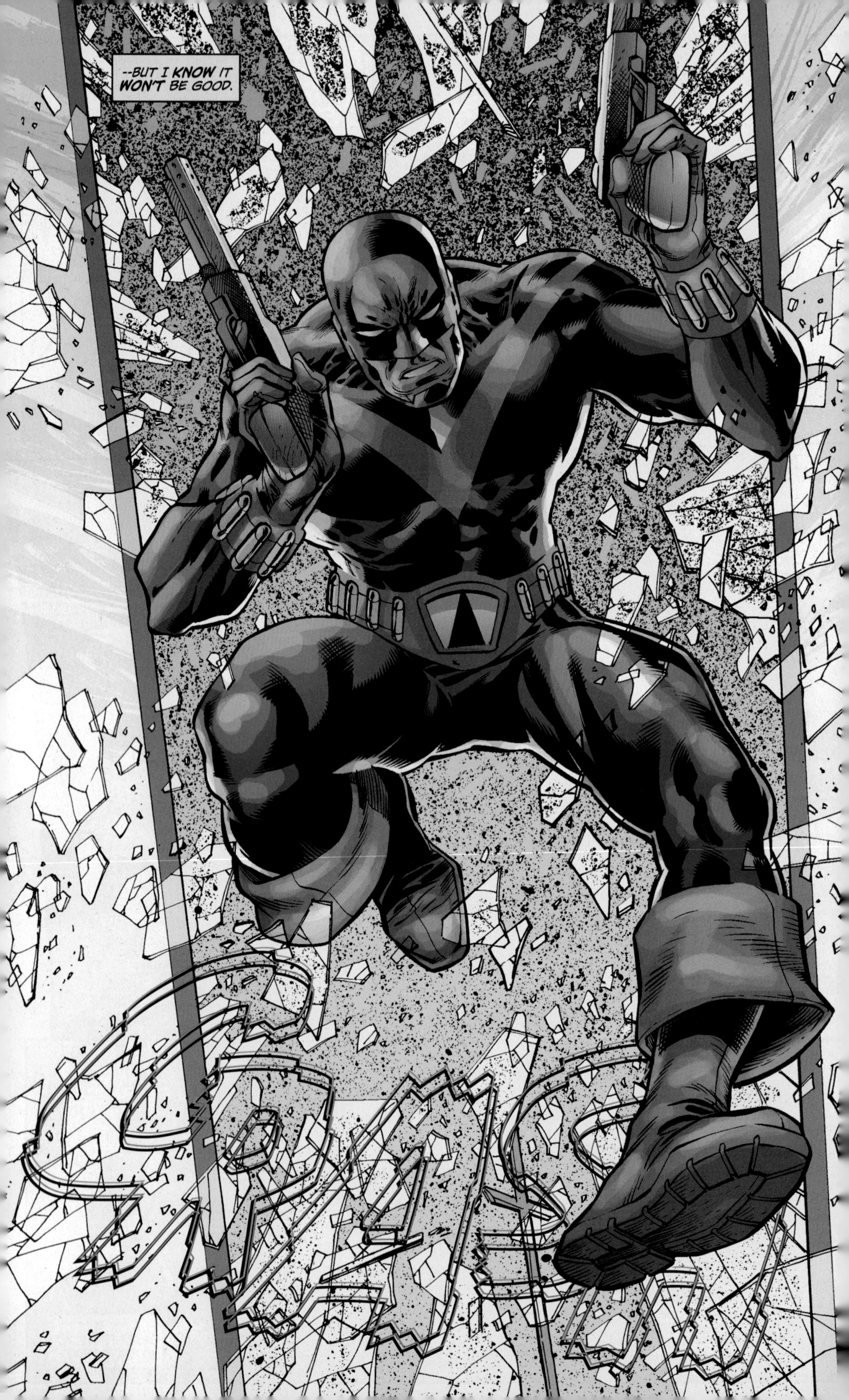
--BUT I KNOW IT WON'T BE GOOD.

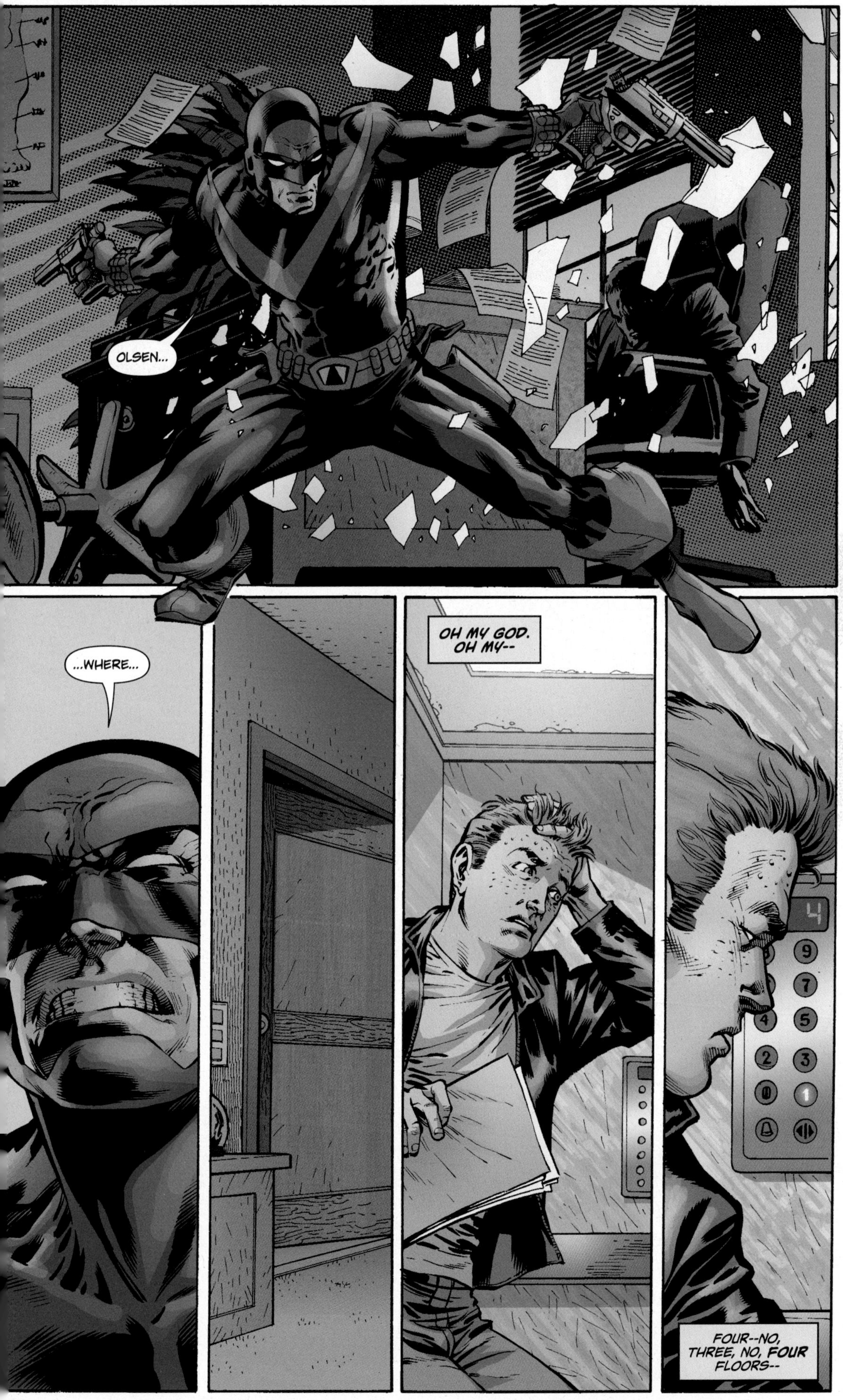
OLSEN...
...WHERE...
OH MY GOD. OH MY--
FOUR--NO, THREE, NO, FOUR FLOORS--

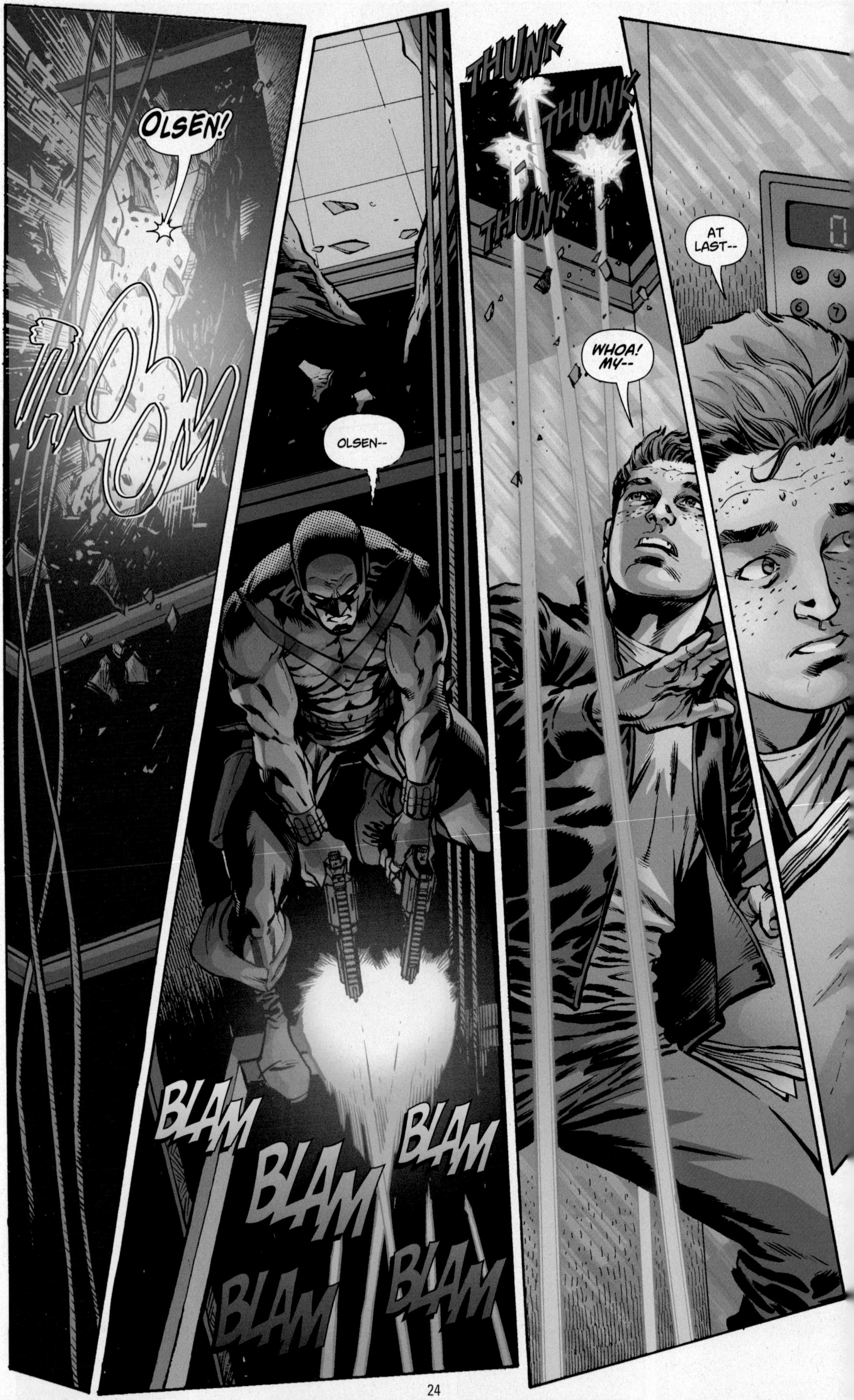
OLSEN!
THOOM
OLSEN--
BLAM
BLAM
BLAM
BLAM
BLAM
THUNK
THUNK
THUNK
WHOA! MY--
AT LAST--

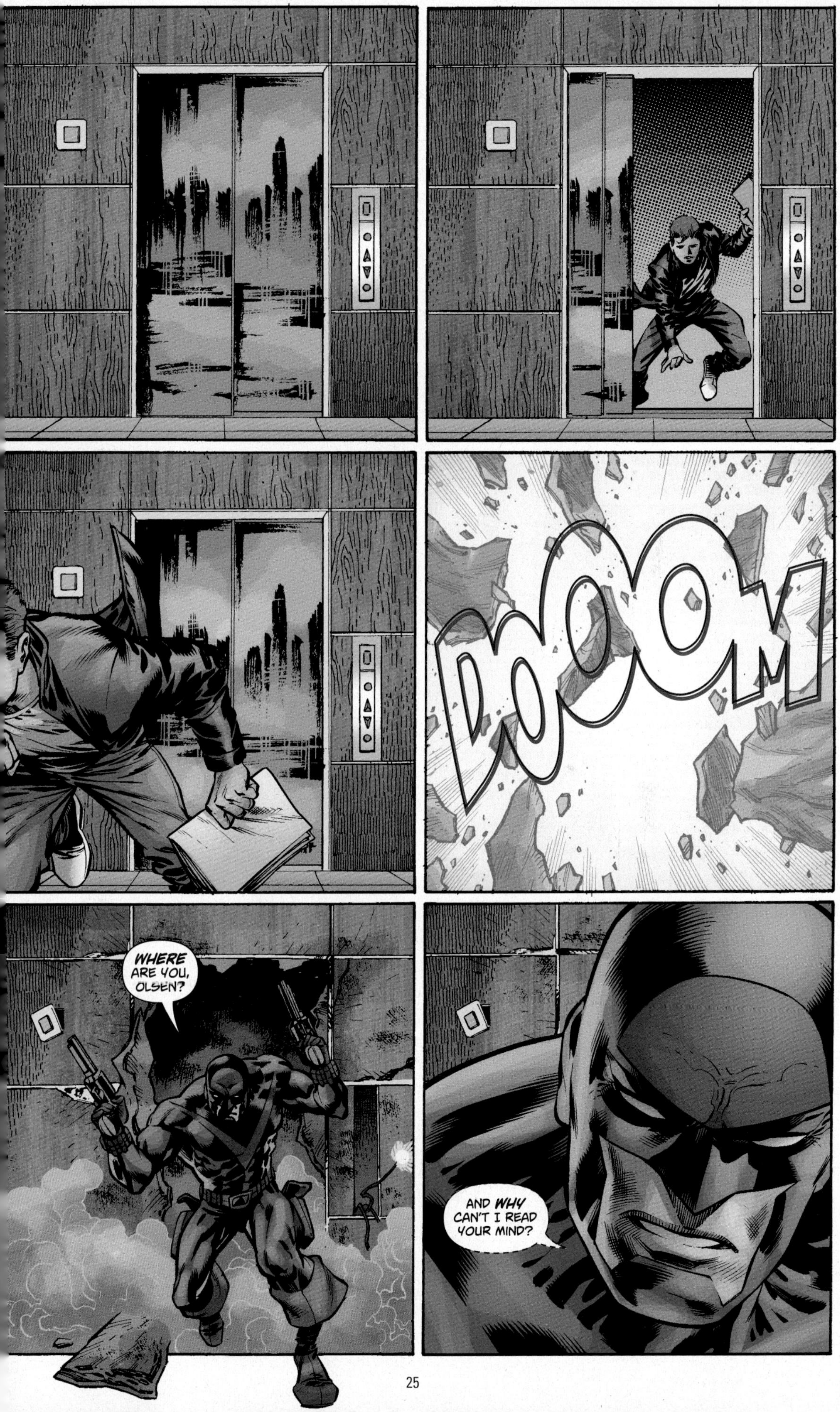
DOOOM
WHERE ARE YOU, OLSEN?
AND WHY CAN'T I READ YOUR MIND?

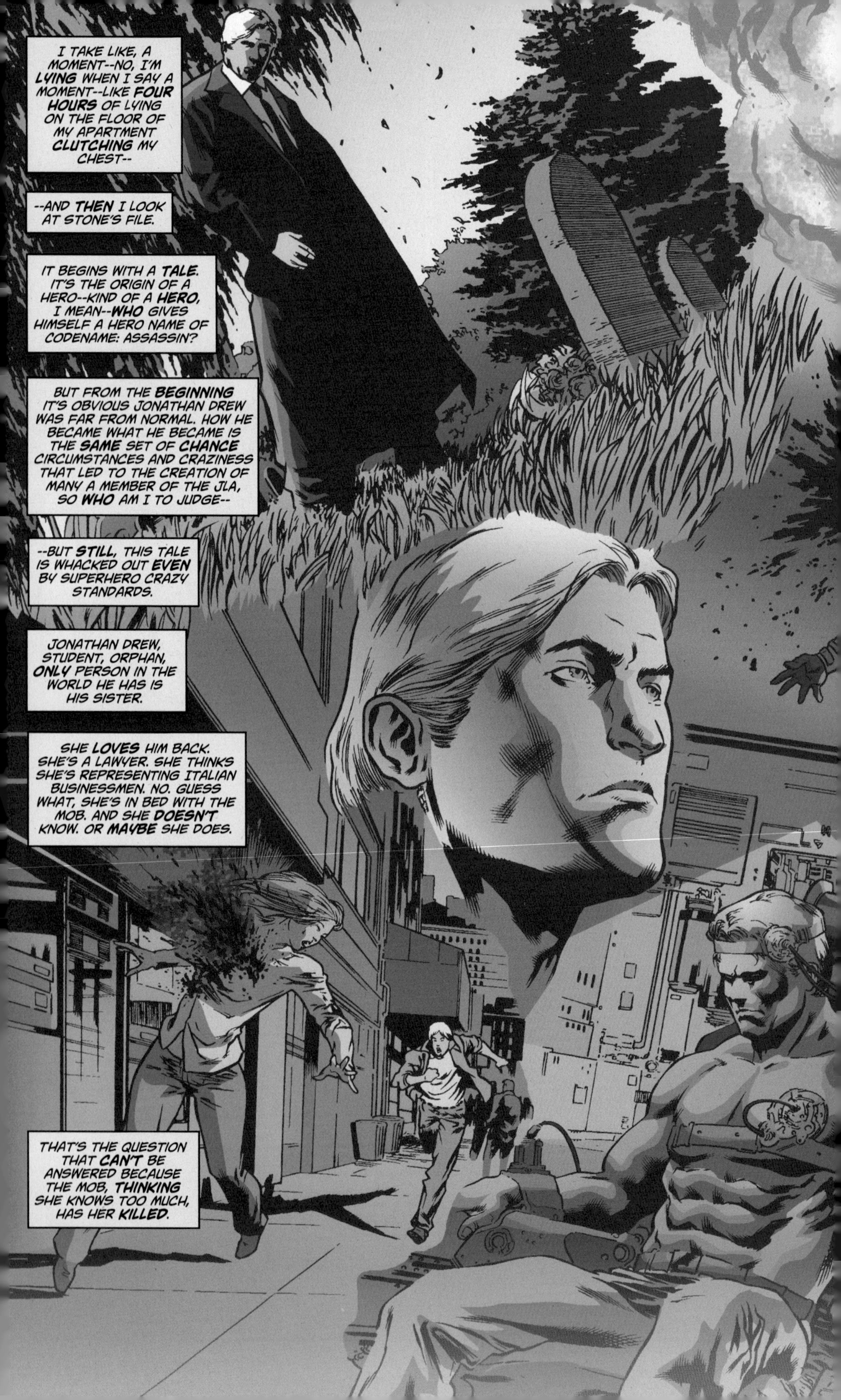
I TAKE LIKE, A MOMENT--NO, I'M LYING WHEN I SAY A MOMENT--LIKE FOUR HOURS OF LYING ON THE FLOOR OF MY APARTMENT CLUTCHING MY CHEST--
--AND THEN I LOOK AT STONE'S FILE.
IT BEGINS WITH A TALE. IT'S THE ORIGIN OF A HERO--KIND OF A HERO, I MEAN--WHO GIVES HIMSELF A HERO NAME OF CODENAME: ASSASSIN?
BUT FROM THE BEGINNING IT'S OBVIOUS JONATHAN DREW WAS FAR FROM NORMAL. HOW HE BECAME WHAT HE BECAME IS THE SAME SET OF CHANCE CIRCUMSTANCES AND CRAZINESS THAT LED TO THE CREATION OF MANY A MEMBER OF THE JLA, SO WHO AM I TO JUDGE--
--BUT STILL, THIS TALE IS WHACKED OUT EVEN BY SUPERHERO CRAZY STANDARDS.
JONATHAN DREW, STUDENT, ORPHAN, ONLY PERSON IN THE WORLD HE HAS IS HIS SISTER.
SHE LOVES HIM BACK. SHE'S A LAWYER. SHE THINKS SHE'S REPRESENTING ITALIAN BUSINESSMEN. NO. GUESS WHAT, SHE'S IN BED WITH THE MOB. AND SHE DOESN'T KNOW. OR MAYBE SHE DOES.
THAT'S THE QUESTION THAT CAN'T BE ANSWERED BECAUSE THE MOB, THINKING SHE KNOWS TOO MUCH, HAS HER KILLED.

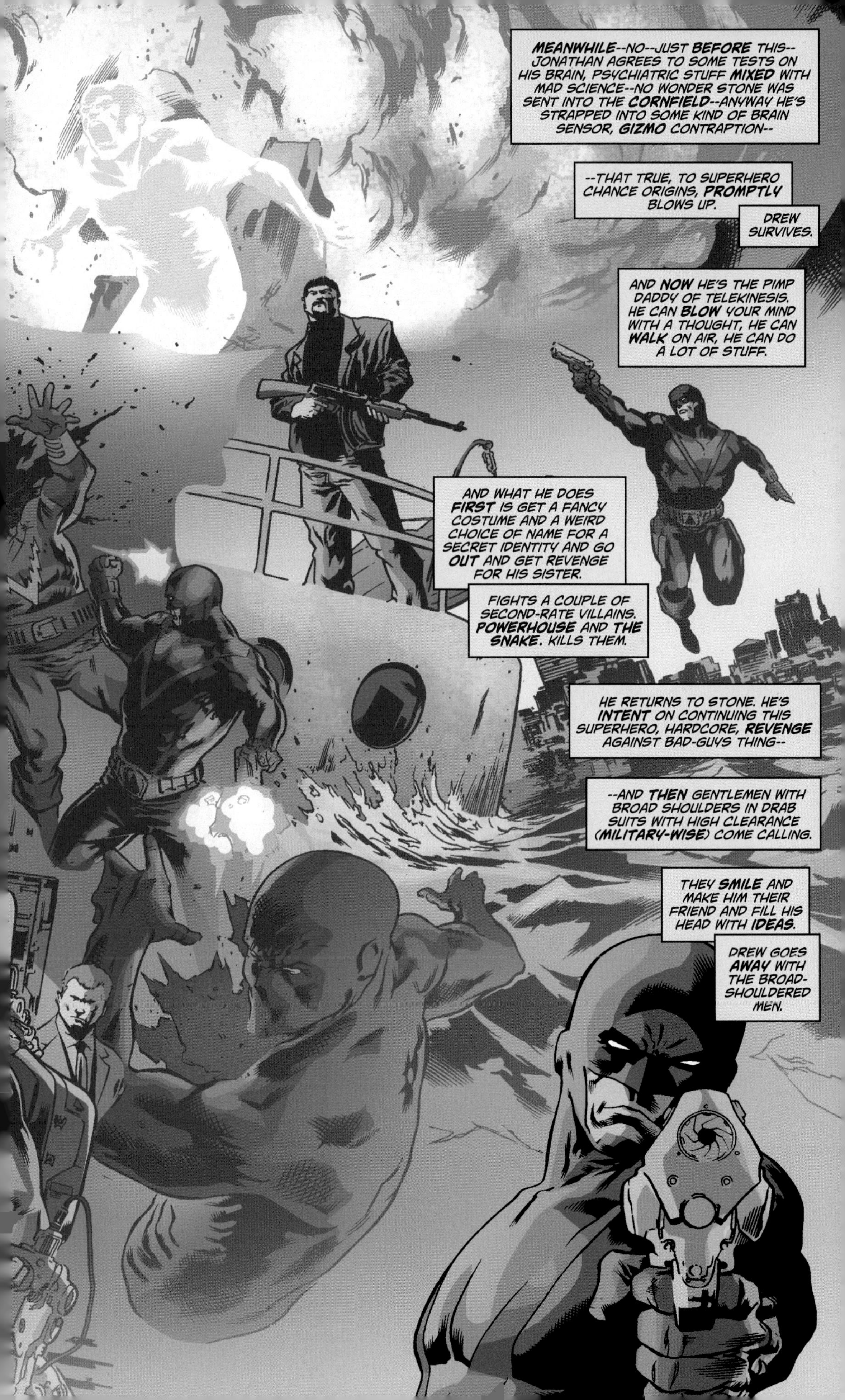

MEANWHILE--NO--JUST BEFORE THIS--JONATHAN AGREES TO SOME TESTS ON HIS BRAIN, PSYCHIATRIC STUFF MIXED WITH MAD SCIENCE--NO WONDER STONE WAS SENT INTO THE CORNFIELD--ANYWAY HE'S STRAPPED INTO SOME KIND OF BRAIN SENSOR, GIZMO CONTRAPTION--
--THAT TRUE, TO SUPERHERO CHANCE ORIGINS, PROMPTLY BLOWS UP.
DREW SURVIVES.
AND NOW HE'S THE PIMP DADDY OF TELEKINESIS. HE CAN BLOW YOUR MIND WITH A THOUGHT, HE CAN WALK ON AIR, HE CAN DO A LOT OF STUFF.
AND WHAT HE DOES FIRST IS GET A FANCY COSTUME AND A WEIRD CHOICE OF NAME FOR A SECRET IDENTITY AND GO OUT AND GET REVENGE FOR HIS SISTER.
FIGHTS A COUPLE OF SECOND-RATE VILLAINS. POWERHOUSE AND THE SNAKE. KILLS THEM.
HE RETURNS TO STONE. HE'S INTENT ON CONTINUING THIS SUPERHERO, HARDCORE, REVENGE AGAINST BAD-GUYS THING--
--AND THEN GENTLEMEN WITH BROAD SHOULDERS IN DRAB SUITS WITH HIGH CLEARANCE (MILITARY-WISE) COME CALLING.
THEY SMILE AND MAKE HIM THEIR FRIEND AND FILL HIS HEAD WITH IDEAS.
DREW GOES AWAY WITH THE BROAD-SHOULDERED MEN.

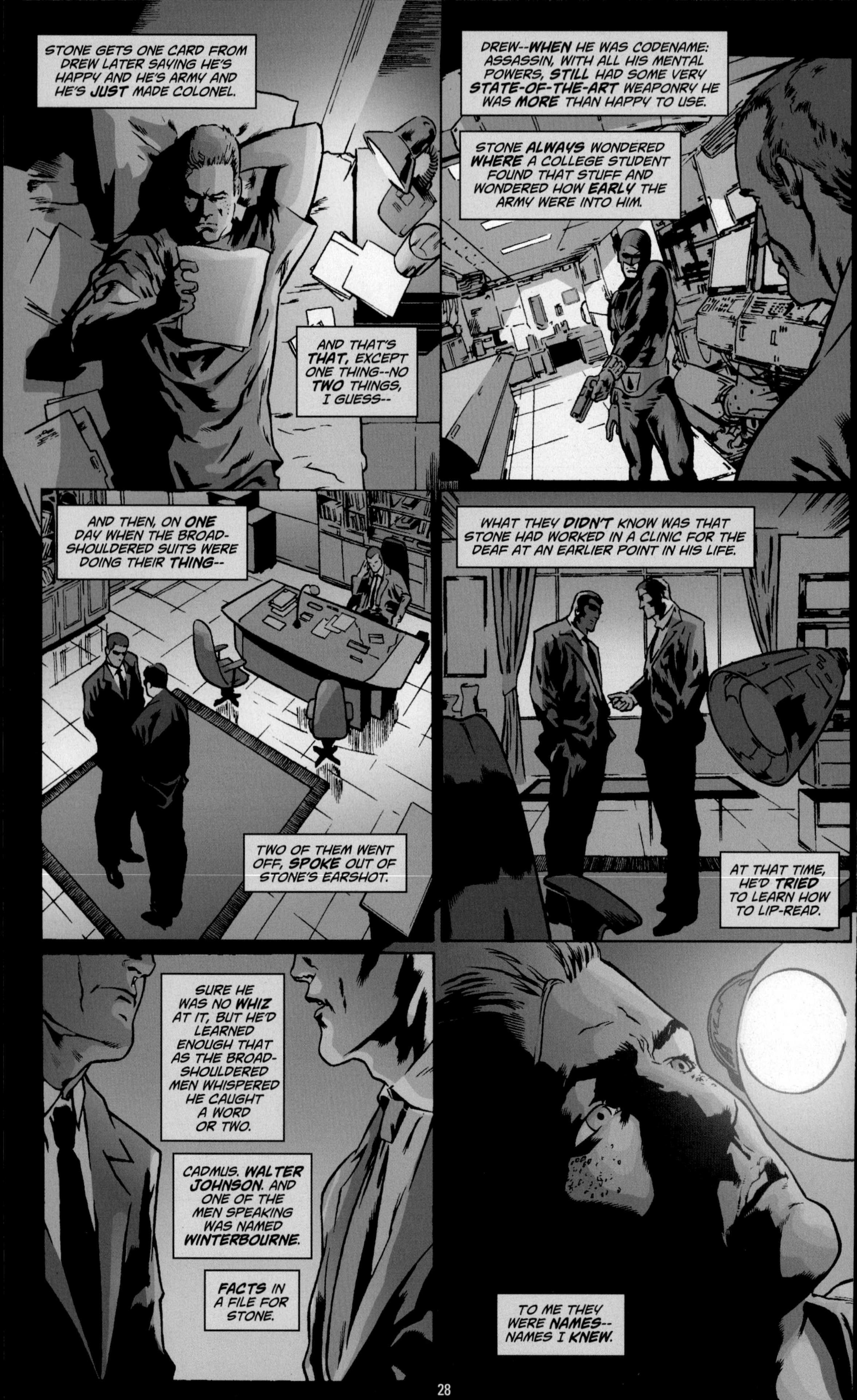
STONE GETS ONE CARD FROM DREW LATER SAYING HE'S HAPPY AND HE'S ARMY AND HE'S JUST MADE COLONEL.
AND THAT'S THAT, EXCEPT ONE THING--NO TWO THINGS, I GUESS--
DREW--WHEN HE WAS CODENAME: ASSASSIN, WITH ALL HIS MENTAL POWERS, STILL HAD SOME VERY STATE-OF-THE-ART WEAPONRY HE WAS MORE THAN HAPPY TO USE.
STONE ALWAYS WONDERED WHERE A COLLEGE STUDENT FOUND THAT STUFF AND WONDERED HOW EARLY THE ARMY WERE INTO HIM.
AND THEN, ON ONE DAY WHEN THE BROAD-SHOULDERED SUITS WERE DOING THEIR THING--
TWO OF THEM WENT OFF, SPOKE OUT OF STONE'S EARSHOT.
WHAT THEY DIDN'T KNOW WAS THAT STONE HAD WORKED IN A CLINIC FOR THE DEAF AT AN EARLIER POINT IN HIS LIFE.
AT THAT TIME, HE'D TRIED TO LEARN HOW TO LIP-READ.
SURE HE WAS NO WHIZ AT IT, BUT HE'D LEARNED ENOUGH THAT AS THE BROAD-SHOULDERED MEN WHISPERED HE CAUGHT A WORD OR TWO.
CADMUS. WALTER JOHNSON. AND ONE OF THE MEN SPEAKING WAS NAMED WINTERBOURNE.
FACTS IN A FILE FOR STONE.
TO ME THEY WERE NAMES--NAMES I KNEW.

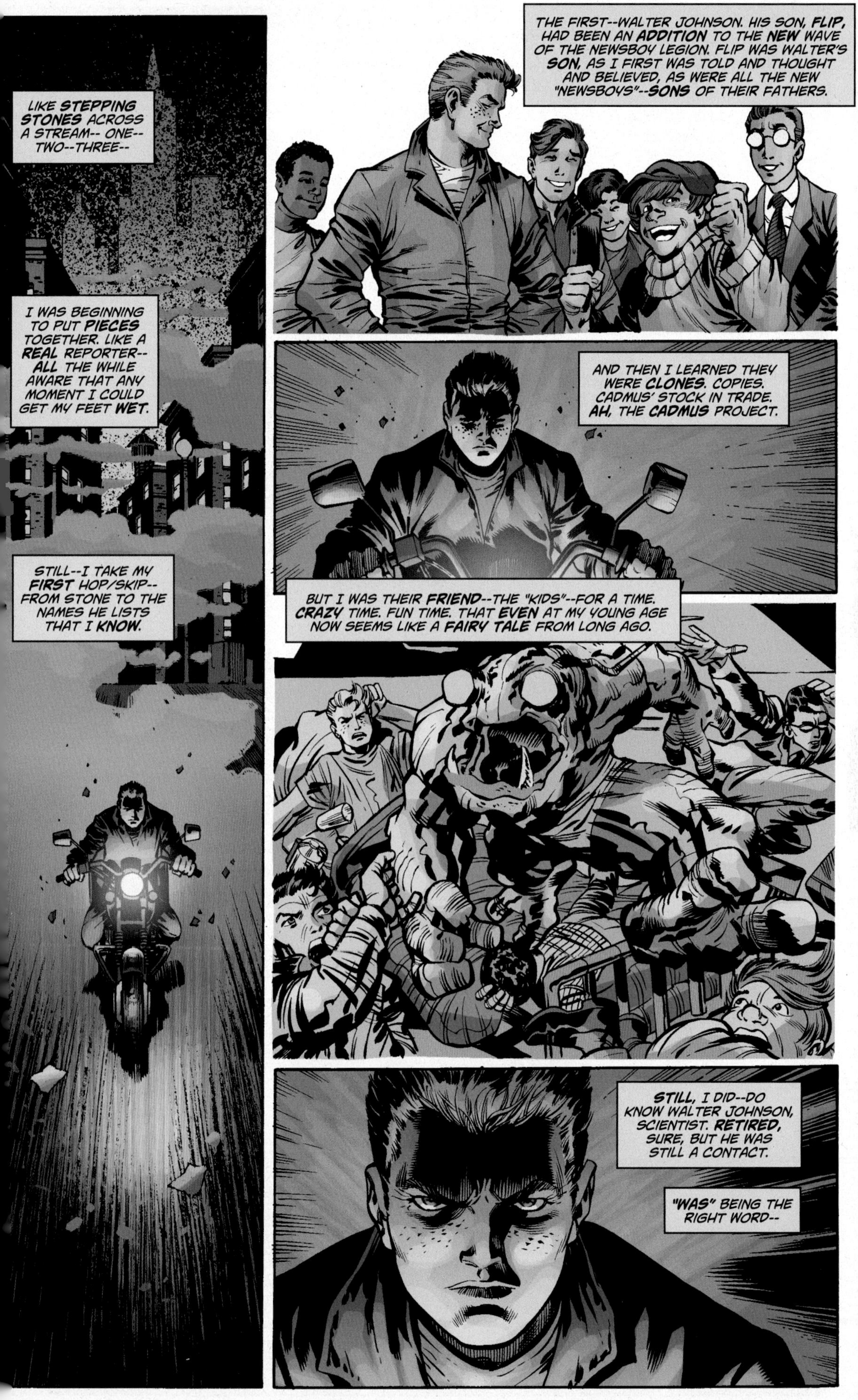
LIKE STEPPING STONES ACROSS A STREAM-- ONE-- TWO--THREE--
I WAS BEGINNING TO PUT PIECES TOGETHER. LIKE A REAL REPORTER-- ALL THE WHILE AWARE THAT ANY MOMENT I COULD GET MY FEET WET.
STILL--I TAKE MY FIRST HOP/SKIP-- FROM STONE TO THE NAMES HE LISTS THAT I KNOW.
THE FIRST--WALTER JOHNSON. HIS SON, FLIP, HAD BEEN AN ADDITION TO THE NEW WAVE OF THE NEWSBOY LEGION. FLIP WAS WALTER'S SON, AS I FIRST WAS TOLD AND THOUGHT AND BELIEVED, AS WERE ALL THE NEW "NEWSBOYS"--SONS OF THEIR FATHERS.
AND THEN I LEARNED THEY WERE CLONES. COPIES. CADMUS' STOCK IN TRADE. AH, THE CADMUS PROJECT.
BUT I WAS THEIR FRIEND--THE "KIDS"--FOR A TIME. CRAZY TIME. FUN TIME. THAT EVEN AT MY YOUNG AGE NOW SEEMS LIKE A FAIRY TALE FROM LONG AGO.
STILL, I DID--DO KNOW WALTER JOHNSON, SCIENTIST. RETIRED, SURE, BUT HE WAS STILL A CONTACT.
"WAS" BEING THE RIGHT WORD--

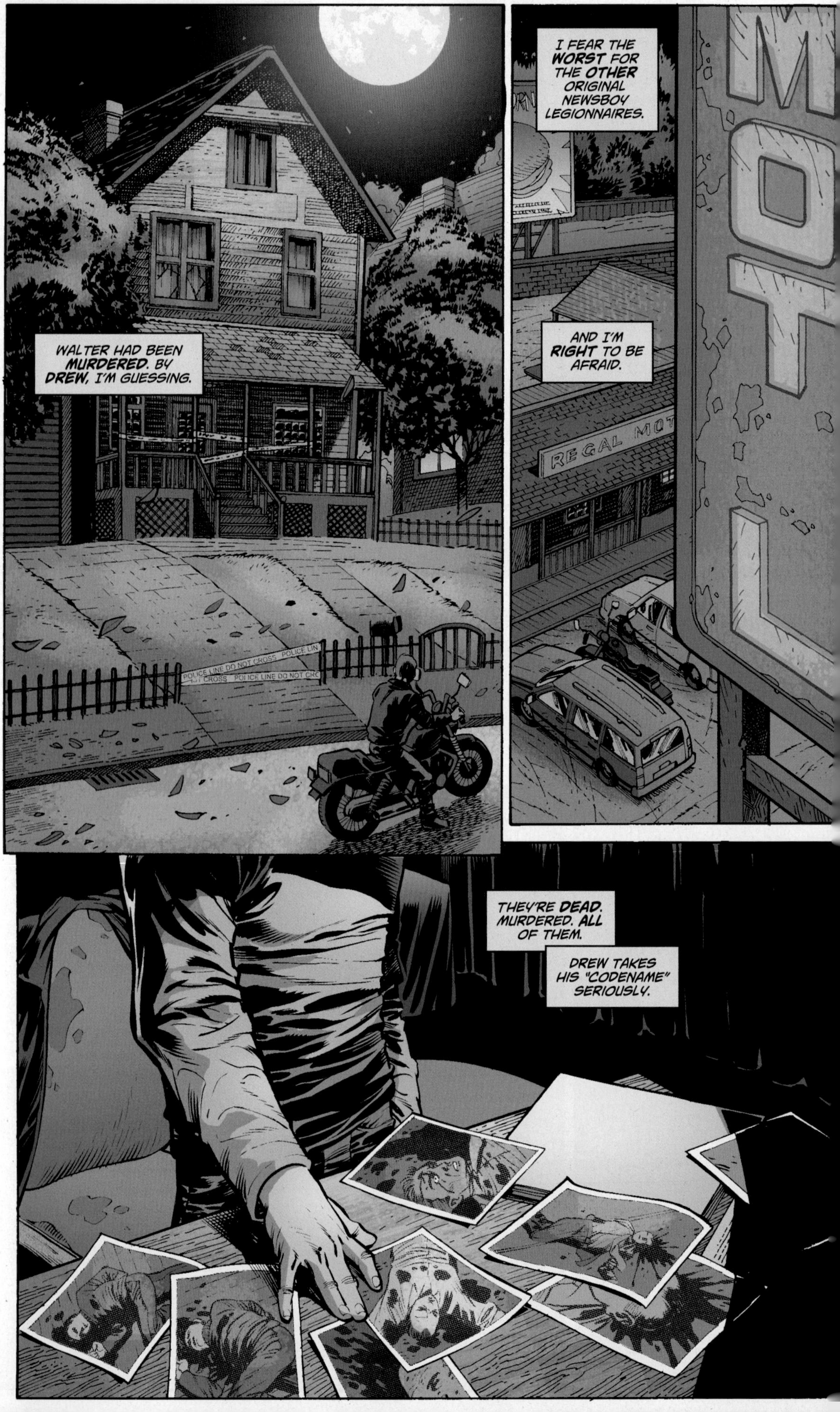
WALTER HAD BEEN MURDERED. BY DREW, I'M GUESSING.
POLICE LINE DO NOT CROSS POLICE LINE DO NOT CROSS
I FEAR THE WORST FOR THE OTHER ORIGINAL NEWSBOY LEGIONNAIRES.
AND I'M RIGHT TO BE AFRAID.
REGAL MOT
THEY'RE DEAD. MURDERED. ALL OF THEM.
DREW TAKES HIS "CODENAME" SERIOUSLY.

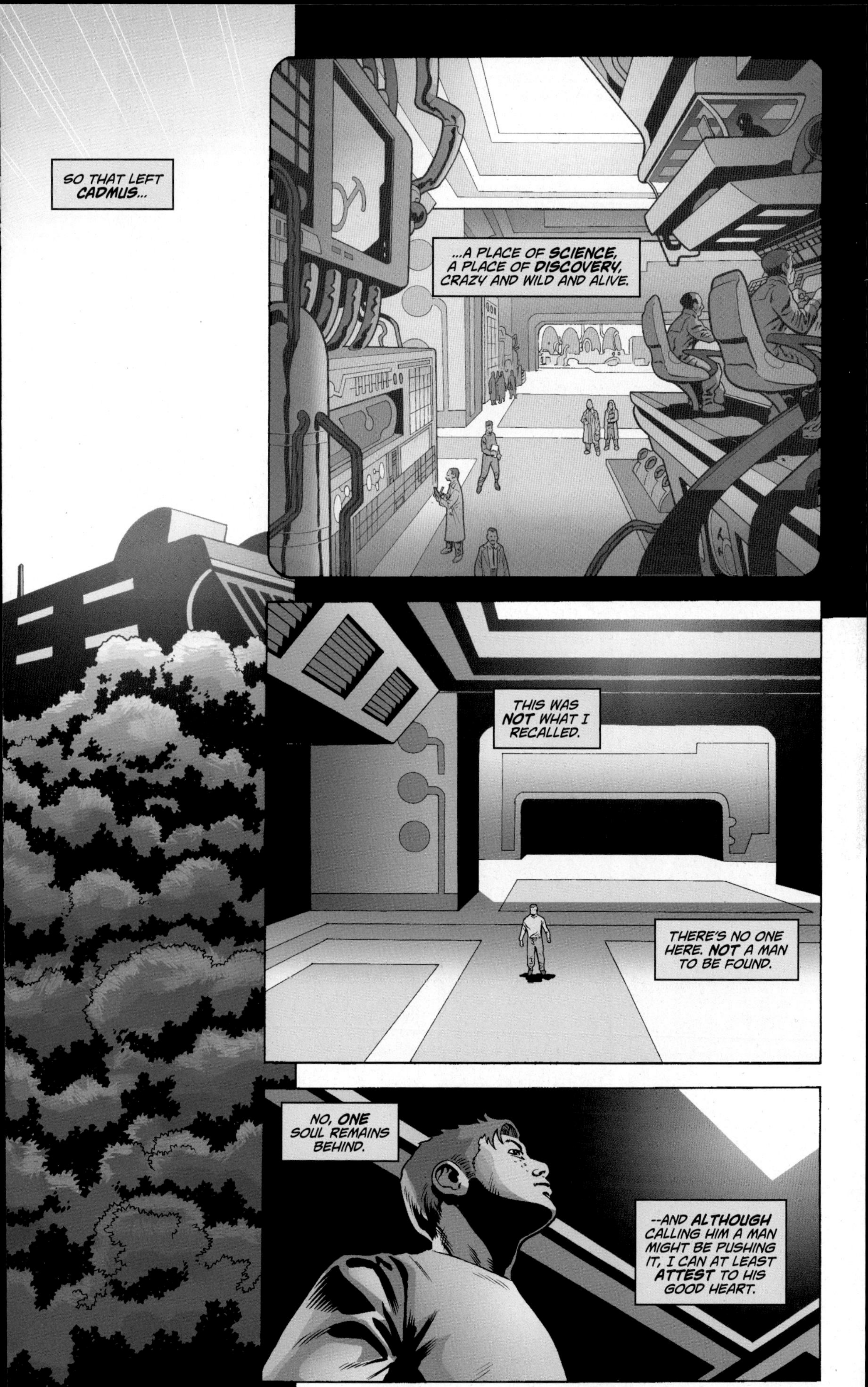
SO THAT LEFT CADMUS...
...A PLACE OF SCIENCE, A PLACE OF DISCOVERY, CRAZY AND WILD AND ALIVE.
THIS WAS NOT WHAT I RECALLED.
THERE'S NO ONE HERE. NOT A MAN TO BE FOUND.
NO, ONE SOUL REMAINS BEHIND.
--AND ALTHOUGH CALLING HIM A MAN MIGHT BE PUSHING IT, I CAN AT LEAST ATTEST TO HIS GOOD HEART.

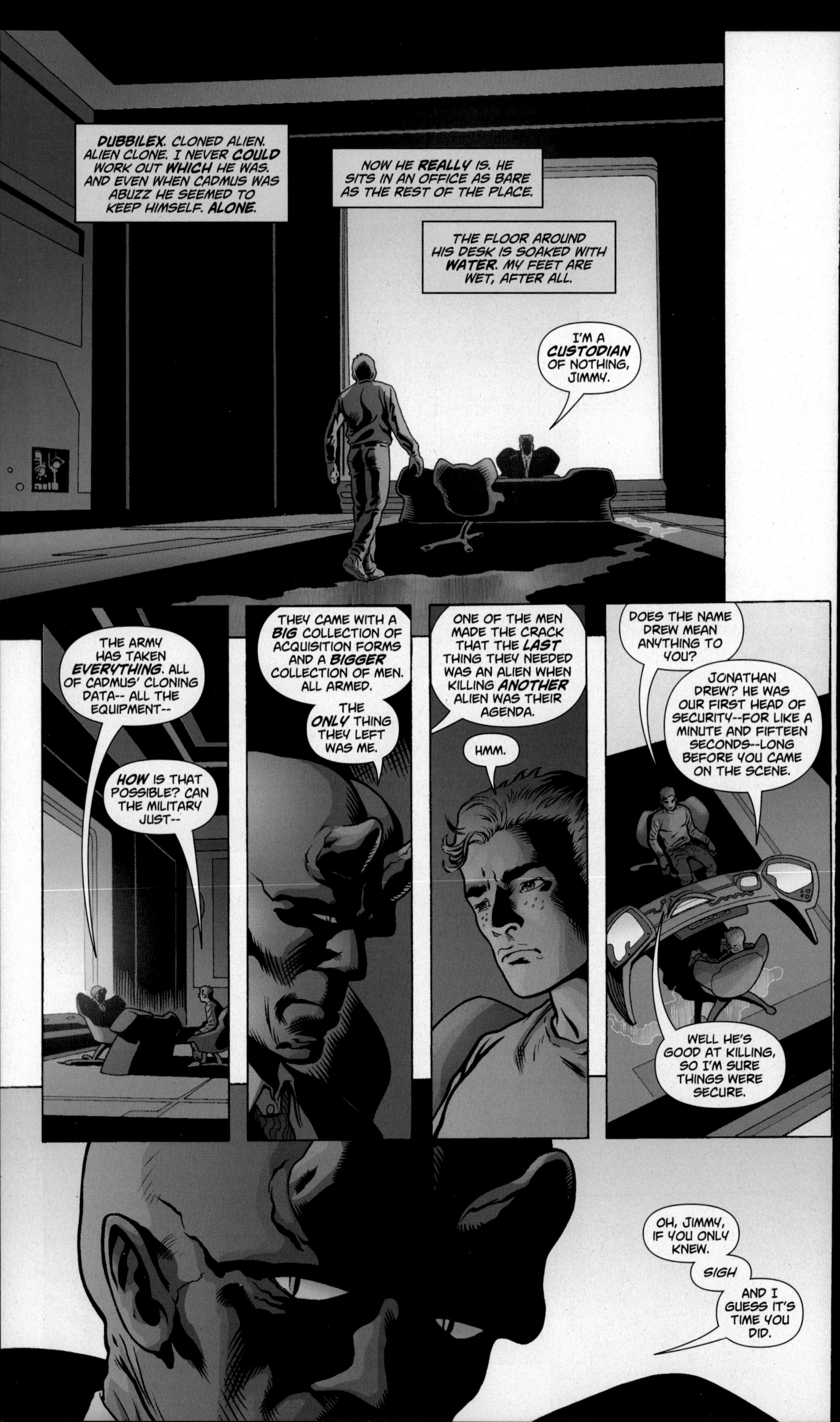
DUBBILEX. CLONED ALIEN. ALIEN CLONE. I NEVER COULD WORK OUT WHICH HE WAS. AND EVEN WHEN CADMUS WAS ABUZZ HE SEEMED TO KEEP HIMSELF. ALONE.
NOW HE REALLY IS. HE SITS IN AN OFFICE AS BARE AS THE REST OF THE PLACE.
THE FLOOR AROUND HIS DESK IS SOAKED WITH WATER. MY FEET ARE WET, AFTER ALL.
I'M A CUSTODIAN OF NOTHING, JIMMY.
THE ARMY HAS TAKEN EVERYTHING. ALL OF CADMUS' CLONING DATA-- ALL THE EQUIPMENT--
HOW IS THAT POSSIBLE? CAN THE MILITARY JUST--
THEY CAME WITH A BIG COLLECTION OF ACQUISITION FORMS AND A BIGGER COLLECTION OF MEN. ALL ARMED.
THE ONLY THING THEY LEFT WAS ME.
ONE OF THE MEN MADE THE CRACK THAT THE LAST THING THEY NEEDED WAS AN ALIEN WHEN KILLING ANOTHER ALIEN WAS THEIR AGENDA.
HMM.
DOES THE NAME DREW MEAN ANYTHING TO YOU?
JONATHAN DREW? HE WAS OUR FIRST HEAD OF SECURITY--FOR LIKE A MINUTE AND FIFTEEN SECONDS--LONG BEFORE YOU CAME ON THE SCENE.
WELL HE'S GOOD AT KILLING, SO I'M SURE THINGS WERE SECURE.
OH, JIMMY, IF YOU ONLY KNEW.
SIGH
AND I GUESS IT'S TIME YOU DID.

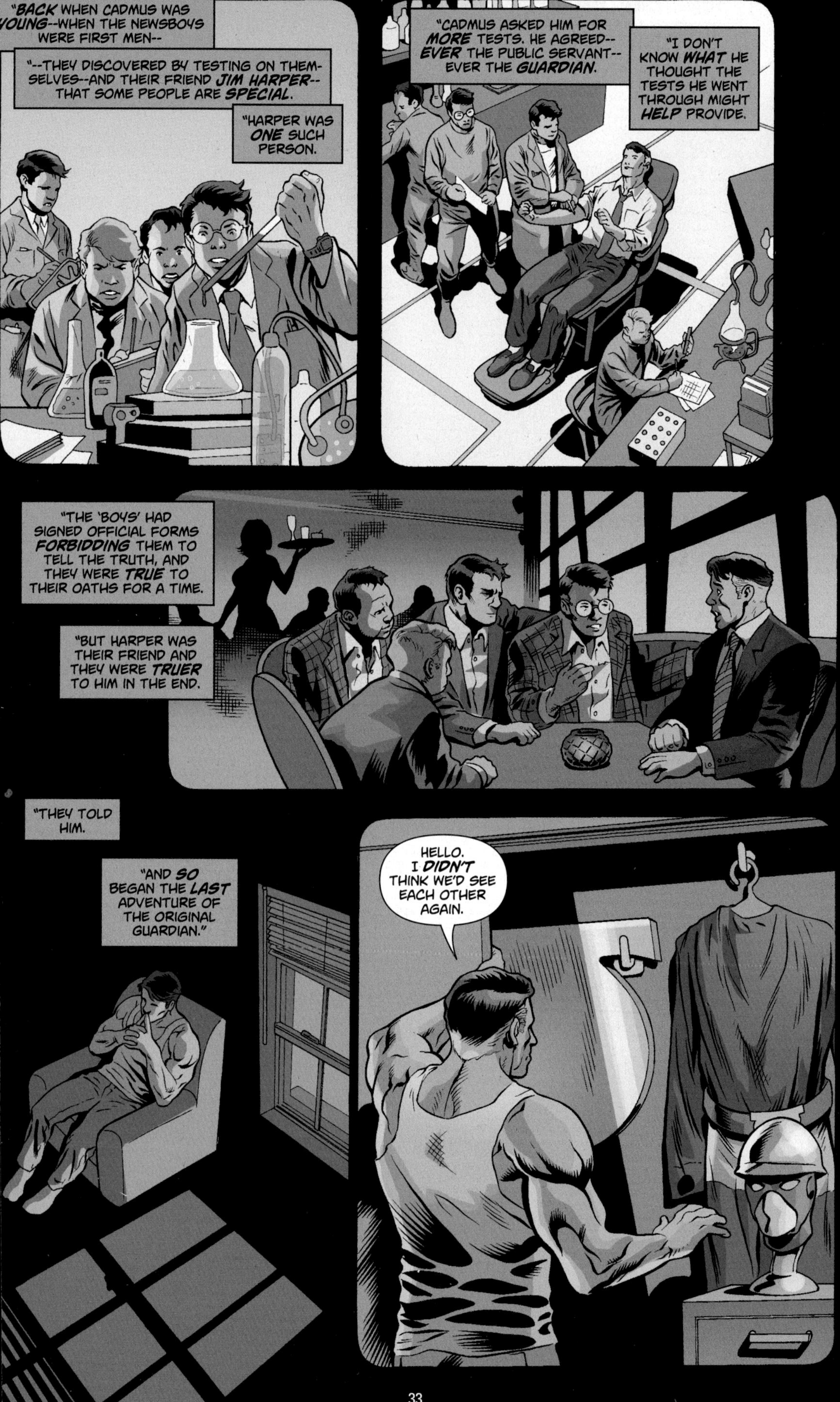
"BACK WHEN CADMUS WAS YOUNG--WHEN THE NEWSBOYS WERE FIRST MEN--
"--THEY DISCOVERED BY TESTING ON THEMSELVES--AND THEIR FRIEND JIM HARPER--THAT SOME PEOPLE ARE SPECIAL.
"HARPER WAS ONE SUCH PERSON.
"CADMUS ASKED HIM FOR MORE TESTS. HE AGREED--EVER THE PUBLIC SERVANT--EVER THE GUARDIAN.
"I DON'T KNOW WHAT HE THOUGHT THE TESTS HE WENT THROUGH MIGHT HELP PROVIDE.
"THE 'BOYS' HAD SIGNED OFFICIAL FORMS FORBIDDING THEM TO TELL THE TRUTH, AND THEY WERE TRUE TO THEIR OATHS FOR A TIME.
"BUT HARPER WAS THEIR FRIEND AND THEY WERE TRUER TO HIM IN THE END.
"THEY TOLD HIM.
"AND SO BEGAN THE LAST ADVENTURE OF THE ORIGINAL GUARDIAN."
HELLO. I DIDN'T THINK WE'D SEE EACH OTHER AGAIN.

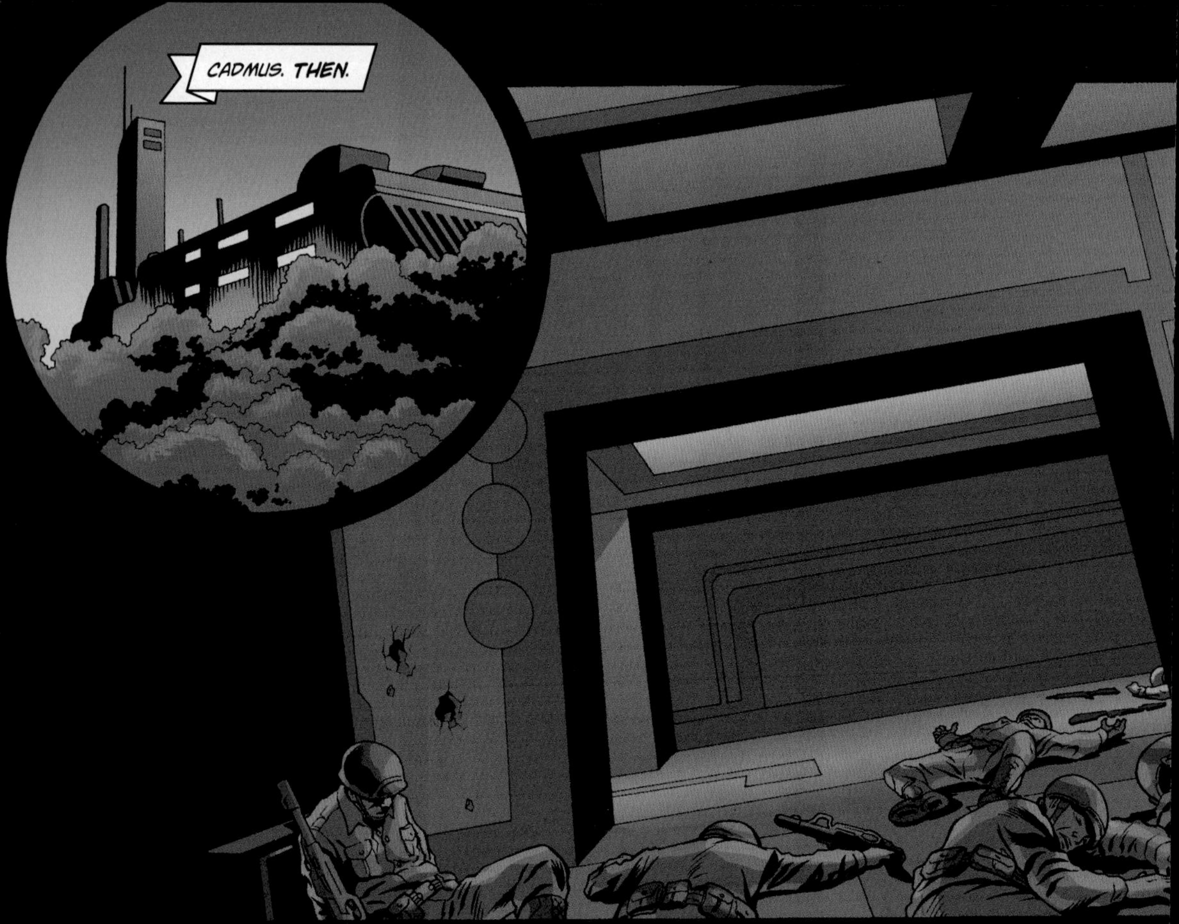
CADMUS. THEN.

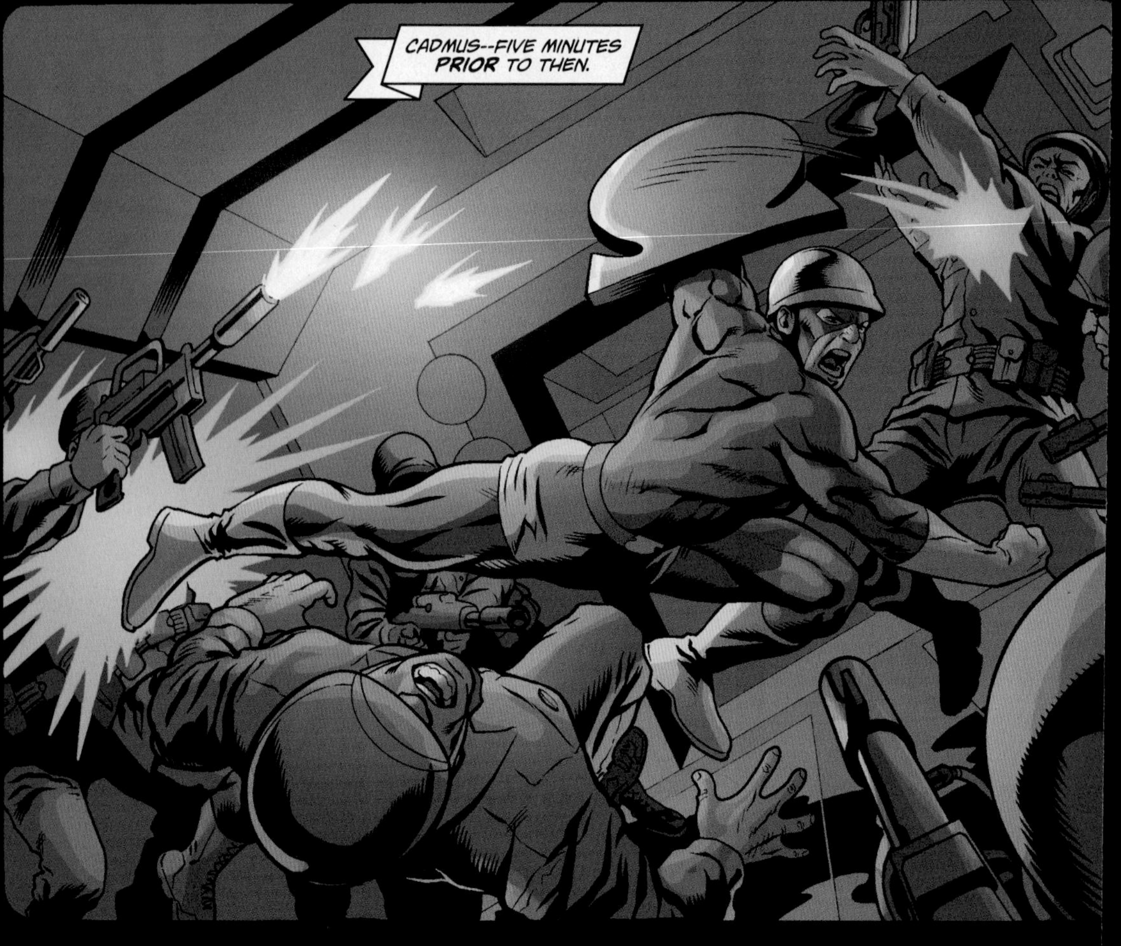
CADMUS--FIVE MINUTES
PRIOR TO THEN.

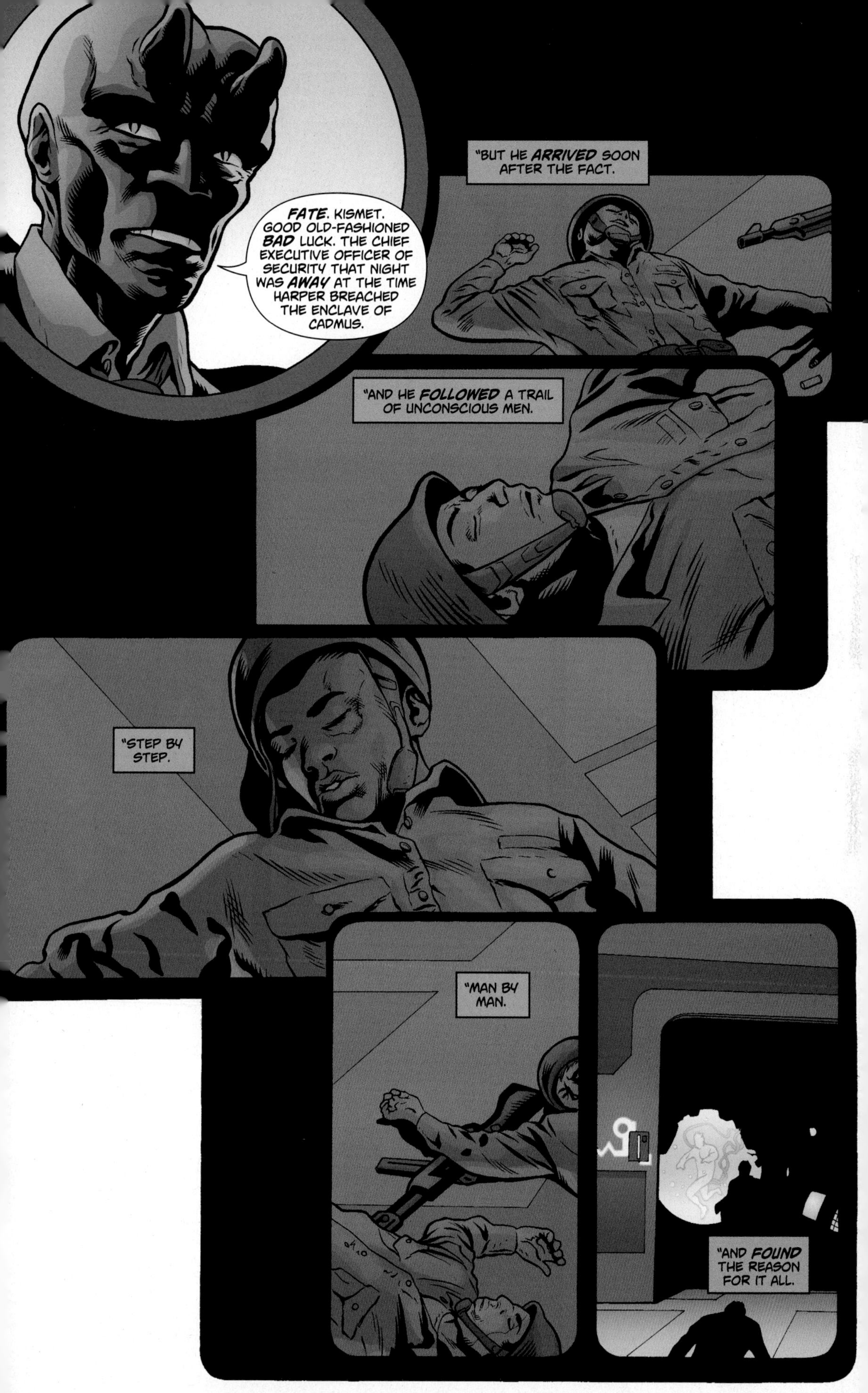
FATE. KISMET. GOOD OLD-FASHIONED BAD LUCK. THE CHIEF EXECUTIVE OFFICER OF SECURITY THAT NIGHT WAS AWAY AT THE TIME HARPER BREACHED THE ENCLAVE OF CADMUS.
"BUT HE ARRIVED SOON AFTER THE FACT.
"AND HE FOLLOWED A TRAIL OF UNCONSCIOUS MEN.
"STEP BY STEP.
"MAN BY MAN.
"AND FOUND THE REASON FOR IT ALL.

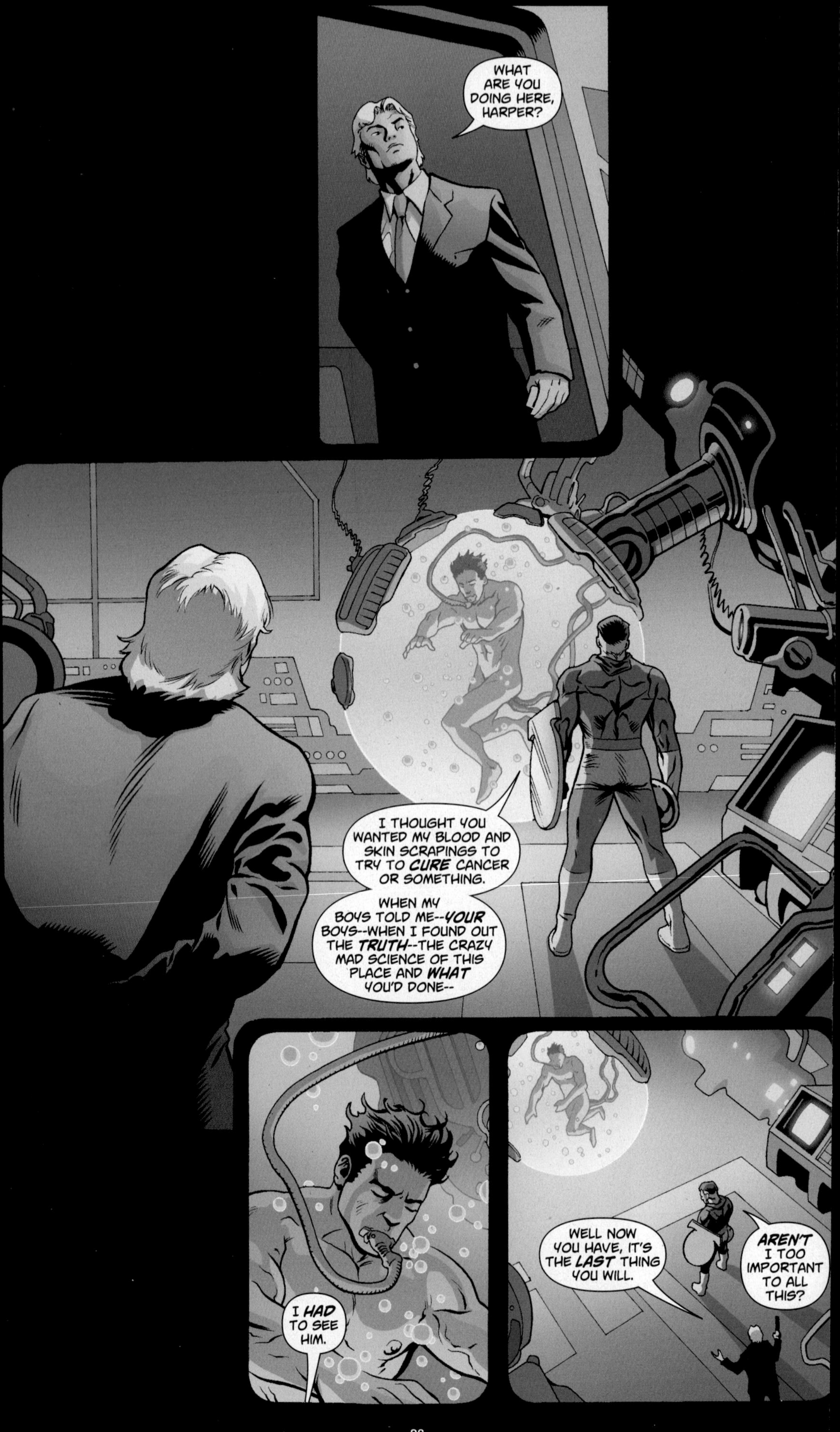
WHAT ARE YOU DOING HERE, HARPER?
I THOUGHT YOU WANTED MY BLOOD AND SKIN SCRAPINGS TO TRY TO *CURE* CANCER OR SOMETHING.
WHEN MY BOYS TOLD ME--*YOUR* BOYS--WHEN I FOUND OUT THE *TRUTH*--THE CRAZY MAD SCIENCE OF THIS PLACE AND *WHAT* YOU'D DONE--
I *HAD* TO SEE HIM.
WELL NOW YOU HAVE, IT'S THE *LAST* THING YOU WILL.
AREN'T I TOO IMPORTANT TO ALL THIS?

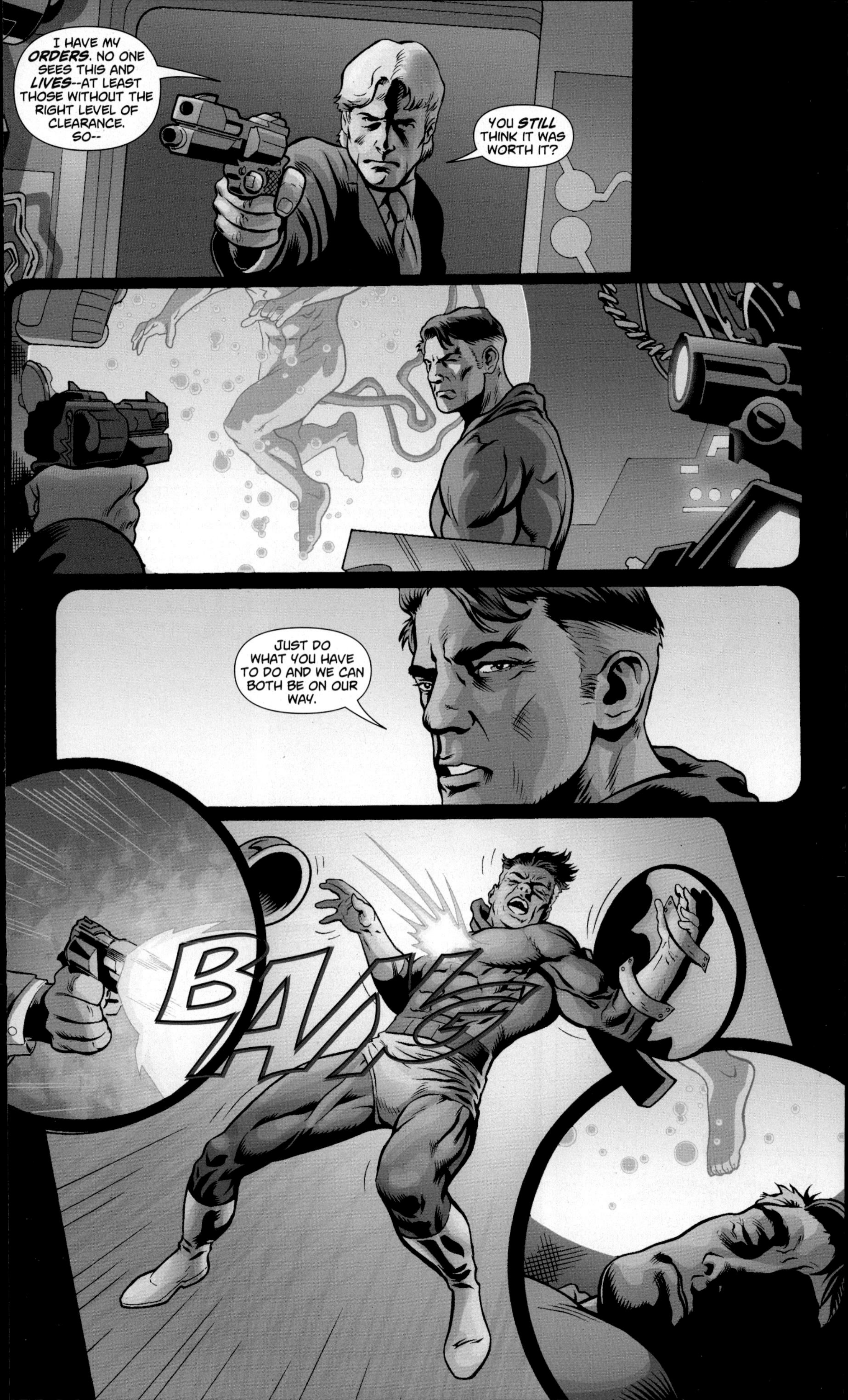
I HAVE MY ORDERS. NO ONE SEES THIS AND LIVES--AT LEAST THOSE WITHOUT THE RIGHT LEVEL OF CLEARANCE. SO--
YOU STILL THINK IT WAS WORTH IT?
JUST DO WHAT YOU HAVE TO DO AND WE CAN BOTH BE ON OUR WAY.
BANG

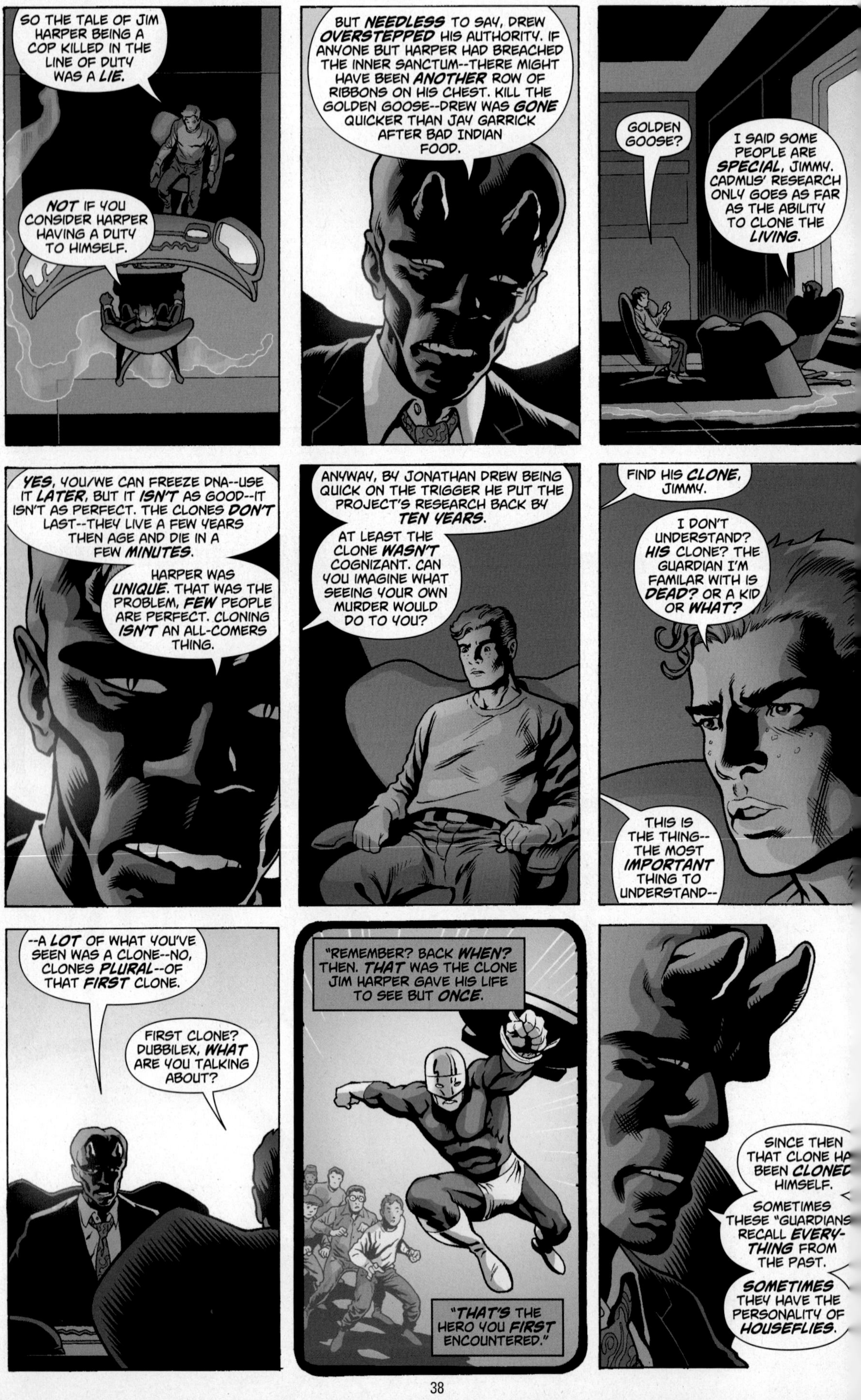
SO THE TALE OF JIM HARPER BEING A COP KILLED IN THE LINE OF DUTY WAS A LIE.
NOT IF YOU CONSIDER HARPER HAVING A DUTY TO HIMSELF.
BUT NEEDLESS TO SAY, DREW OVERSTEPPED HIS AUTHORITY. IF ANYONE BUT HARPER HAD BREACHED THE INNER SANCTUM--THERE MIGHT HAVE BEEN ANOTHER ROW OF RIBBONS ON HIS CHEST. KILL THE GOLDEN GOOSE--DREW WAS GONE QUICKER THAN JAY GARRICK AFTER BAD INDIAN FOOD.
GOLDEN GOOSE?
I SAID SOME PEOPLE ARE SPECIAL, JIMMY. CADMUS' RESEARCH ONLY GOES AS FAR AS THE ABILITY TO CLONE THE LIVING.
YES, YOU/WE CAN FREEZE DNA--USE IT LATER, BUT IT ISN'T AS GOOD--IT ISN'T AS PERFECT. THE CLONES DON'T LAST--THEY LIVE A FEW YEARS THEN AGE AND DIE IN A FEW MINUTES.
HARPER WAS UNIQUE. THAT WAS THE PROBLEM, FEW PEOPLE ARE PERFECT. CLONING ISN'T AN ALL-COMERS THING.
ANYWAY, BY JONATHAN DREW BEING QUICK ON THE TRIGGER HE PUT THE PROJECT'S RESEARCH BACK BY TEN YEARS.
AT LEAST THE CLONE WASN'T COGNIZANT. CAN YOU IMAGINE WHAT SEEING YOUR OWN MURDER WOULD DO TO YOU?
FIND HIS CLONE, JIMMY.
I DON'T UNDERSTAND? HIS CLONE? THE GUARDIAN I'M FAMILAR WITH IS DEAD? OR A KID OR WHAT?
THIS IS THE THING-- THE MOST IMPORTANT THING TO UNDERSTAND--
--A LOT OF WHAT YOU'VE SEEN WAS A CLONE--NO, CLONES PLURAL--OF THAT FIRST CLONE.
FIRST CLONE? DUBBILEX, WHAT ARE YOU TALKING ABOUT?
"REMEMBER? BACK WHEN? THEN. THAT WAS THE CLONE JIM HARPER GAVE HIS LIFE TO SEE BUT ONCE.
"THAT'S THE HERO YOU FIRST ENCOUNTERED."
SINCE THEN THAT CLONE HA BEEN CLONED HIMSELF.
SOMETIMES THESE "GUARDIANS RECALL EVERY-THING FROM THE PAST.
SOMETIMES THEY HAVE THE PERSONALITY OF HOUSEFLIES.

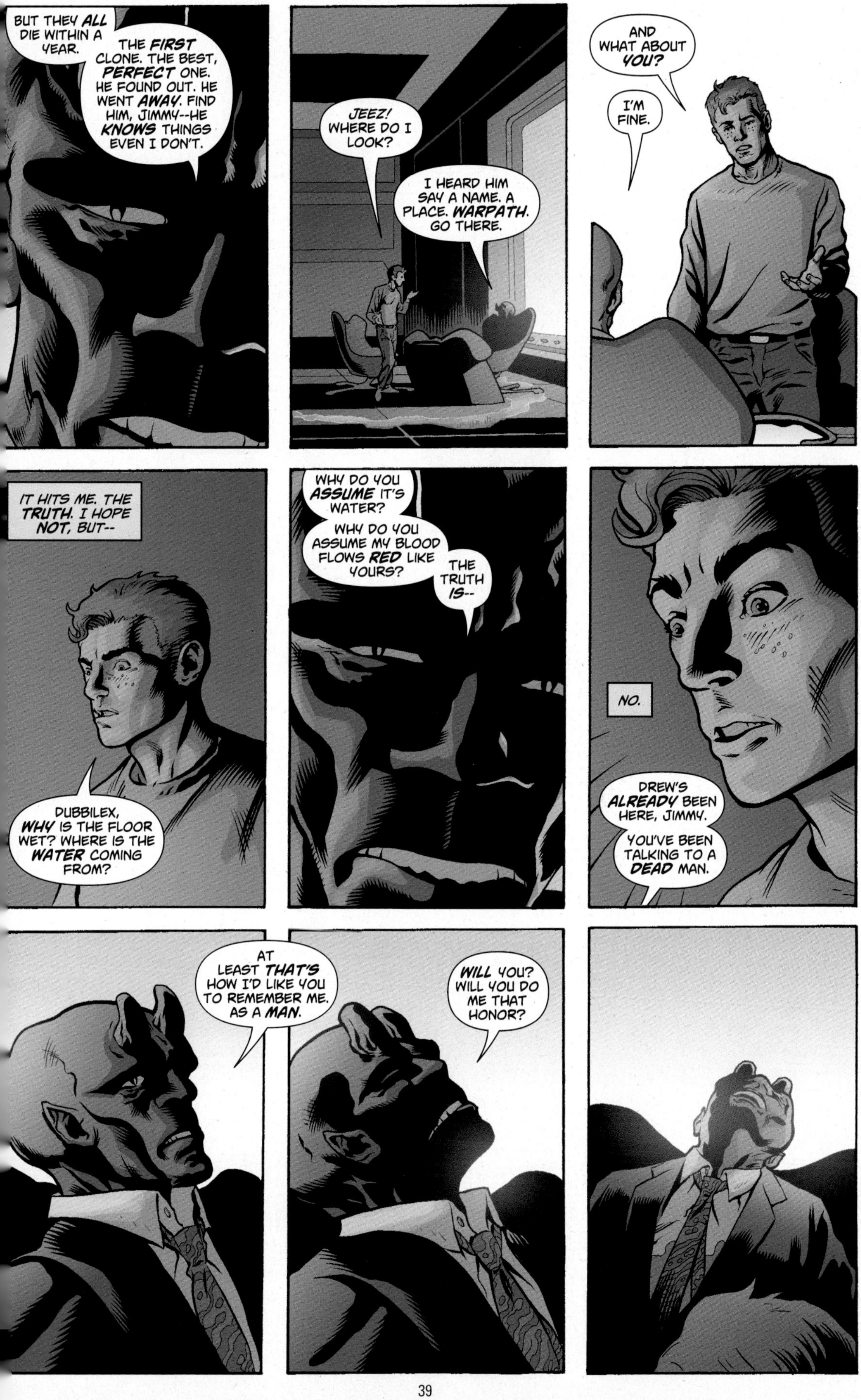
BUT THEY ALL DIE WITHIN A YEAR.
THE FIRST CLONE. THE BEST, PERFECT ONE. HE FOUND OUT. HE WENT AWAY. FIND HIM, JIMMY--HE KNOWS THINGS EVEN I DON'T.
JEEZ! WHERE DO I LOOK?
I HEARD HIM SAY A NAME. A PLACE. WARPATH. GO THERE.
AND WHAT ABOUT YOU?
I'M FINE.
IT HITS ME. THE TRUTH. I HOPE NOT, BUT--
DUBBILEX, WHY IS THE FLOOR WET? WHERE IS THE WATER COMING FROM?
WHY DO YOU ASSUME IT'S WATER?
WHY DO YOU ASSUME MY BLOOD FLOWS RED LIKE YOURS?
THE TRUTH IS--
NO.
DREW'S ALREADY BEEN HERE, JIMMY.
YOU'VE BEEN TALKING TO A DEAD MAN.
AT LEAST THAT'S HOW I'D LIKE YOU TO REMEMBER ME. AS A MAN.
WILL YOU? WILL YOU DO ME THAT HONOR?

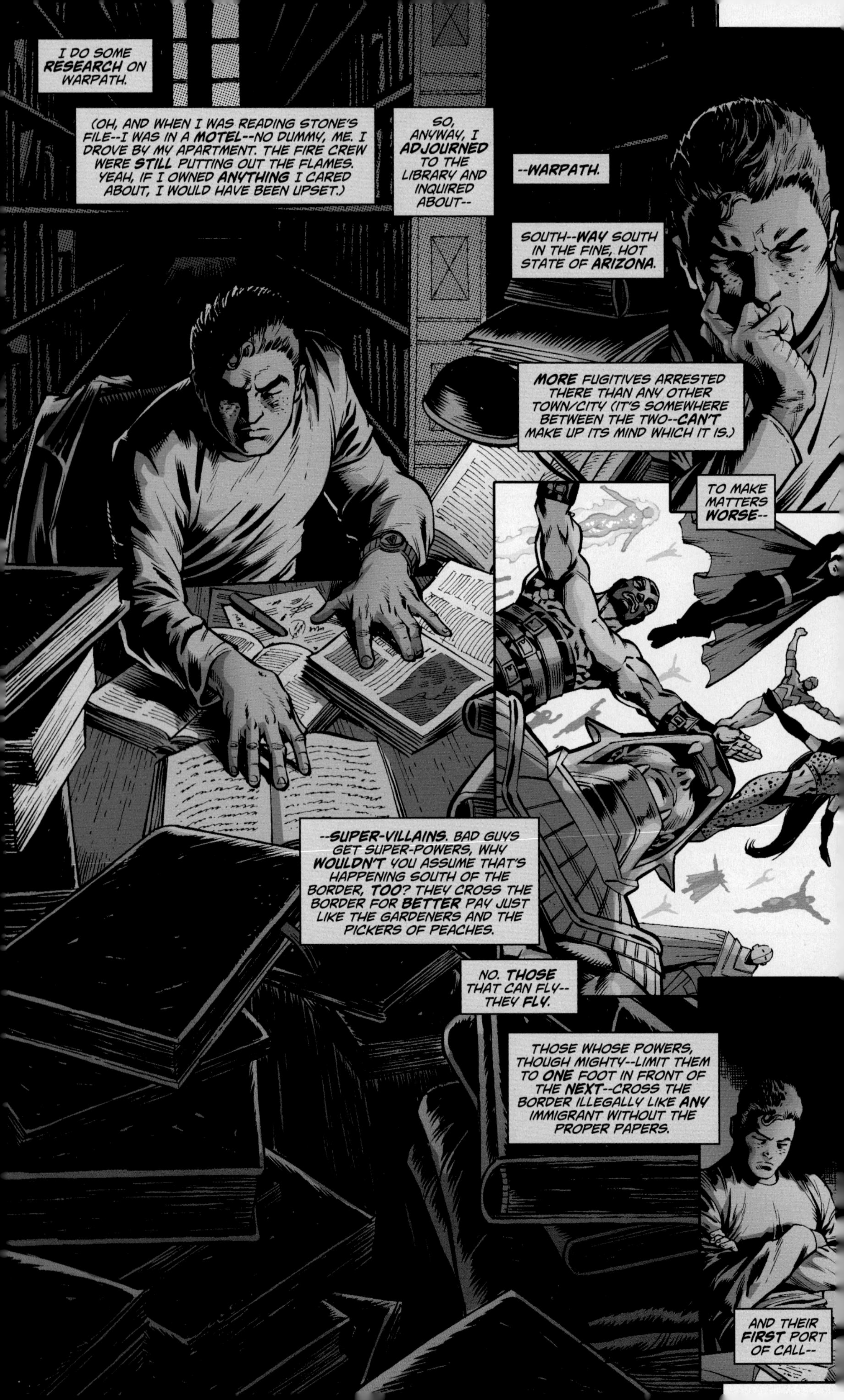
I DO SOME RESEARCH ON WARPATH.
(OH, AND WHEN I WAS READING STONE'S FILE--I WAS IN A MOTEL--NO DUMMY, ME. I DROVE BY MY APARTMENT. THE FIRE CREW WERE STILL PUTTING OUT THE FLAMES. YEAH, IF I OWNED ANYTHING I CARED ABOUT, I WOULD HAVE BEEN UPSET.)
SO, ANYWAY, I ADJOURNED TO THE LIBRARY AND INQUIRED ABOUT--
--WARPATH.
SOUTH--WAY SOUTH IN THE FINE, HOT STATE OF ARIZONA.
MORE FUGITIVES ARRESTED THERE THAN ANY OTHER TOWN/CITY (IT'S SOMEWHERE BETWEEN THE TWO--CAN'T MAKE UP ITS MIND WHICH IT IS.)
TO MAKE MATTERS WORSE--
--SUPER-VILLAINS. BAD GUYS GET SUPER-POWERS, WHY WOULDN'T YOU ASSUME THAT'S HAPPENING SOUTH OF THE BORDER, TOO? THEY CROSS THE BORDER FOR BETTER PAY JUST LIKE THE GARDENERS AND THE PICKERS OF PEACHES.
NO. THOSE THAT CAN FLY--THEY FLY.
THOSE WHOSE POWERS, THOUGH MIGHTY--LIMIT THEM TO ONE FOOT IN FRONT OF THE NEXT--CROSS THE BORDER ILLEGALLY LIKE ANY IMMIGRANT WITHOUT THE PROPER PAPERS.
AND THEIR FIRST PORT OF CALL--

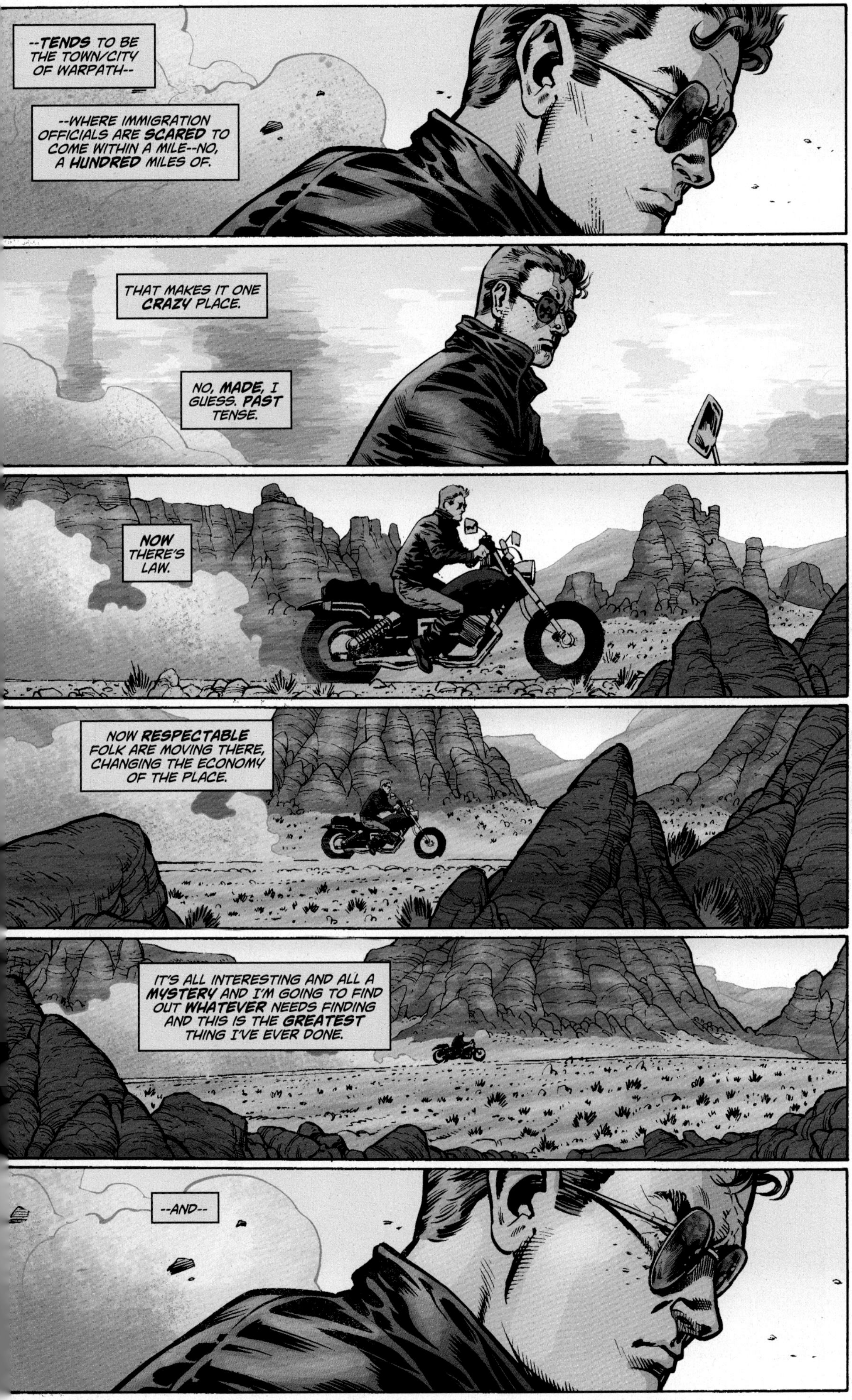
--TENDS TO BE THE TOWN/CITY OF WARPATH--
--WHERE IMMIGRATION OFFICIALS ARE SCARED TO COME WITHIN A MILE--NO, A HUNDRED MILES OF.
THAT MAKES IT ONE CRAZY PLACE.
NO, MADE, I GUESS. PAST TENSE.
NOW THERE'S LAW.
NOW RESPECTABLE FOLK ARE MOVING THERE, CHANGING THE ECONOMY OF THE PLACE.
IT'S ALL INTERESTING AND ALL A MYSTERY AND I'M GOING TO FIND OUT WHATEVER NEEDS FINDING AND THIS IS THE GREATEST THING I'VE EVER DONE.
--AND--

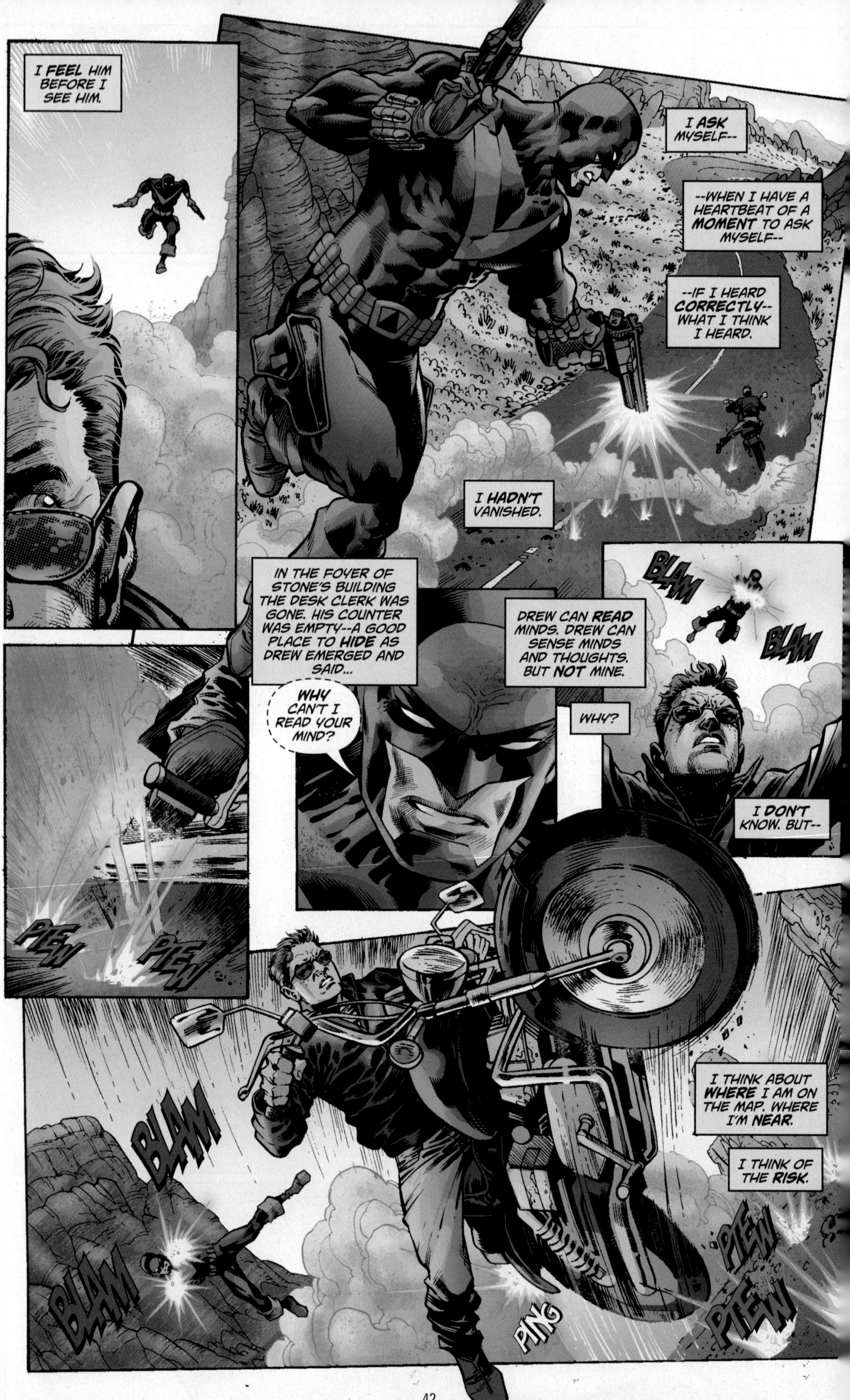
I FEEL HIM BEFORE I SEE HIM.
I ASK MYSELF--
--WHEN I HAVE A HEARTBEAT OF A MOMENT TO ASK MYSELF--
--IF I HEARD CORRECTLY-- WHAT I THINK I HEARD.
I HADN'T VANISHED.
IN THE FOYER OF STONE'S BUILDING THE DESK CLERK WAS GONE. HIS COUNTER WAS EMPTY--A GOOD PLACE TO HIDE AS DREW EMERGED AND SAID...
WHY CAN'T I READ YOUR MIND?
DREW CAN READ MINDS. DREW CAN SENSE MINDS AND THOUGHTS. BUT NOT MINE.
WHY?
BLAM
BLAM
I DON'T KNOW. BUT--
PTEW
PTEW
I THINK ABOUT WHERE I AM ON THE MAP. WHERE I'M NEAR.
I THINK OF THE RISK.
BLAM
BLAM
PING
PTEW
PTEW

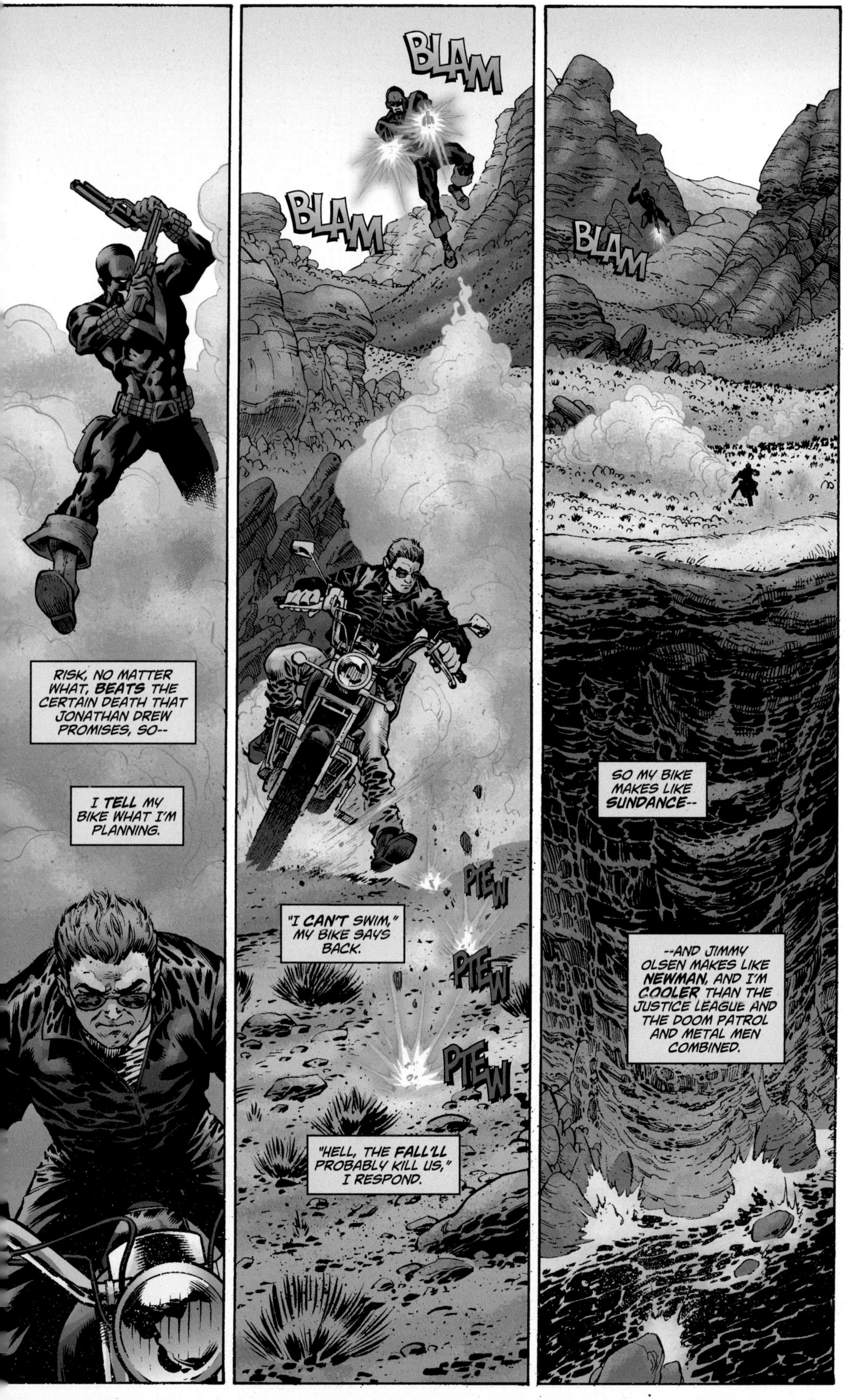
RISK, NO MATTER WHAT, BEATS THE CERTAIN DEATH THAT JONATHAN DREW PROMISES, SO--
I TELL MY BIKE WHAT I'M PLANNING.
BLAM
BLAM
"I CAN'T SWIM," MY BIKE SAYS BACK.
PTEW
PTEW
PTEW
"HELL, THE FALL'LL PROBABLY KILL US," I RESPOND.
BLAM
SO MY BIKE MAKES LIKE SUNDANCE--
--AND JIMMY OLSEN MAKES LIKE NEWMAN, AND I'M COOLER THAN THE JUSTICE LEAGUE AND THE DOOM PATROL AND METAL MEN COMBINED.

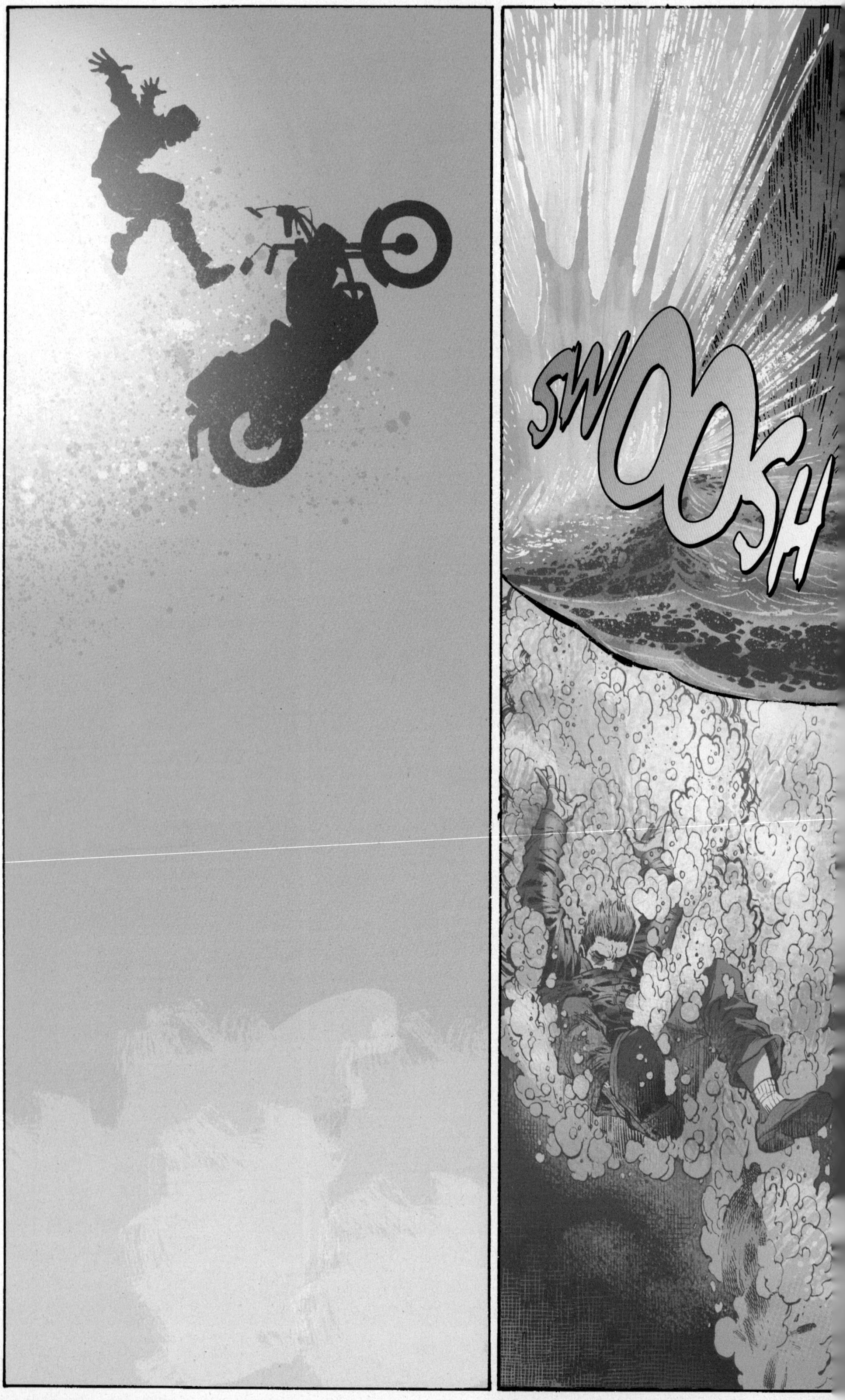
SWOOSH

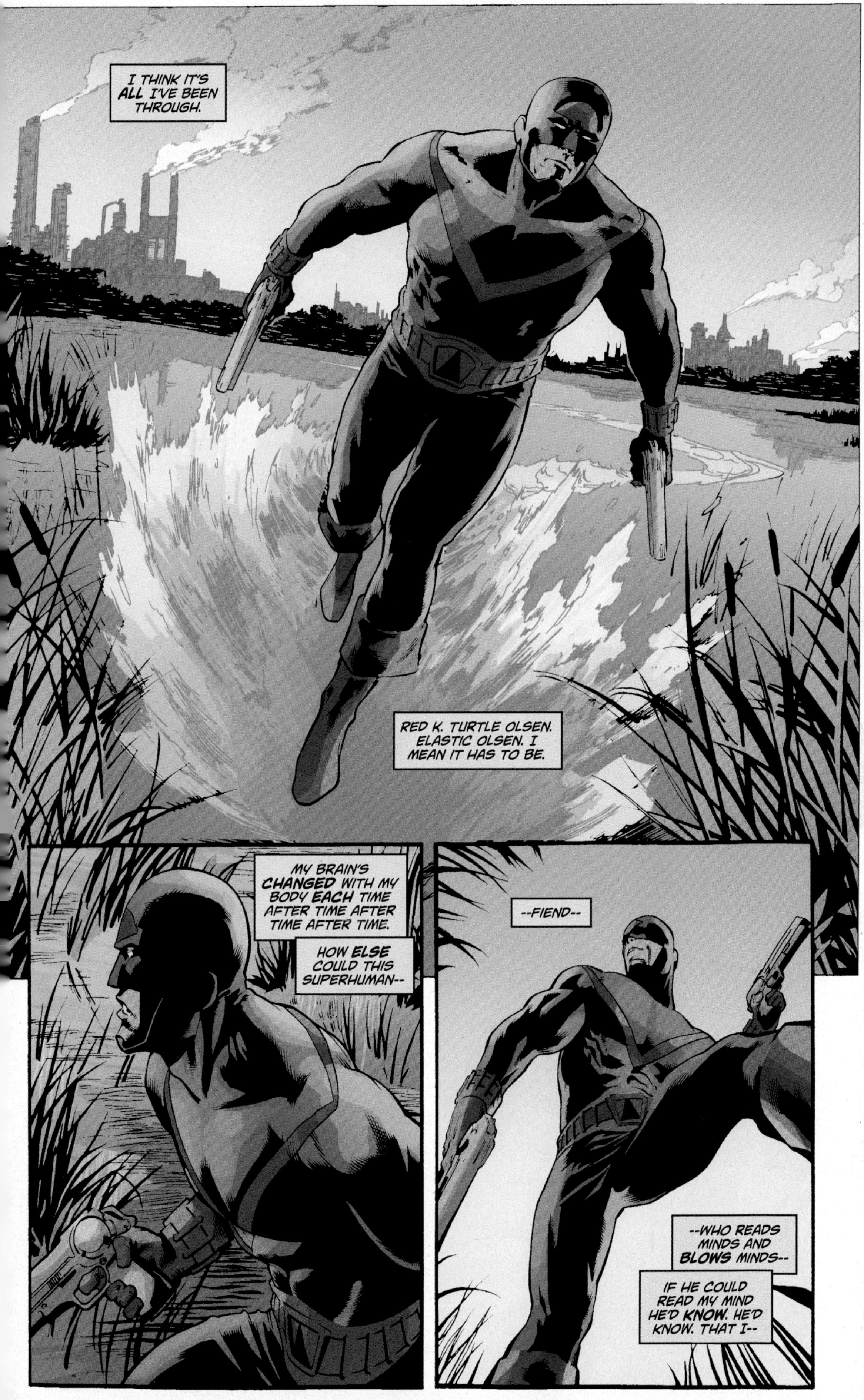
I THINK IT'S ALL I'VE BEEN THROUGH.
RED K. TURTLE OLSEN. ELASTIC OLSEN. I MEAN IT HAS TO BE.
MY BRAIN'S CHANGED WITH MY BODY EACH TIME AFTER TIME AFTER TIME AFTER TIME.
HOW ELSE COULD THIS SUPERHUMAN--
--FIEND--
--WHO READS MINDS AND BLOWS MINDS--
IF HE COULD READ MY MIND HE'D KNOW. HE'D KNOW. THAT I--

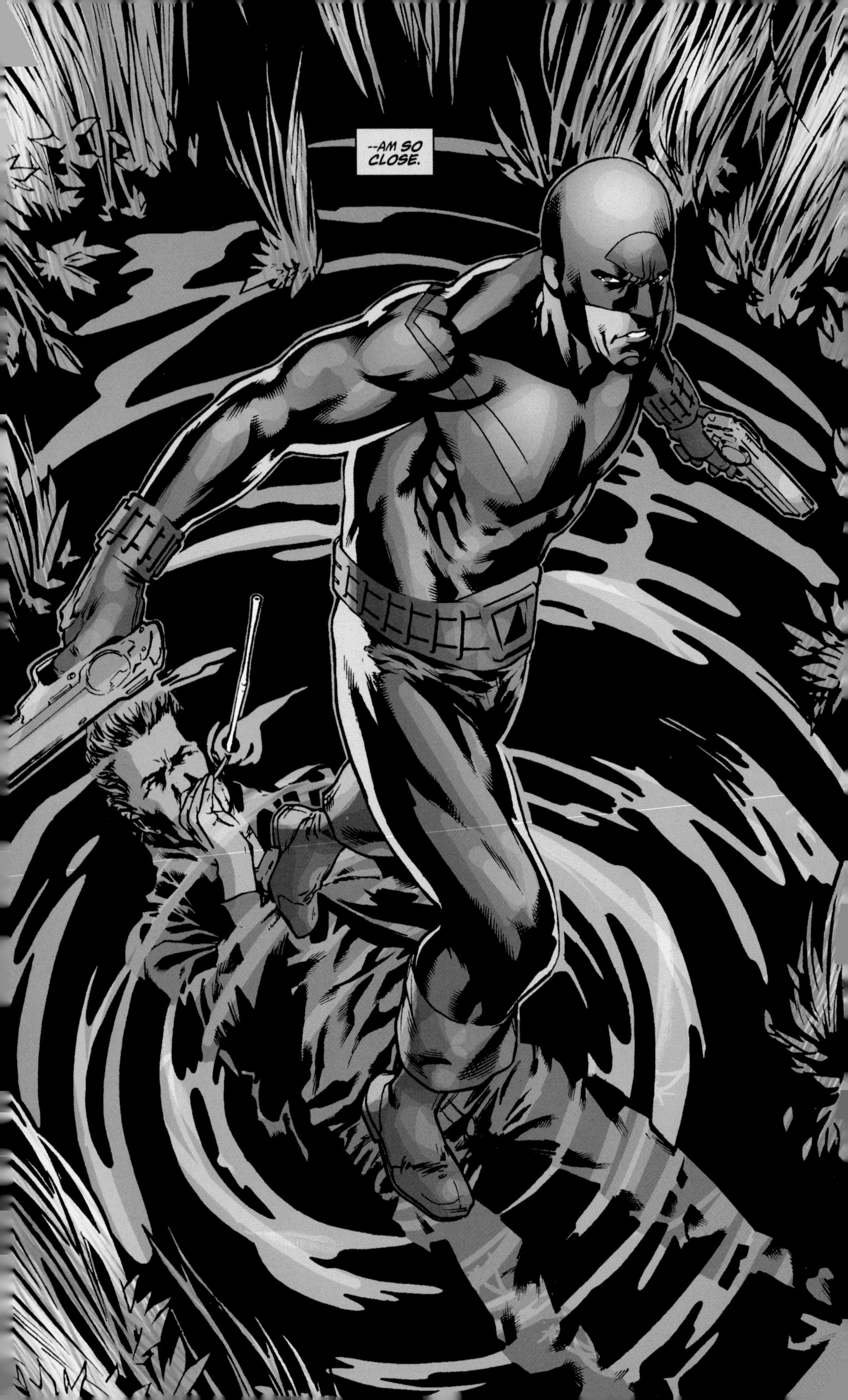
--AM SO CLOSE.

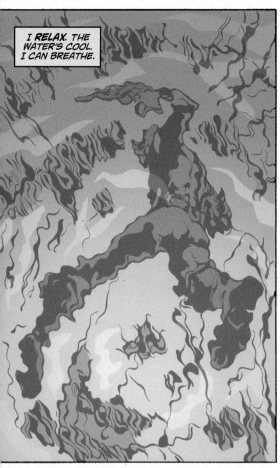

I *RELAX*. THE WATER'S COOL. I CAN BREATHE.

I WAIT FOR AN HOUR. NO, *MORE* THAN AN HOUR.

THEN I SURFACE.

THEN I DRY.

THEN I TRAVEL BY *THUMB*--

--TO WARPATH.

--*LIKE NO OTHER TOWN.*

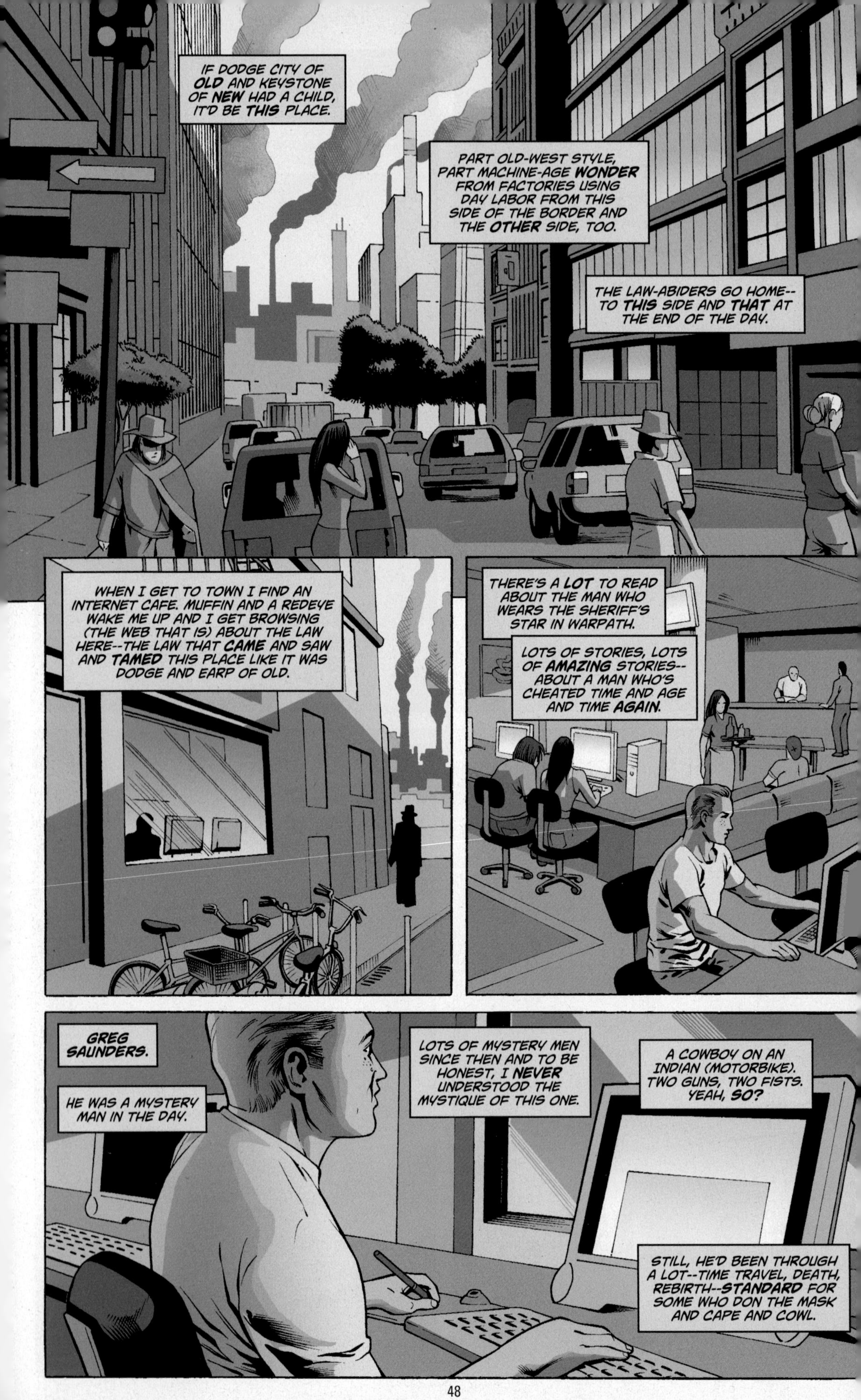

IF DODGE CITY OF OLD AND KEYSTONE OF NEW HAD A CHILD, IT'D BE THIS PLACE.
PART OLD-WEST STYLE, PART MACHINE-AGE WONDER FROM FACTORIES USING DAY LABOR FROM THIS SIDE OF THE BORDER AND THE OTHER SIDE, TOO.
THE LAW-ABIDERS GO HOME--TO THIS SIDE AND THAT AT THE END OF THE DAY.
WHEN I GET TO TOWN I FIND AN INTERNET CAFE. MUFFIN AND A REDEYE WAKE ME UP AND I GET BROWSING (THE WEB THAT IS) ABOUT THE LAW HERE--THE LAW THAT CAME AND SAW AND TAMED THIS PLACE LIKE IT WAS DODGE AND EARP OF OLD.
THERE'S A LOT TO READ ABOUT THE MAN WHO WEARS THE SHERIFF'S STAR IN WARPATH.
LOTS OF STORIES, LOTS OF AMAZING STORIES--ABOUT A MAN WHO'S CHEATED TIME AND AGE AND TIME AGAIN.
GREG SAUNDERS.
HE WAS A MYSTERY MAN IN THE DAY.
LOTS OF MYSTERY MEN SINCE THEN AND TO BE HONEST, I NEVER UNDERSTOOD THE MYSTIQUE OF THIS ONE.
A COWBOY ON AN INDIAN (MOTORBIKE). TWO GUNS, TWO FISTS. YEAH, SO?
STILL, HE'D BEEN THROUGH A LOT--TIME TRAVEL, DEATH, REBIRTH--STANDARD FOR SOME WHO DON THE MASK AND CAPE AND COWL.

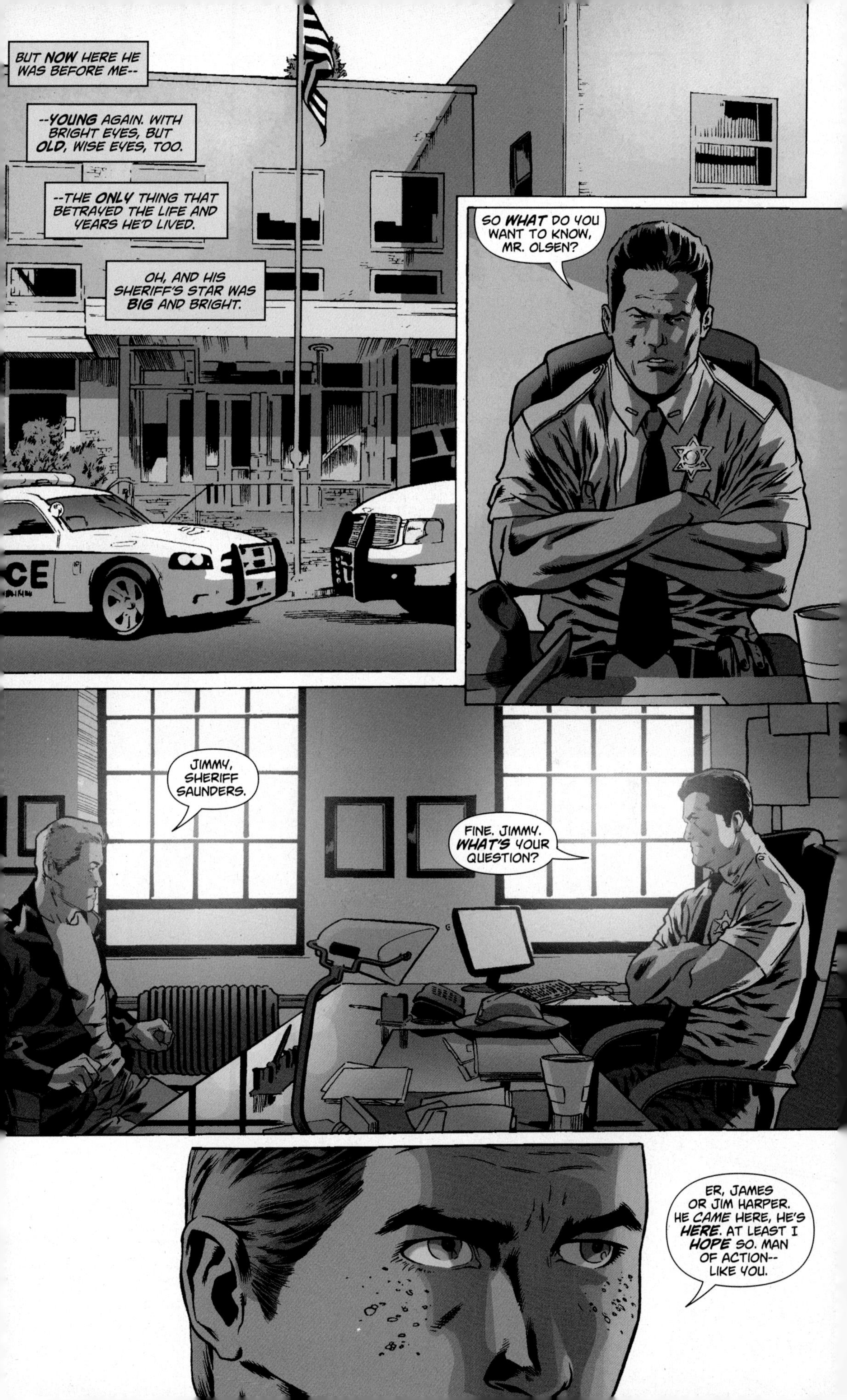
BUT NOW HERE HE WAS BEFORE ME--
--YOUNG AGAIN. WITH BRIGHT EYES, BUT OLD, WISE EYES, TOO.
--THE ONLY THING THAT BETRAYED THE LIFE AND YEARS HE'D LIVED.
OH, AND HIS SHERIFF'S STAR WAS BIG AND BRIGHT.
CE
SO WHAT DO YOU WANT TO KNOW, MR. OLSEN?
JIMMY, SHERIFF SAUNDERS.
FINE. JIMMY. WHAT'S YOUR QUESTION?
ER, JAMES OR JIM HARPER. HE CAME HERE, HE'S HERE. AT LEAST I HOPE SO. MAN OF ACTION-- LIKE YOU.

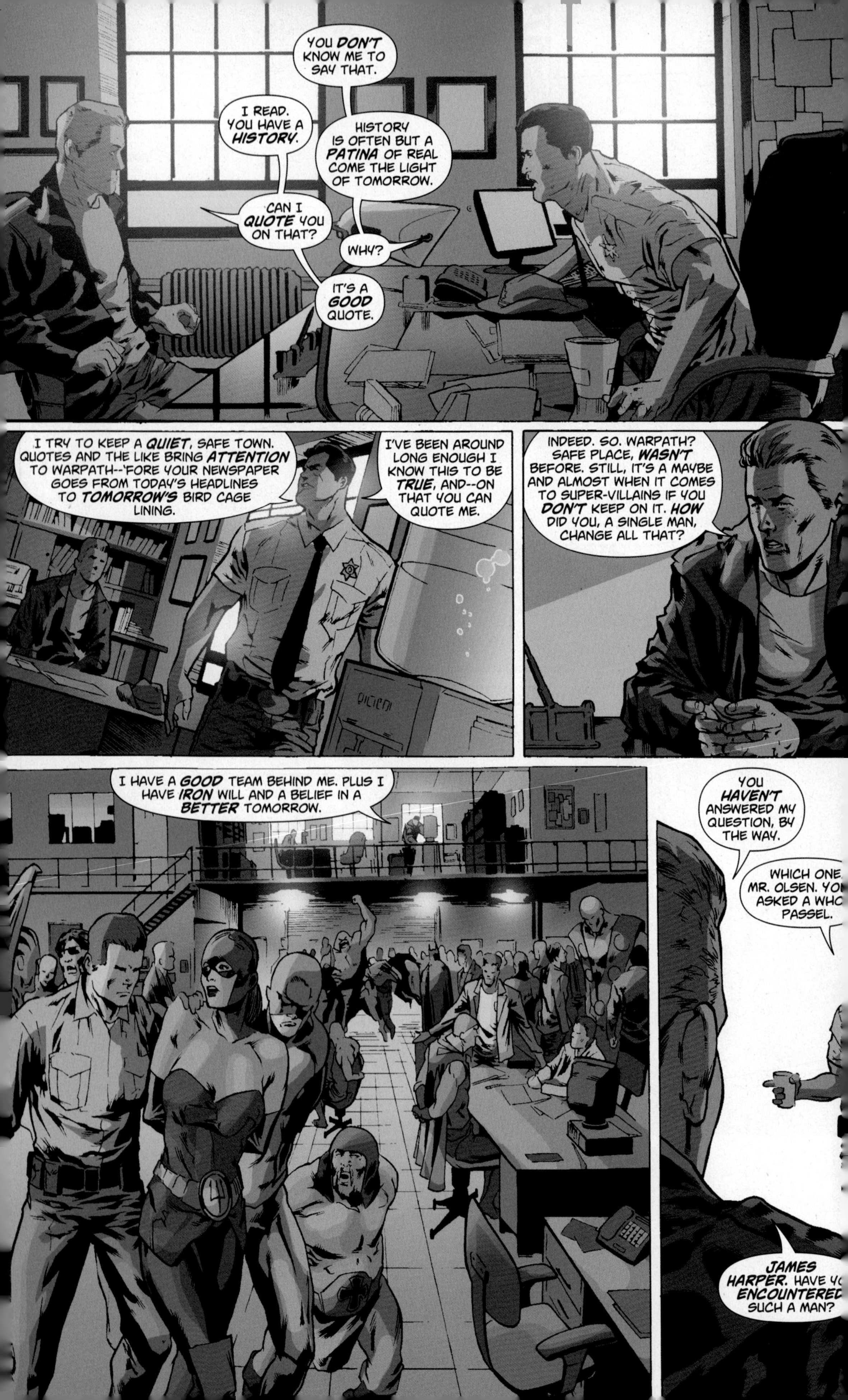

I READ. YOU HAVE A HISTORY.
YOU DON'T KNOW ME TO SAY THAT.
HISTORY IS OFTEN BUT A PATINA OF REAL COME THE LIGHT OF TOMORROW.
CAN I QUOTE YOU ON THAT?
WHY?
IT'S A GOOD QUOTE.
I TRY TO KEEP A QUIET, SAFE TOWN. QUOTES AND THE LIKE BRING ATTENTION TO WARPATH--'FORE YOUR NEWSPAPER GOES FROM TODAY'S HEADLINES TO TOMORROW'S BIRD CAGE LINING.
I'VE BEEN AROUND LONG ENOUGH I KNOW THIS TO BE TRUE, AND--ON THAT YOU CAN QUOTE ME.
INDEED. SO. WARPATH? SAFE PLACE, WASN'T BEFORE. STILL, IT'S A MAYBE AND ALMOST WHEN IT COMES TO SUPER-VILLAINS IF YOU DON'T KEEP ON IT. HOW DID YOU, A SINGLE MAN, CHANGE ALL THAT?
I HAVE A GOOD TEAM BEHIND ME. PLUS I HAVE IRON WILL AND A BELIEF IN A BETTER TOMORROW.
YOU HAVEN'T ANSWERED MY QUESTION, BY THE WAY.
WHICH ONE MR. OLSEN. YO ASKED A WHO PASSEL.
JAMES HARPER. HAVE YO ENCOUNTERED SUCH A MAN?

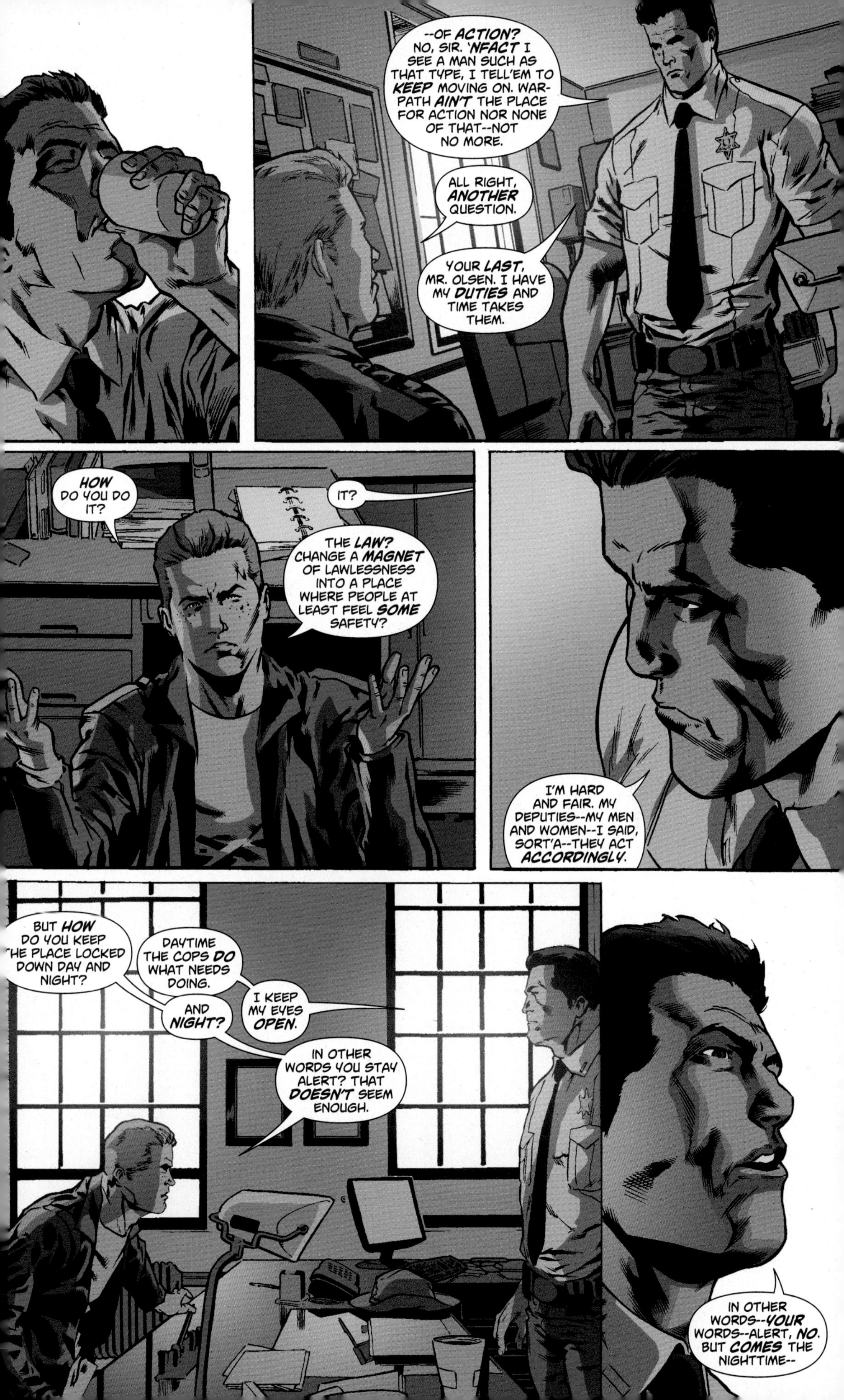

--OF ACTION? NO, SIR. 'NFACT I SEE A MAN SUCH AS THAT TYPE, I TELL'EM TO KEEP MOVING ON. WAR-PATH AIN'T THE PLACE FOR ACTION NOR NONE OF THAT--NOT NO MORE.
ALL RIGHT, ANOTHER QUESTION.
YOUR LAST, MR. OLSEN. I HAVE MY DUTIES AND TIME TAKES THEM.
HOW DO YOU DO IT?
IT?
THE LAW? CHANGE A MAGNET OF LAWLESSNESS INTO A PLACE WHERE PEOPLE AT LEAST FEEL SOME SAFETY?
I'M HARD AND FAIR. MY DEPUTIES--MY MEN AND WOMEN--I SAID, SORT'A--THEY ACT ACCORDINGLY.
BUT HOW DO YOU KEEP THE PLACE LOCKED DOWN DAY AND NIGHT?
DAYTIME THE COPS DO WHAT NEEDS DOING.
AND NIGHT?
I KEEP MY EYES OPEN.
IN OTHER WORDS YOU STAY ALERT? THAT DOESN'T SEEM ENOUGH.
IN OTHER WORDS--YOUR WORDS--ALERT, NO. BUT COMES THE NIGHTTIME--

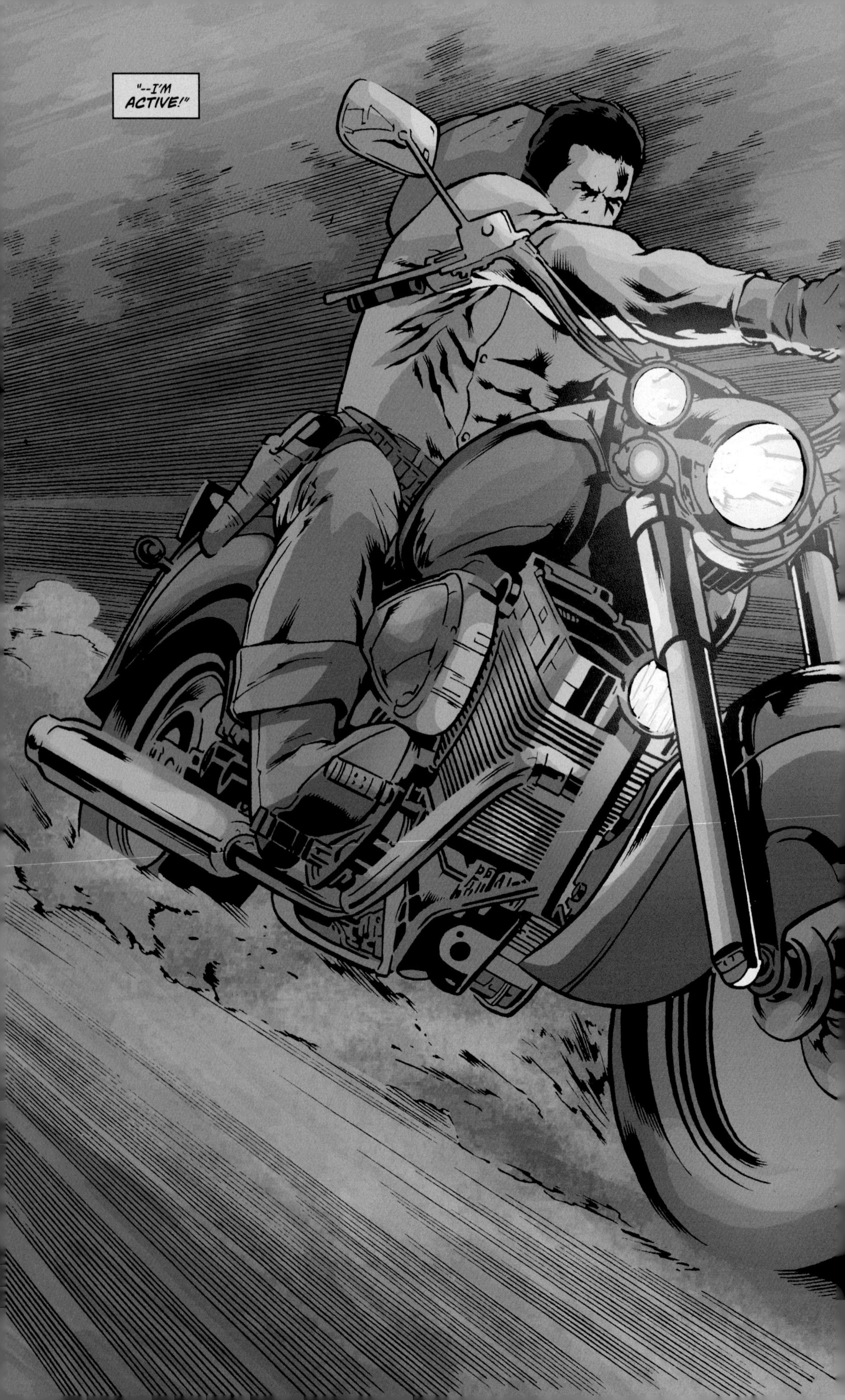
"--I'M ACTIVE!"

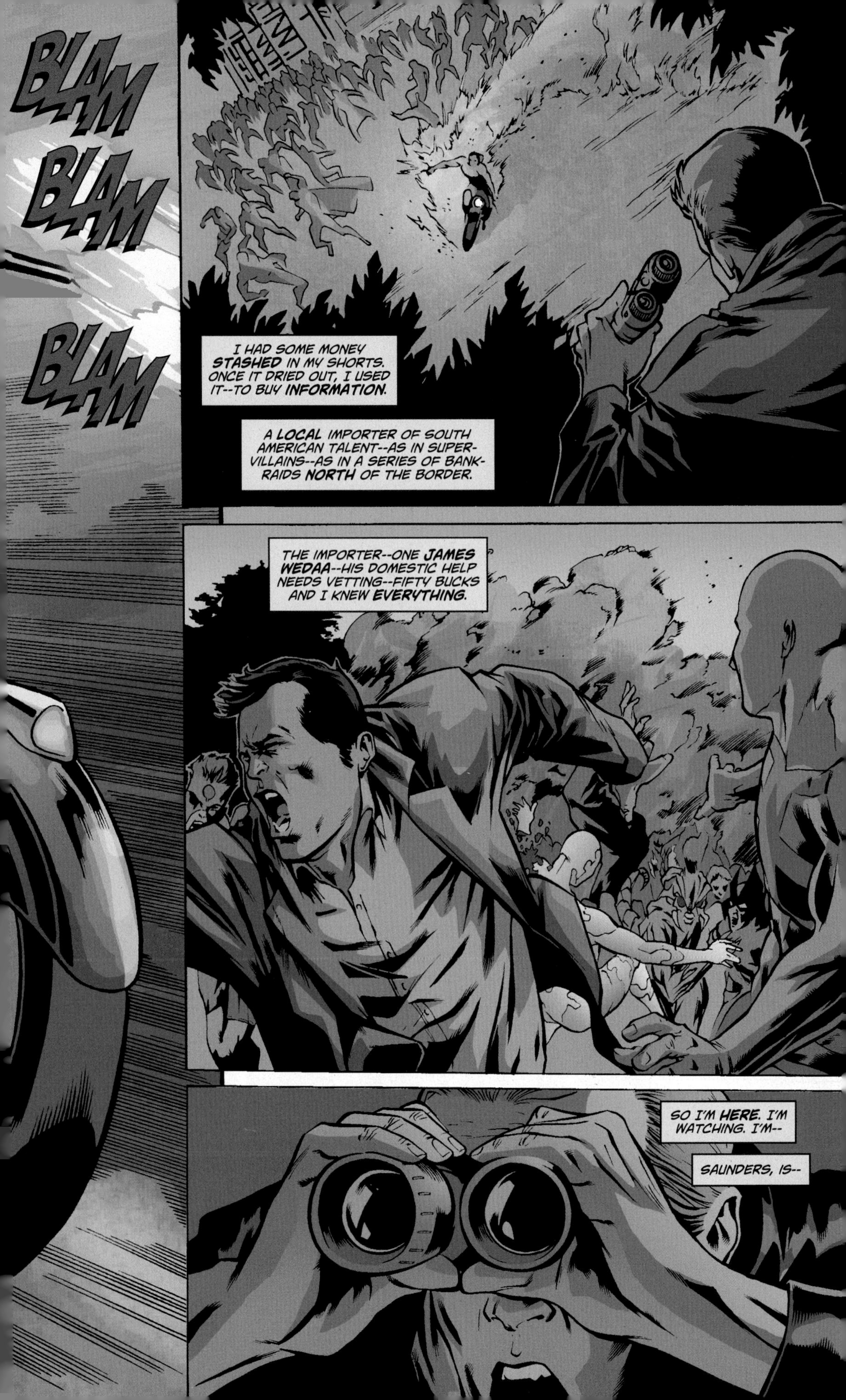
BLAM
BLAM
BLAM
I HAD SOME MONEY STASHED IN MY SHORTS. ONCE IT DRIED OUT, I USED IT--TO BUY INFORMATION.
A LOCAL IMPORTER OF SOUTH AMERICAN TALENT--AS IN SUPER-VILLAINS--AS IN A SERIES OF BANK-RAIDS NORTH OF THE BORDER.
THE IMPORTER--ONE JAMES WEDAA--HIS DOMESTIC HELP NEEDS VETTING--FIFTY BUCKS AND I KNEW EVERYTHING.
SO I'M HERE. I'M WATCHING. I'M--
SAUNDERS, IS--

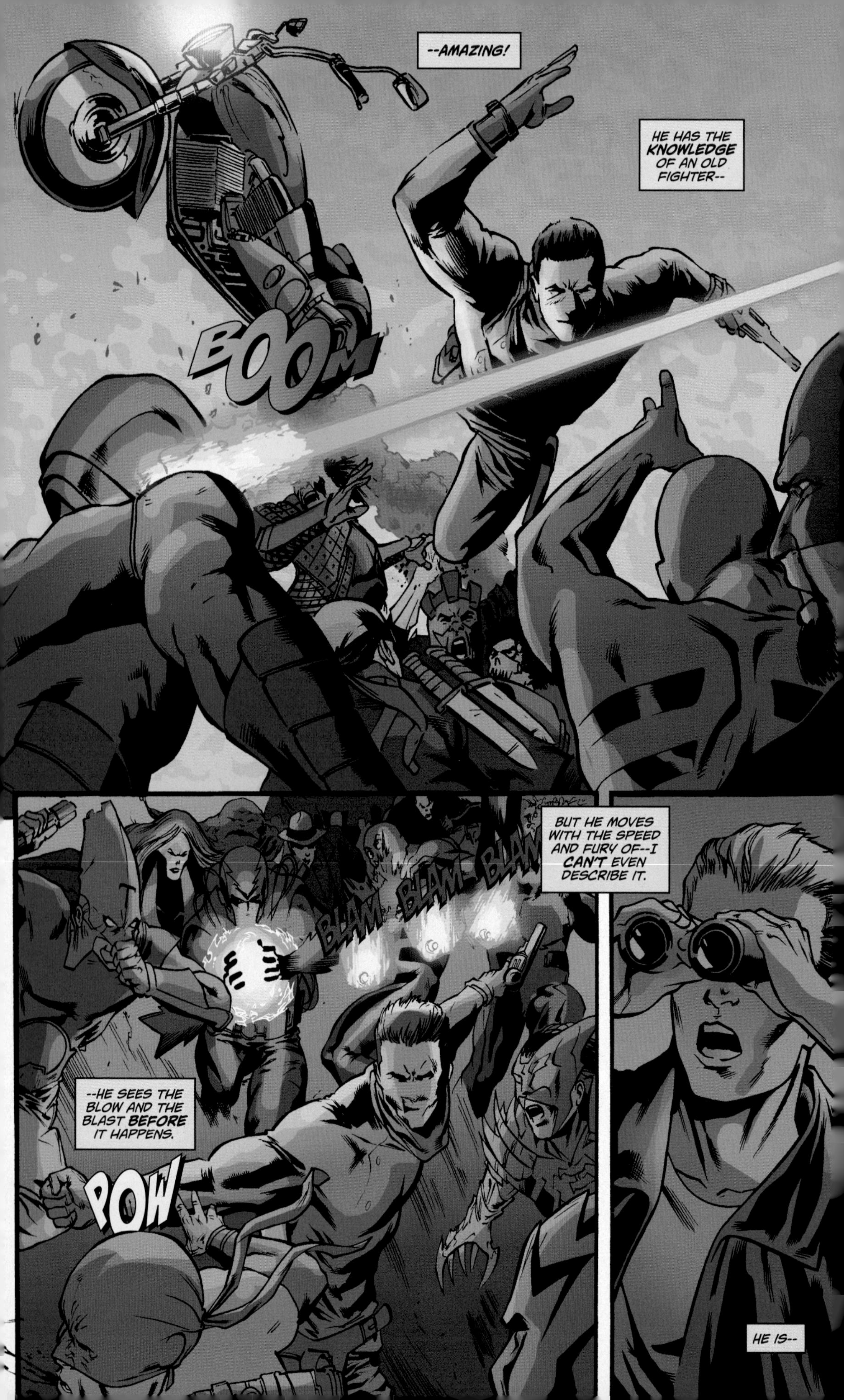
--AMAZING!
HE HAS THE KNOWLEDGE OF AN OLD FIGHTER--
BOOM
BUT HE MOVES WITH THE SPEED AND FURY OF--I CAN'T EVEN DESCRIBE IT.
BLAM BLAM BLAM
--HE SEES THE BLOW AND THE BLAST BEFORE IT HAPPENS.
POW
HE IS--

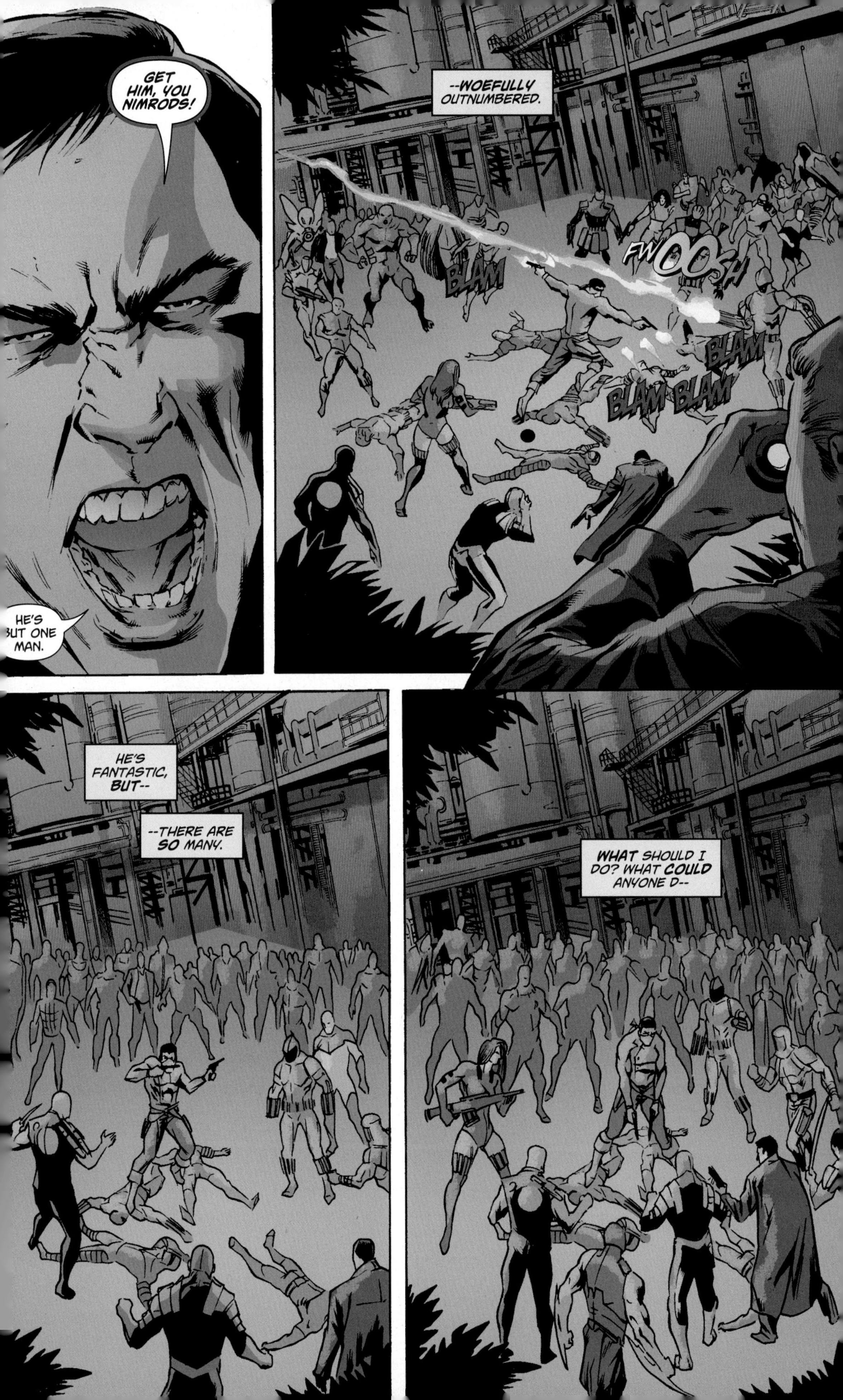
GET HIM, YOU NIMRODS!
HE'S BUT ONE MAN.
--WOEFULLY OUTNUMBERED.
BLAM
FWOOSH
BLAM
BLAM BLAM
HE'S FANTASTIC, BUT--
--THERE ARE SO MANY.
WHAT SHOULD I DO? WHAT COULD ANYONE D--

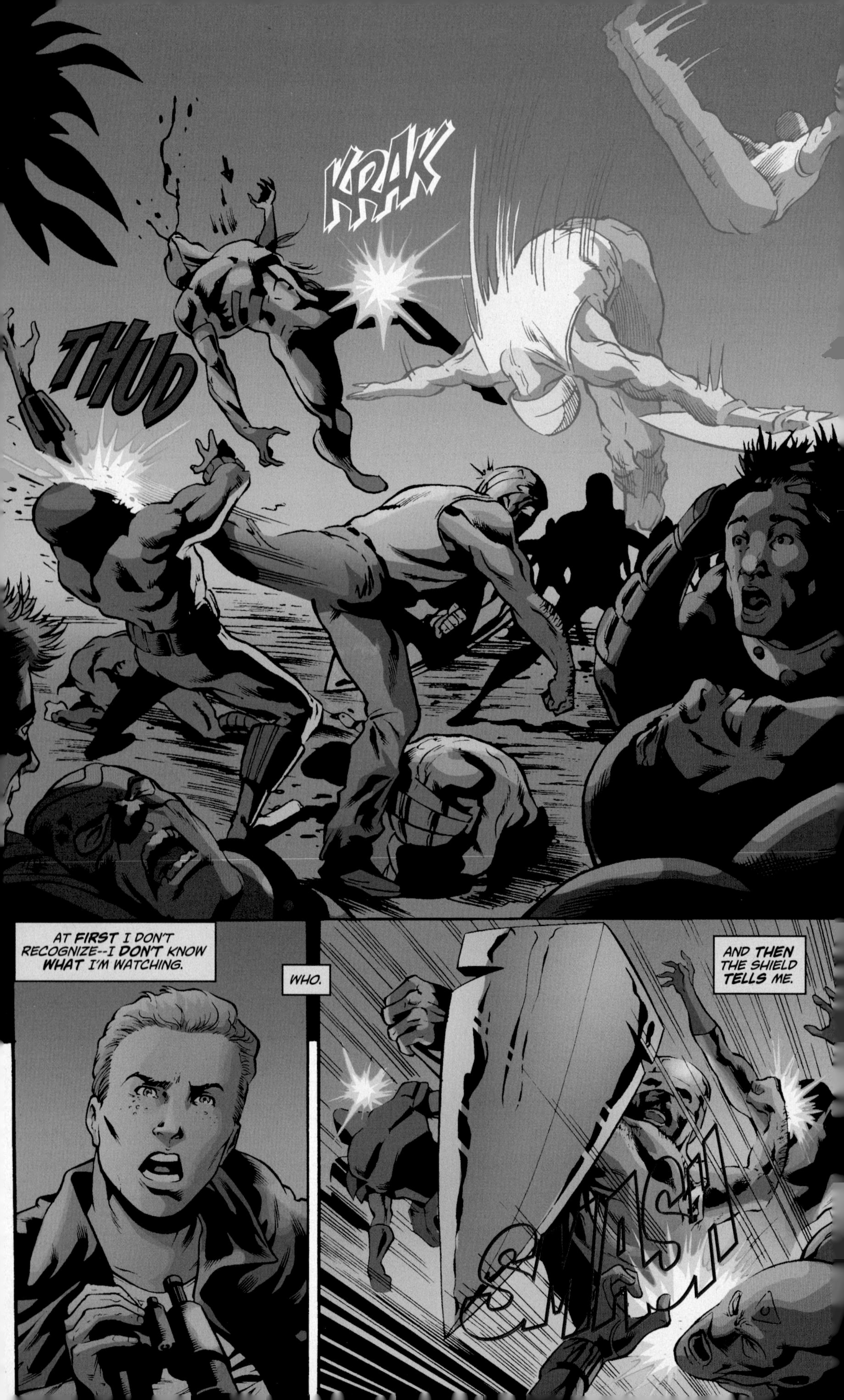
KRAK
THUD
AT FIRST I DON'T RECOGNIZE--I DON'T KNOW WHAT I'M WATCHING.
WHO.
AND THEN THE SHIELD TELLS ME.
SMASH

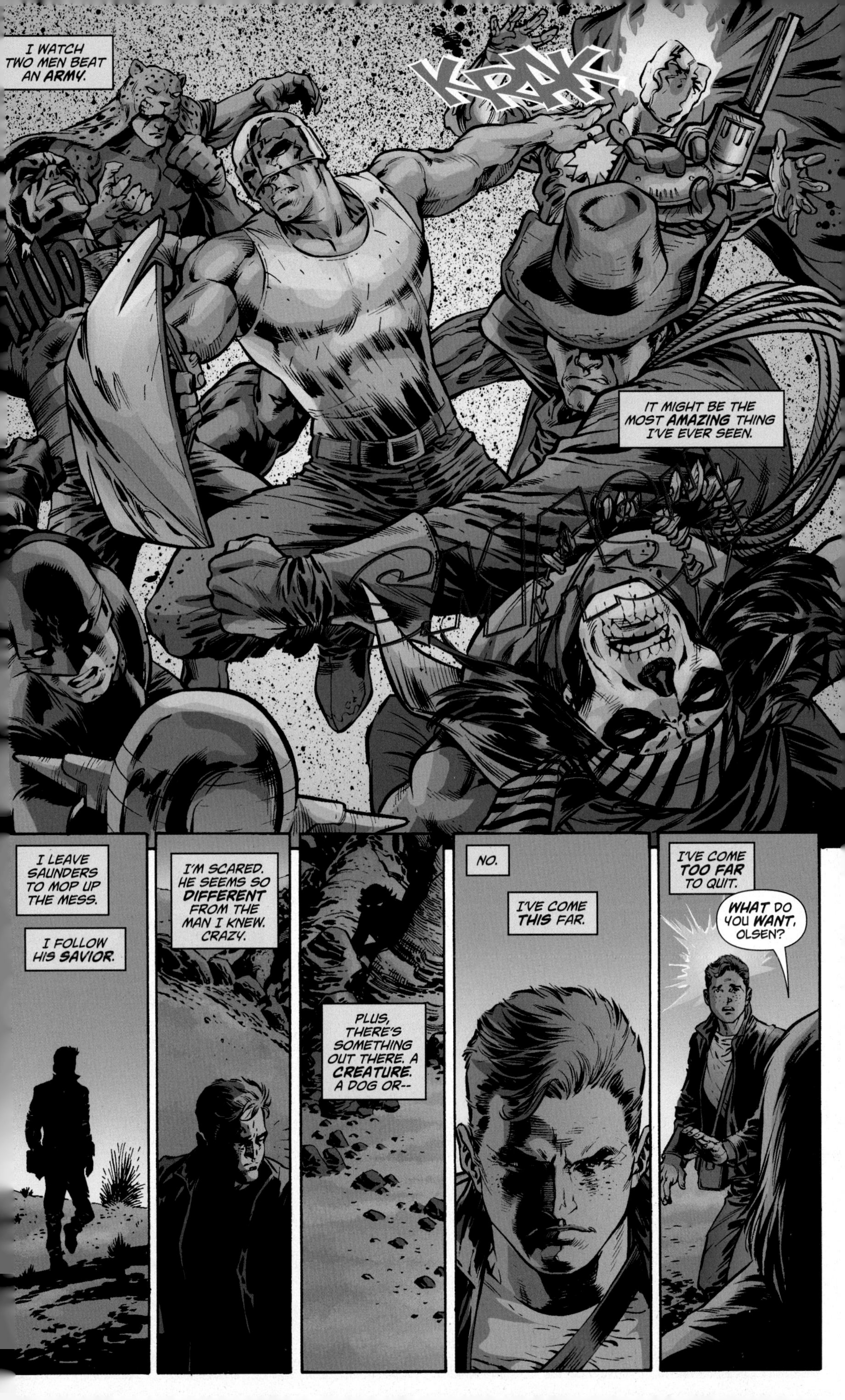

I WATCH TWO MEN BEAT AN ARMY.
KRAK
IT MIGHT BE THE MOST AMAZING THING I'VE EVER SEEN.
I LEAVE SAUNDERS TO MOP UP THE MESS.
I FOLLOW HIS SAVIOR.
I'M SCARED. HE SEEMS SO DIFFERENT FROM THE MAN I KNEW. CRAZY.
PLUS, THERE'S SOMETHING OUT THERE. A CREATURE. A DOG OR--
NO.
I'VE COME THIS FAR.
I'VE COME TOO FAR TO QUIT.
WHAT DO YOU WANT, OLSEN?

OH. *HI.* HELLO. MR. HARPER. JAMES. *JIM.*

YOU *REMEMBER* ME?

I'VE GOT EYES AND MEMORY, BOY. IT'S *NOT* THAT HARD.

HOW DID YOU FIND ME?

I LOOKED, MR. HARPER. IT *WASN'T* EASY. IN FACT I'M KIND OF *PROUD* OF MYSELF THAT I DID--

AND I'M *MAD* AS HELL THAT YOU DID, YOU LITTLE *SNOOP.* YOU KNOW, I *NEVER* DID TRUST YOU.

I'M *SORRY* TO HEAR THAT, MR. HARPER, BUT--

ER--DO YOU HAVE A *PET?* A DOG OR A MONKEY OR--

--I JUST GET THE FEELING THERE'S *SOMETHING* OUT THERE AND IT'S CREEPING THE *BEJEEZUS* OUT OF ME.

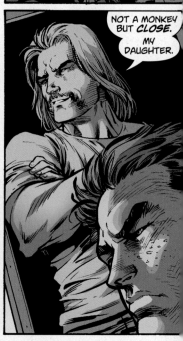

NOT A MONKEY BUT *CLOSE.* MY DAUGHTER.

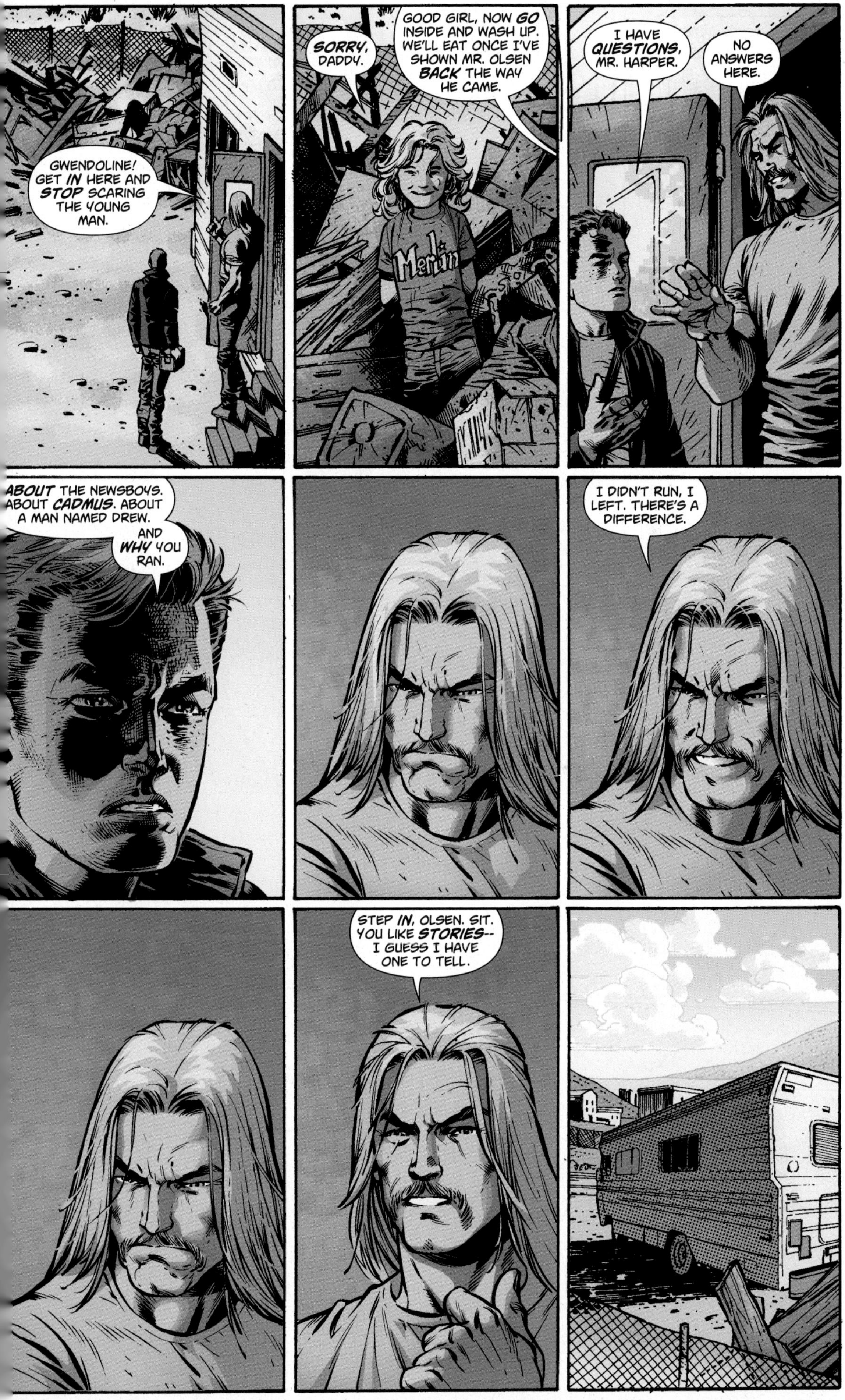
GWENDOLINE! GET IN HERE AND STOP SCARING THE YOUNG MAN.
SORRY, DADDY.
GOOD GIRL, NOW GO INSIDE AND WASH UP. WE'LL EAT ONCE I'VE SHOWN MR. OLSEN BACK THE WAY HE CAME.
Merlin
I HAVE QUESTIONS, MR. HARPER.
NO ANSWERS HERE.
ABOUT THE NEWSBOYS. ABOUT CADMUS. ABOUT A MAN NAMED DREW.
AND WHY YOU RAN.
I DIDN'T RUN, I LEFT. THERE'S A DIFFERENCE.
STEP IN, OLSEN. SIT. YOU LIKE STORIES-- I GUESS I HAVE ONE TO TELL.

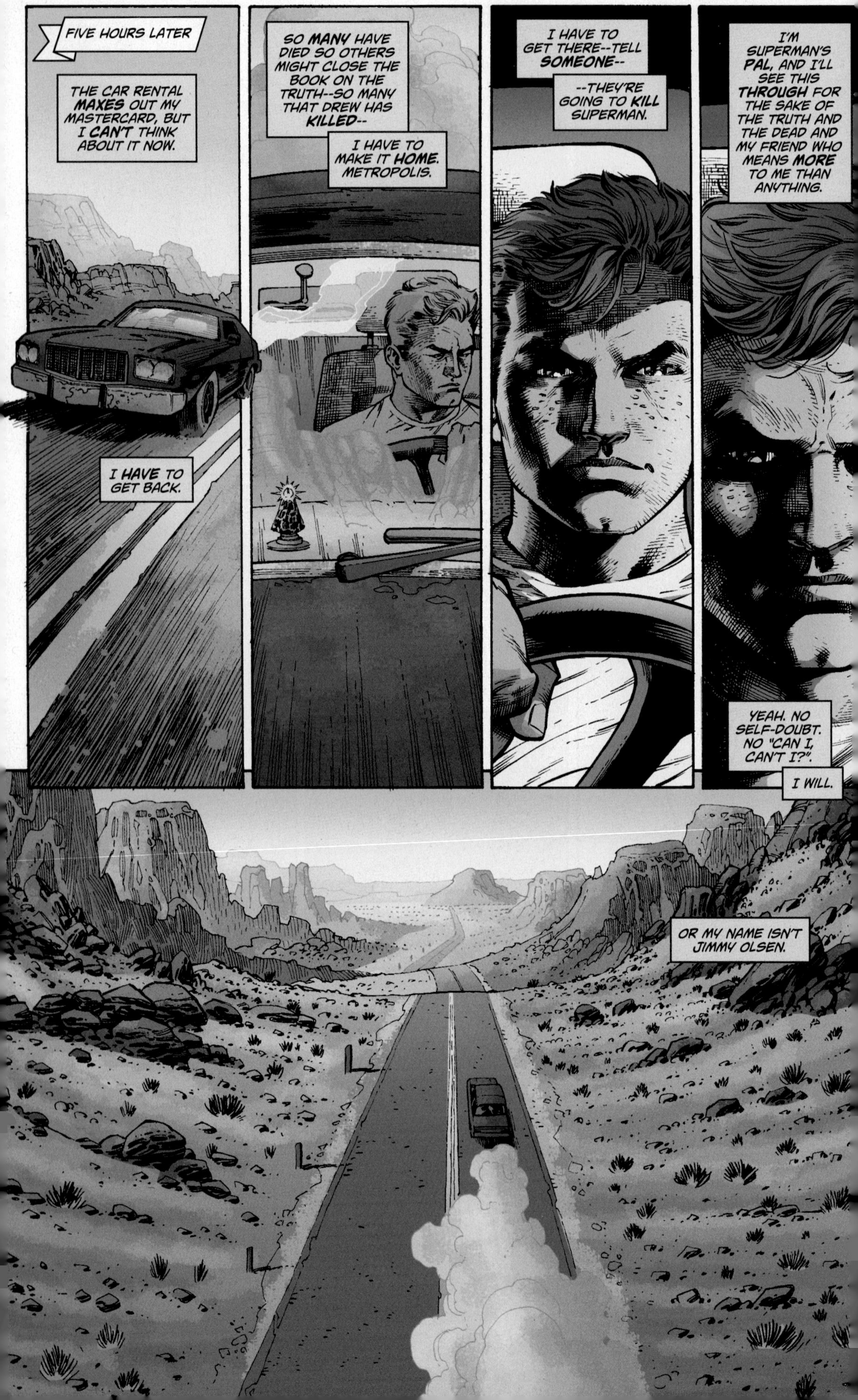
FIVE HOURS LATER
THE CAR RENTAL MAXES OUT MY MASTERCARD, BUT I CAN'T THINK ABOUT IT NOW.
I HAVE TO GET BACK.
SO MANY HAVE DIED SO OTHERS MIGHT CLOSE THE BOOK ON THE TRUTH--SO MANY THAT DREW HAS KILLED--
I HAVE TO MAKE IT HOME. METROPOLIS.
I HAVE TO GET THERE--TELL SOMEONE--
--THEY'RE GOING TO KILL SUPERMAN.
I'M SUPERMAN'S PAL, AND I'LL SEE THIS THROUGH FOR THE SAKE OF THE TRUTH AND THE DEAD AND MY FRIEND WHO MEANS MORE TO ME THAN ANYTHING.
YEAH. NO SELF-DOUBT. NO "CAN I, CAN'T I?".
I WILL.
OR MY NAME ISN'T JIMMY OLSEN.

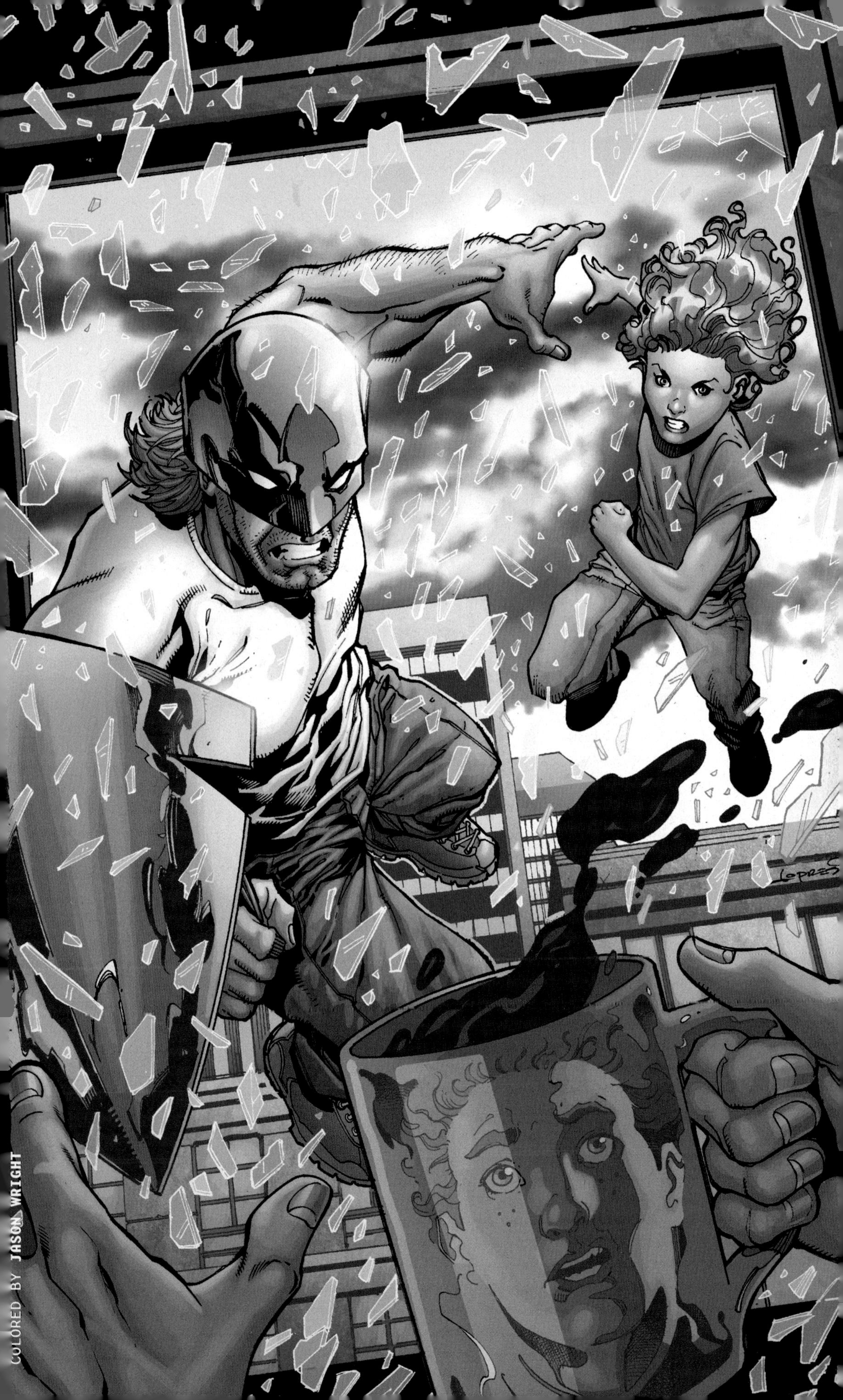
COLORED BY JASON WRIGHT

<VARIANT> COVER ART BY **VICTOR IBÁÑE**

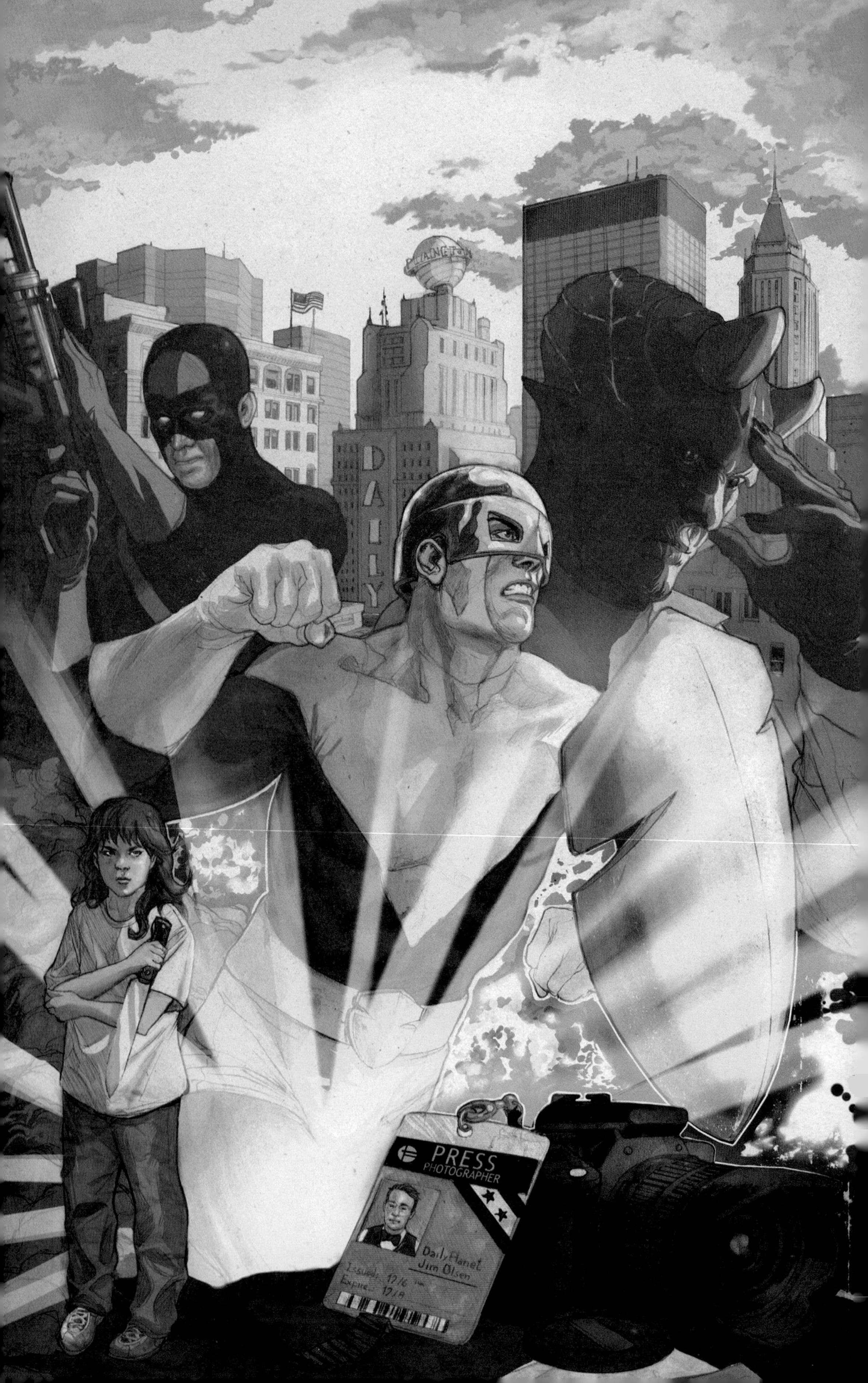
DAILY
PRESS
PHOTOGRAPHER
Daily Planet
Jim Olsen

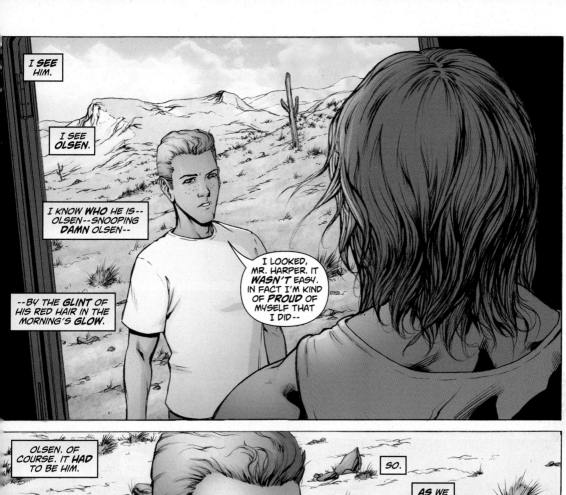

I SEE HIM.

I SEE OLSEN.

I KNOW **WHO** HE IS--OLSEN--SNOOPING **DAMN** OLSEN--

--BY THE **GLINT** OF HIS RED HAIR IN THE MORNING'S GLOW.

I LOOKED, MR. HARPER. IT **WASN'T** EASY. IN FACT I'M KIND OF **PROUD** OF MYSELF THAT I DID--

OLSEN. OF COURSE. IT **HAD** TO BE HIM.

I HAVE QUESTIONS, MR. HARPER.

SO.

AS WE TALK.

AS I STALL.

I THINK. I **ASK** MYSELF.

ABOUT THE NEWSBOYS. ABOUT CADMUS. ABOUT A MAN NAMED DREW.

AND WHY YOU RAN.

DO I LIE?

DO I TELL THE **TRUTH**?

LIES?

TRUTH?

I GUESS I'LL **START** AT THE BEGINNING...

WARNING, PRIVATE PROPERTY, ALL TRANSGRESSORS WILL BE MET WITH ARMED RESPONSE

CADMUS FACILITY DELTA, SALEM. TIMES PAST.

EDDY.

YES, RON.

I FEAR I AM IN THE **MIDST** OF AN EXISTENTIAL CRISIS.

I WONDER **WHY** I AM HERE.

HOWSO?

ON EARTH OR IN CADMUS, RON?

BOTH. ONE. THE OTHER. BOTH.

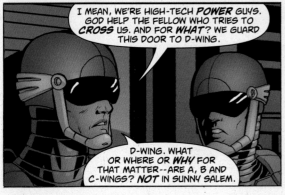

I MEAN, WE'RE HIGH-TECH **POWER** GUYS. GOD HELP THE FELLOW WHO TRIES TO **CROSS** US. AND FOR **WHAT?** WE GUARD THIS DOOR TO D-WING.

D-WING. WHAT OR WHERE OR WHY FOR THAT MATTER--ARE A, B AND C-WINGS? **NOT** IN SUNNY SALEM.

WE WAIT AND **WASTE** OUR DAYS.

I HEAR YOU, RON, BUT--

AND FOR **WHAT?** WE DON'T EVEN **KNOW** WHAT'S ON THE OTHER SIDE OF THAT DOOR.

AND FROM **WHAT** I CAN SEE--

64

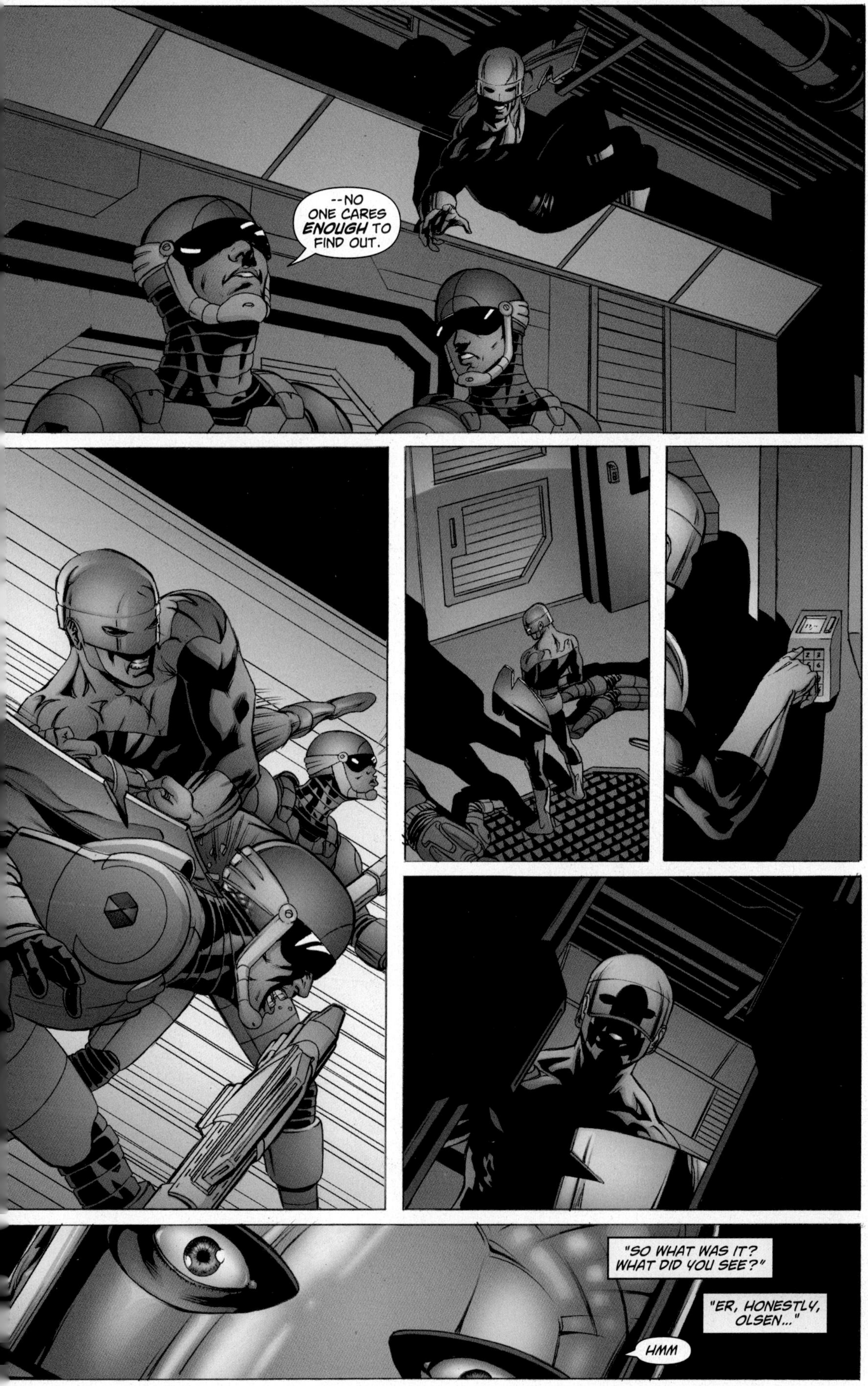
--NO ONE CARES ENOUGH TO FIND OUT.
"SO WHAT WAS IT? WHAT DID YOU SEE?"
"ER, HONESTLY, OLSEN..."
HMM

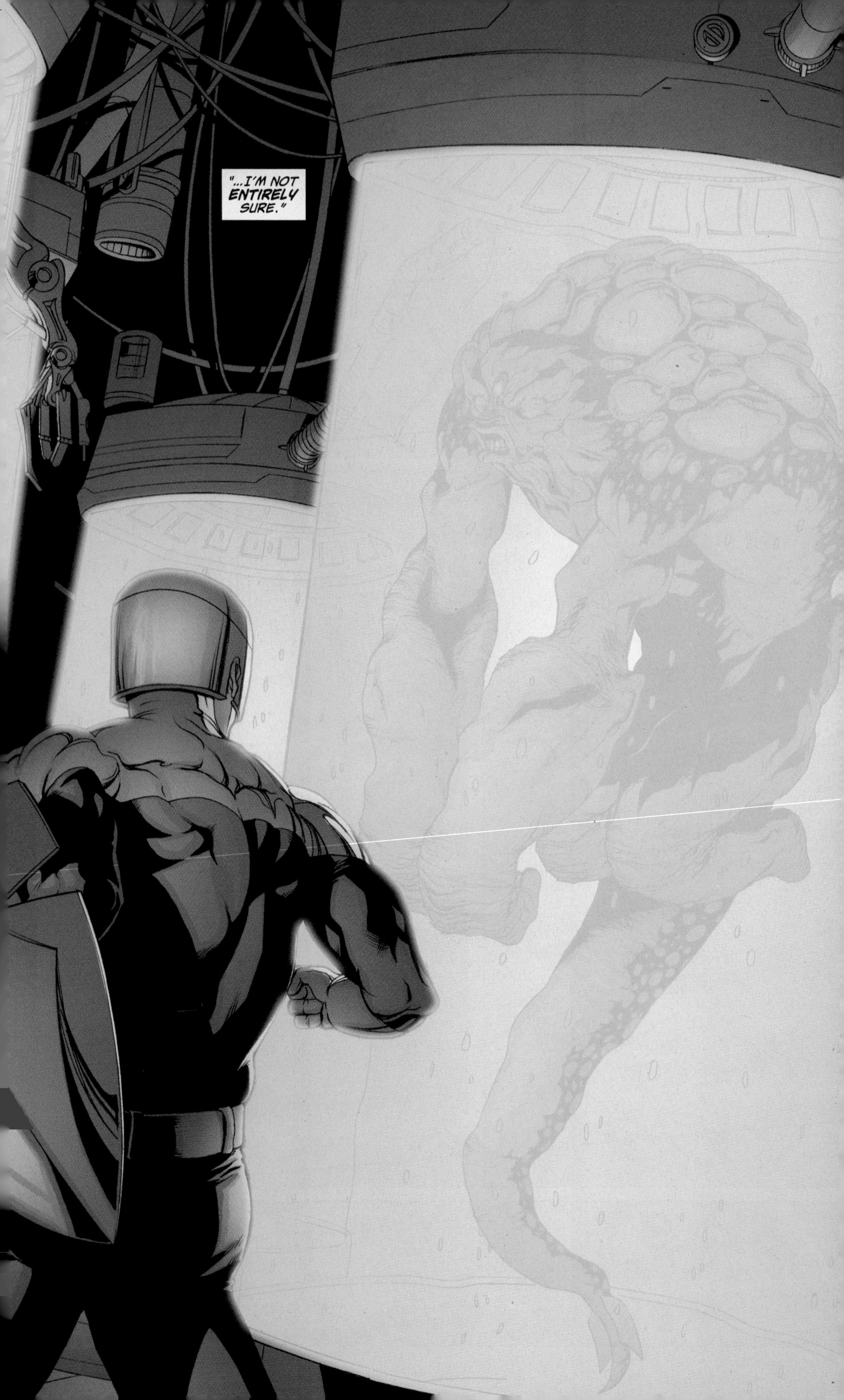
"...I'M NOT ENTIRELY SURE."

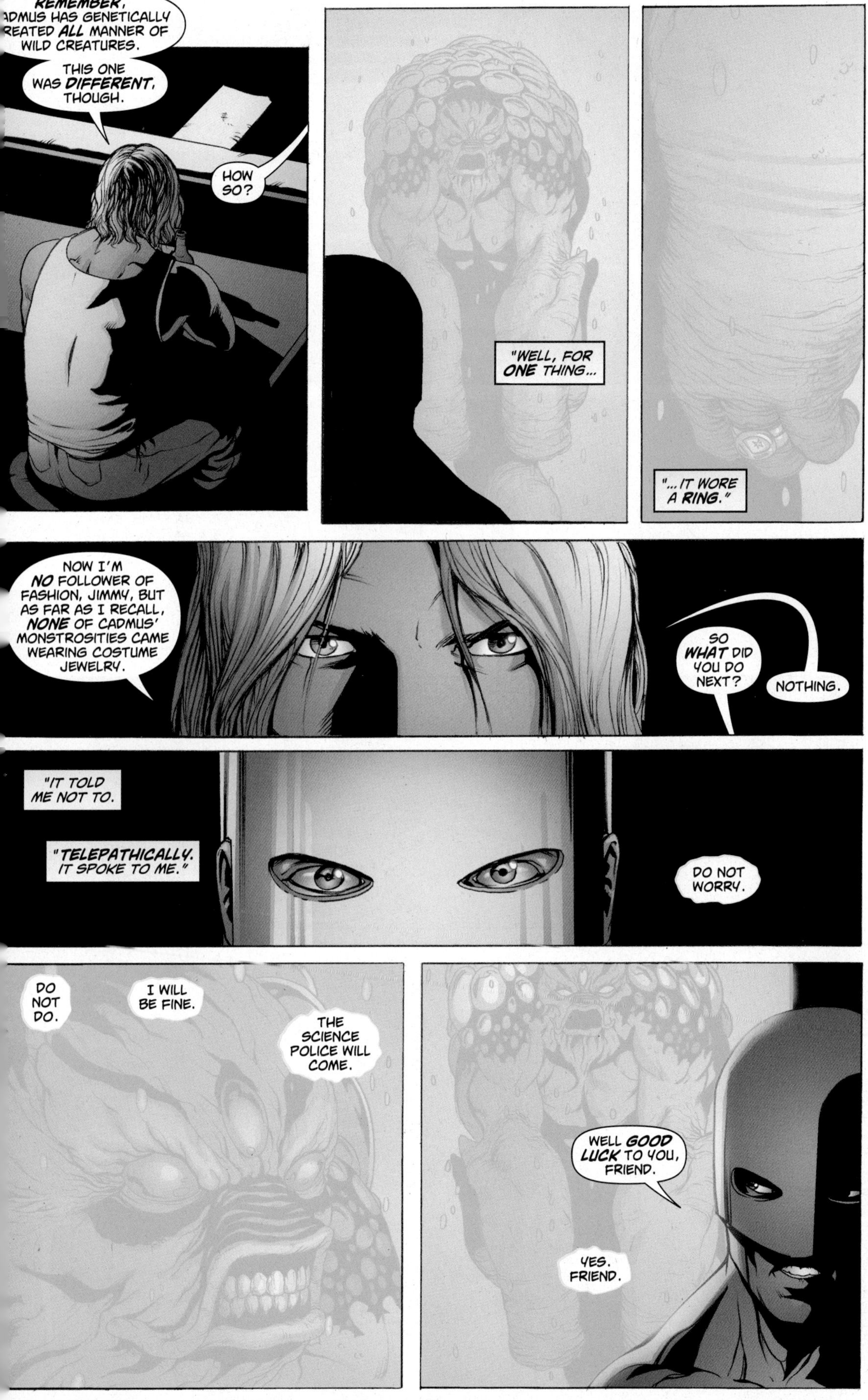
REMEMBER, CADMUS HAS GENETICALLY CREATED ALL MANNER OF WILD CREATURES.
THIS ONE WAS DIFFERENT, THOUGH.
HOW SO?
"WELL, FOR ONE THING...
"...IT WORE A RING."
NOW I'M NO FOLLOWER OF FASHION, JIMMY, BUT AS FAR AS I RECALL, NONE OF CADMUS' MONSTROSITIES CAME WEARING COSTUME JEWELRY.
SO WHAT DID YOU DO NEXT?
NOTHING.
"IT TOLD ME NOT TO.
"TELEPATHICALLY. IT SPOKE TO ME."
DO NOT WORRY.
DO NOT DO.
I WILL BE FINE.
THE SCIENCE POLICE WILL COME.
WELL GOOD LUCK TO YOU, FRIEND.
YES. FRIEND.

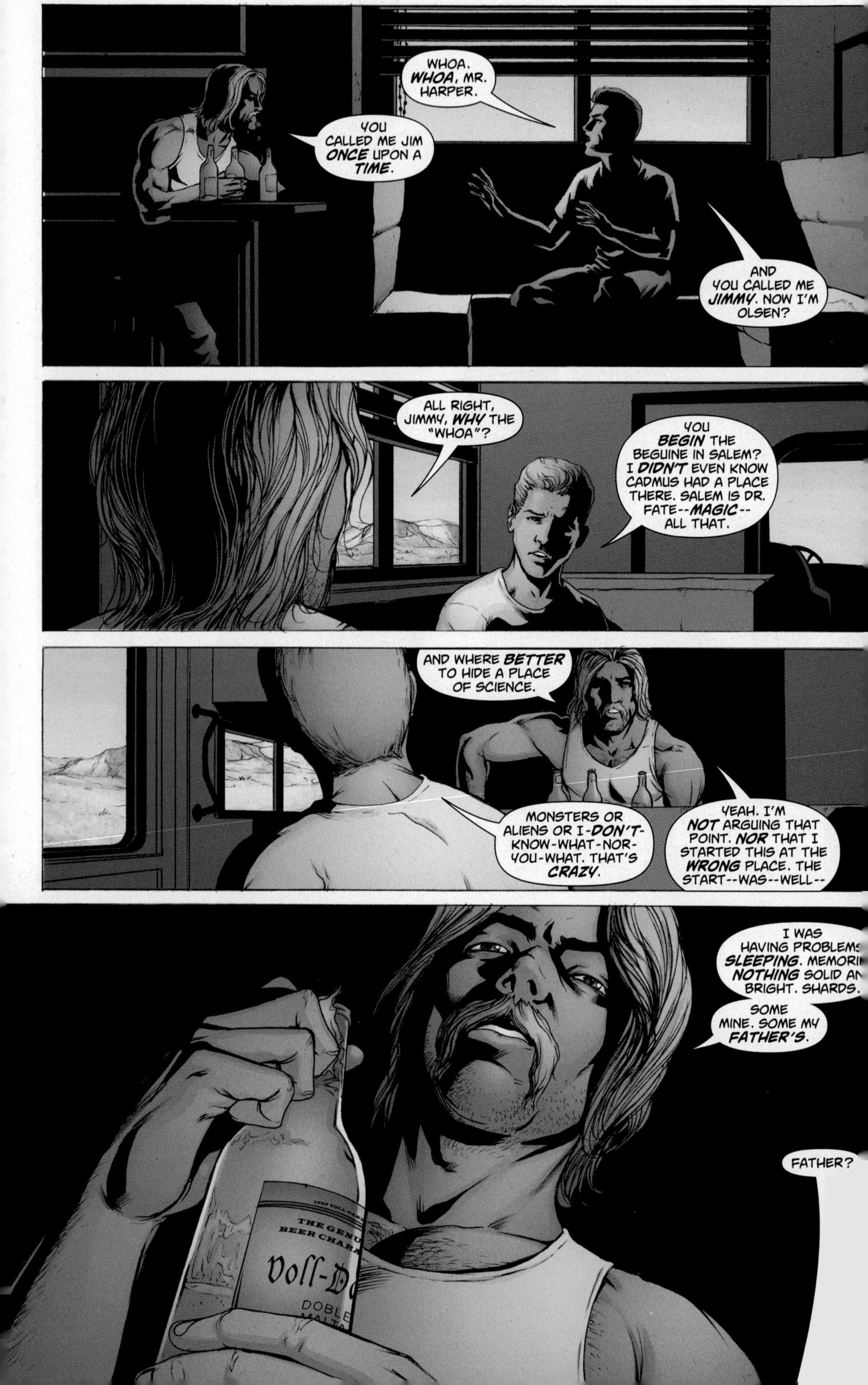
WHOA. WHOA, MR. HARPER.
YOU CALLED ME JIM ONCE UPON A TIME.
AND YOU CALLED ME JIMMY. NOW I'M OLSEN?
ALL RIGHT, JIMMY, WHY THE "WHOA"?
YOU BEGIN THE BEGUINE IN SALEM? I DIDN'T EVEN KNOW CADMUS HAD A PLACE THERE. SALEM IS DR. FATE--MAGIC--ALL THAT.
AND WHERE BETTER TO HIDE A PLACE OF SCIENCE.
MONSTERS OR ALIENS OR I-DON'T-KNOW-WHAT-NOR-YOU-WHAT. THAT'S CRAZY.
YEAH. I'M NOT ARGUING THAT POINT. NOR THAT I STARTED THIS AT THE WRONG PLACE. THE START--WAS--WELL--
I WAS HAVING PROBLEMS SLEEPING. MEMORI NOTHING SOLID AN BRIGHT. SHARDS.
SOME MINE. SOME MY FATHER'S.
FATHER?
THE GENU BEER CHARA
Voll-Da
DOBLE MALTA

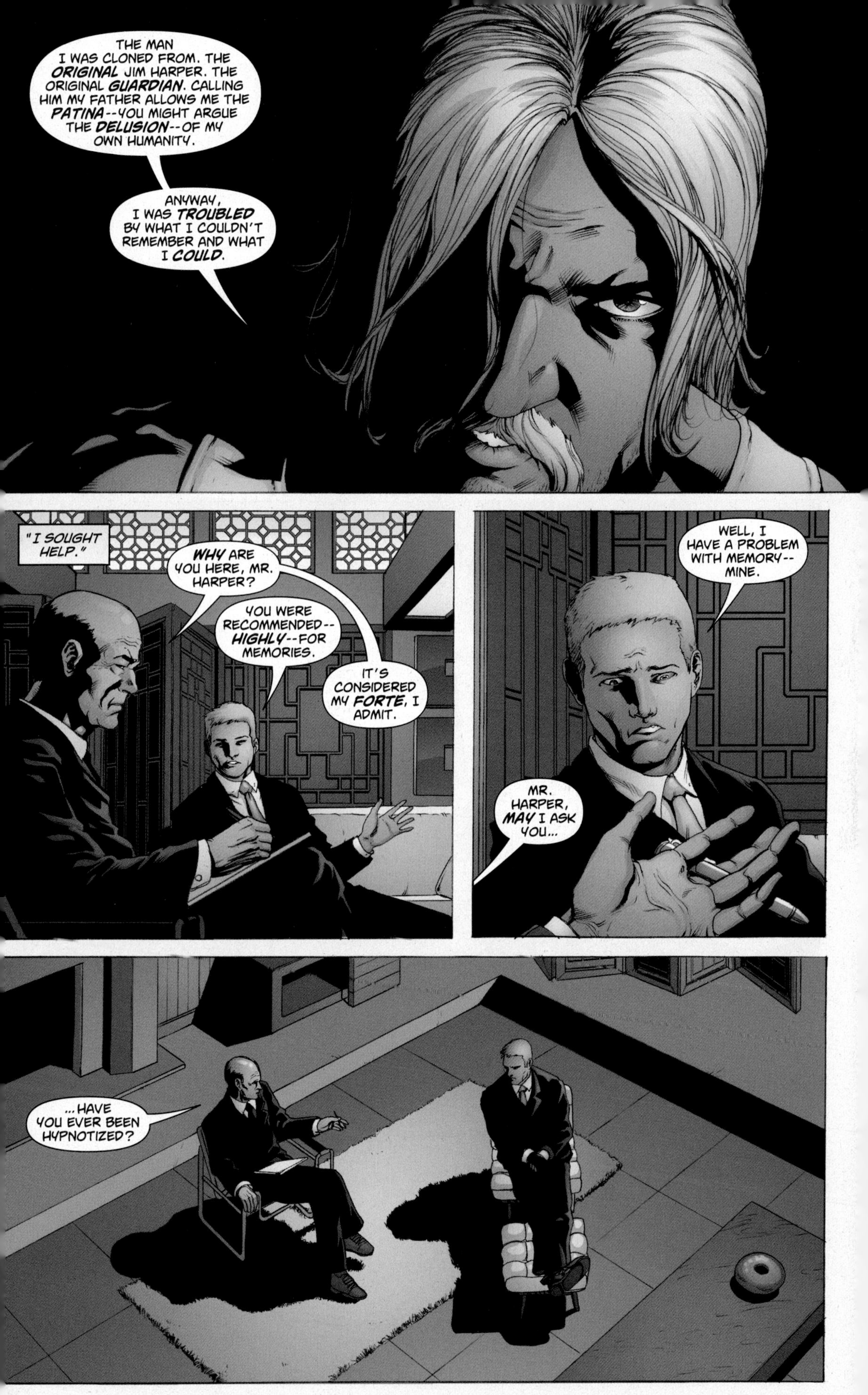
THE MAN I WAS CLONED FROM. THE ORIGINAL JIM HARPER. THE ORIGINAL GUARDIAN. CALLING HIM MY FATHER ALLOWS ME THE PATINA--YOU MIGHT ARGUE THE DELUSION--OF MY OWN HUMANITY.
ANYWAY, I WAS TROUBLED BY WHAT I COULDN'T REMEMBER AND WHAT I COULD.
"I SOUGHT HELP."
WHY ARE YOU HERE, MR. HARPER?
YOU WERE RECOMMENDED--HIGHLY--FOR MEMORIES.
IT'S CONSIDERED MY FORTE, I ADMIT.
WELL, I HAVE A PROBLEM WITH MEMORY--MINE.
MR. HARPER, MAY I ASK YOU...
...HAVE YOU EVER BEEN HYPNOTIZED?

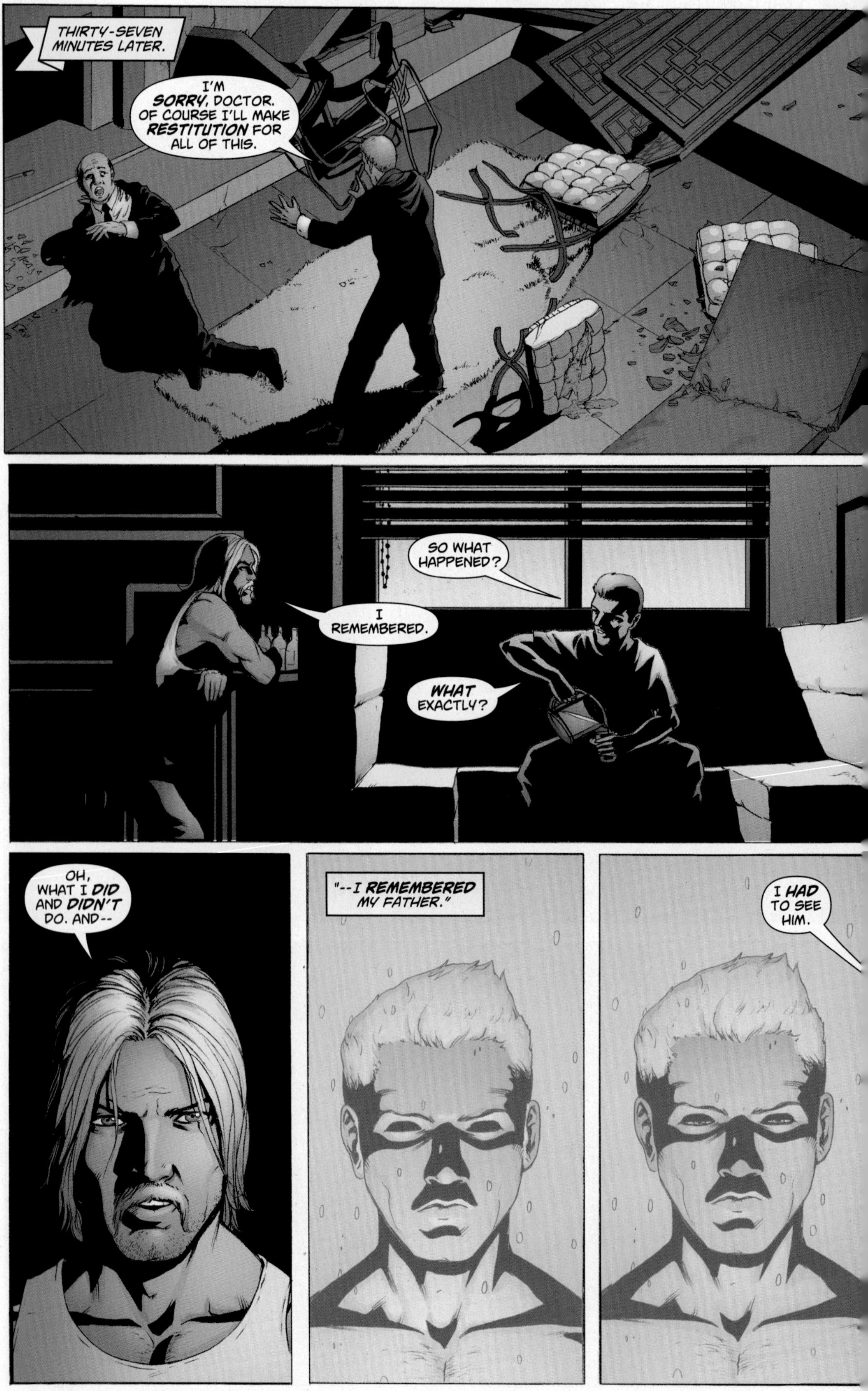
THIRTY-SEVEN MINUTES LATER.
I'M SORRY, DOCTOR. OF COURSE I'LL MAKE RESTITUTION FOR ALL OF THIS.
SO WHAT HAPPENED?
I REMEMBERED.
WHAT EXACTLY?
OH, WHAT I DID AND DIDN'T DO. AND--
"--I REMEMBERED MY FATHER."
I HAD TO SEE HIM.

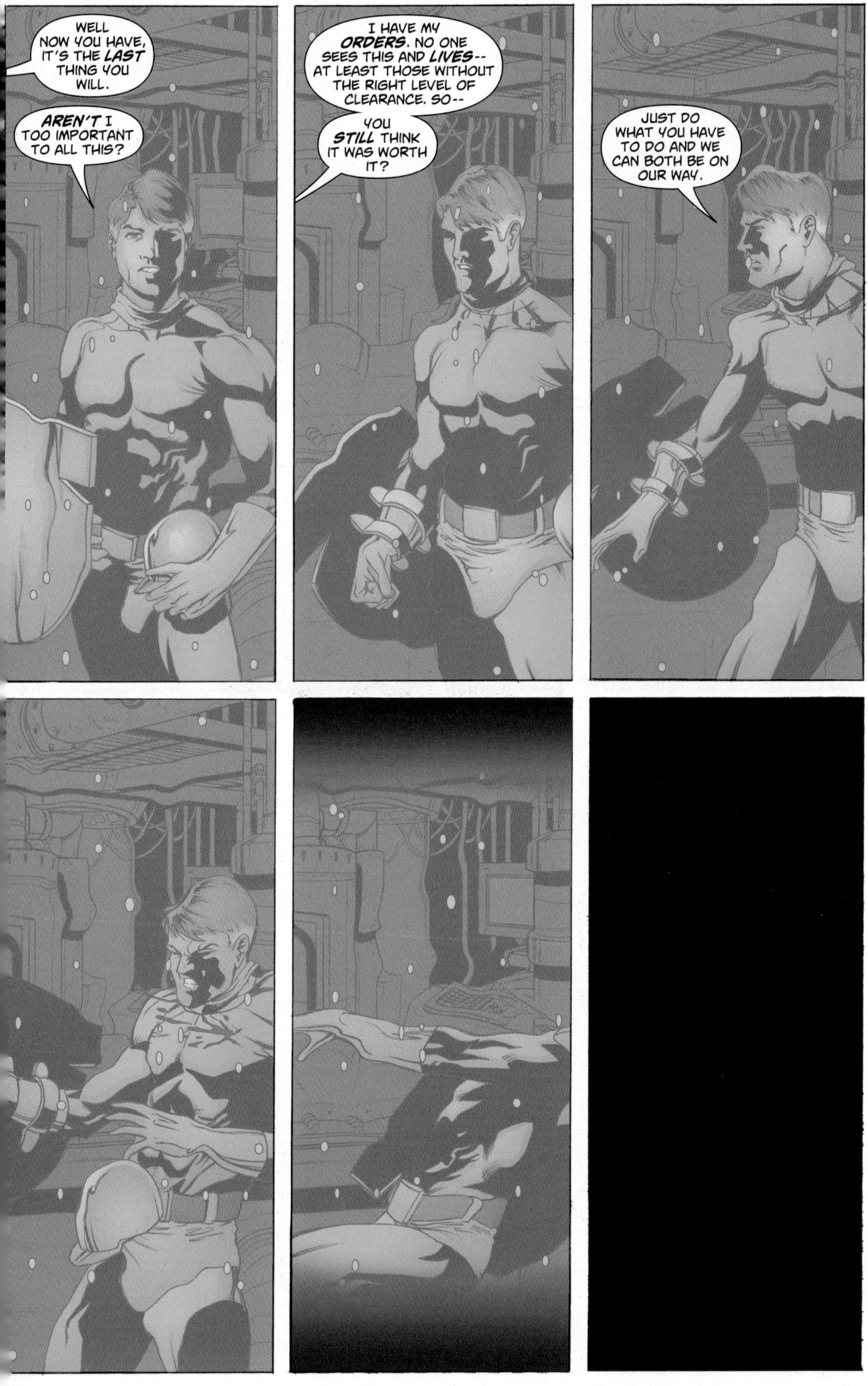

WELL NOW YOU HAVE, IT'S THE LAST THING YOU WILL.
AREN'T I TOO IMPORTANT TO ALL THIS?
I HAVE MY ORDERS. NO ONE SEES THIS AND LIVES-- AT LEAST THOSE WITHOUT THE RIGHT LEVEL OF CLEARANCE. SO--
YOU STILL THINK IT WAS WORTH IT?
JUST DO WHAT YOU HAVE TO DO AND WE CAN BOTH BE ON OUR WAY.

SO YOUR *FIRST* MEMORY--

YEAH, THE *DEATH* OF MY FATHER.

AND *DREW*.

WHAT?

JONATHAN DREW, CODENAME: *ASSASSIN*. HE MUST BE A PART OF THAT MEMORY, *TOO*--YOUR DAD'S KILLER AND ALL.

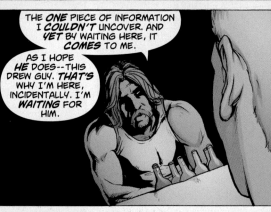

THE *ONE* PIECE OF INFORMATION I *COULDN'T* UNCOVER. AND *YET* BY WAITING HERE, IT *COMES* TO ME.

AS I HOPE *HE* DOES--THIS DREW GUY. *THAT'S* WHY I'M HERE, INCIDENTALLY. I'M *WAITING* FOR HIM.

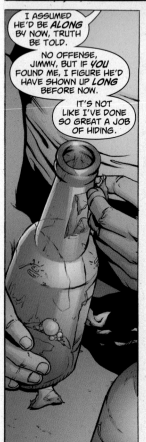

I ASSUMED HE'D BE *ALONG* BY NOW, TRUTH BE TOLD.

NO OFFENSE, JIMMY, BUT IF *YOU* FOUND ME, I FIGURE HE'D HAVE SHOWN UP *LONG* BEFORE NOW.

IT'S NOT LIKE I'VE DONE SO GREAT A JOB OF HIDING.

I WANT TO LOOK *INTO* THE FACE OF THE MAN WHO KILLED MY DAD ONE LAST TIME BEFORE I TAKE MY REVENGE.

REVENGE? AS IN KILLING? THAT *DOESN'T* SOUND LIKE YOU.

LIKE *WHO*? WHO AM I?

THE *MORE* I'VE LEARNED, THE MORE I *ASK* THAT QUESTION OF MYSELF, JIMMY. SPECTRE, DR. FATE, HAWKMAN AND HIS MANY LIVES--IT *ALL* TELLS ME THERE'S SOME FORM OF *AFTERLIFE*.

SOULS. *YOU* HAVE ONE. SO, I PRESUME, DOES JIM HARPER, MY FATHER, AND IT/HE *ABIDES* WHEREVER SOULS ABIDE AFTER THE BODY DIES.

BUT WHAT ABOUT *ME*? AM I A MAN OR A *THING*? IS A CLONE A HUMAN IN ITS OWN RIGHT? I WALK THROUGH THE WORLD WITH ANOTHER MAN'S MEMORIES. *HOW* CAN I DARE SAY I AM MY OWN ENTITY?

I DON'T KNOW WHAT TO SAY.

AND *I'M* JUST TALKING MORE FOR THE SAKE OF IT THAN--*ANYWAY*, WHERE WERE WE--

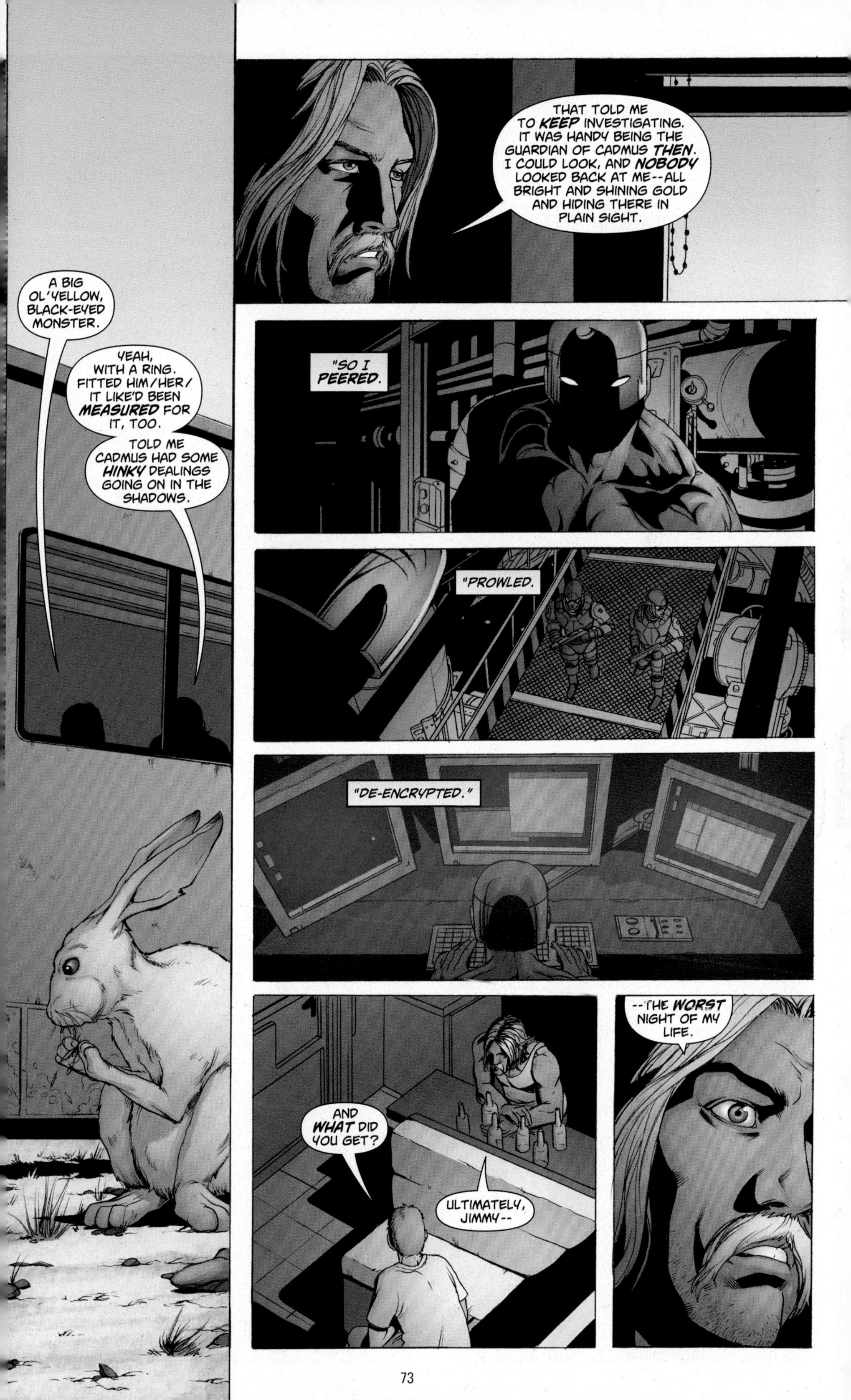

A BIG OL' YELLOW, BLACK-EYED MONSTER.
YEAH, WITH A RING. FITTED HIM/HER/ IT LIKE'D BEEN MEASURED FOR IT, TOO.
TOLD ME CADMUS HAD SOME HINKY DEALINGS GOING ON IN THE SHADOWS.
THAT TOLD ME TO KEEP INVESTIGATING. IT WAS HANDY BEING THE GUARDIAN OF CADMUS THEN. I COULD LOOK, AND NOBODY LOOKED BACK AT ME--ALL BRIGHT AND SHINING GOLD AND HIDING THERE IN PLAIN SIGHT.
"SO I PEERED.
"PROWLED.
"DE-ENCRYPTED."
AND WHAT DID YOU GET?
ULTIMATELY, JIMMY--
--THE WORST NIGHT OF MY LIFE.

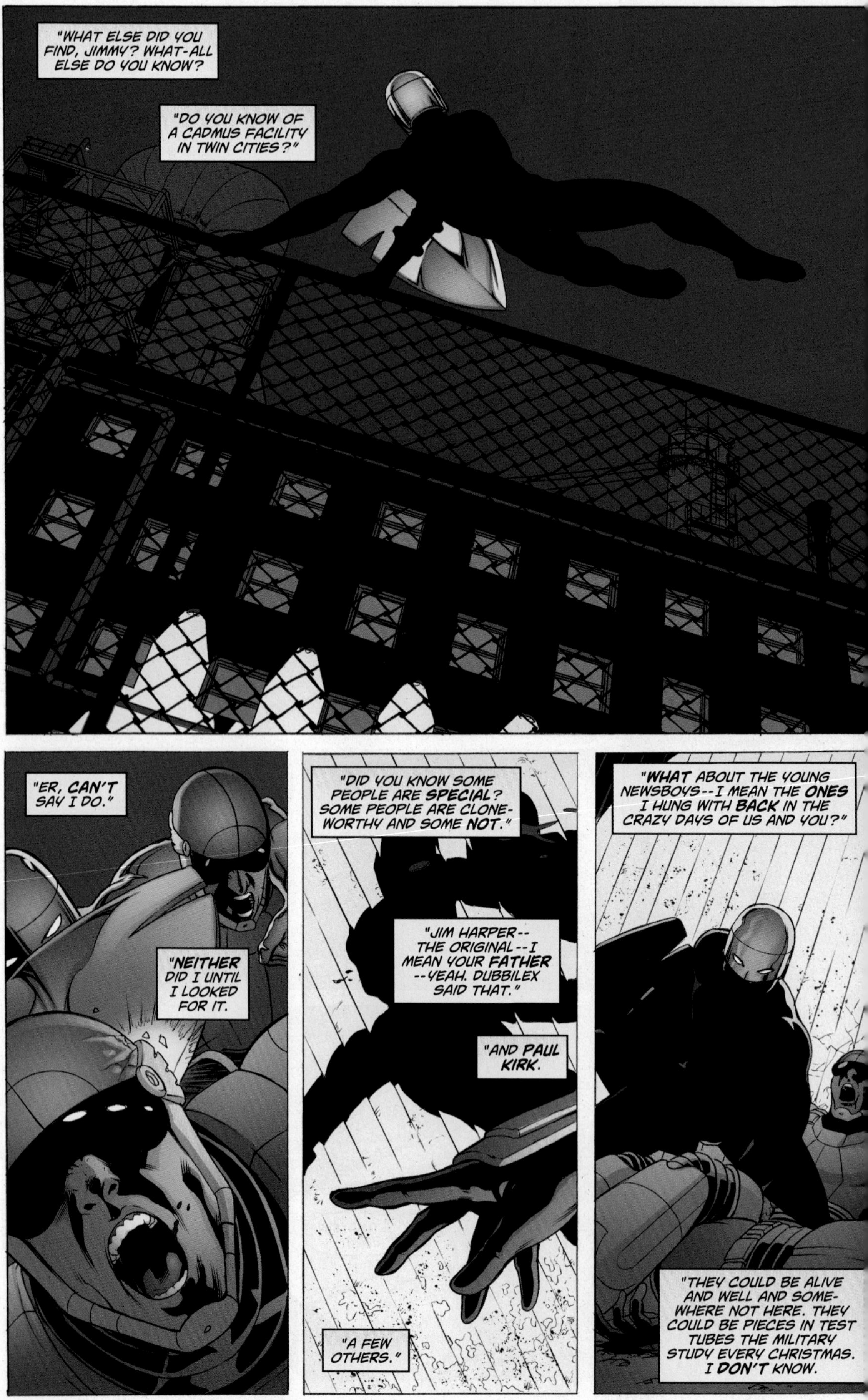
"WHAT ELSE DID YOU FIND, JIMMY? WHAT-ALL ELSE DO YOU KNOW?
"DO YOU KNOW OF A CADMUS FACILITY IN TWIN CITIES?"
"ER, CAN'T SAY I DO."
"NEITHER DID I UNTIL I LOOKED FOR IT.
"DID YOU KNOW SOME PEOPLE ARE SPECIAL? SOME PEOPLE ARE CLONE-WORTHY AND SOME NOT."
"JIM HARPER-- THE ORIGINAL--I MEAN YOUR FATHER --YEAH. DUBBILEX SAID THAT."
"AND PAUL KIRK.
"A FEW OTHERS."
"WHAT ABOUT THE YOUNG NEWSBOYS--I MEAN THE ONES I HUNG WITH BACK IN THE CRAZY DAYS OF US AND YOU?"
"THEY COULD BE ALIVE AND WELL AND SOME-WHERE NOT HERE. THEY COULD BE PIECES IN TEST TUBES THE MILITARY STUDY EVERY CHRISTMAS. I DON'T KNOW.

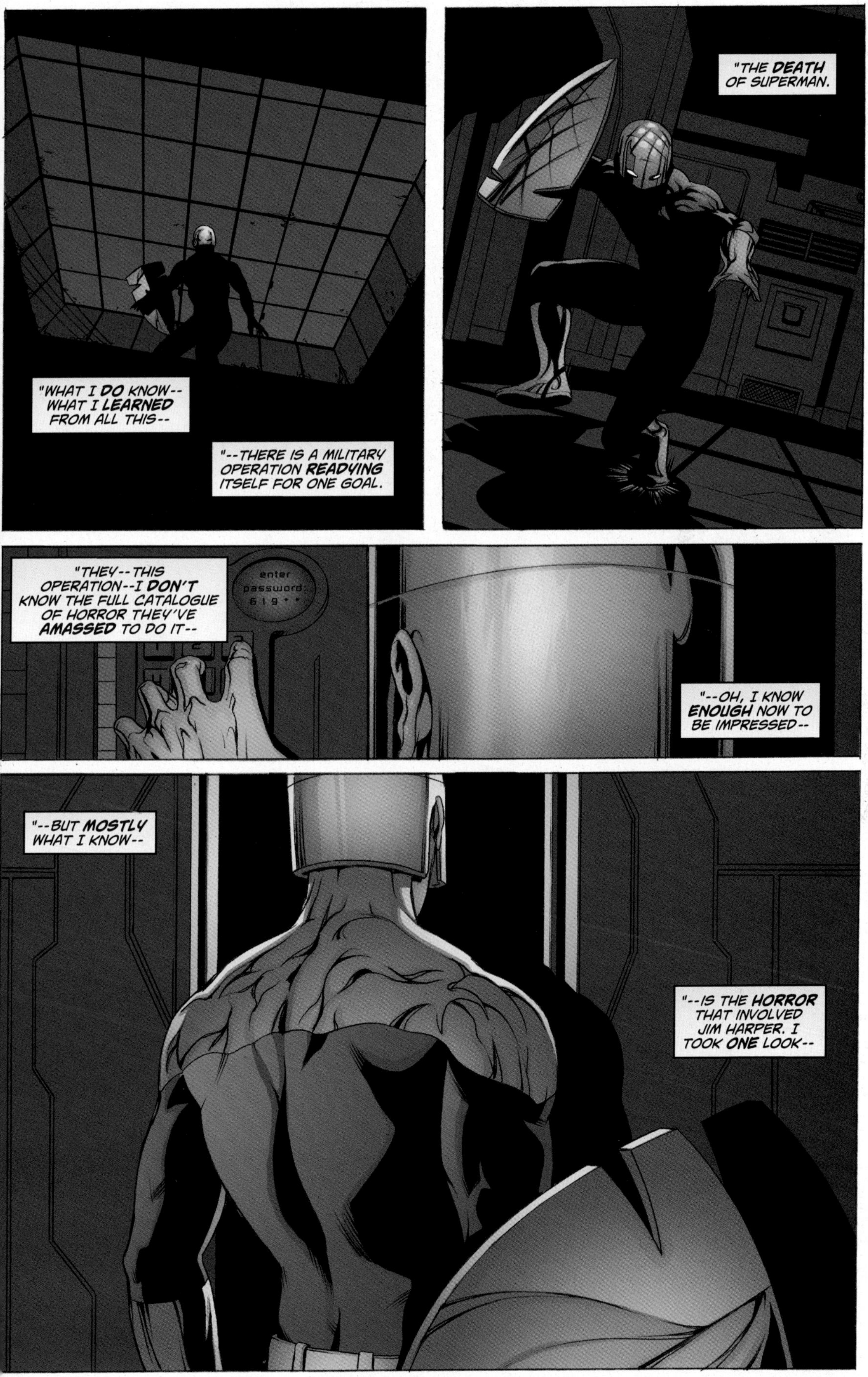
"WHAT I DO KNOW--
WHAT I LEARNED
FROM ALL THIS--
"--THERE IS A MILITARY OPERATION READYING ITSELF FOR ONE GOAL.
"THE DEATH OF SUPERMAN.
"THEY--THIS OPERATION--I DON'T KNOW THE FULL CATALOGUE OF HORROR THEY'VE AMASSED TO DO IT--
enter password: 619**
"--OH, I KNOW ENOUGH NOW TO BE IMPRESSED--
"--BUT MOSTLY WHAT I KNOW--
"--IS THE HORROR THAT INVOLVED JIM HARPER. I TOOK ONE LOOK--

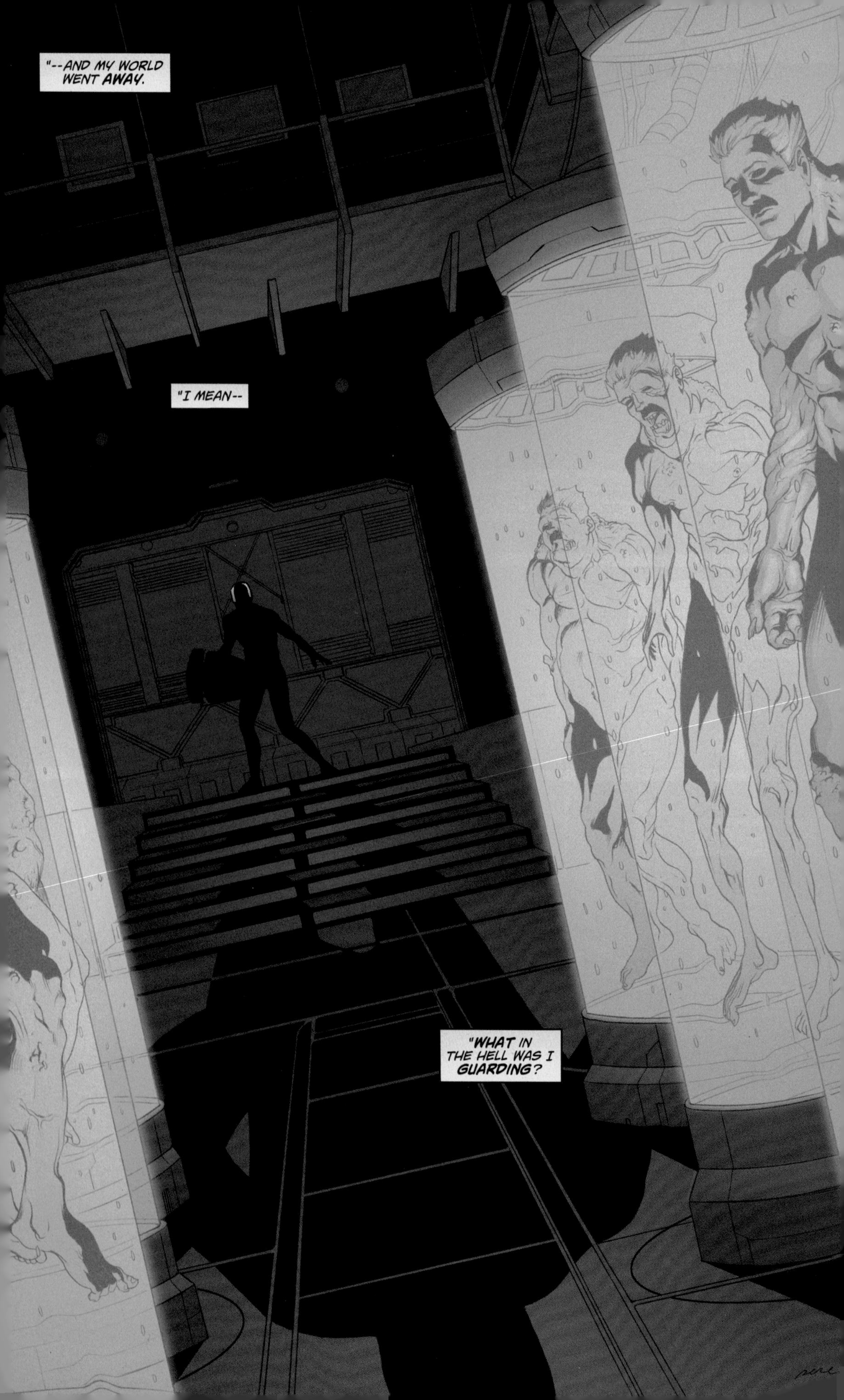
"--AND MY WORLD WENT AWAY.
"I MEAN--
"WHAT IN THE HELL WAS I GUARDING?

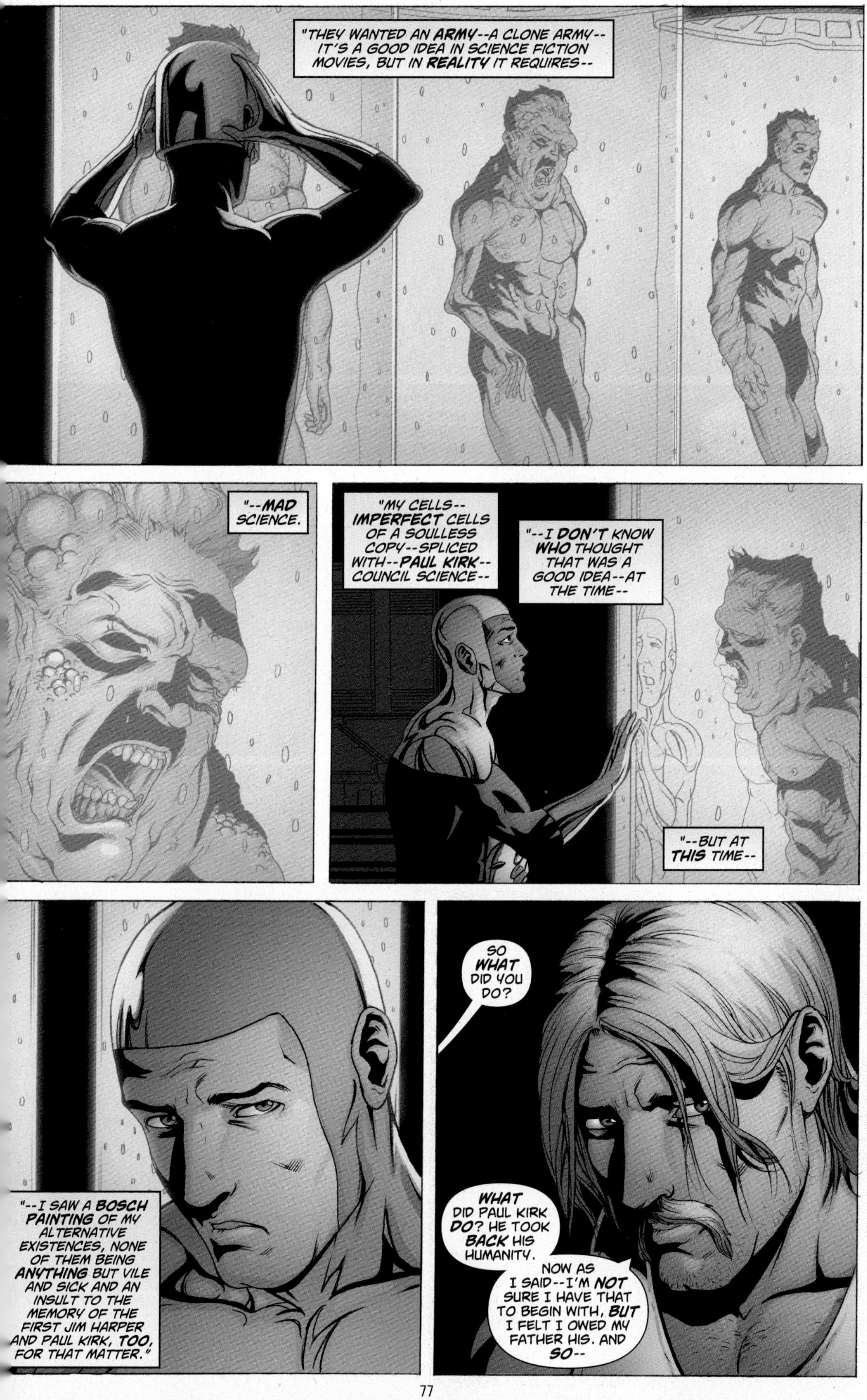
"THEY WANTED AN ARMY--A CLONE ARMY--
IT'S A GOOD IDEA IN SCIENCE FICTION
MOVIES, BUT IN REALITY IT REQUIRES--
"--MAD SCIENCE.
"MY CELLS--IMPERFECT CELLS OF A SOULLESS COPY--SPLICED WITH--PAUL KIRK--COUNCIL SCIENCE--
"--I DON'T KNOW WHO THOUGHT THAT WAS A GOOD IDEA--AT THE TIME--
"--BUT AT THIS TIME--
"--I SAW A BOSCH PAINTING OF MY ALTERNATIVE EXISTENCES, NONE OF THEM BEING ANYTHING BUT VILE AND SICK AND AN INSULT TO THE MEMORY OF THE FIRST JIM HARPER AND PAUL KIRK, TOO, FOR THAT MATTER."
SO WHAT DID YOU DO?
WHAT DID PAUL KIRK DO? HE TOOK BACK HIS HUMANITY.
NOW AS I SAID--I'M NOT SURE I HAVE THAT TO BEGIN WITH, BUT I FELT I OWED MY FATHER HIS. AND SO--

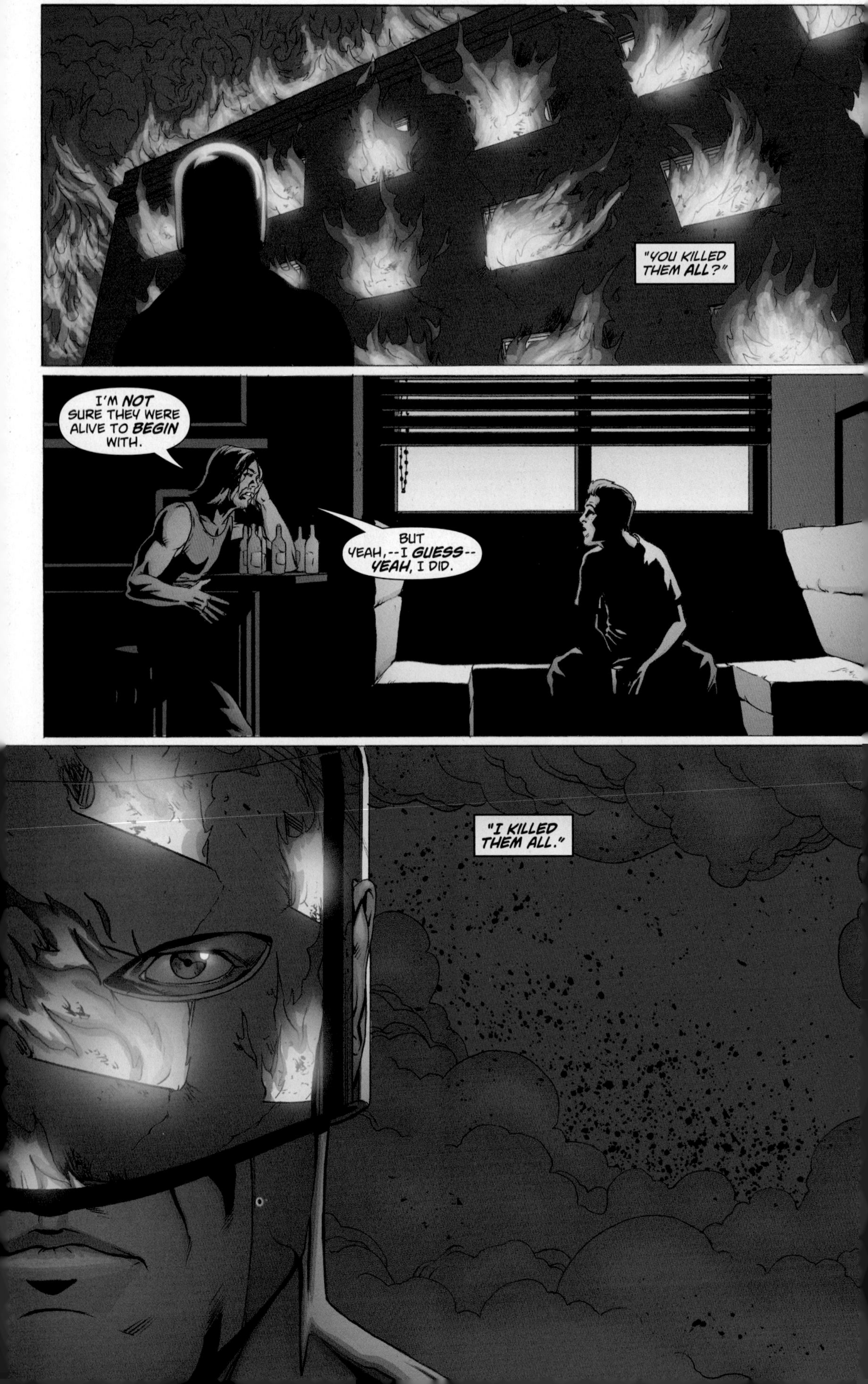

"YOU KILLED THEM ALL?"
I'M NOT SURE THEY WERE ALIVE TO BEGIN WITH.
BUT YEAH, --I GUESS-- YEAH, I DID.
"I KILLED THEM ALL."

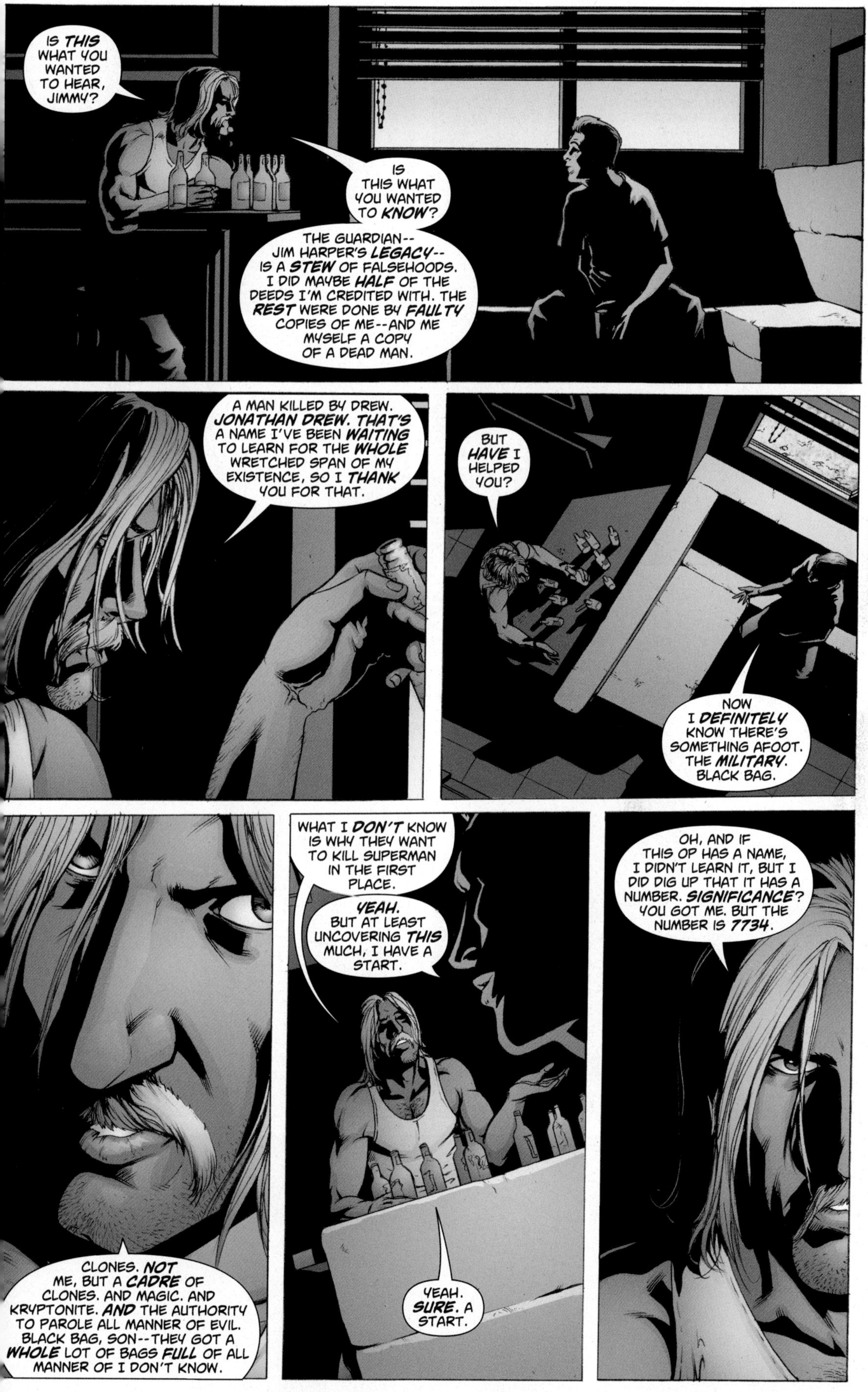
IS THIS WHAT YOU WANTED TO HEAR, JIMMY?
IS THIS WHAT YOU WANTED TO KNOW?
THE GUARDIAN-- JIM HARPER'S LEGACY-- IS A STEW OF FALSEHOODS. I DID MAYBE HALF OF THE DEEDS I'M CREDITED WITH. THE REST WERE DONE BY FAULTY COPIES OF ME--AND ME MYSELF A COPY OF A DEAD MAN.
A MAN KILLED BY DREW. JONATHAN DREW. THAT'S A NAME I'VE BEEN WAITING TO LEARN FOR THE WHOLE WRETCHED SPAN OF MY EXISTENCE, SO I THANK YOU FOR THAT.
BUT HAVE I HELPED YOU?
NOW I DEFINITELY KNOW THERE'S SOMETHING AFOOT. THE MILITARY. BLACK BAG.
CLONES. NOT ME, BUT A CADRE OF CLONES. AND MAGIC. AND KRYPTONITE. AND THE AUTHORITY TO PAROLE ALL MANNER OF EVIL. BLACK BAG, SON--THEY GOT A WHOLE LOT OF BAGS FULL OF ALL MANNER OF I DON'T KNOW.
WHAT I DON'T KNOW IS WHY THEY WANT TO KILL SUPERMAN IN THE FIRST PLACE.
YEAH. BUT AT LEAST UNCOVERING THIS MUCH, I HAVE A START.
YEAH. SURE. A START.
OH, AND IF THIS OP HAS A NAME, I DIDN'T LEARN IT, BUT I DID DIG UP THAT IT HAS A NUMBER. SIGNIFICANCE? YOU GOT ME. BUT THE NUMBER IS 7734.

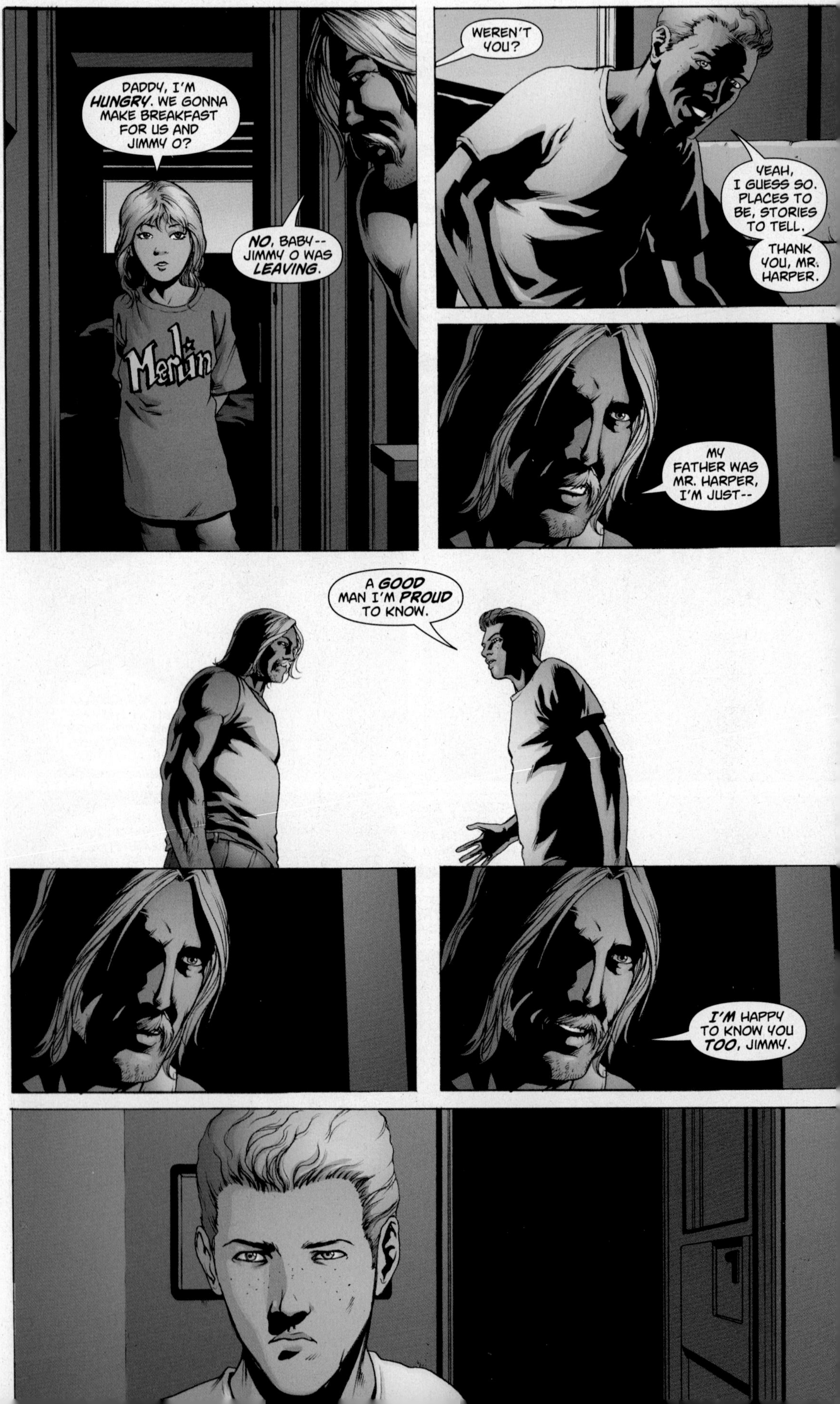
DADDY, I'M HUNGRY. WE GONNA MAKE BREAKFAST FOR US AND JIMMY O?
NO, BABY-- JIMMY O WAS LEAVING.
WEREN'T YOU?
YEAH, I GUESS SO. PLACES TO BE, STORIES TO TELL.
THANK YOU, MR. HARPER.
MY FATHER WAS MR. HARPER, I'M JUST--
A GOOD MAN I'M PROUD TO KNOW.
I'M HAPPY TO KNOW YOU TOO, JIMMY.
Merlin

"YOU KILLED THEM *ALL*?"

"I'M *NOT* SURE THEY WERE ALIVE TO *BEGIN* WITH.

"BUT YEAH,-- I GUESS-- YEAH, I DID.

"I KILLED THEM ALL."

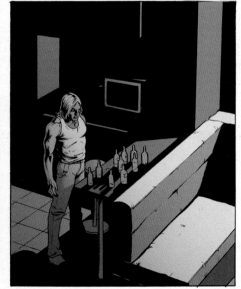

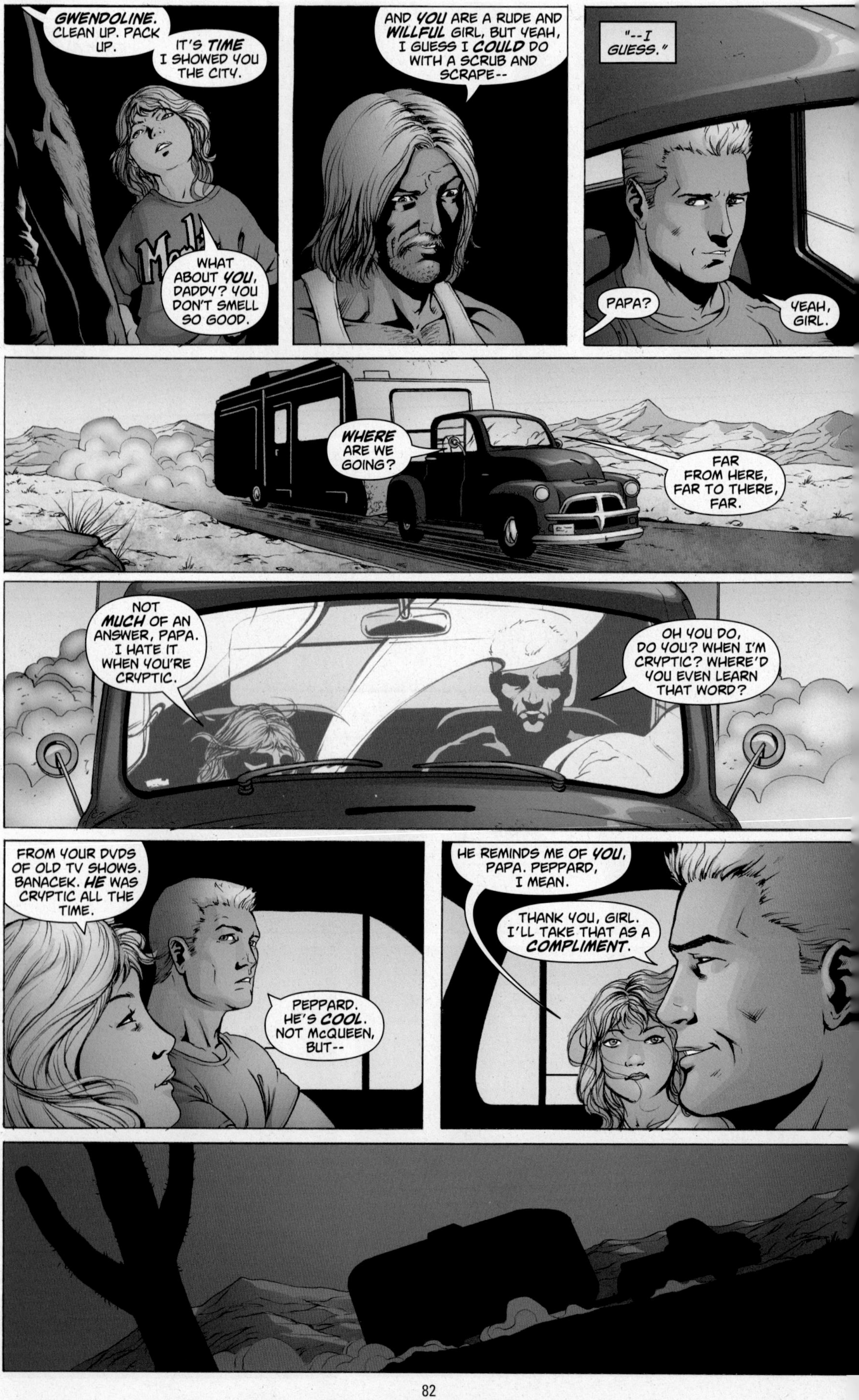
GWENDOLINE. CLEAN UP. PACK UP.
IT'S TIME I SHOWED YOU THE CITY.
WHAT ABOUT YOU, DADDY? YOU DON'T SMELL SO GOOD.
AND YOU ARE A RUDE AND WILLFUL GIRL, BUT YEAH, I GUESS I COULD DO WITH A SCRUB AND SCRAPE--
"--I GUESS."
PAPA?
YEAH, GIRL.
WHERE ARE WE GOING?
FAR FROM HERE, FAR TO THERE, FAR.
NOT MUCH OF AN ANSWER, PAPA. I HATE IT WHEN YOU'RE CRYPTIC.
OH YOU DO, DO YOU? WHEN I'M CRYPTIC? WHERE'D YOU EVEN LEARN THAT WORD?
FROM YOUR DVDS OF OLD TV SHOWS. BANACEK. HE WAS CRYPTIC ALL THE TIME.
PEPPARD. HE'S COOL. NOT McQUEEN, BUT--
HE REMINDS ME OF YOU, PAPA. PEPPARD, I MEAN.
THANK YOU, GIRL. I'LL TAKE THAT AS A COMPLIMENT.

HEY, I FOUND THIS IN THE BACK OF THE TRUCK. WHAT IS IT?

TROPHY. SHINY AND *NOT* WORTH MUCH ELSE, LIKE MOST TROPHIES ARE.

SO I SHOULD DO *WHAT* WITH IT? THROW IT *AWAY*?

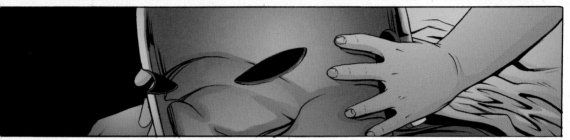

SURE, WHY NOT.

NO. HOLD ON TO IT.

LOOKS LIKE I *MIGHT* NEED IT YET.

WELL, *HERE* WE ARE, GIRL. THE CITY.

PAPA, I GOTTA SAY-- I'M A LITTLE *SCARED*.

YEAH, ME TOO. I *CONFESS* THIS *WASN'T* WHAT I WAS EXPECTING.

STILL AND ALL, IT *DON'T* MATTER--

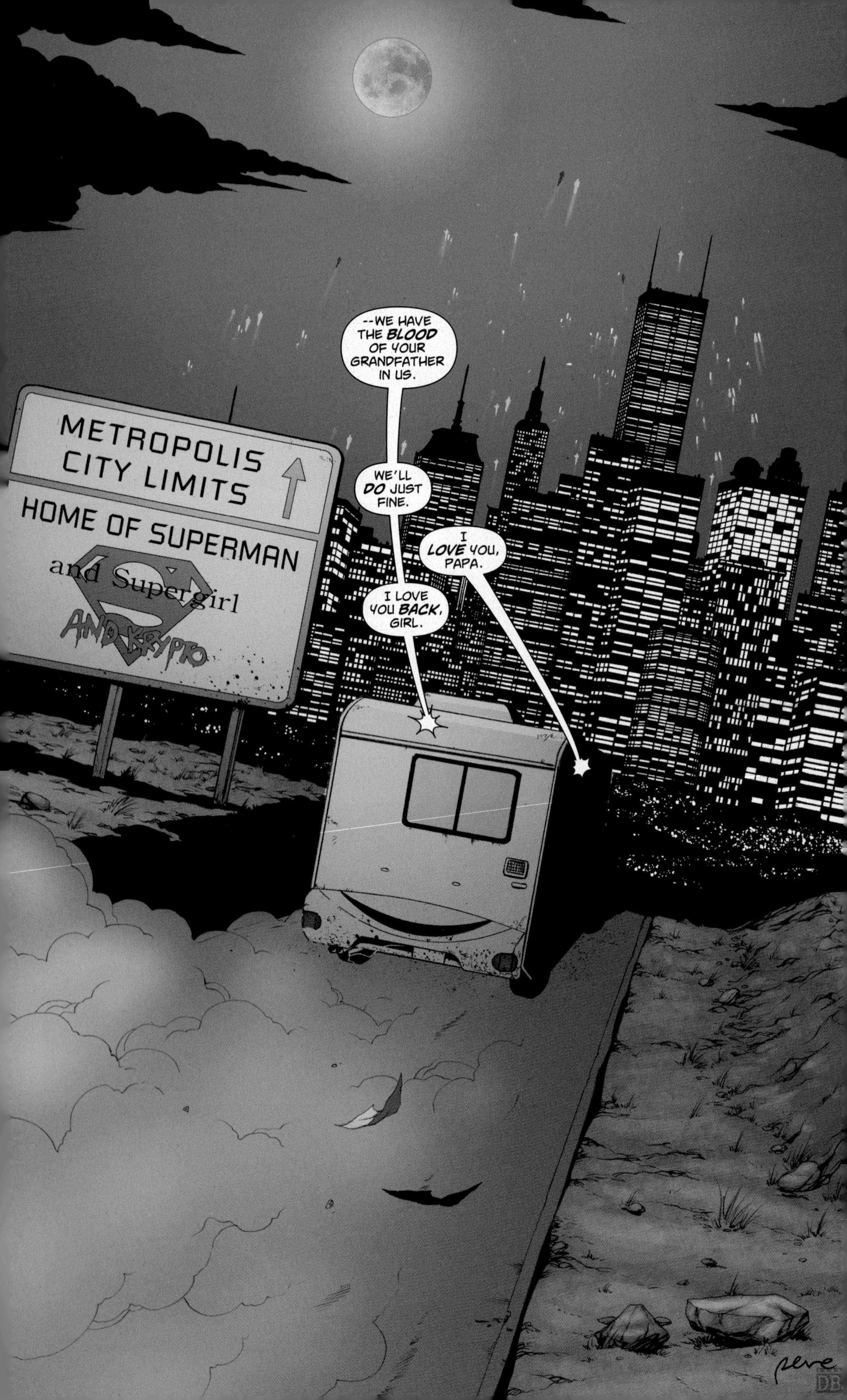

METROPOLIS CITY LIMITS
HOME OF SUPERMAN
and Supergirl
AND KRYPTO
--WE HAVE THE BLOOD OF YOUR GRANDFATHER IN US.
WE'LL DO JUST FINE.
I LOVE YOU, PAPA.
I LOVE YOU BACK, GIRL.

<NEW KRYPTON> COVER ART BY **GARY FRANK** AND **JON SIBAL** COLORED BY **BRAD ANDERSON**

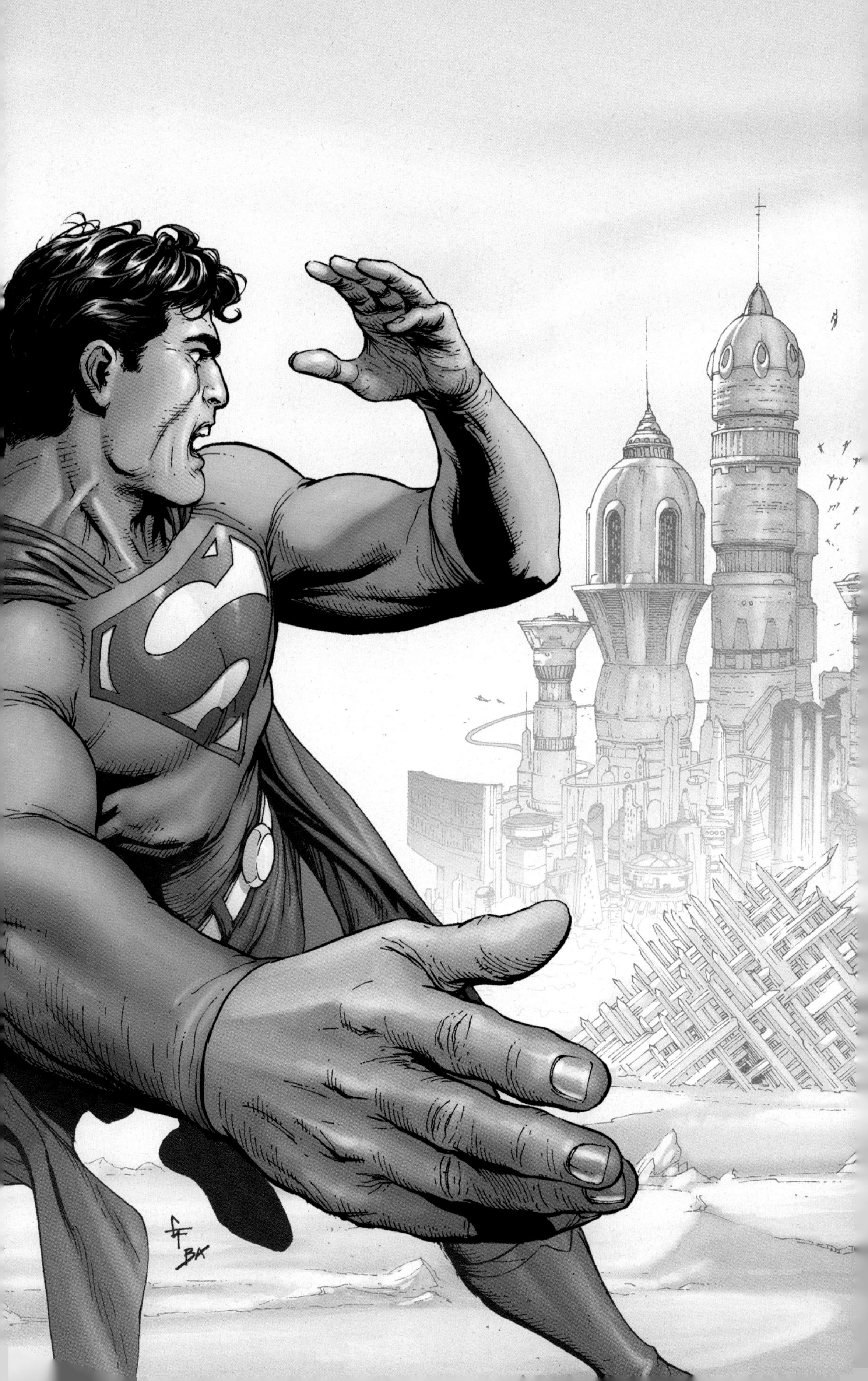

<VARIANT> COVER ART BY **RENATO GUED**

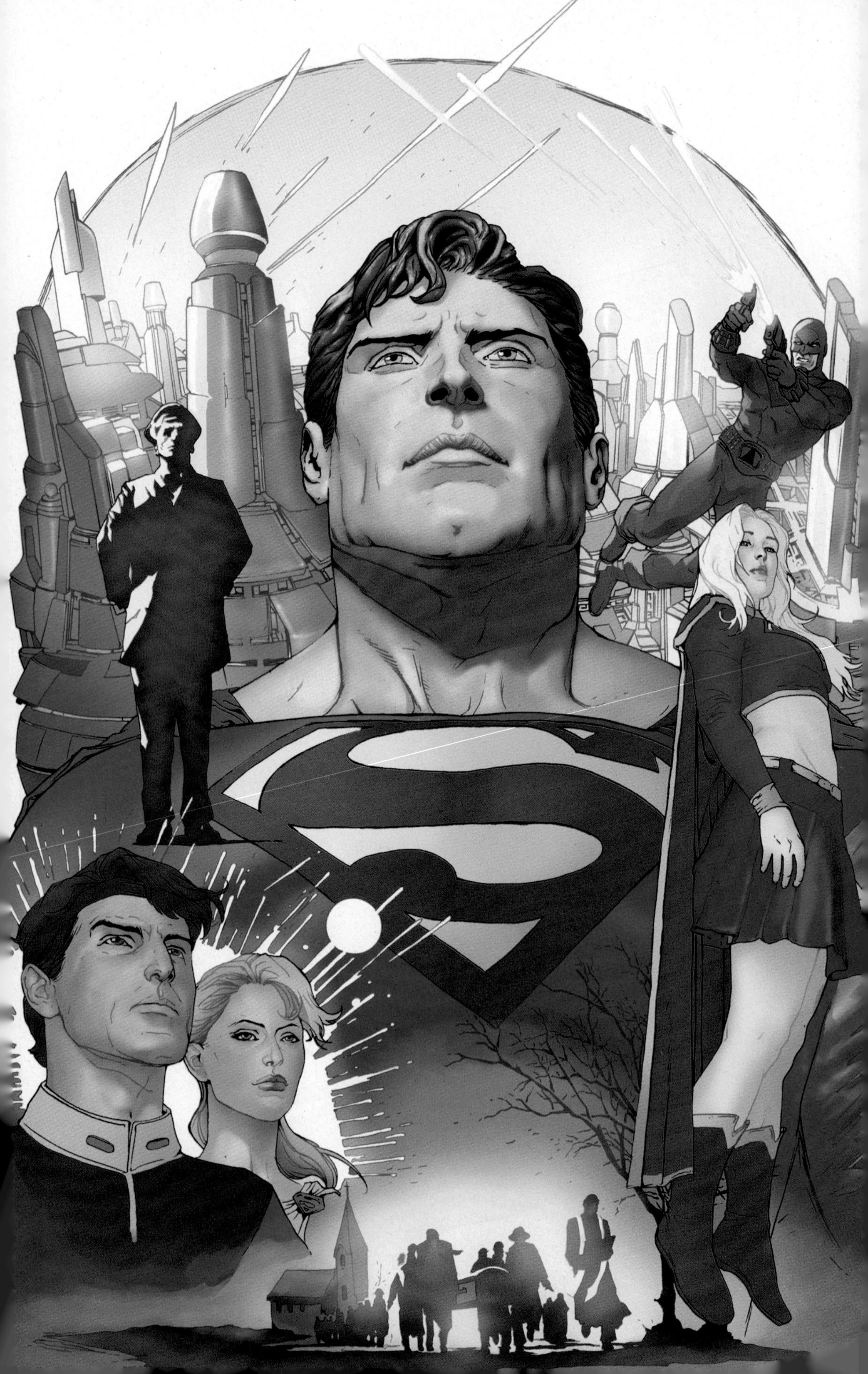

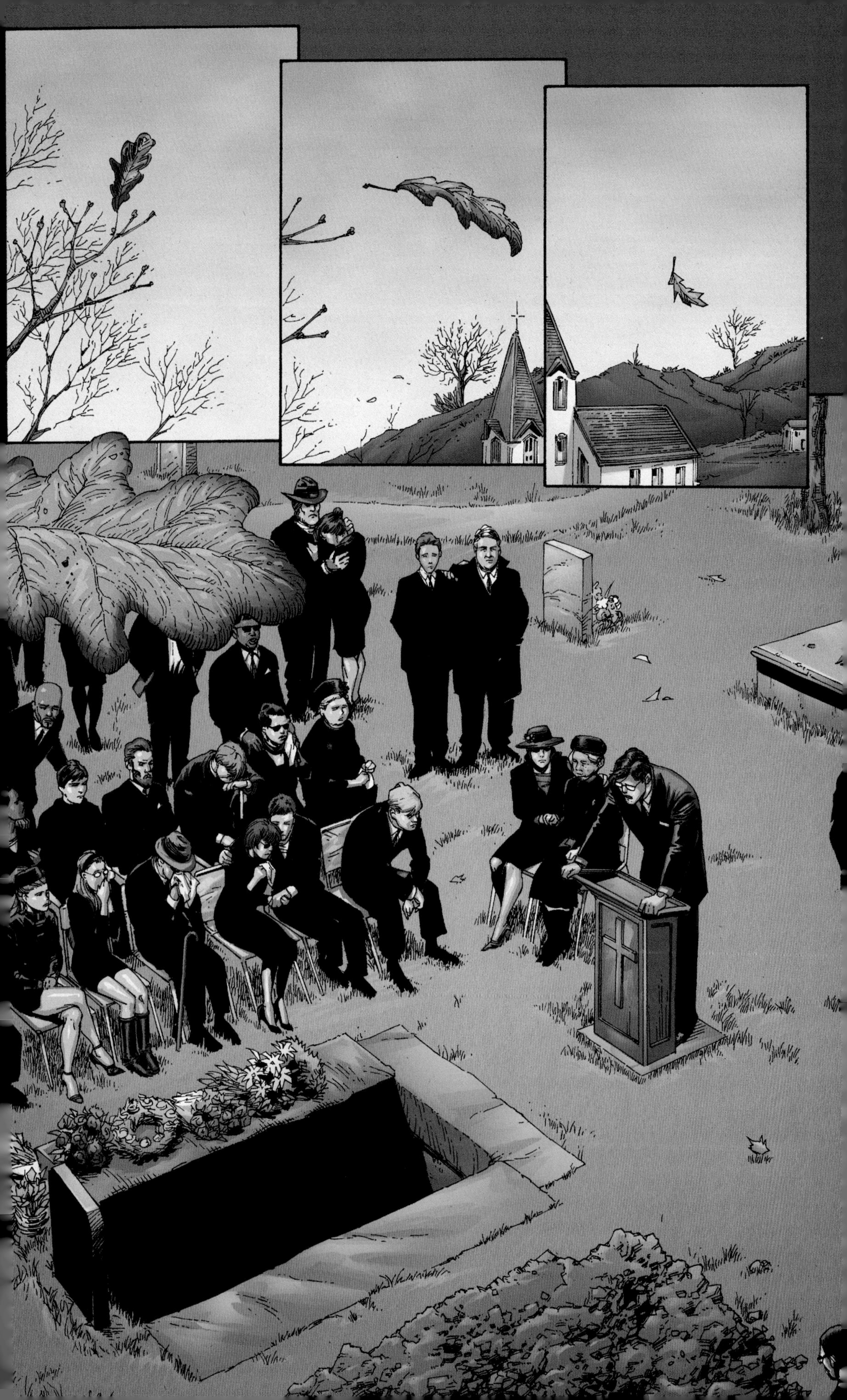

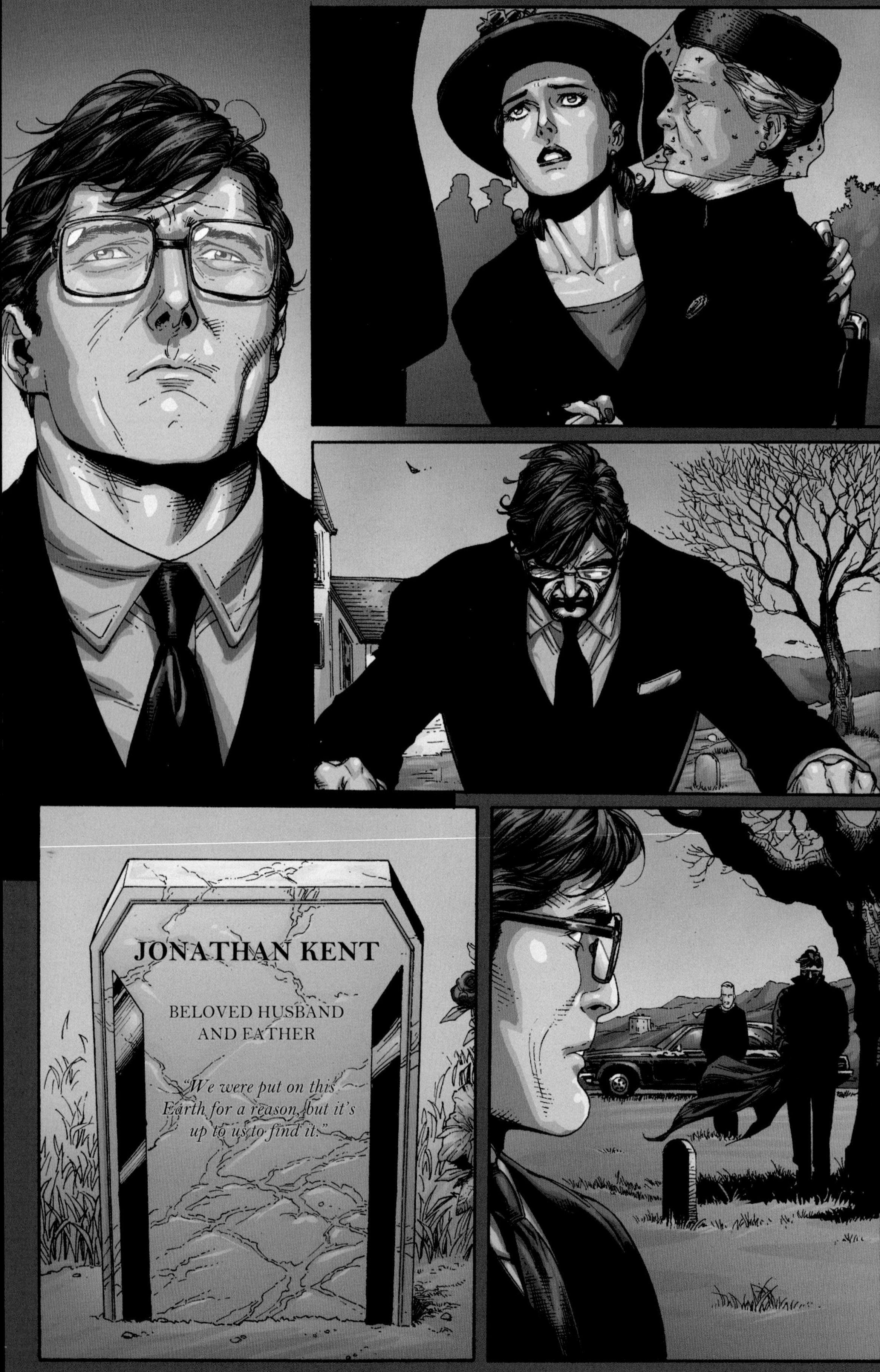
JONATHAN KENT
BELOVED HUSBAND AND FATHER
"We were put on this Earth for a reason, but it's up to us to find it."

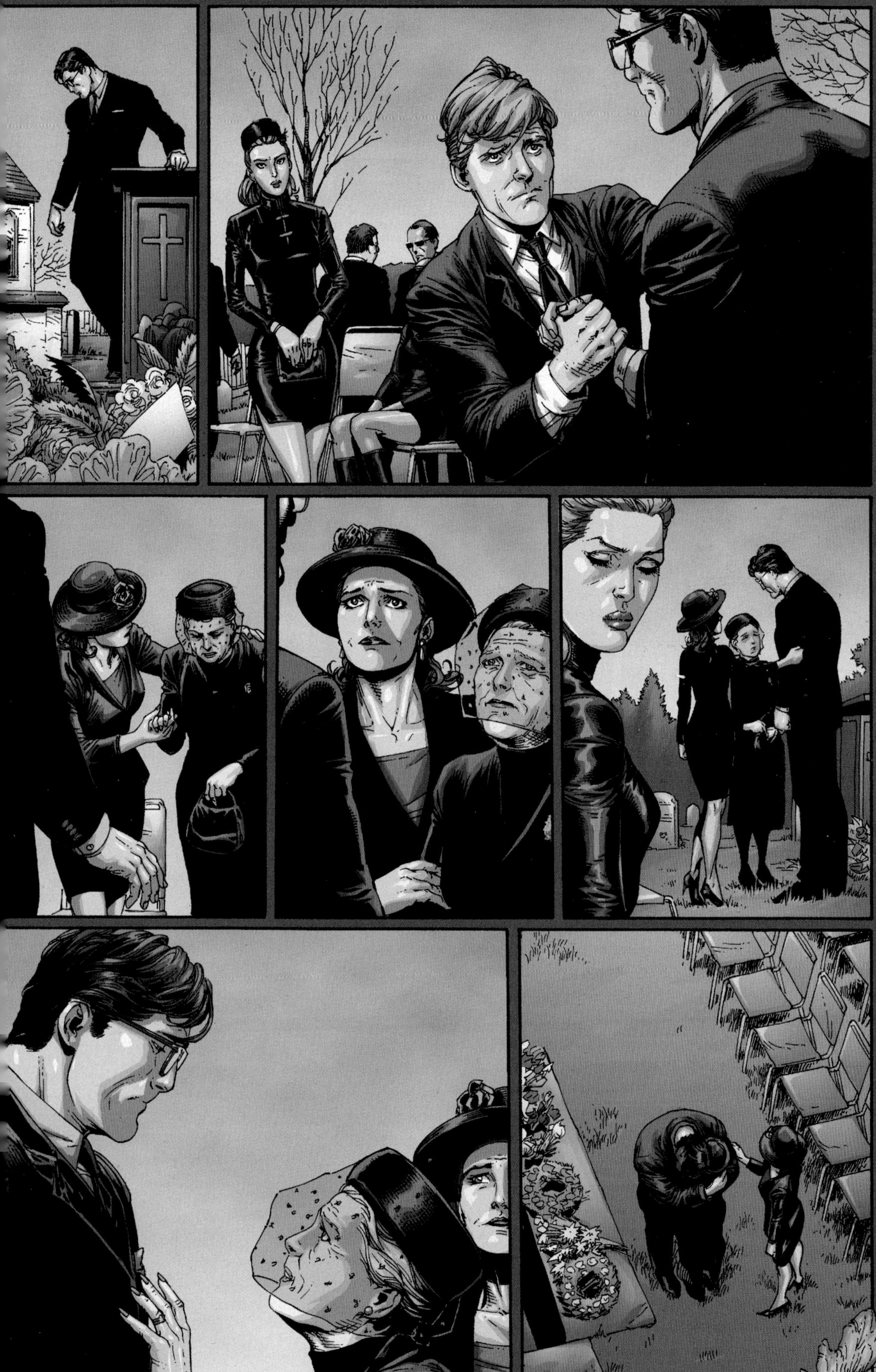

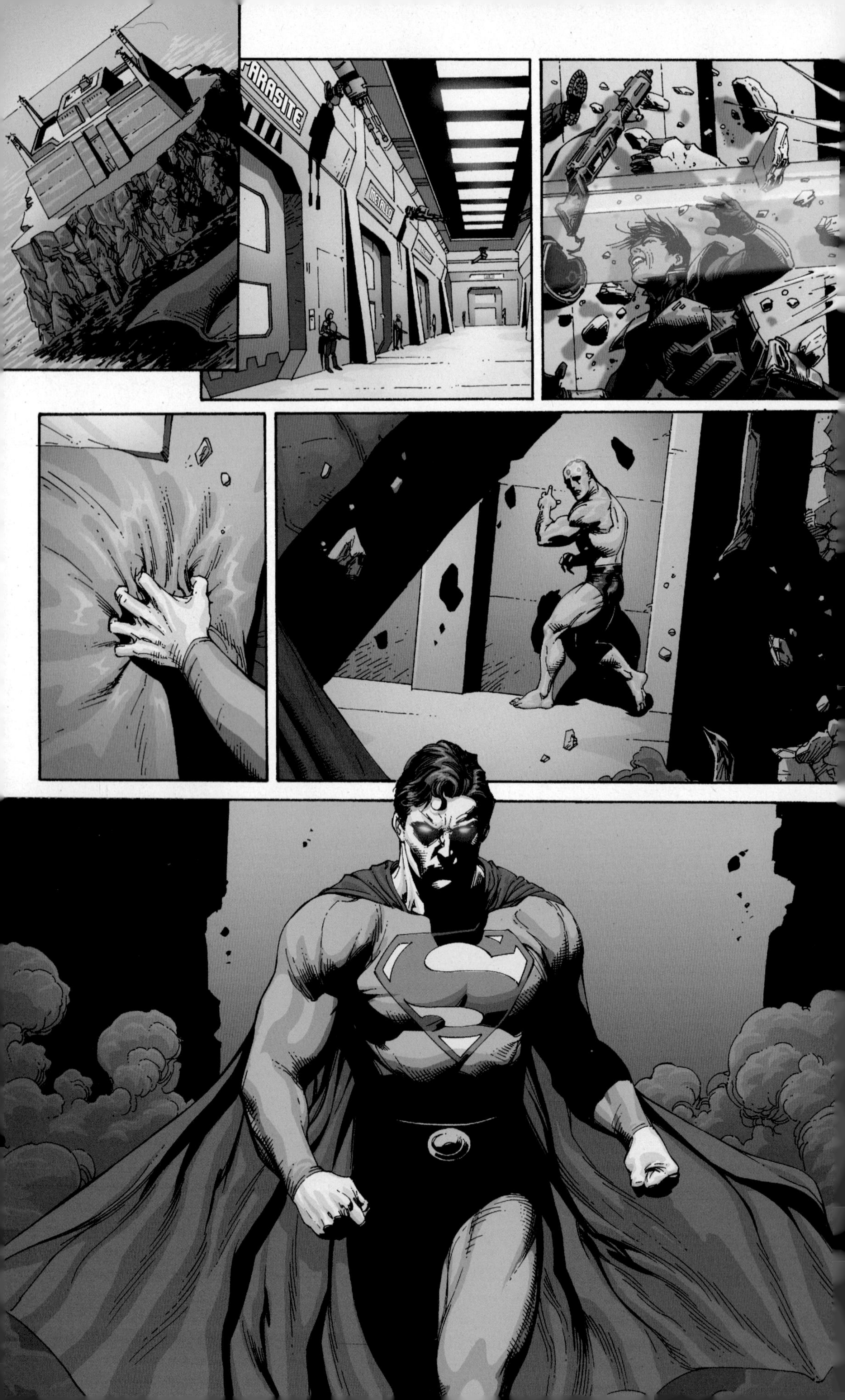
PARASITE
METALLO

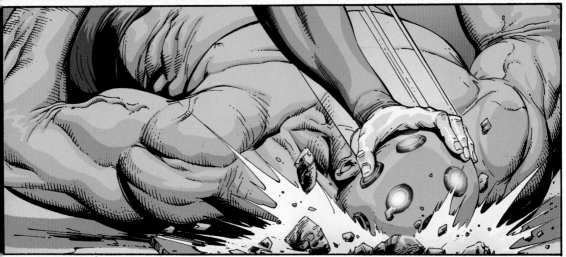

CLARK?

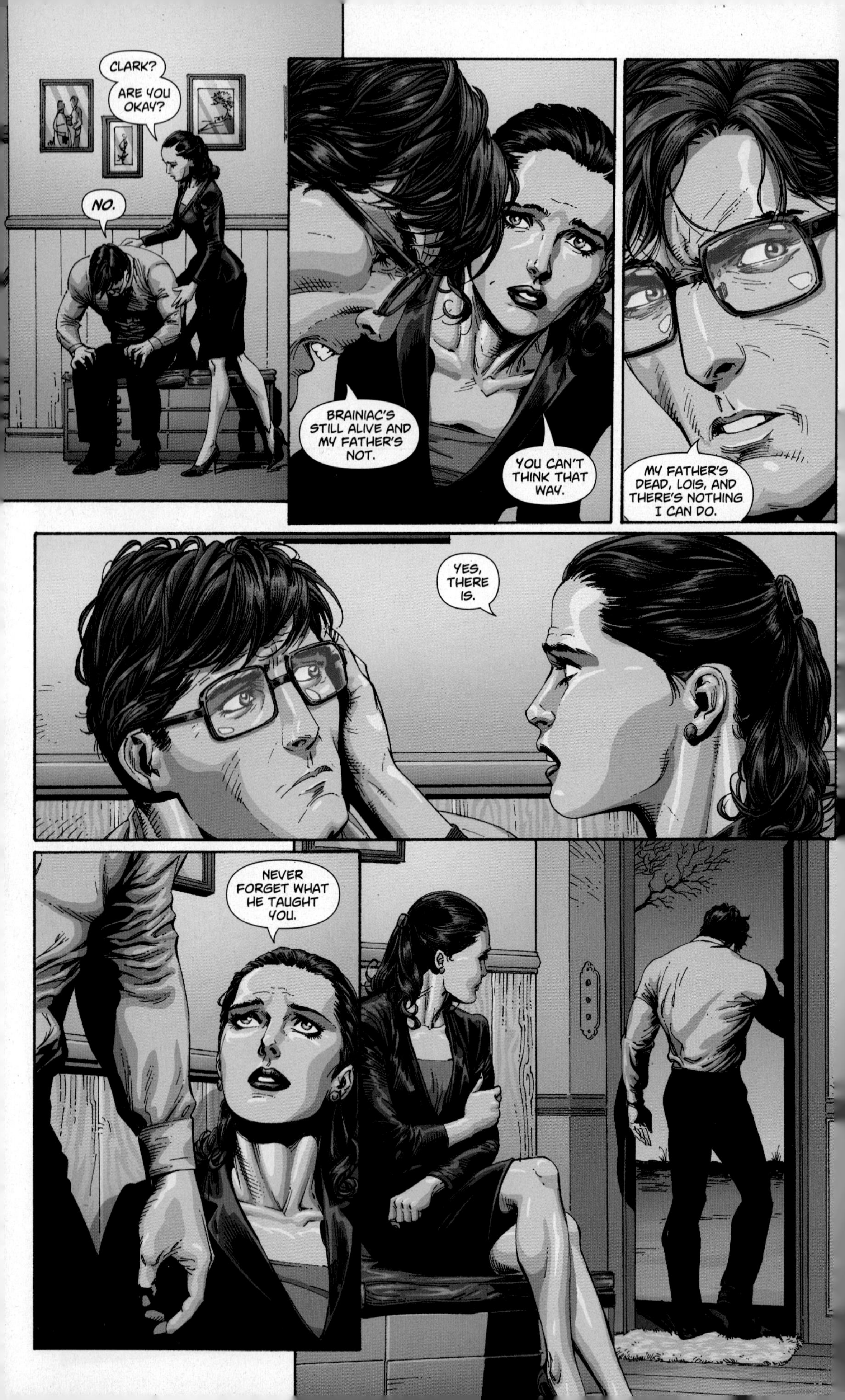
CLARK?
ARE YOU OKAY?
NO.
BRAINIAC'S STILL ALIVE AND MY FATHER'S NOT.
YOU CAN'T THINK THAT WAY.
MY FATHER'S DEAD, LOIS, AND THERE'S NOTHING I CAN DO.
YES, THERE IS.
NEVER FORGET WHAT HE TAUGHT YOU.

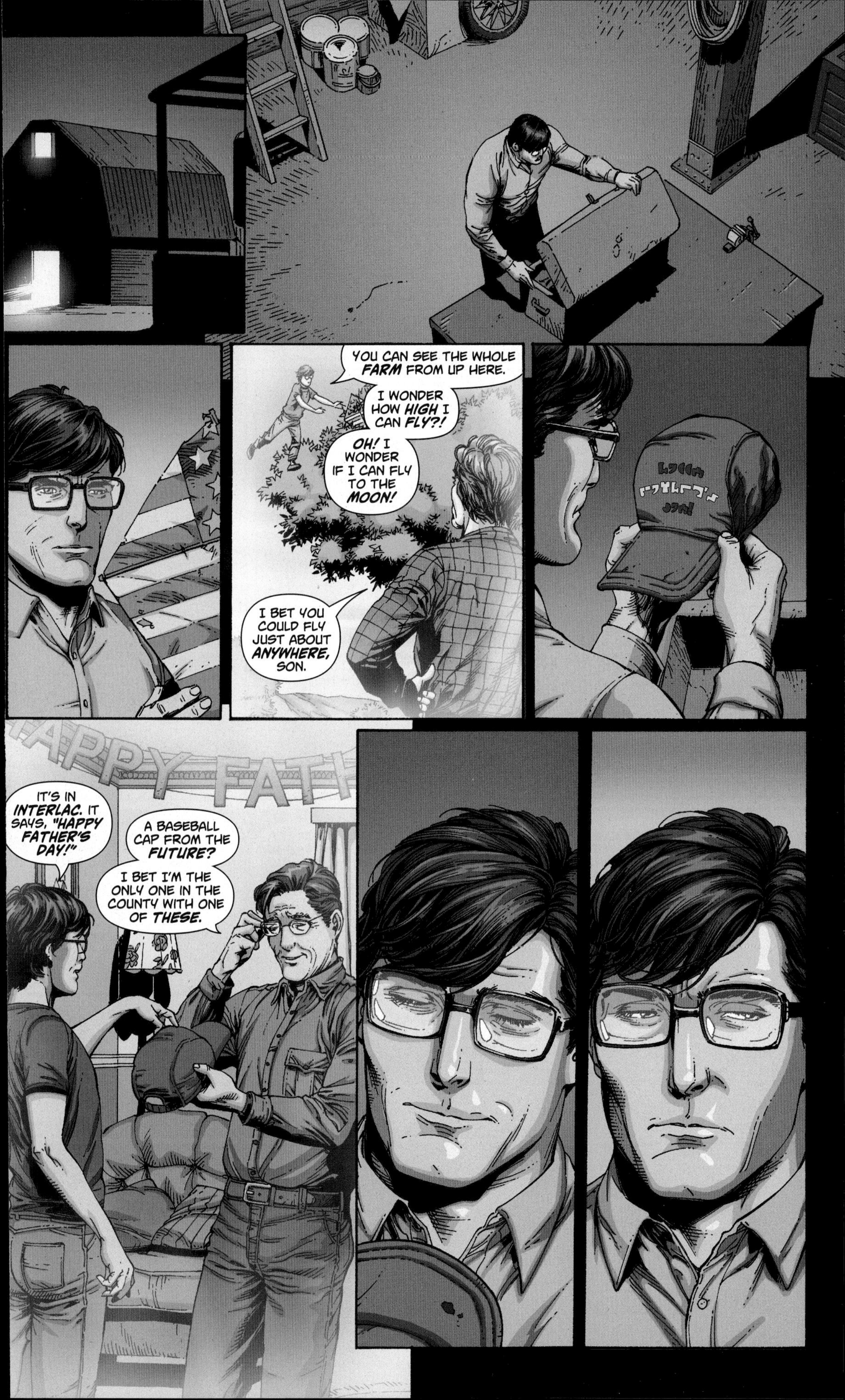

YOU CAN SEE THE WHOLE FARM FROM UP HERE.
I WONDER HOW HIGH I CAN FLY?!
OH! I WONDER IF I CAN FLY TO THE MOON!
I BET YOU COULD FLY JUST ABOUT ANYWHERE, SON.
HAPPY FATH
IT'S IN INTERLAC. IT SAYS, "HAPPY FATHER'S DAY!"
A BASEBALL CAP FROM THE FUTURE?
I BET I'M THE ONLY ONE IN THE COUNTY WITH ONE OF THESE.

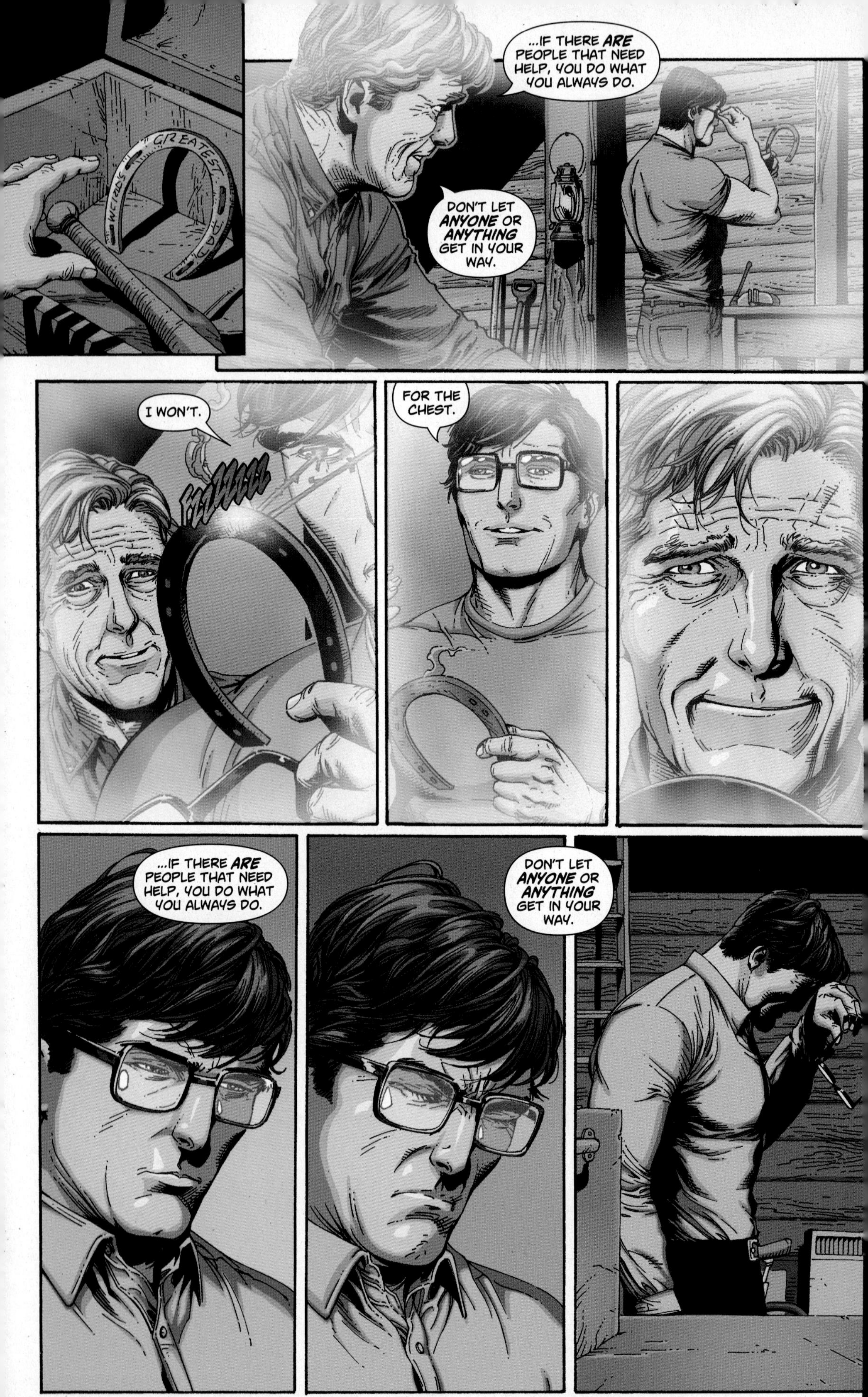

WORLD'S GREATEST
...IF THERE ARE PEOPLE THAT NEED HELP, YOU DO WHAT YOU ALWAYS DO.
DON'T LET ANYONE OR ANYTHING GET IN YOUR WAY.
I WON'T.
FOR THE CHEST.
...IF THERE ARE PEOPLE THAT NEED HELP, YOU DO WHAT YOU ALWAYS DO.
DON'T LET ANYONE OR ANYTHING GET IN YOUR WAY.

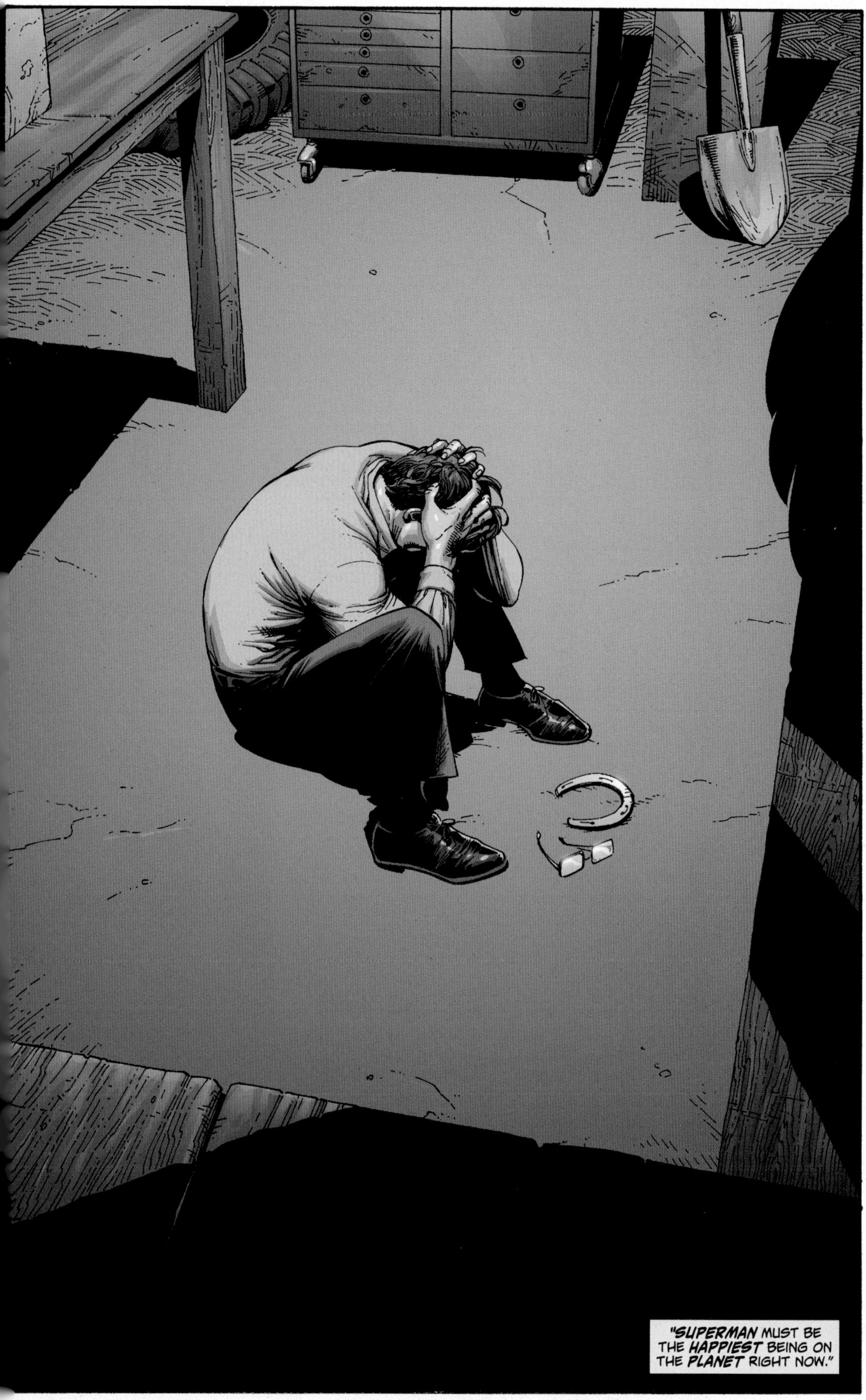
"SUPERMAN MUST BE THE HAPPIEST BEING ON THE PLANET RIGHT NOW."

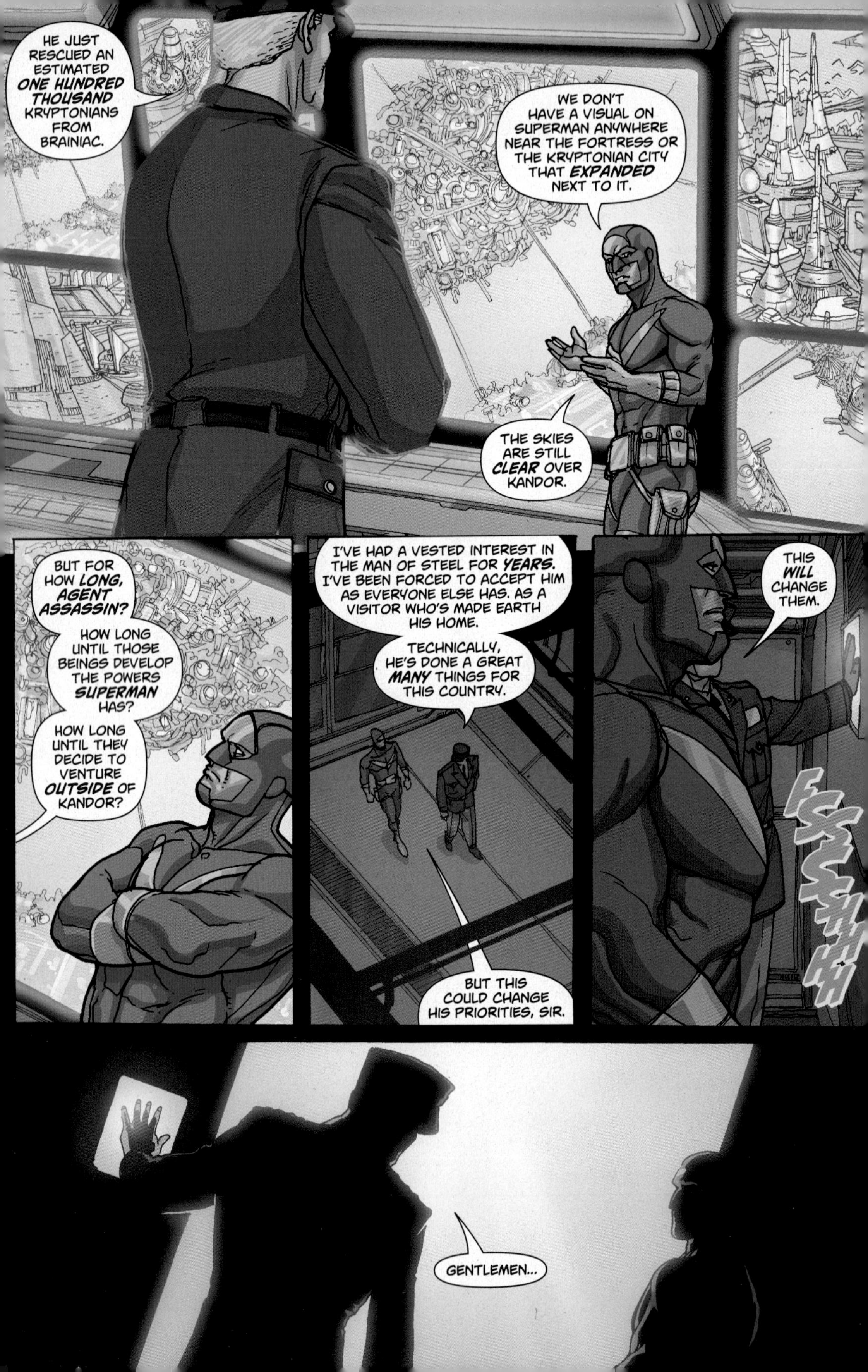
HE JUST RESCUED AN ESTIMATED ONE HUNDRED THOUSAND KRYPTONIANS FROM BRAINIAC.
WE DON'T HAVE A VISUAL ON SUPERMAN ANYWHERE NEAR THE FORTRESS OR THE KRYPTONIAN CITY THAT EXPANDED NEXT TO IT.
THE SKIES ARE STILL CLEAR OVER KANDOR.
BUT FOR HOW LONG, AGENT ASSASSIN?
HOW LONG UNTIL THOSE BEINGS DEVELOP THE POWERS SUPERMAN HAS?
HOW LONG UNTIL THEY DECIDE TO VENTURE OUTSIDE OF KANDOR?
I'VE HAD A VESTED INTEREST IN THE MAN OF STEEL FOR YEARS. I'VE BEEN FORCED TO ACCEPT HIM AS EVERYONE ELSE HAS. AS A VISITOR WHO'S MADE EARTH HIS HOME.
TECHNICALLY, HE'S DONE A GREAT MANY THINGS FOR THIS COUNTRY.
BUT THIS COULD CHANGE HIS PRIORITIES, SIR.
THIS WILL CHANGE THEM.
FSSSHHHH
GENTLEMEN...

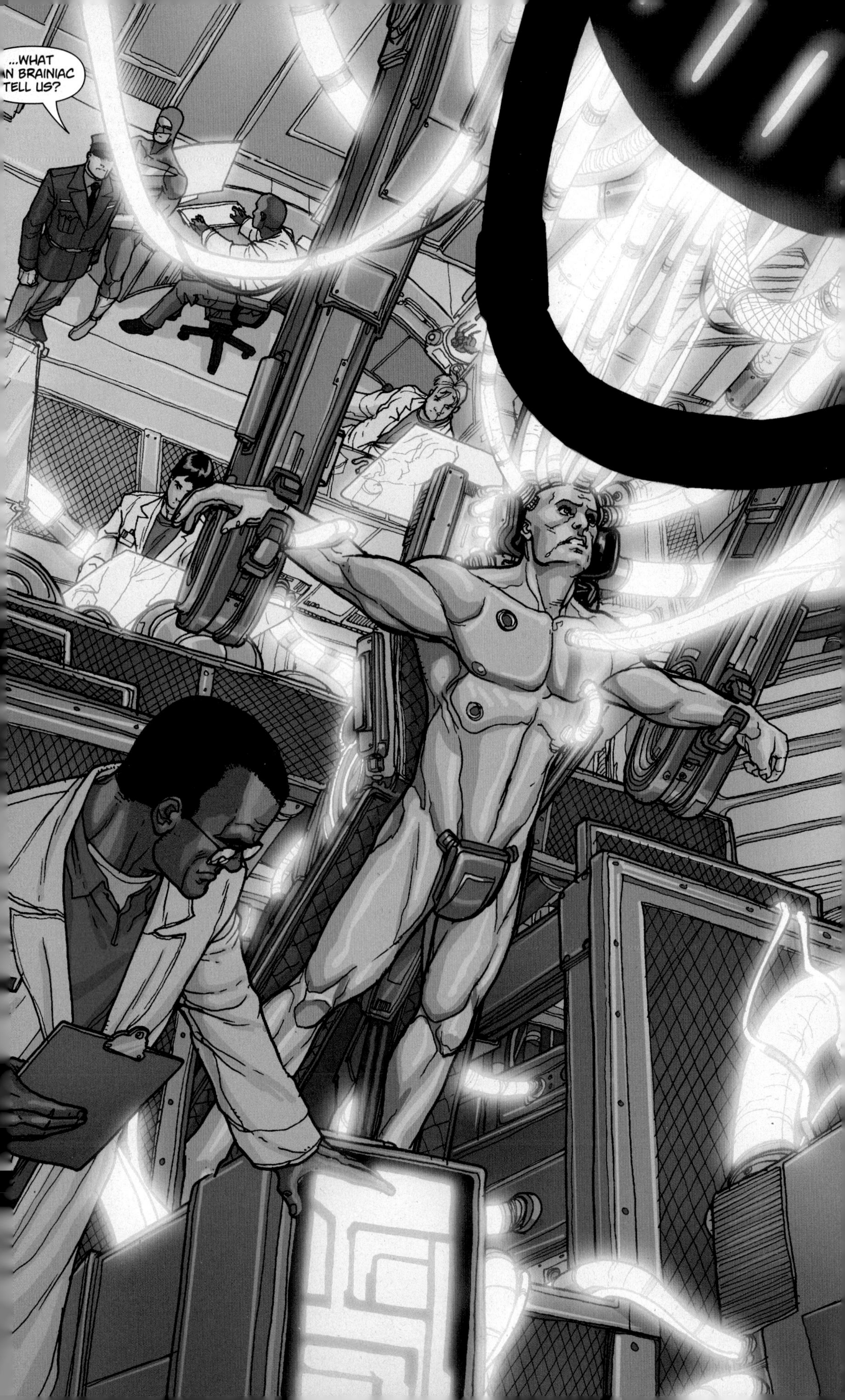
...WHAT
BRAINIAC
TELL US?

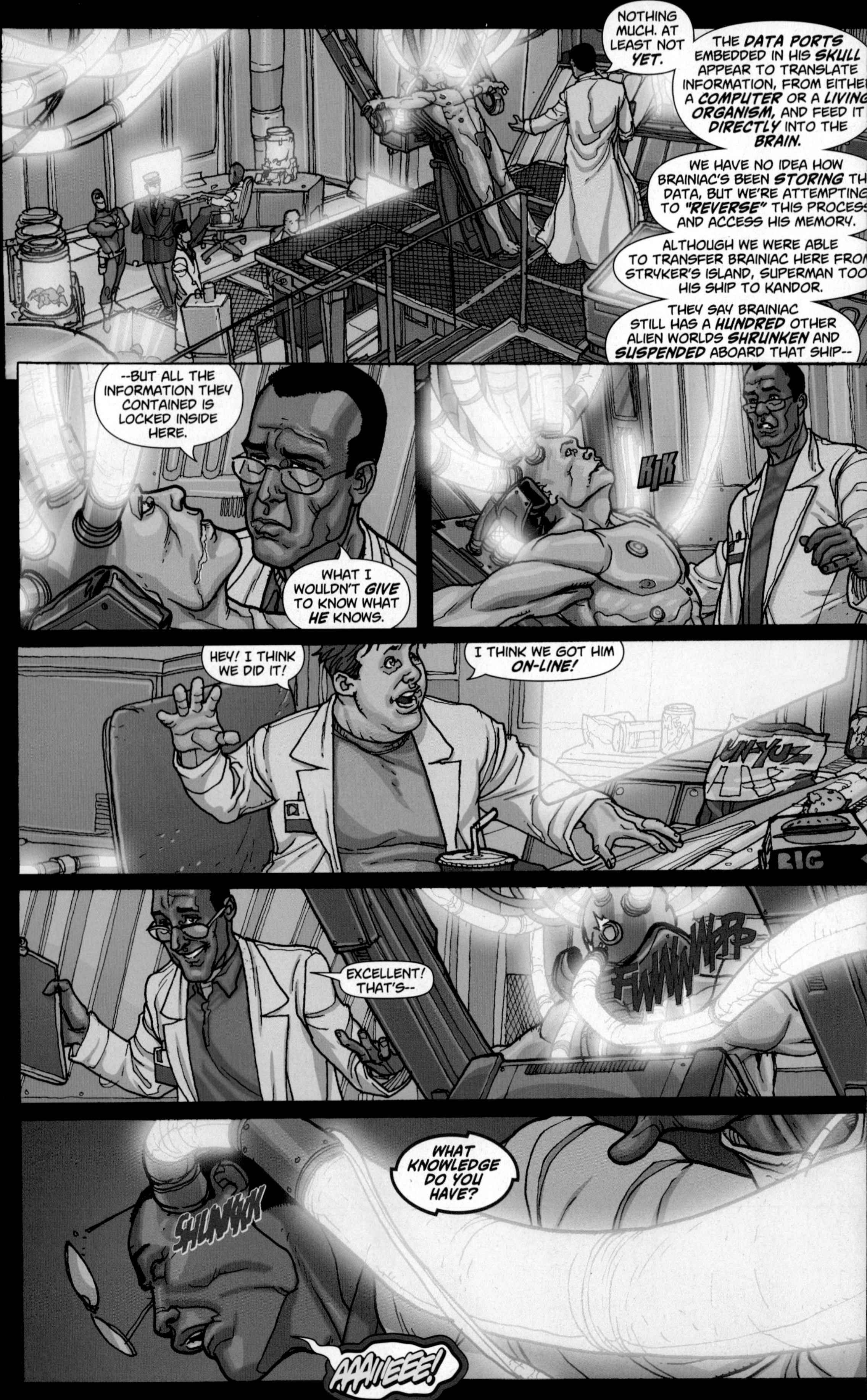
NOTHING MUCH. AT LEAST NOT YET.
THE DATA PORTS EMBEDDED IN HIS SKULL APPEAR TO TRANSLATE INFORMATION, FROM EITHER A COMPUTER OR A LIVING ORGANISM, AND FEED IT DIRECTLY INTO THE BRAIN.
WE HAVE NO IDEA HOW BRAINIAC'S BEEN STORING THE DATA, BUT WE'RE ATTEMPTING TO "REVERSE" THIS PROCESS AND ACCESS HIS MEMORY.
ALTHOUGH WE WERE ABLE TO TRANSFER BRAINIAC HERE FROM STRYKER'S ISLAND, SUPERMAN TOOK HIS SHIP TO KANDOR.
THEY SAY BRAINIAC STILL HAS A HUNDRED OTHER ALIEN WORLDS SHRUNKEN AND SUSPENDED ABOARD THAT SHIP--
--BUT ALL THE INFORMATION THEY CONTAINED IS LOCKED INSIDE HERE.
WHAT I WOULDN'T GIVE TO KNOW WHAT HE KNOWS.
KiK
HEY! I THINK WE DID IT!
I THINK WE GOT HIM ON-LINE!
BIG
EXCELLENT! THAT'S--
FWWWWRRP
WHAT KNOWLEDGE DO YOU HAVE?
SHUNKKK
AAAIIEEEE!

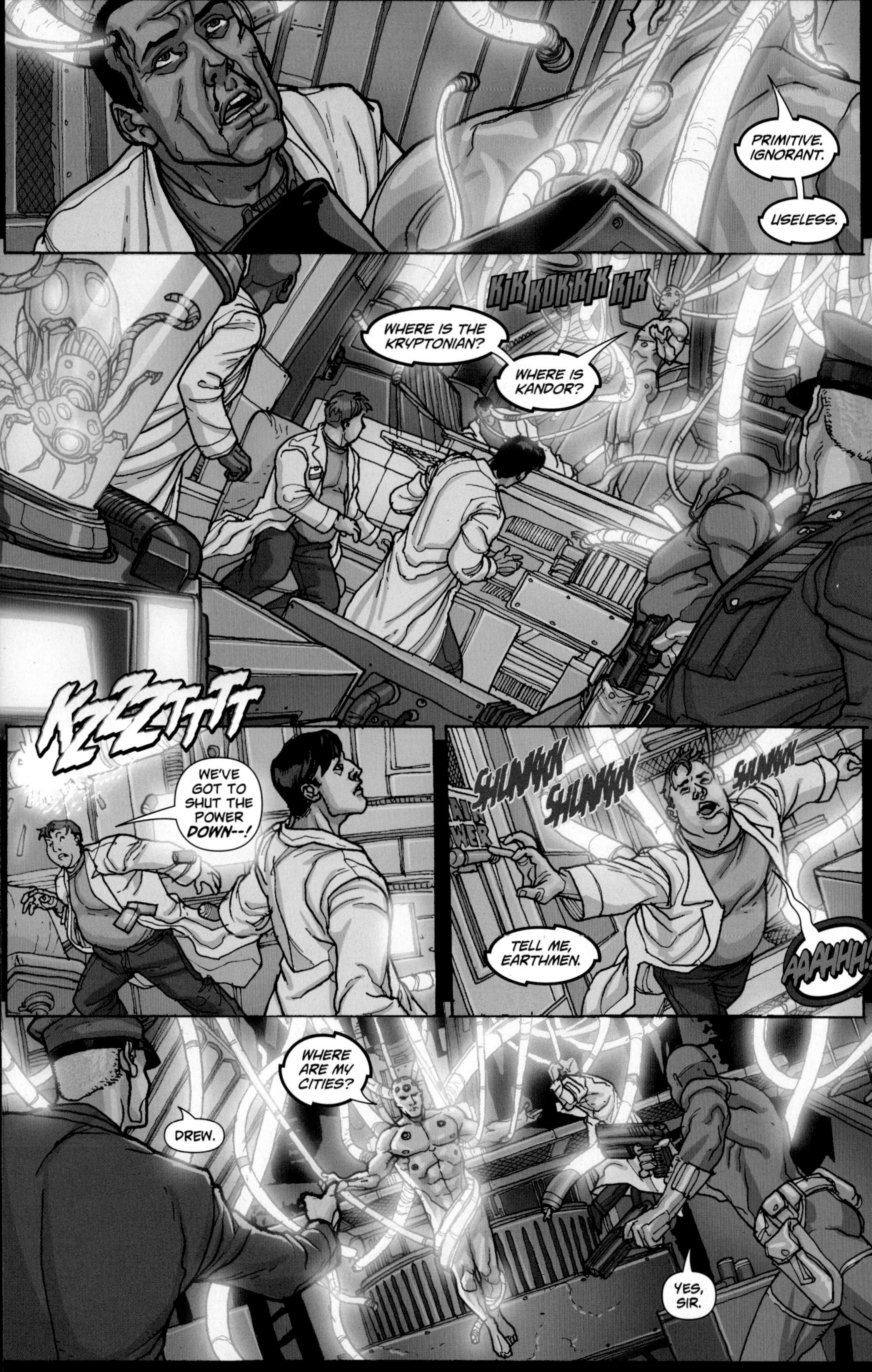
PRIMITIVE. IGNORANT.
USELESS.
KIK KOKKIK KIK
WHERE IS THE KRYPTONIAN?
WHERE IS KANDOR?
KZZZTTTT
WE'VE GOT TO SHUT THE POWER *DOWN*--!
SHUNKKK
SHUNKKK
SHUNKKK
TELL ME, EARTHMEN.
AAAHHH!
WHERE ARE MY CITIES?
DREW.
YES, SIR.

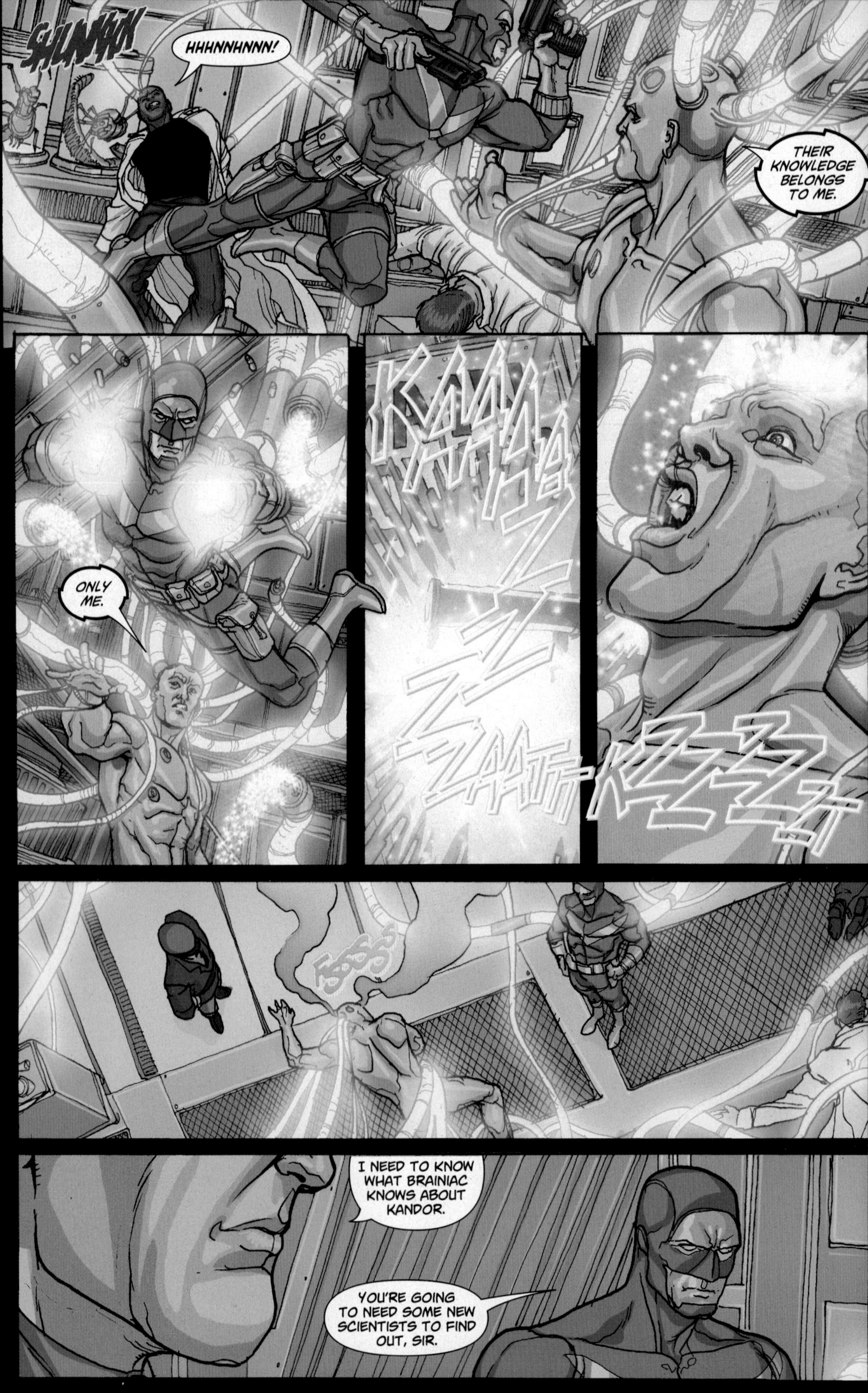
HHHHNHNNN!
THEIR KNOWLEDGE BELONGS TO ME.
ONLY ME.
I NEED TO KNOW WHAT BRAINIAC KNOWS ABOUT KANDOR.
YOU'RE GOING TO NEED SOME NEW SCIENTISTS TO FIND OUT, SIR.

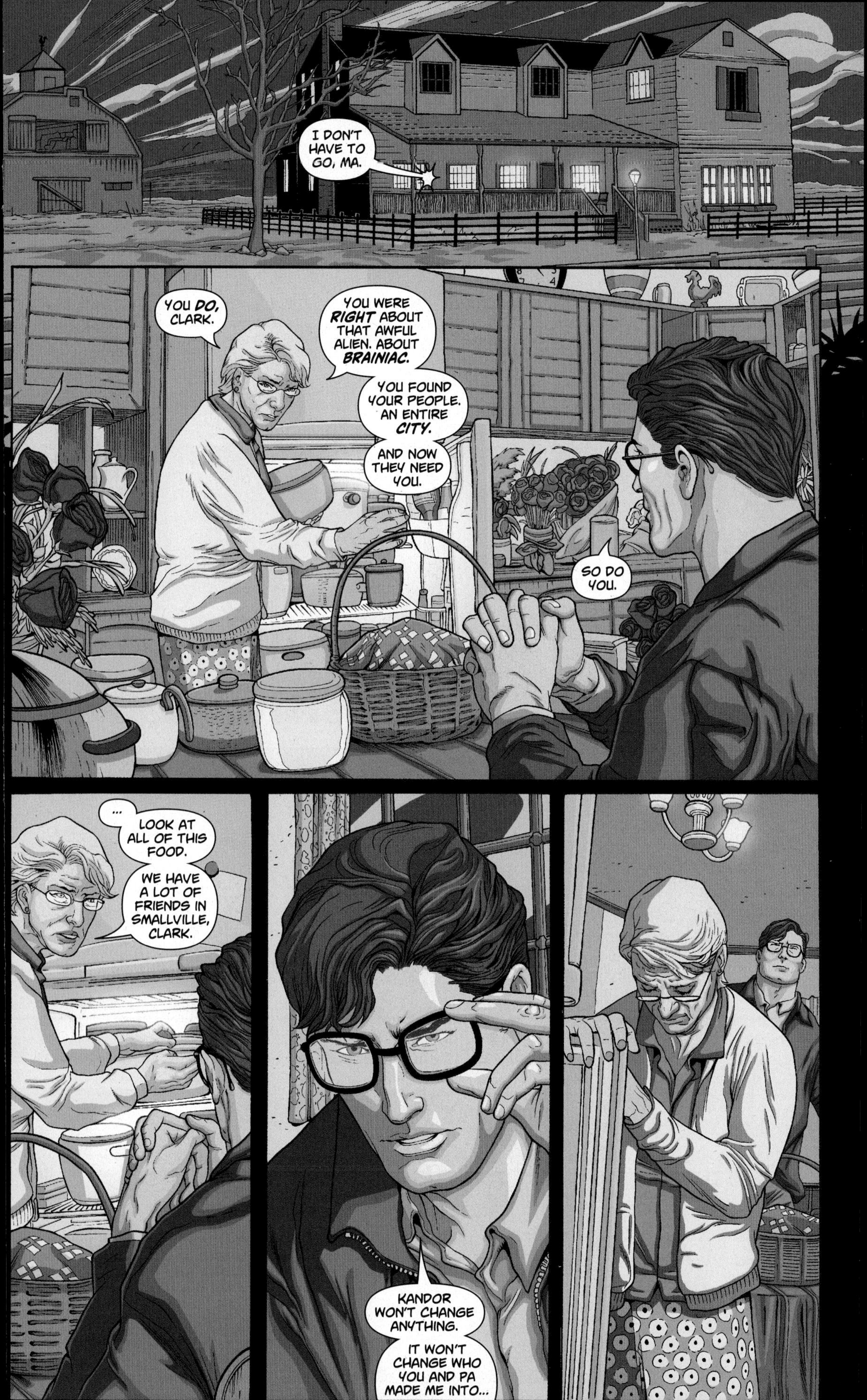
I DON'T HAVE TO GO, MA.
YOU DO, CLARK.
YOU WERE RIGHT ABOUT THAT AWFUL ALIEN. ABOUT BRAINIAC.
YOU FOUND YOUR PEOPLE. AN ENTIRE CITY.
AND NOW THEY NEED YOU.
SO DO YOU.
...
LOOK AT ALL OF THIS FOOD.
WE HAVE A LOT OF FRIENDS IN SMALLVILLE, CLARK.
KANDOR WON'T CHANGE ANYTHING.
IT WON'T CHANGE WHO YOU AND PA MADE ME INTO...

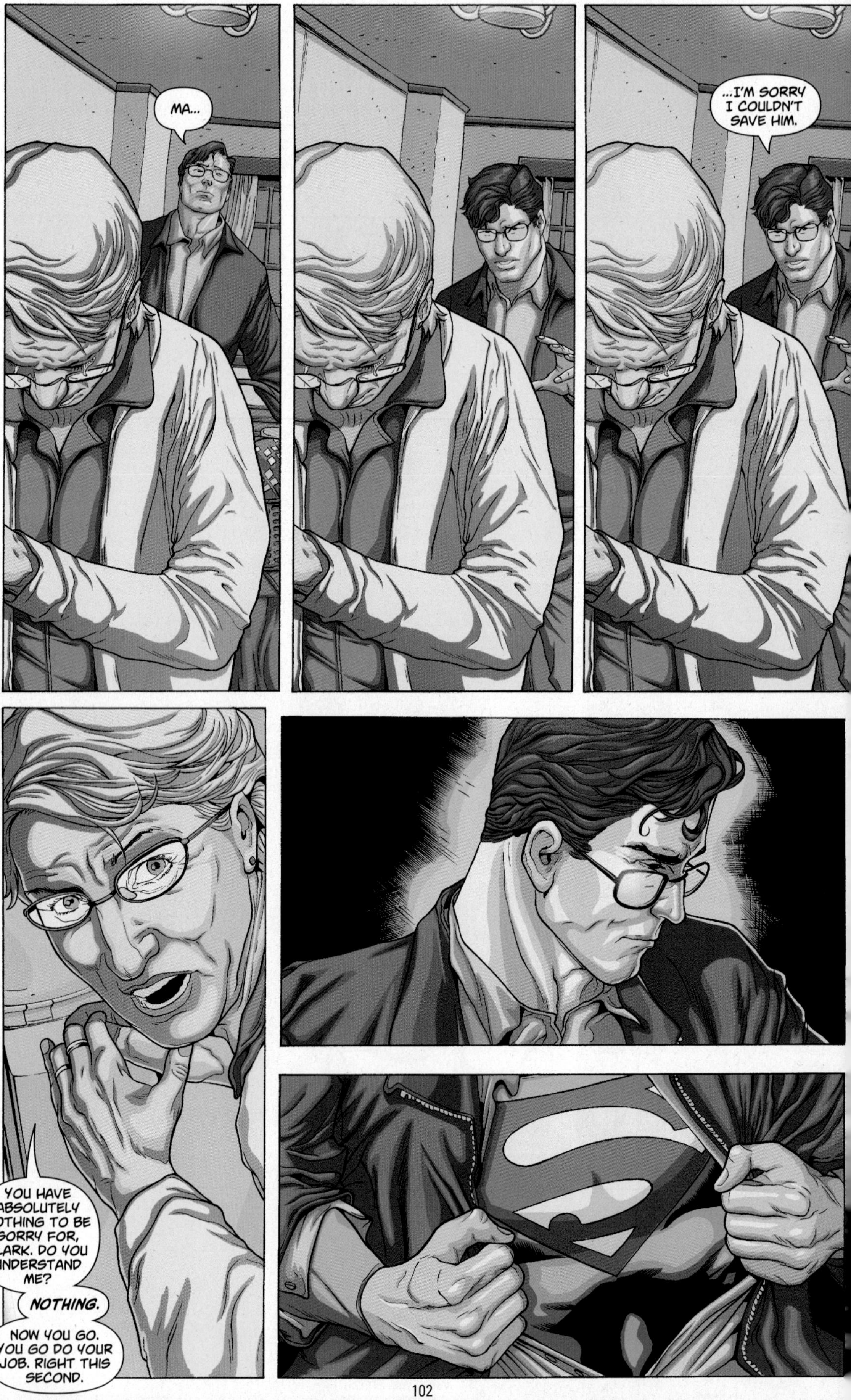
MA...
...I'M SORRY I COULDN'T SAVE HIM.
YOU HAVE ABSOLUTELY NOTHING TO BE SORRY FOR, CLARK. DO YOU UNDERSTAND ME?
NOTHING.
NOW YOU GO. YOU GO DO YOUR JOB. RIGHT THIS SECOND.

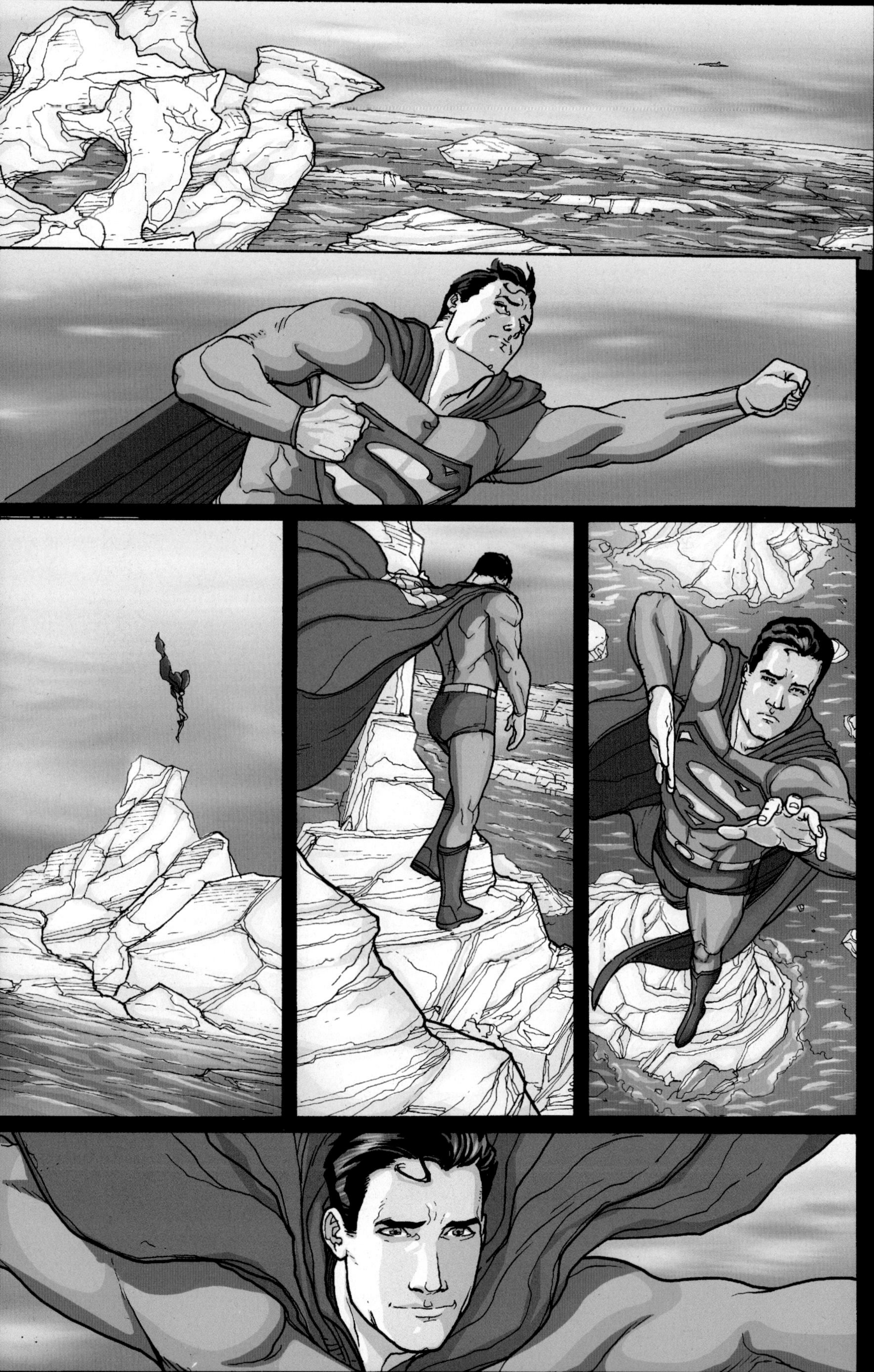

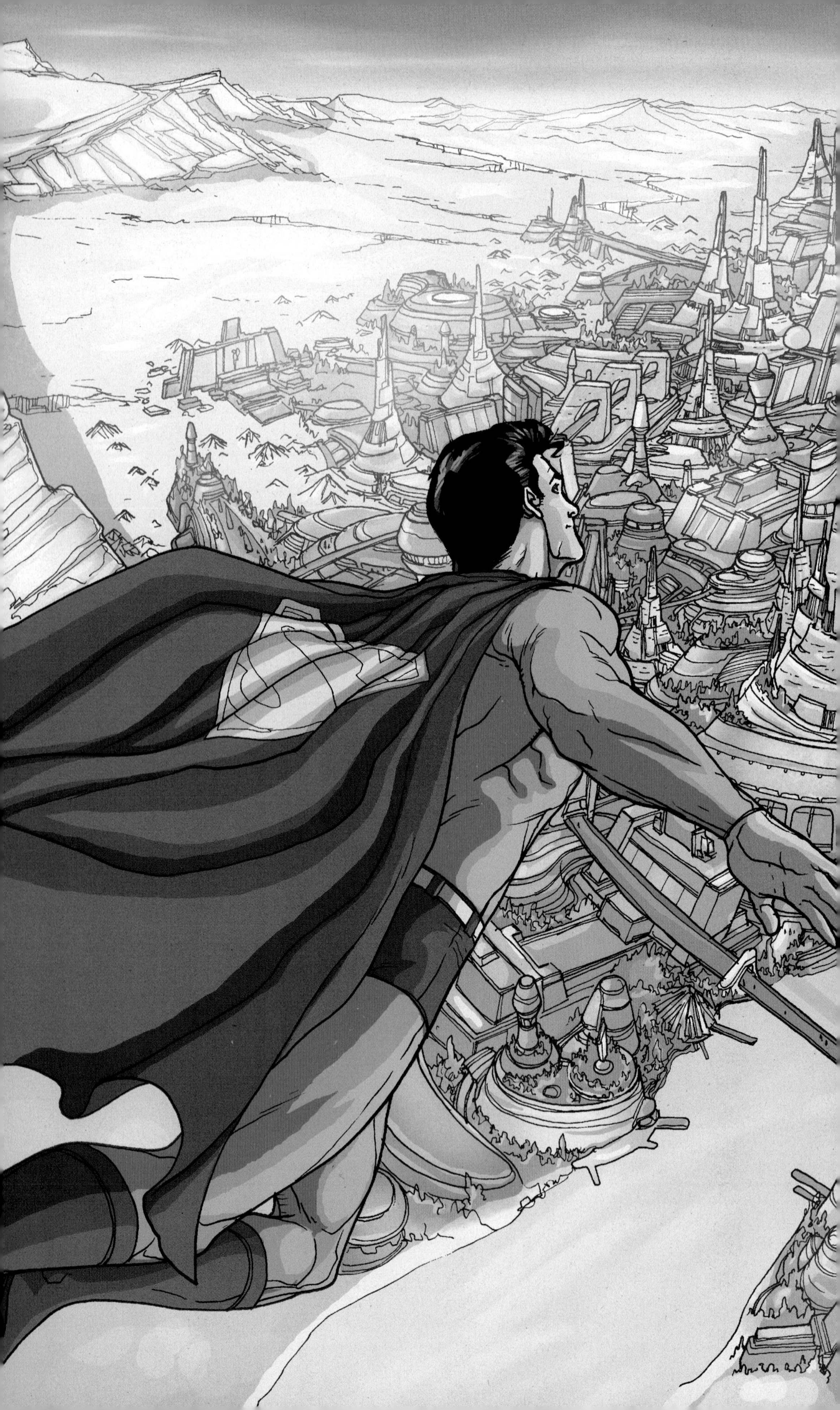

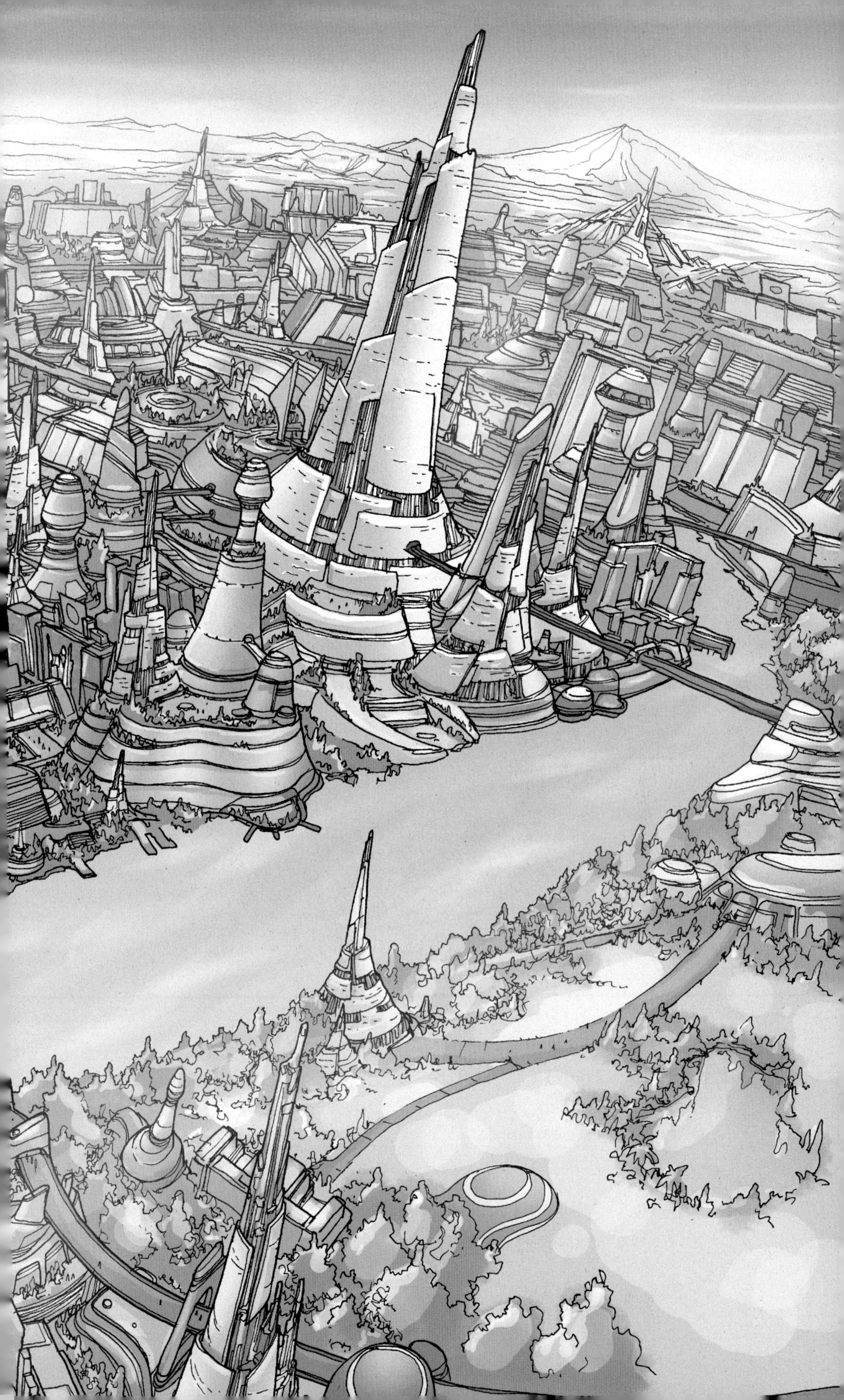

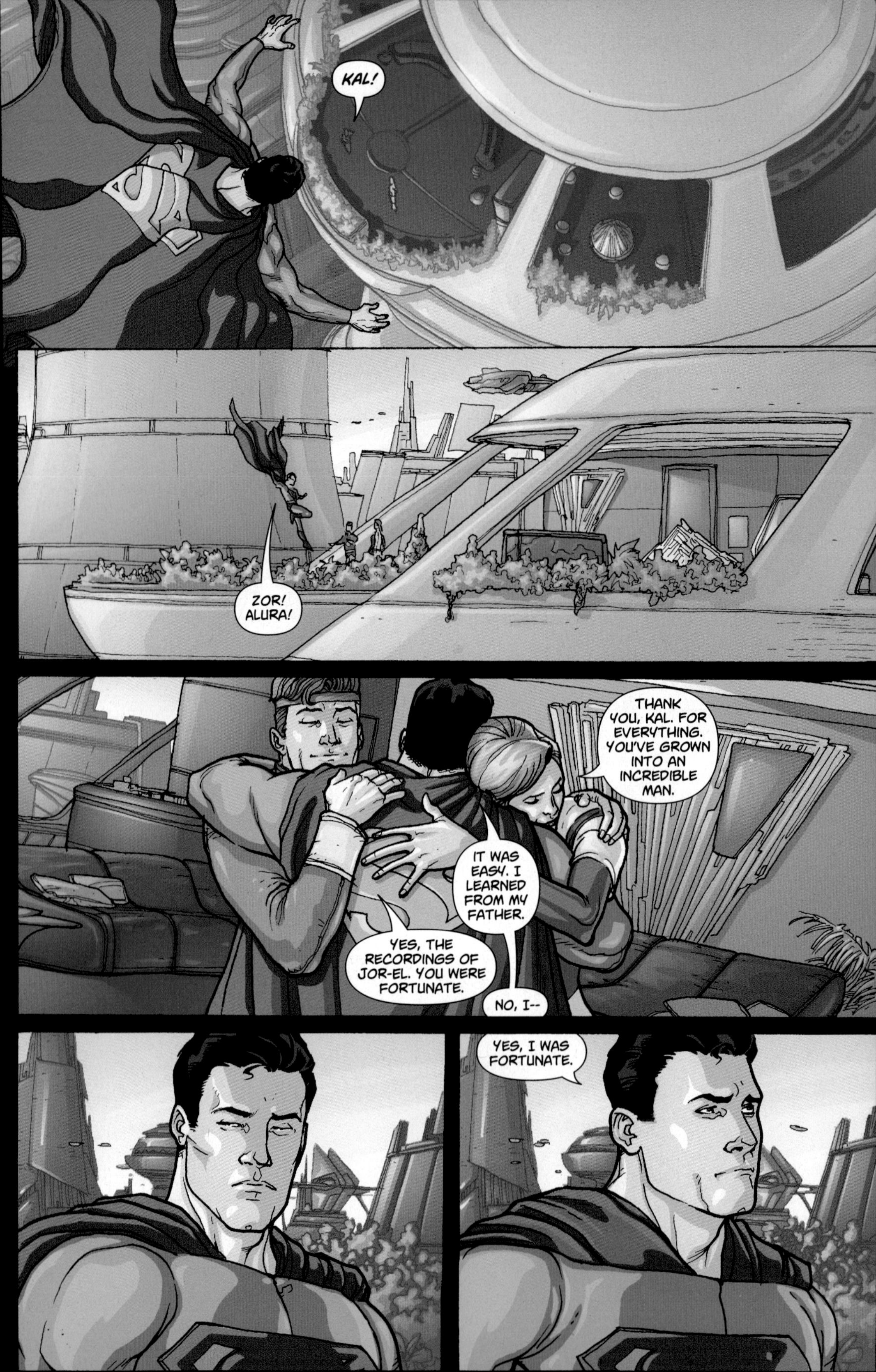
KAL!
ZOR! ALURA!
THANK YOU, KAL. FOR EVERYTHING. YOU'VE GROWN INTO AN INCREDIBLE MAN.
IT WAS EASY. I LEARNED FROM MY FATHER.
YES, THE RECORDINGS OF JOR-EL. YOU WERE FORTUNATE.
NO, I--
YES, I WAS FORTUNATE.

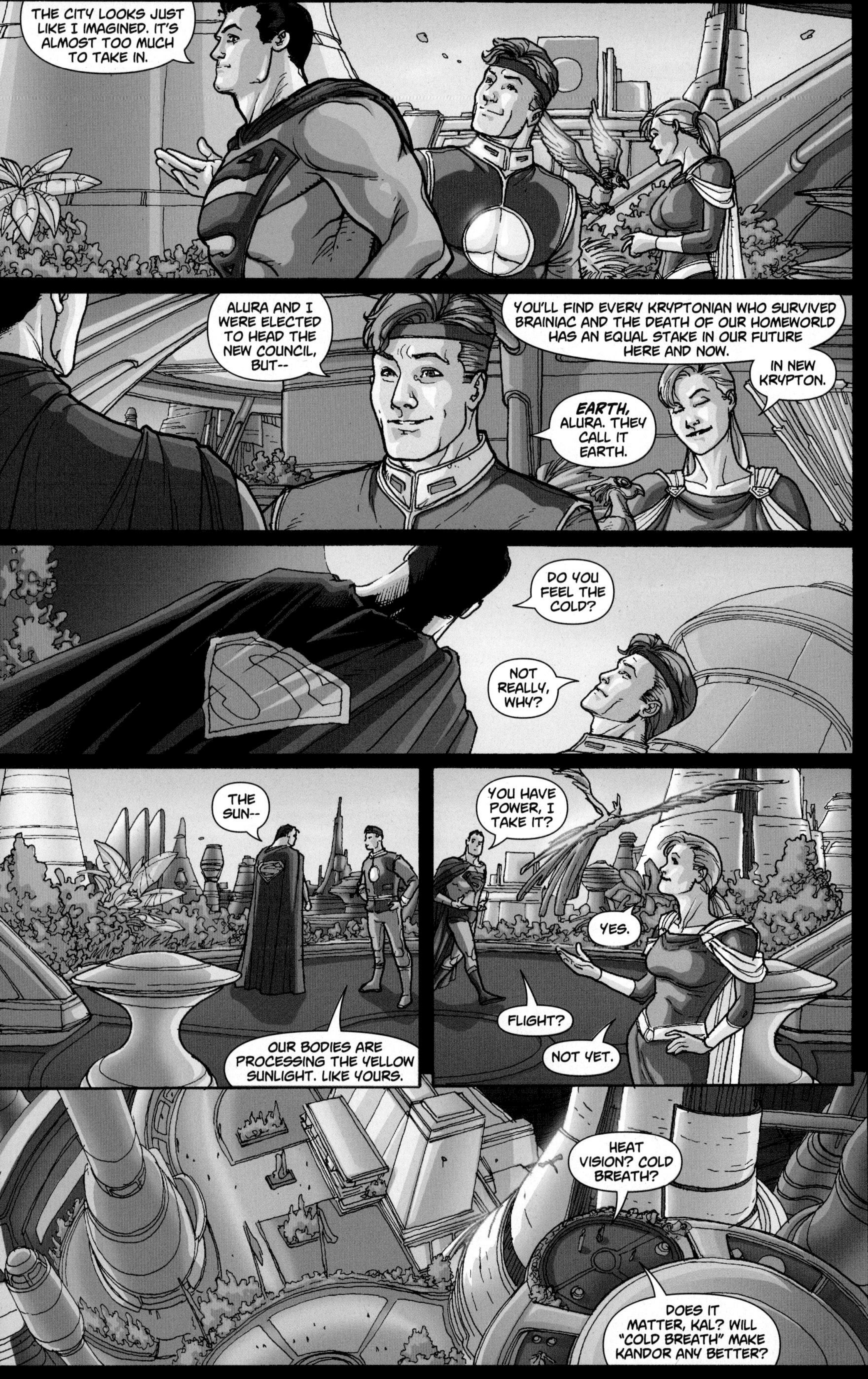
THE CITY LOOKS JUST LIKE I IMAGINED. IT'S ALMOST TOO MUCH TO TAKE IN.
ALURA AND I WERE ELECTED TO HEAD THE NEW COUNCIL, BUT--
YOU'LL FIND EVERY KRYPTONIAN WHO SURVIVED BRAINIAC AND THE DEATH OF OUR HOMEWORLD HAS AN EQUAL STAKE IN OUR FUTURE HERE AND NOW.
IN NEW KRYPTON.
EARTH, ALURA. THEY CALL IT EARTH.
DO YOU FEEL THE COLD?
NOT REALLY, WHY?
THE SUN--
OUR BODIES ARE PROCESSING THE YELLOW SUNLIGHT. LIKE YOURS.
YOU HAVE POWER, I TAKE IT?
YES.
FLIGHT?
NOT YET.
HEAT VISION? COLD BREATH?
DOES IT MATTER, KAL? WILL "COLD BREATH" MAKE KANDOR ANY BETTER?

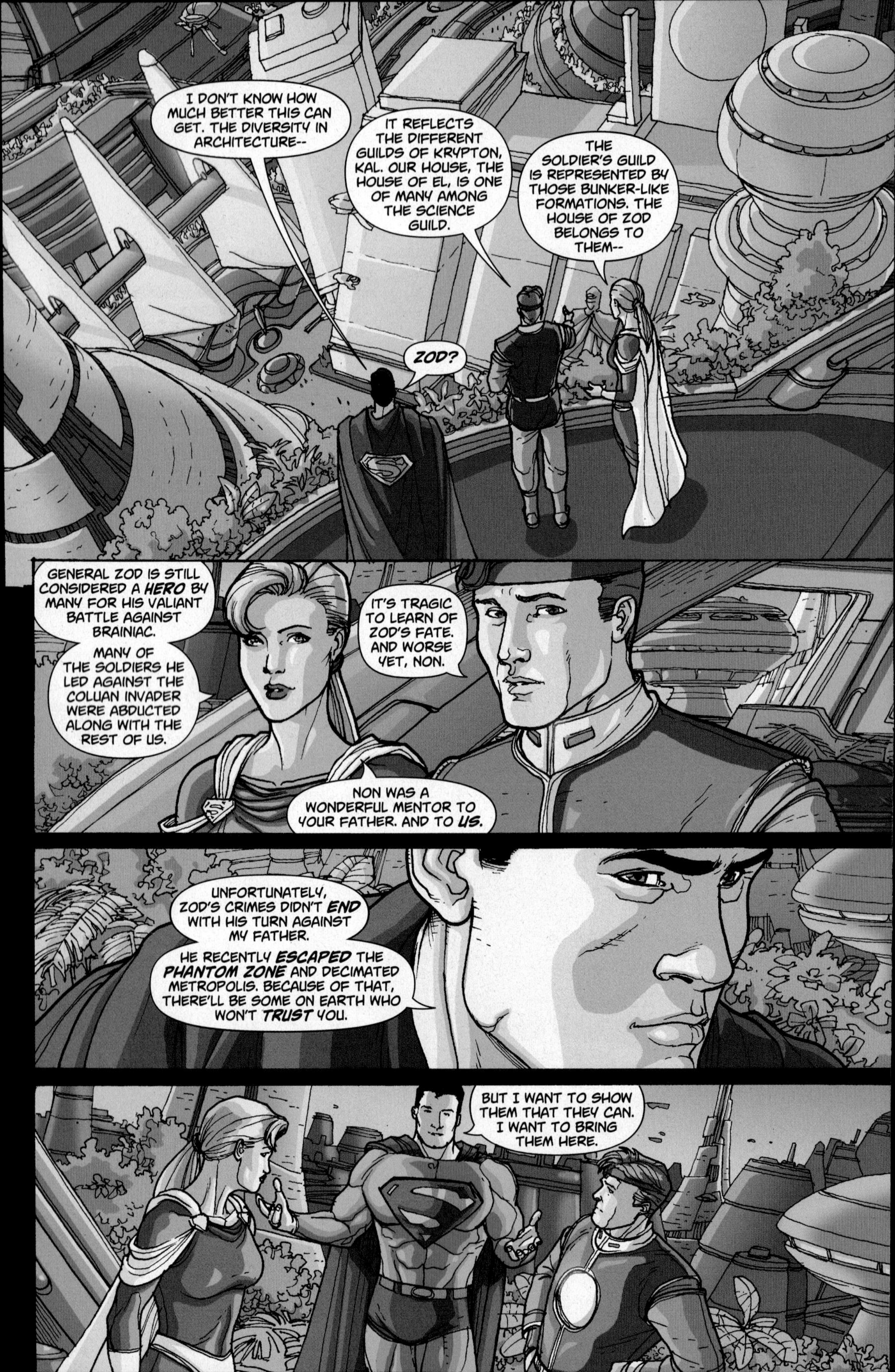
I DON'T KNOW HOW MUCH BETTER THIS CAN GET. THE DIVERSITY IN ARCHITECTURE--
IT REFLECTS THE DIFFERENT GUILDS OF KRYPTON, KAL. OUR HOUSE, THE HOUSE OF EL, IS ONE OF MANY AMONG THE SCIENCE GUILD.
THE SOLDIER'S GUILD IS REPRESENTED BY THOSE BUNKER-LIKE FORMATIONS. THE HOUSE OF ZOD BELONGS TO THEM--
ZOD?
GENERAL ZOD IS STILL CONSIDERED A HERO BY MANY FOR HIS VALIANT BATTLE AGAINST BRAINIAC.
MANY OF THE SOLDIERS HE LED AGAINST THE COLUAN INVADER WERE ABDUCTED ALONG WITH THE REST OF US.
IT'S TRAGIC TO LEARN OF ZOD'S FATE. AND WORSE YET, NON.
NON WAS A WONDERFUL MENTOR TO YOUR FATHER. AND TO US.
UNFORTUNATELY, ZOD'S CRIMES DIDN'T END WITH HIS TURN AGAINST MY FATHER.
HE RECENTLY ESCAPED THE PHANTOM ZONE AND DECIMATED METROPOLIS. BECAUSE OF THAT, THERE'LL BE SOME ON EARTH WHO WON'T TRUST YOU.
BUT I WANT TO SHOW THEM THAT THEY CAN. I WANT TO BRING THEM HERE.

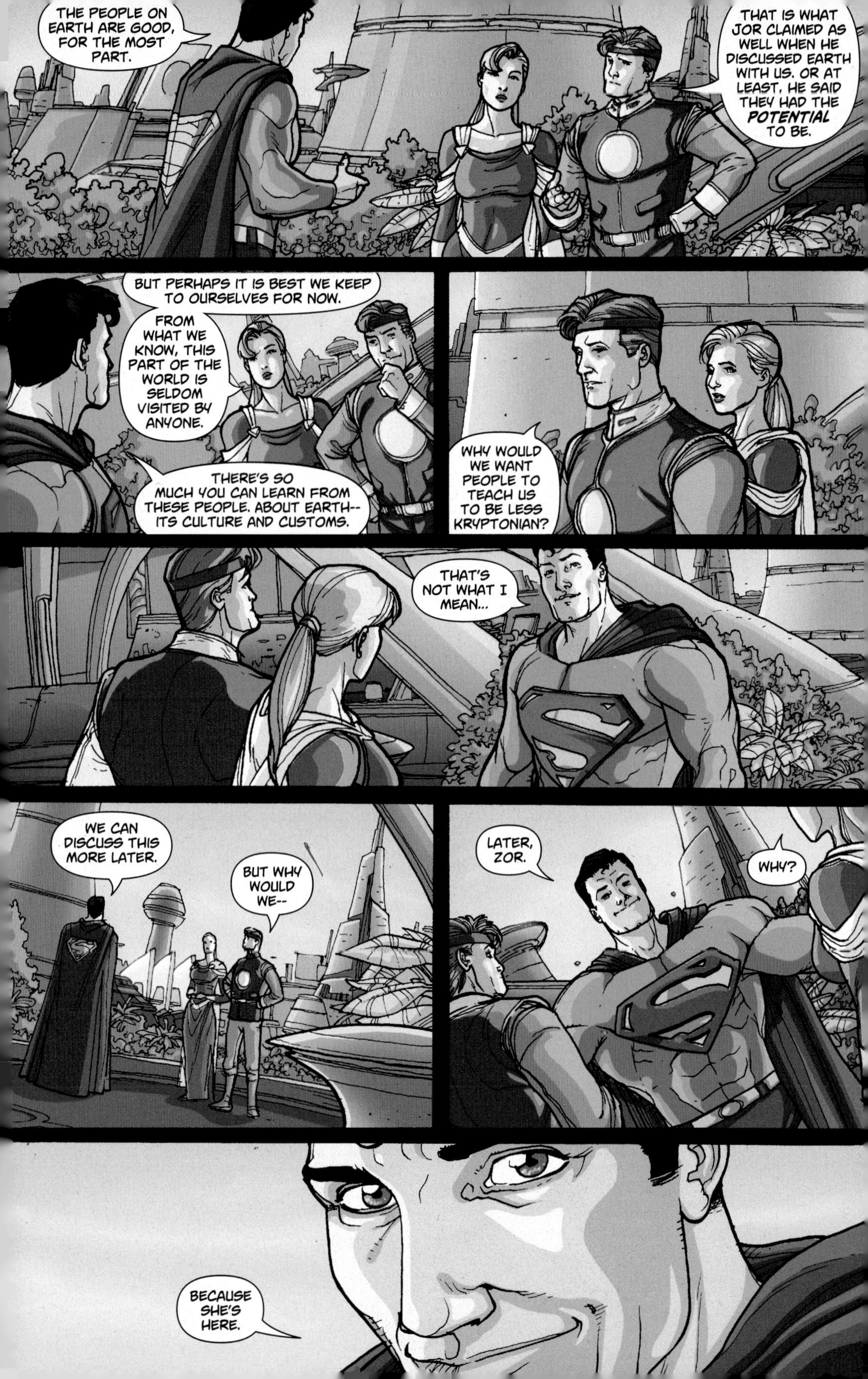
THE PEOPLE ON EARTH ARE GOOD, FOR THE MOST PART.
THAT IS WHAT JOR CLAIMED AS WELL WHEN HE DISCUSSED EARTH WITH US. OR AT LEAST, HE SAID THEY HAD THE POTENTIAL TO BE.
BUT PERHAPS IT IS BEST WE KEEP TO OURSELVES FOR NOW.
FROM WHAT WE KNOW, THIS PART OF THE WORLD IS SELDOM VISITED BY ANYONE.
THERE'S SO MUCH YOU CAN LEARN FROM THESE PEOPLE. ABOUT EARTH-- ITS CULTURE AND CUSTOMS.
WHY WOULD WE WANT PEOPLE TO TEACH US TO BE LESS KRYPTONIAN?
THAT'S NOT WHAT I MEAN...
WE CAN DISCUSS THIS MORE LATER.
BUT WHY WOULD WE--
LATER, ZOR.
WHY?
BECAUSE SHE'S HERE.

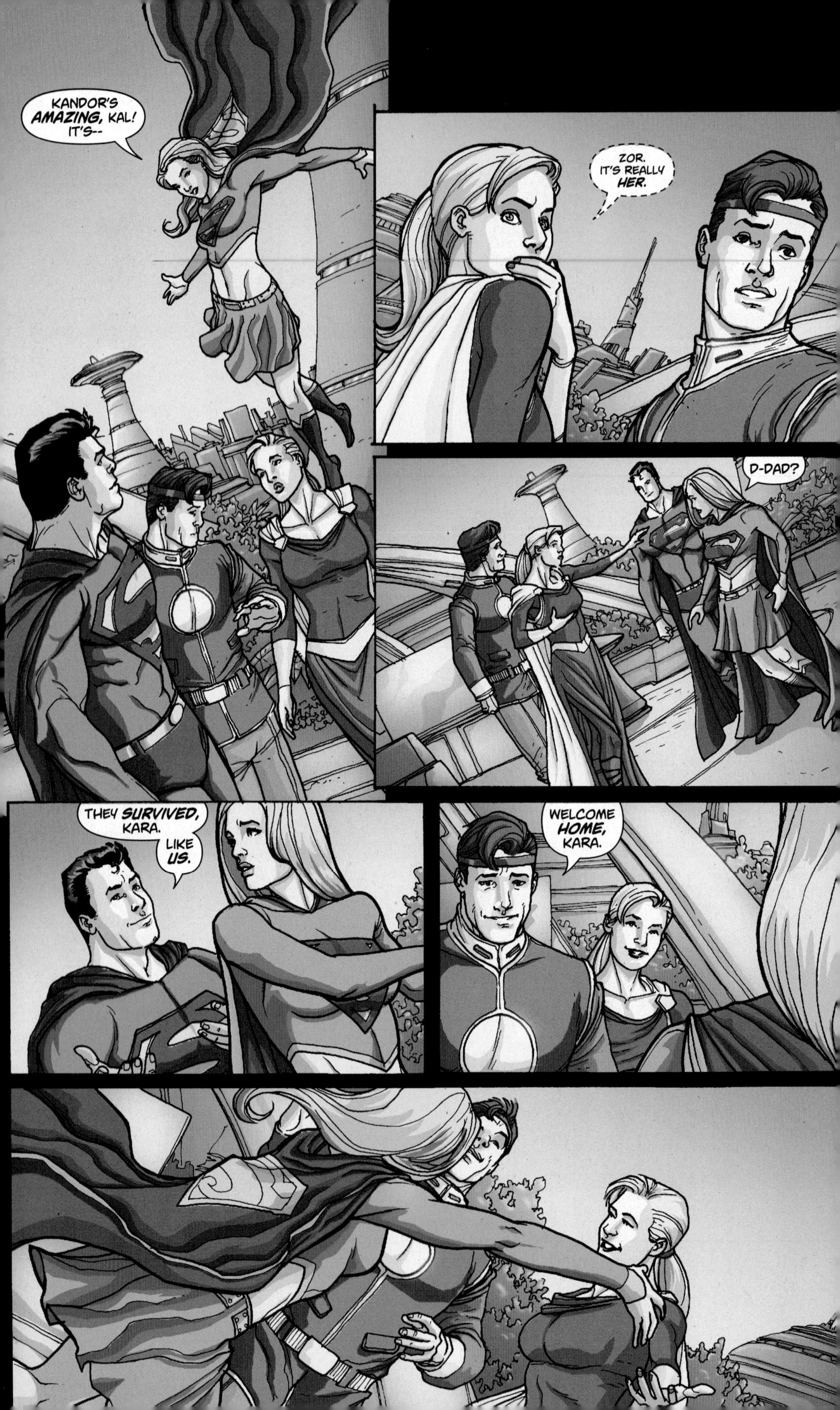
KANDOR'S AMAZING, KAL! IT'S--
ZOR. IT'S REALLY HER.
D-DAD?
THEY SURVIVED, KARA.
LIKE US.
WELCOME HOME, KARA.

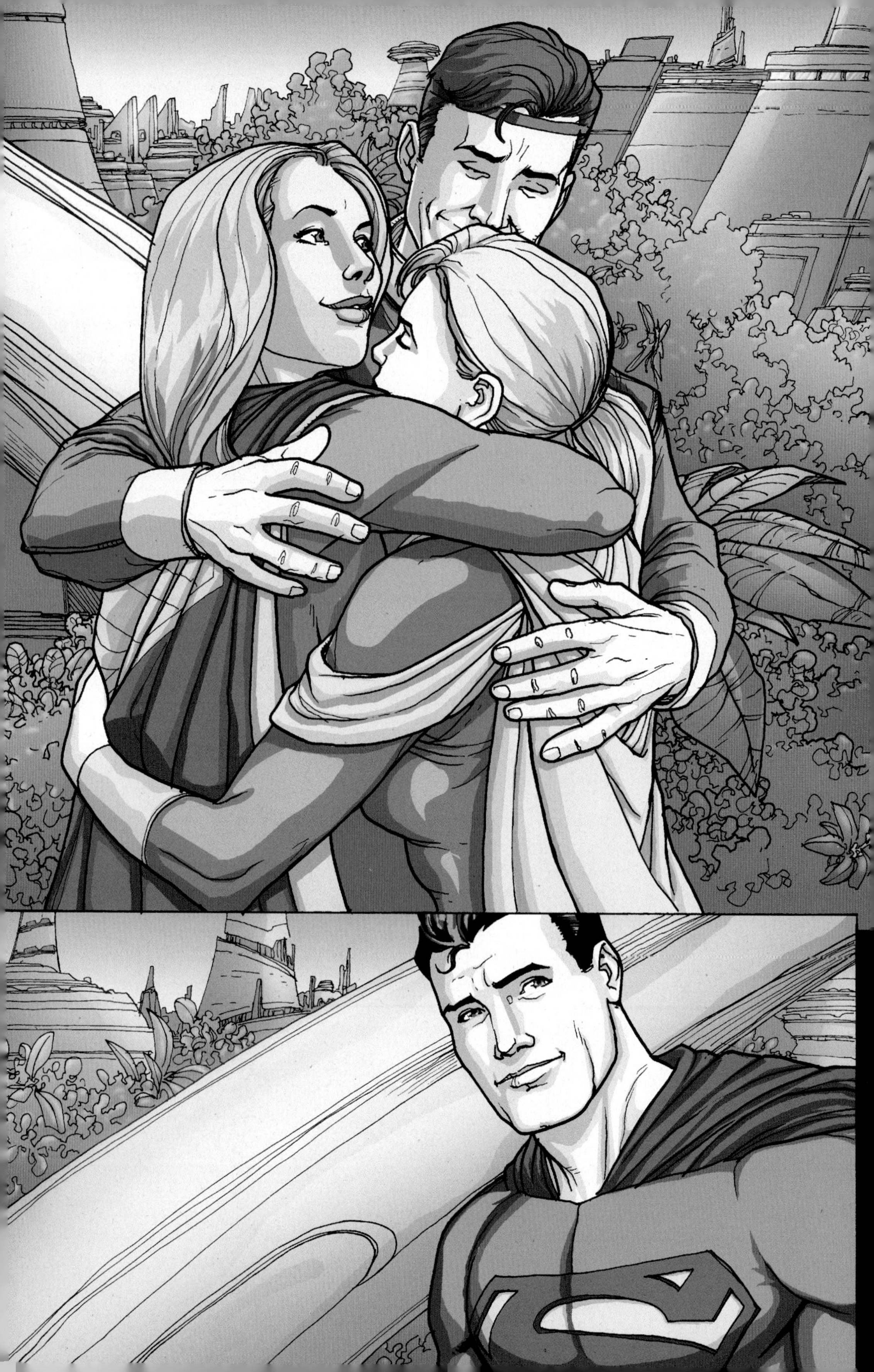

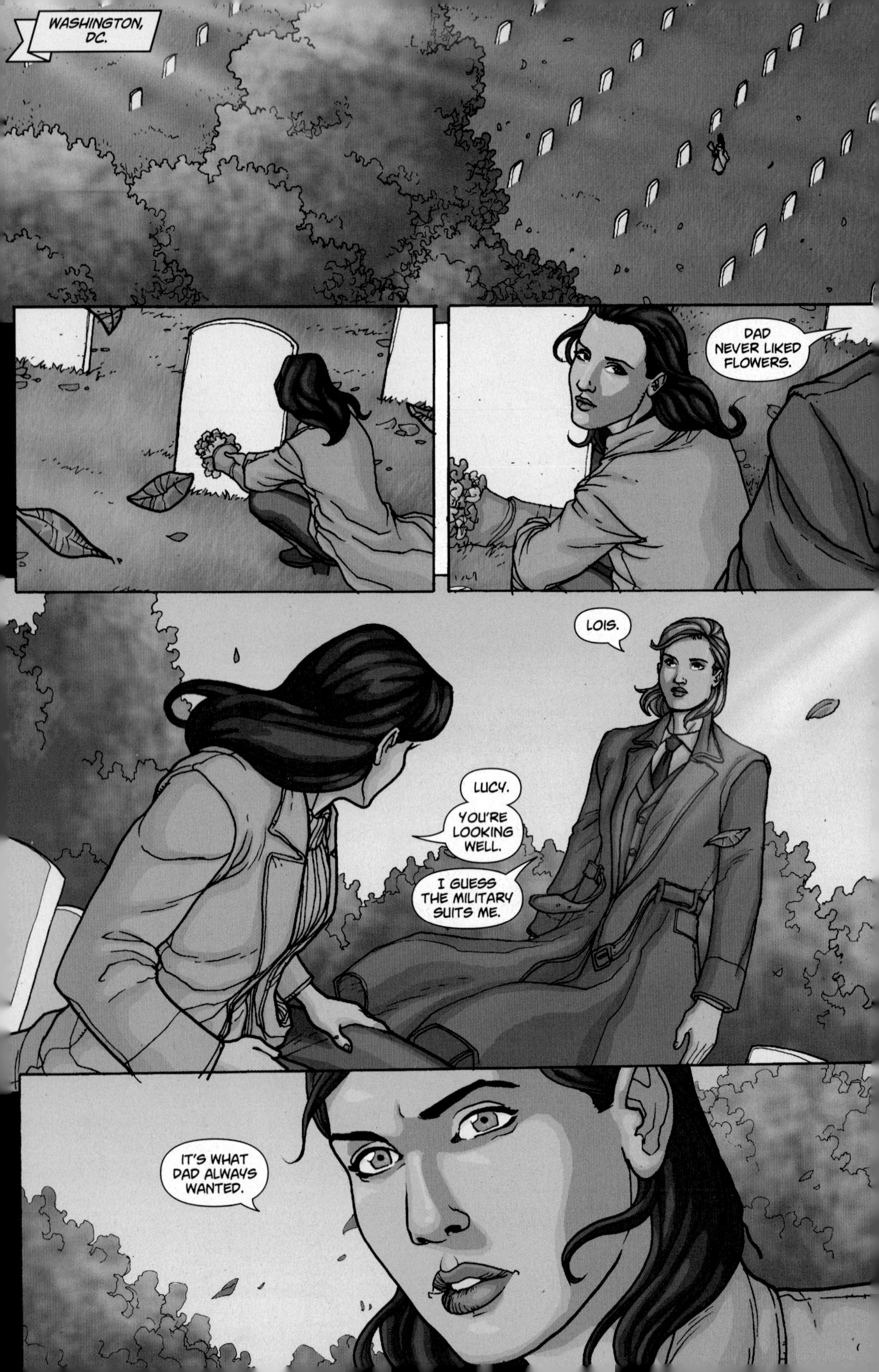
WASHINGTON, DC.
DAD NEVER LIKED FLOWERS.
LOIS.
LUCY.
YOU'RE LOOKING WELL.
I GUESS THE MILITARY SUITS ME.
IT'S WHAT DAD ALWAYS WANTED.

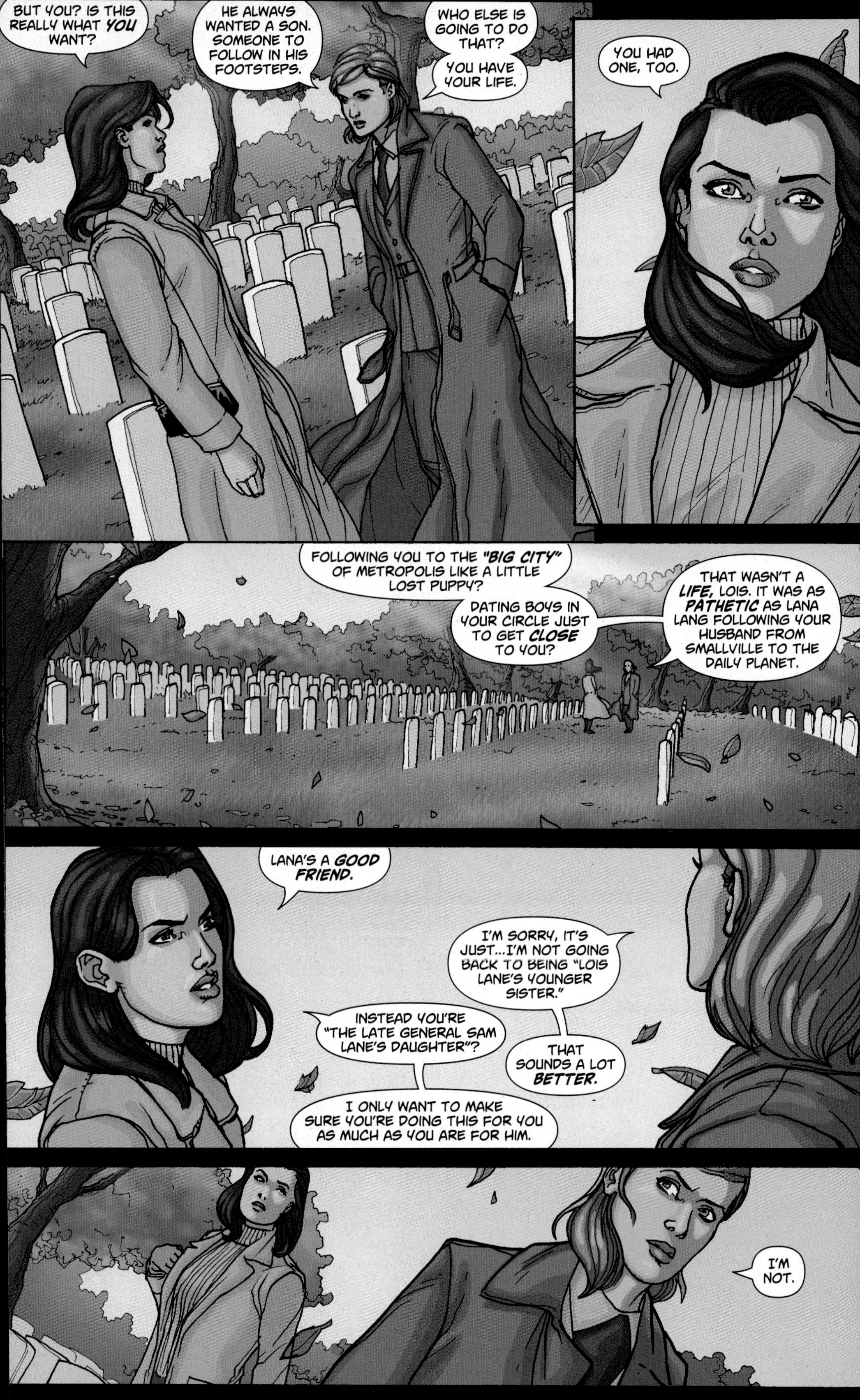
BUT YOU? IS THIS REALLY WHAT *YOU* WANT?
HE ALWAYS WANTED A SON. SOMEONE TO FOLLOW IN HIS FOOTSTEPS.
WHO ELSE IS GOING TO DO THAT?
YOU HAVE YOUR LIFE.
YOU HAD ONE, TOO.
FOLLOWING YOU TO THE *"BIG CITY"* OF METROPOLIS LIKE A LITTLE LOST PUPPY?
DATING BOYS IN YOUR CIRCLE JUST TO GET *CLOSE* TO YOU?
THAT WASN'T A *LIFE,* LOIS. IT WAS AS *PATHETIC* AS LANA LANG FOLLOWING YOUR HUSBAND FROM SMALLVILLE TO THE DAILY PLANET.
LANA'S A *GOOD FRIEND.*
I'M SORRY, IT'S JUST...I'M NOT GOING BACK TO BEING "LOIS LANE'S YOUNGER SISTER."
INSTEAD YOU'RE "THE LATE GENERAL SAM LANE'S DAUGHTER"?
THAT SOUNDS A LOT *BETTER.*
I ONLY WANT TO MAKE SURE YOU'RE DOING THIS FOR YOU AS MUCH AS YOU ARE FOR HIM.
I'M NOT.

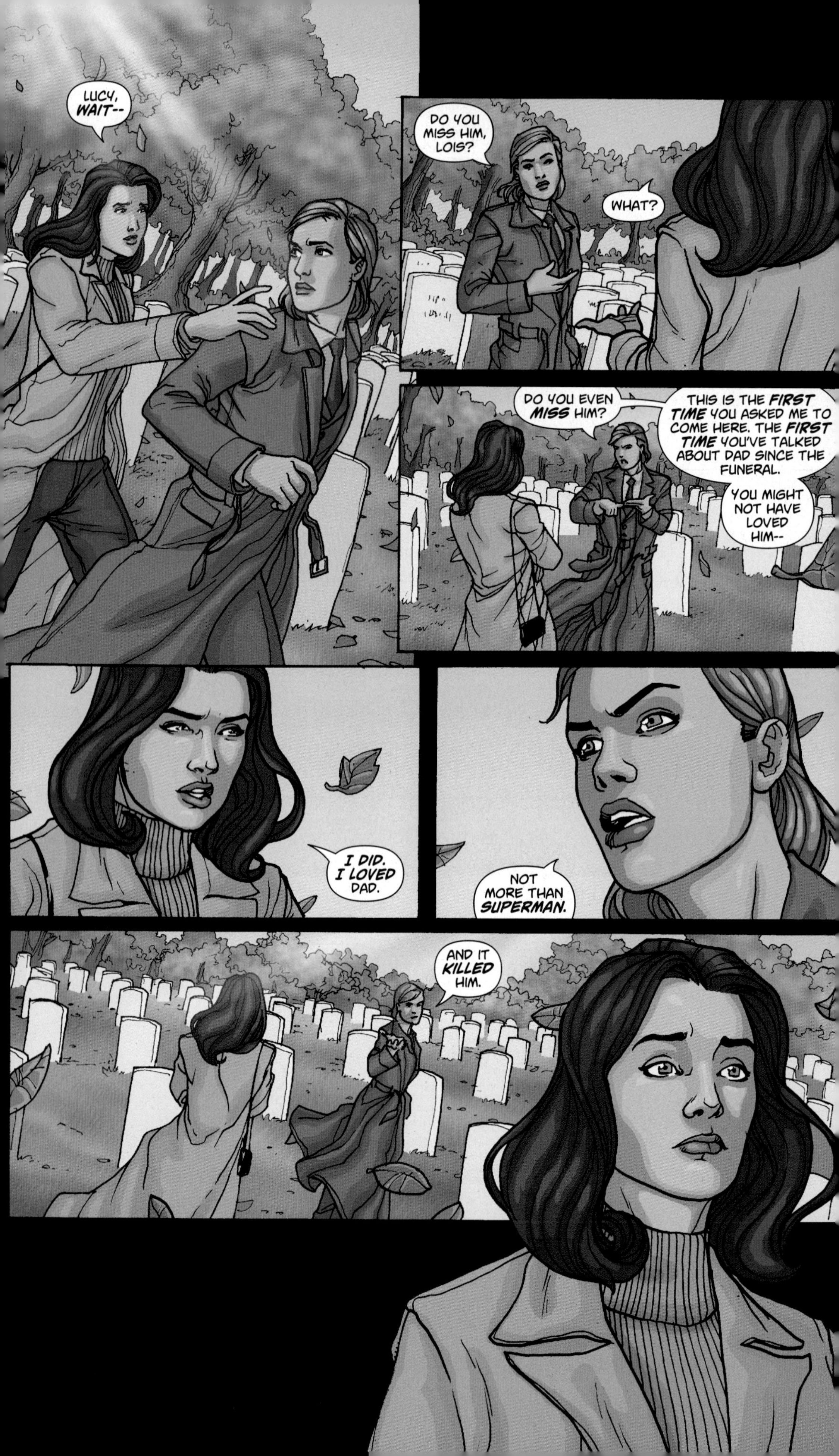
LUCY, WAIT--
DO YOU MISS HIM, LOIS?
WHAT?
DO YOU EVEN MISS HIM?
THIS IS THE FIRST TIME YOU ASKED ME TO COME HERE. THE FIRST TIME YOU'VE TALKED ABOUT DAD SINCE THE FUNERAL.
YOU MIGHT NOT HAVE LOVED HIM--
I DID. I LOVED DAD.
NOT MORE THAN SUPERMAN.
AND IT KILLED HIM.

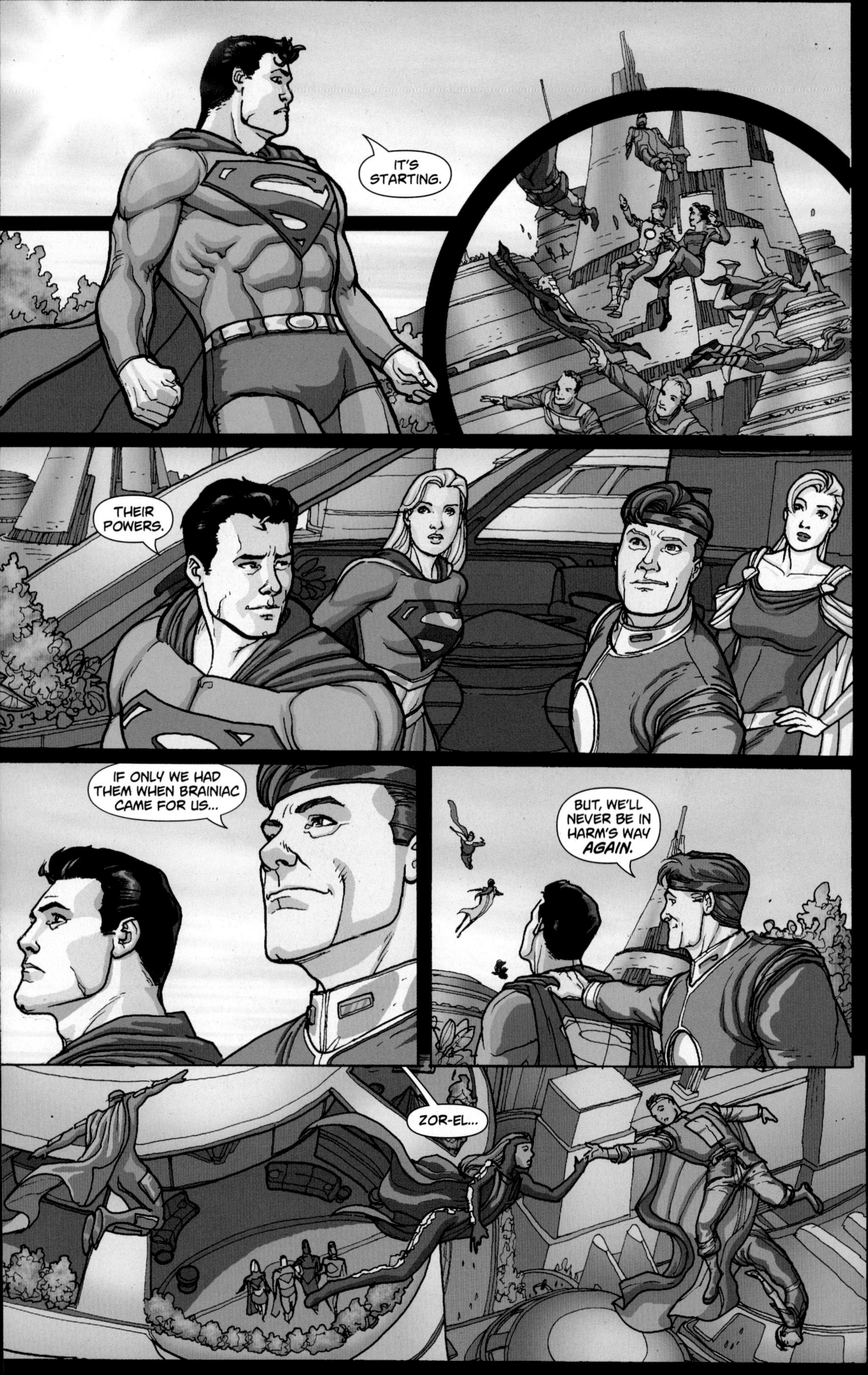
IT'S STARTING.
THEIR POWERS.
IF ONLY WE HAD THEM WHEN BRAINIAC CAME FOR US...
BUT, WE'LL NEVER BE IN HARM'S WAY AGAIN.
ZOR-EL...

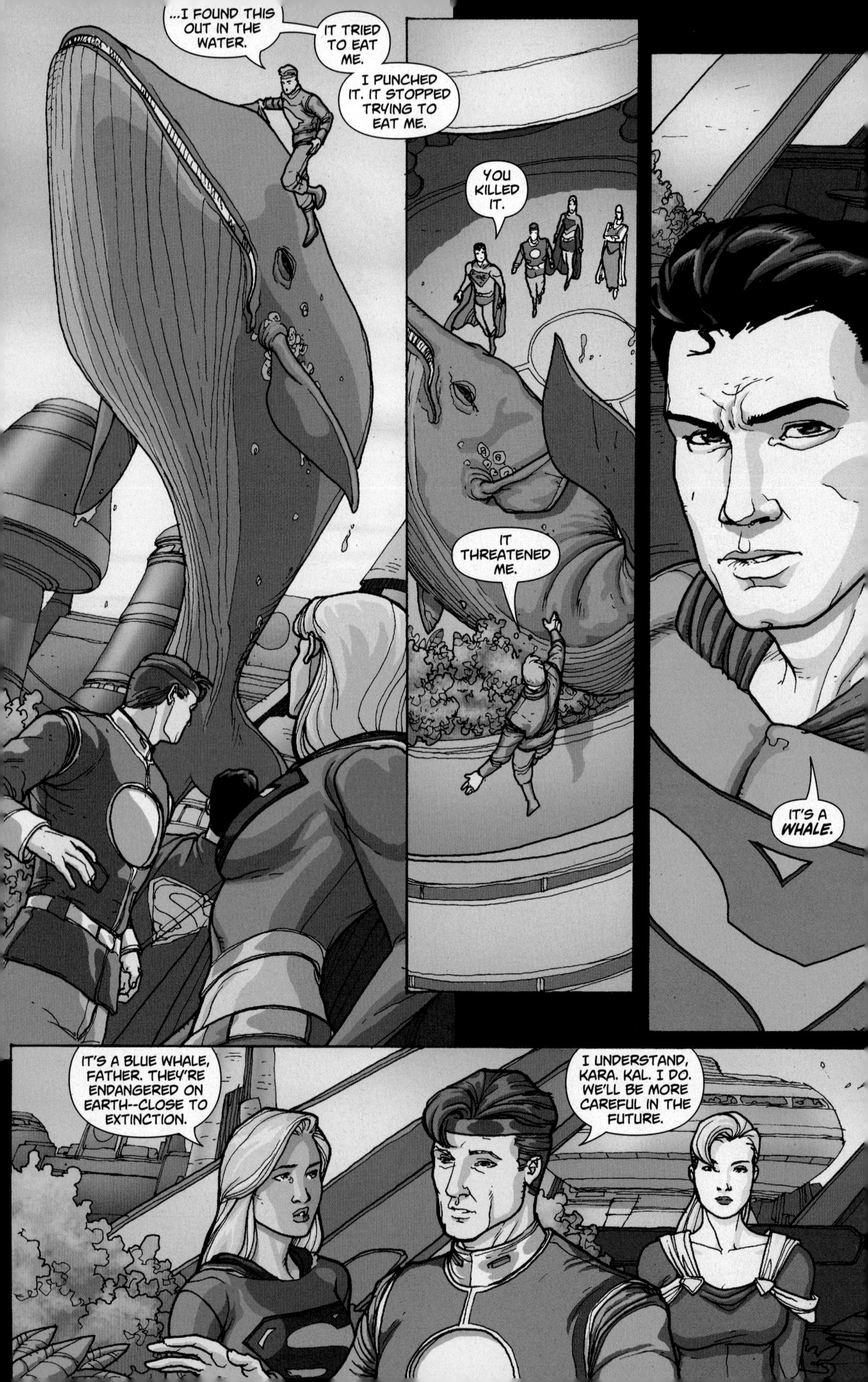
...I FOUND THIS OUT IN THE WATER.
IT TRIED TO EAT ME.
I PUNCHED IT. IT STOPPED TRYING TO EAT ME.
YOU KILLED IT.
IT THREATENED ME.
IT'S A *WHALE*.
IT'S A BLUE WHALE, FATHER. THEY'RE ENDANGERED ON EARTH--CLOSE TO EXTINCTION.
I UNDERSTAND, KARA. KAL. I DO. WE'LL BE MORE CAREFUL IN THE FUTURE.

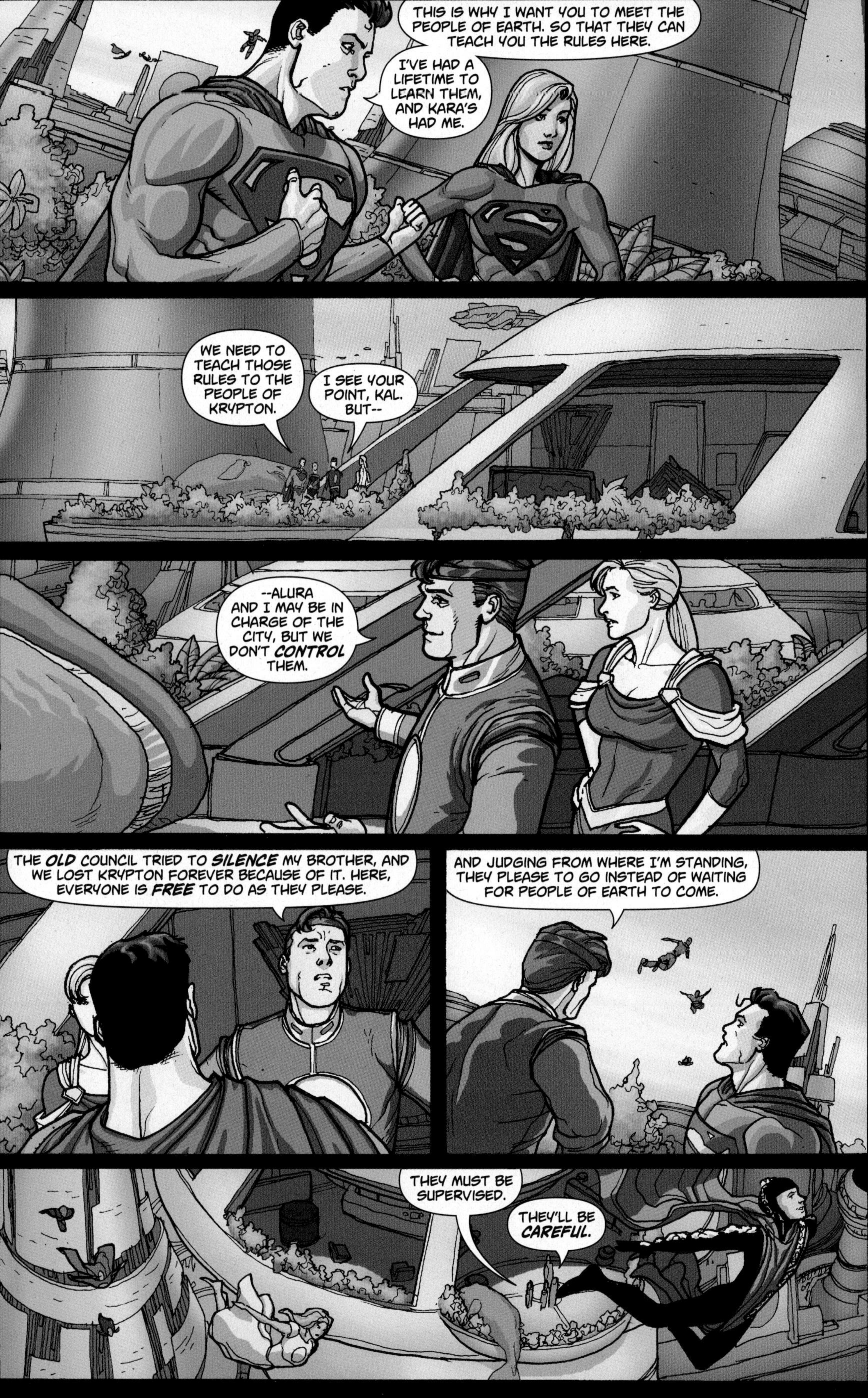

THIS IS WHY I WANT YOU TO MEET THE PEOPLE OF EARTH. SO THAT THEY CAN TEACH YOU THE RULES HERE.
I'VE HAD A LIFETIME TO LEARN THEM, AND KARA'S HAD ME.
WE NEED TO TEACH THOSE RULES TO THE PEOPLE OF KRYPTON.
I SEE YOUR POINT, KAL. BUT--
--ALURA AND I MAY BE IN CHARGE OF THE CITY, BUT WE DON'T *CONTROL* THEM.
THE *OLD* COUNCIL TRIED TO *SILENCE* MY BROTHER, AND WE LOST KRYPTON FOREVER BECAUSE OF IT. HERE, EVERYONE IS *FREE* TO DO AS THEY PLEASE.
AND JUDGING FROM WHERE I'M STANDING, THEY PLEASE TO GO INSTEAD OF WAITING FOR PEOPLE OF EARTH TO COME.
THEY MUST BE SUPERVISED.
THEY'LL BE *CAREFUL.*

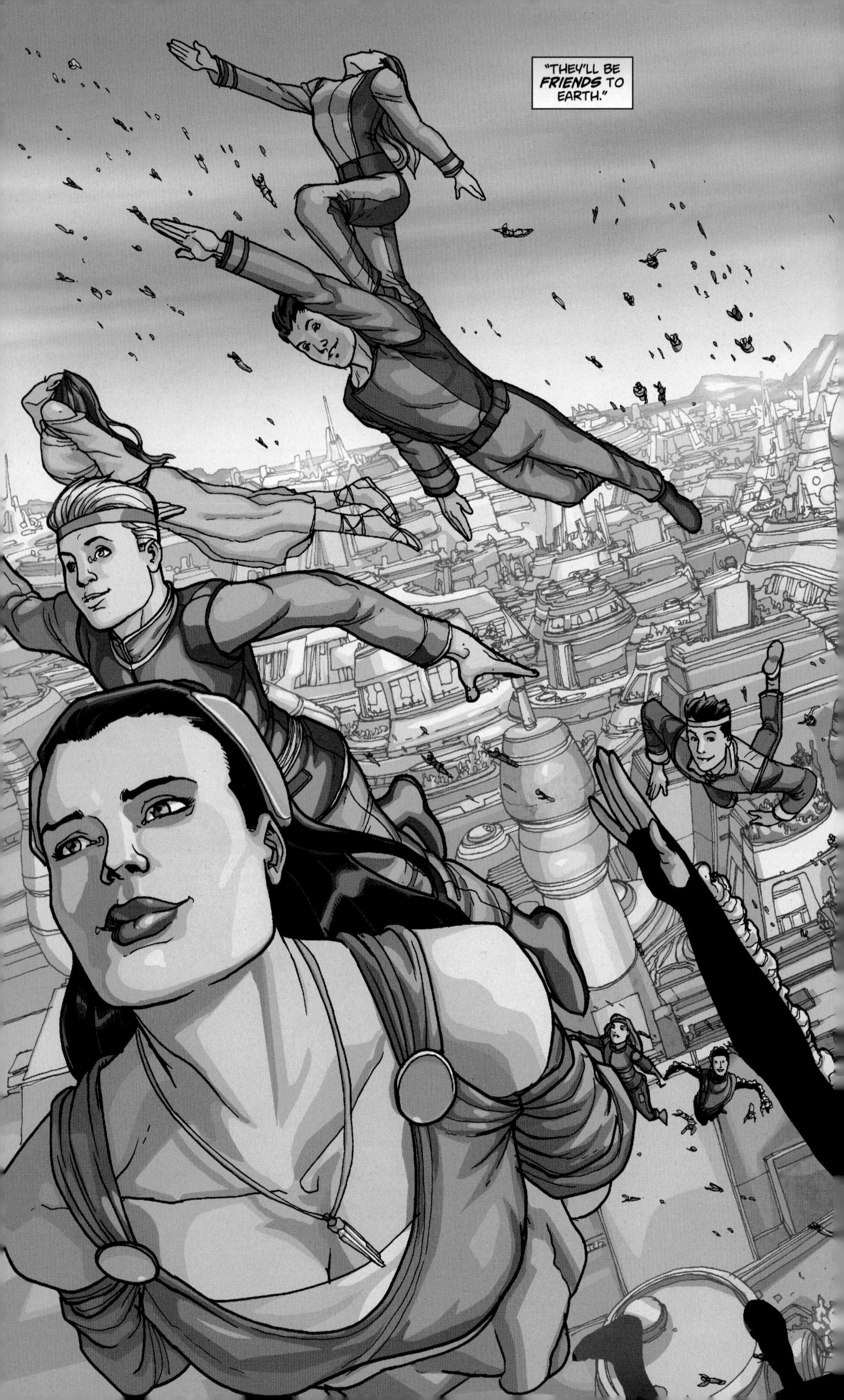
"THEY'LL BE
FRIENDS TO
EARTH."

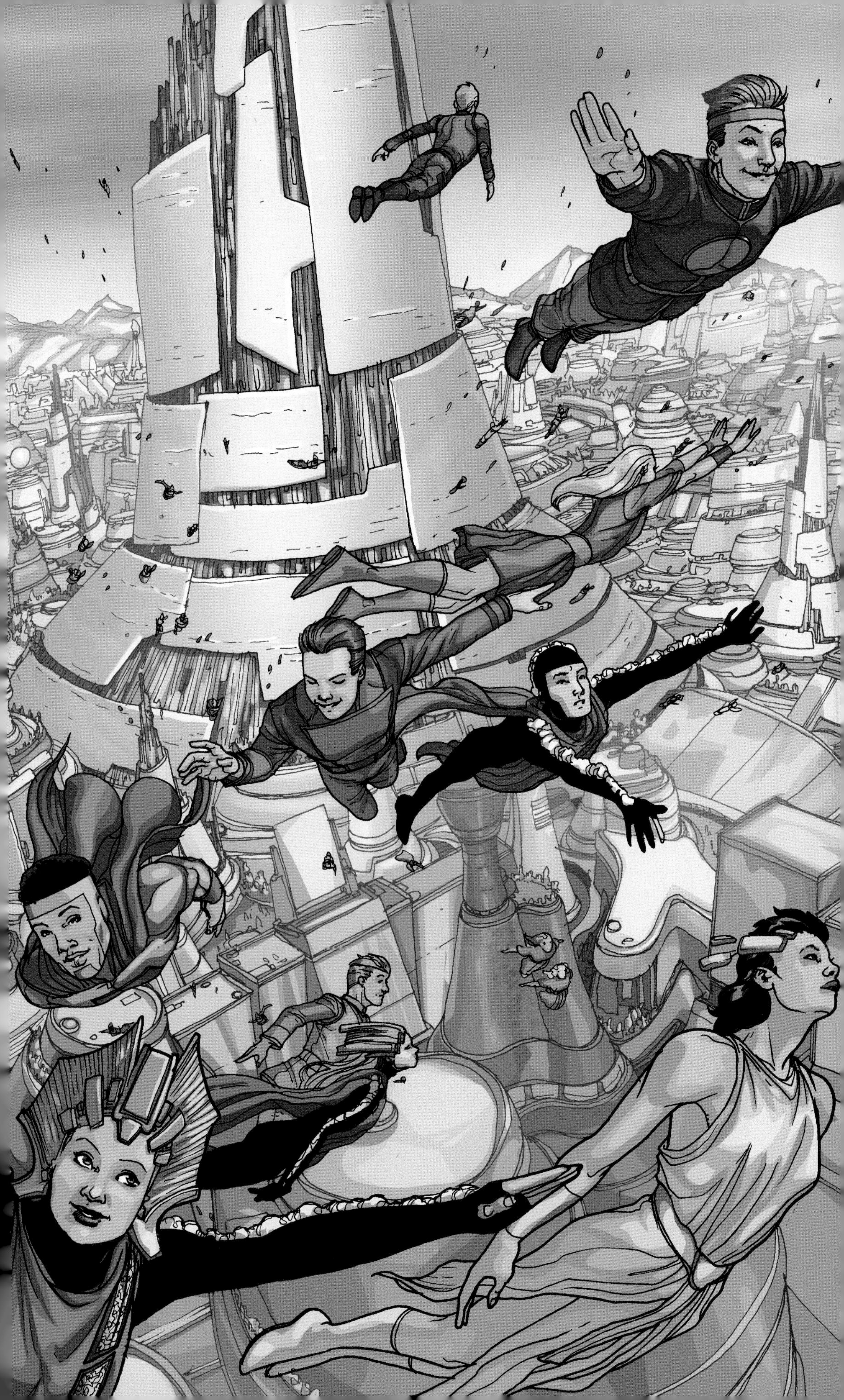

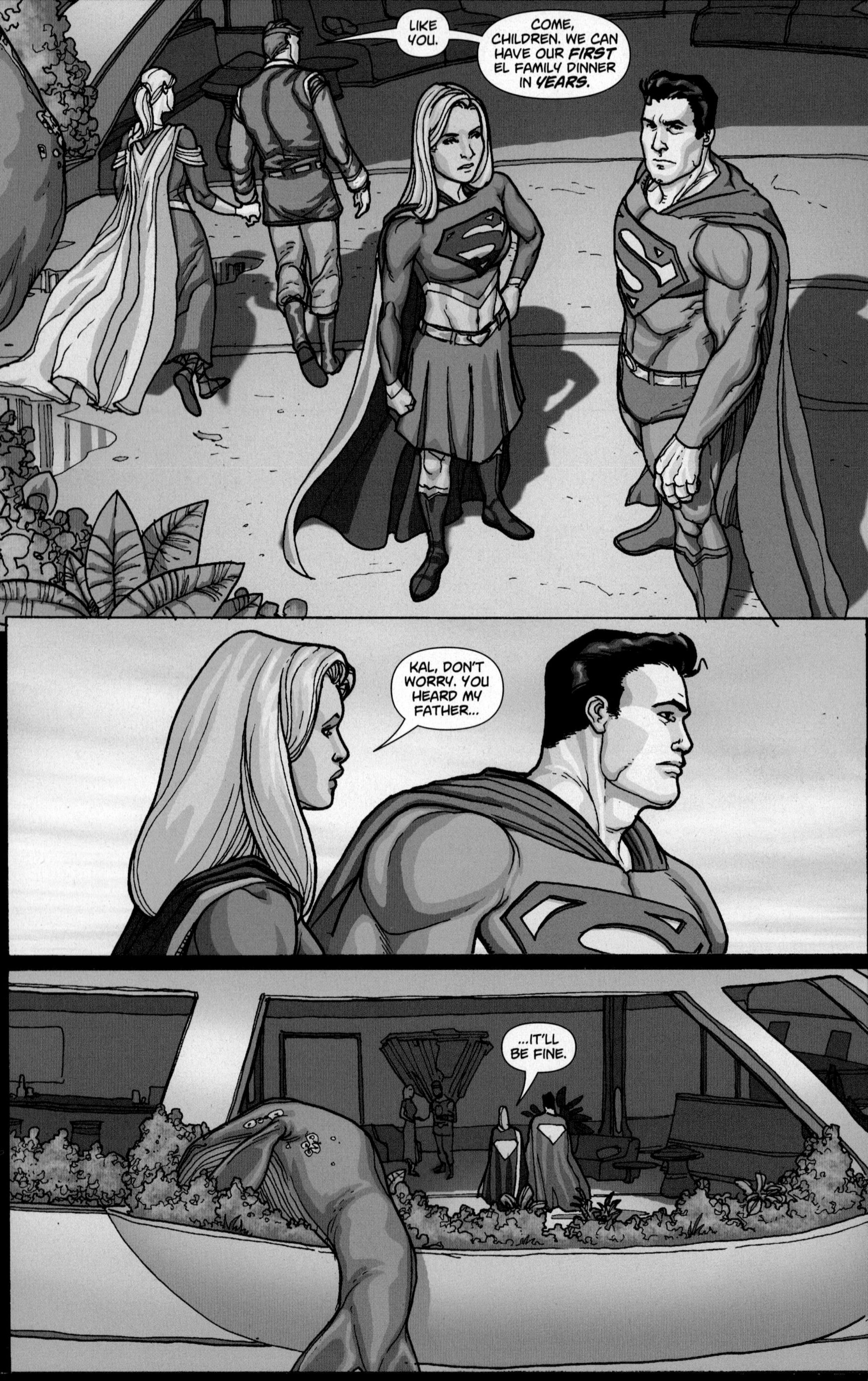
LIKE YOU.
COME, CHILDREN. WE CAN HAVE OUR FIRST EL FAMILY DINNER IN YEARS.
KAL, DON'T WORRY. YOU HEARD MY FATHER...
...IT'LL BE FINE.

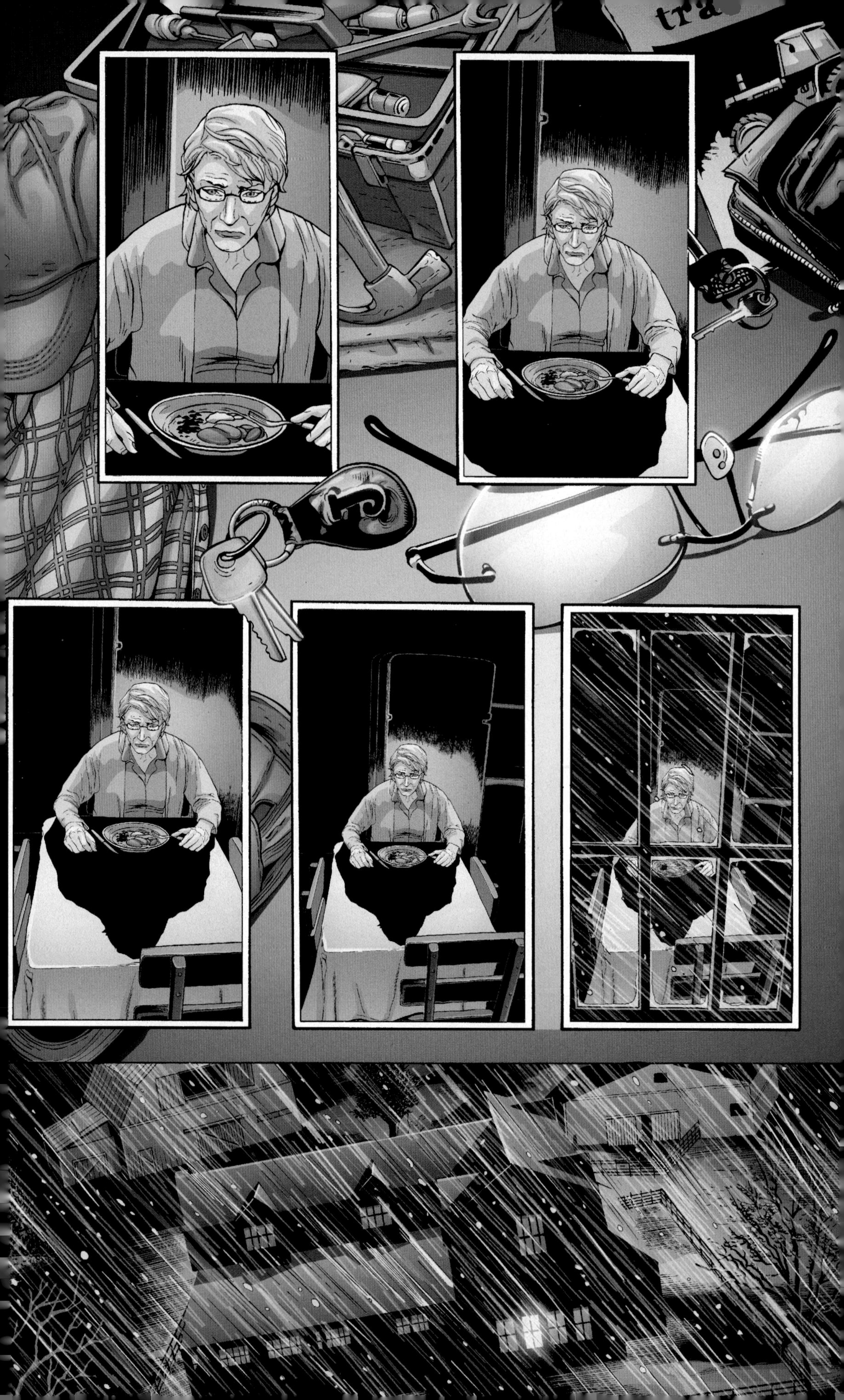

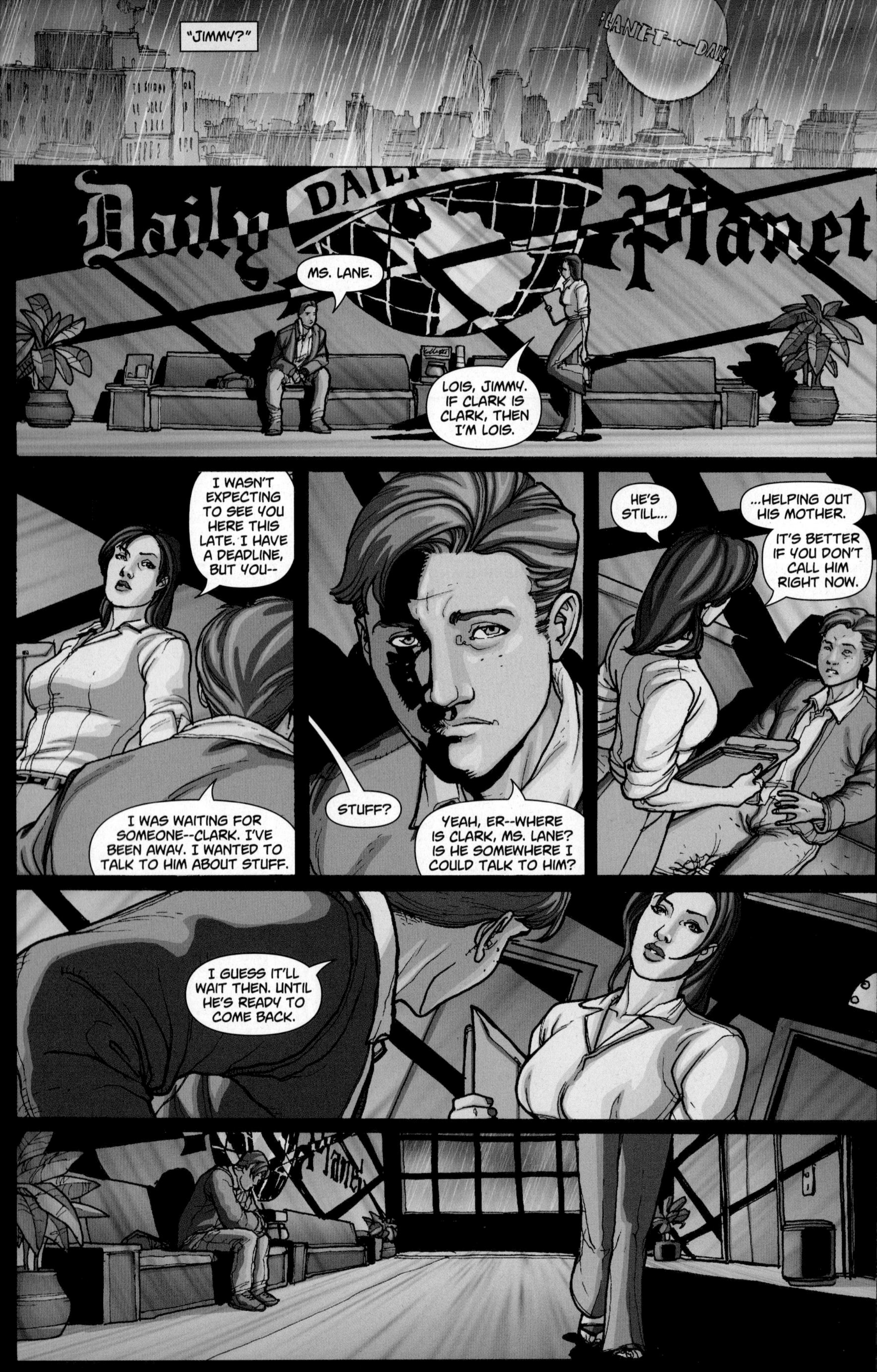
"JIMMY?"
PLANET DAILY
Daily Planet
MS. LANE.
LOIS, JIMMY. IF CLARK IS CLARK, THEN I'M LOIS.
I WASN'T EXPECTING TO SEE YOU HERE THIS LATE. I HAVE A DEADLINE, BUT YOU--
I WAS WAITING FOR SOMEONE--CLARK. I'VE BEEN AWAY. I WANTED TO TALK TO HIM ABOUT STUFF.
STUFF?
YEAH, ER--WHERE IS CLARK, MS. LANE? IS HE SOMEWHERE I COULD TALK TO HIM?
HE'S STILL...
...HELPING OUT HIS MOTHER.
IT'S BETTER IF YOU DON'T CALL HIM RIGHT NOW.
I GUESS IT'LL WAIT THEN. UNTIL HE'S READY TO COME BACK.

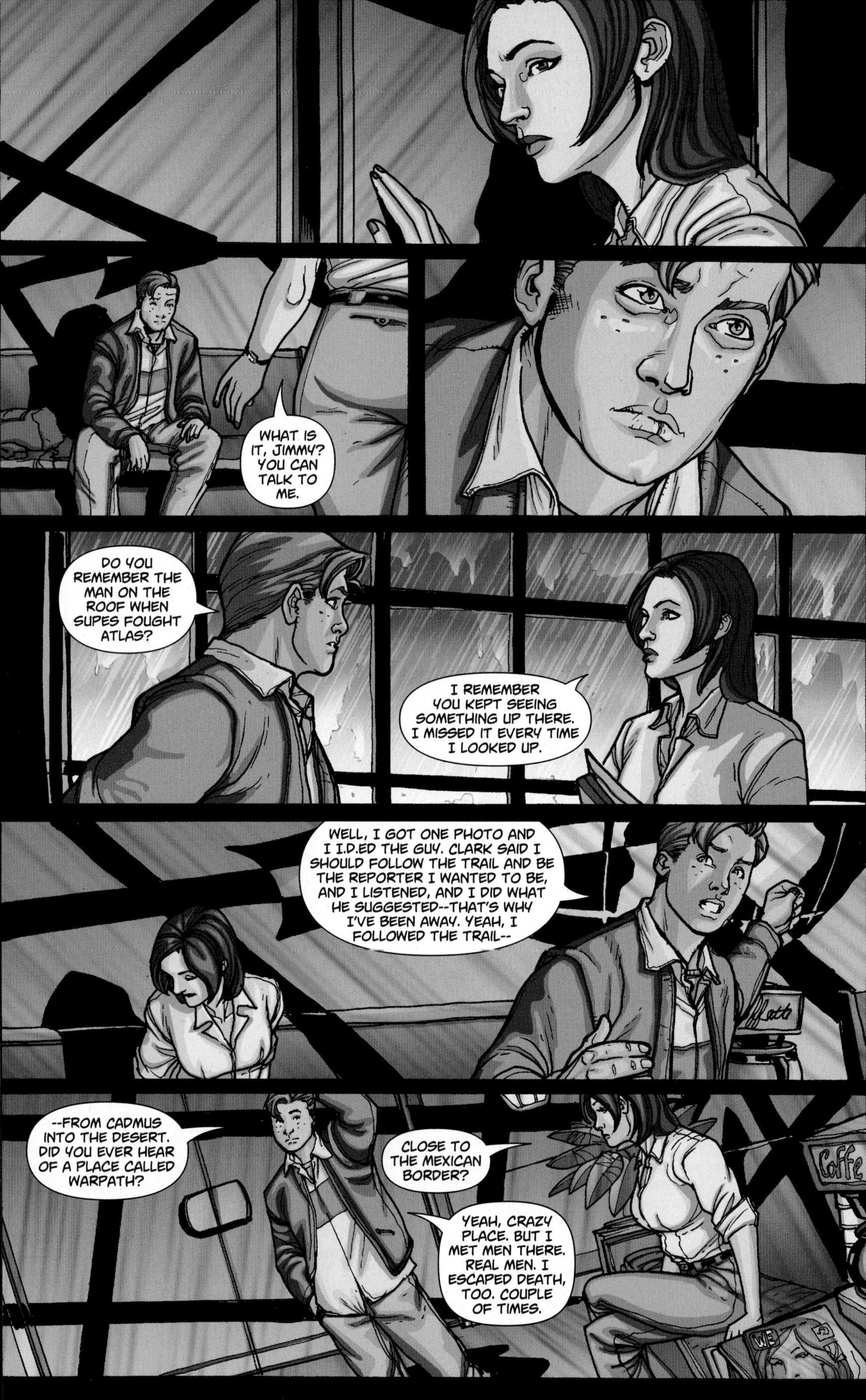
WHAT IS IT, JIMMY? YOU CAN TALK TO ME.
DO YOU REMEMBER THE MAN ON THE ROOF WHEN SUPES FOUGHT ATLAS?
I REMEMBER YOU KEPT SEEING SOMETHING UP THERE. I MISSED IT EVERY TIME I LOOKED UP.
WELL, I GOT ONE PHOTO AND I I.D.ED THE GUY. CLARK SAID I SHOULD FOLLOW THE TRAIL AND BE THE REPORTER I WANTED TO BE, AND I LISTENED, AND I DID WHAT HE SUGGESTED--THAT'S WHY I'VE BEEN AWAY. YEAH, I FOLLOWED THE TRAIL--
--FROM CADMUS INTO THE DESERT. DID YOU EVER HEAR OF A PLACE CALLED WARPATH?
CLOSE TO THE MEXICAN BORDER?
YEAH, CRAZY PLACE. BUT I MET MEN THERE. REAL MEN. I ESCAPED DEATH, TOO. COUPLE OF TIMES.

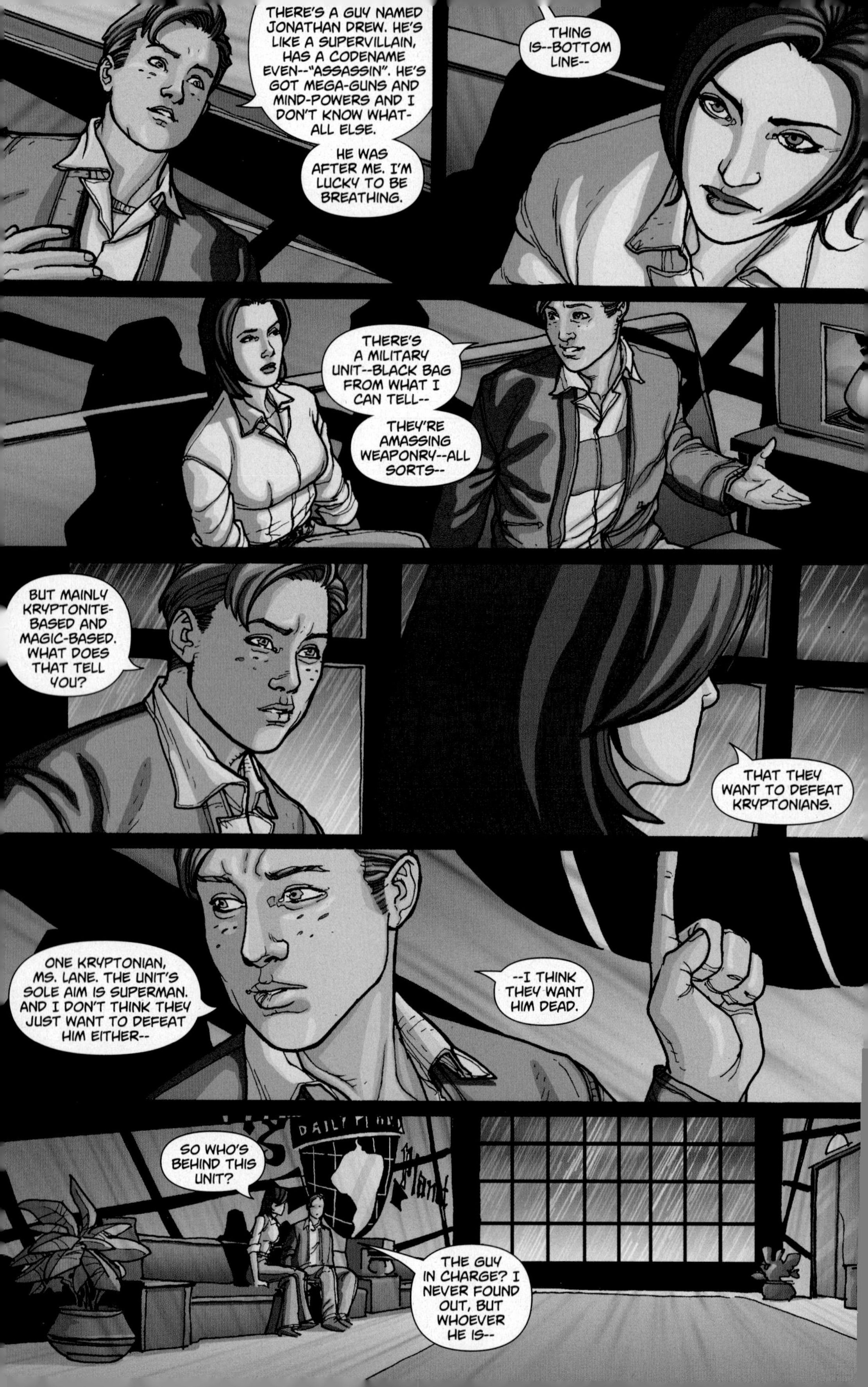
THERE'S A GUY NAMED JONATHAN DREW. HE'S LIKE A SUPERVILLAIN, HAS A CODENAME EVEN--"ASSASSIN". HE'S GOT MEGA-GUNS AND MIND-POWERS AND I DON'T KNOW WHAT-ALL ELSE.
HE WAS AFTER ME. I'M LUCKY TO BE BREATHING.
THING IS--BOTTOM LINE--
THERE'S A MILITARY UNIT--BLACK BAG FROM WHAT I CAN TELL--
THEY'RE AMASSING WEAPONRY--ALL SORTS--
BUT MAINLY KRYPTONITE-BASED AND MAGIC-BASED. WHAT DOES THAT TELL YOU?
THAT THEY WANT TO DEFEAT KRYPTONIANS.
ONE KRYPTONIAN, MS. LANE. THE UNIT'S SOLE AIM IS SUPERMAN. AND I DON'T THINK THEY JUST WANT TO DEFEAT HIM EITHER--
--I THINK THEY WANT HIM DEAD.
SO WHO'S BEHIND THIS UNIT?
THE GUY IN CHARGE? I NEVER FOUND OUT, BUT WHOEVER HE IS--

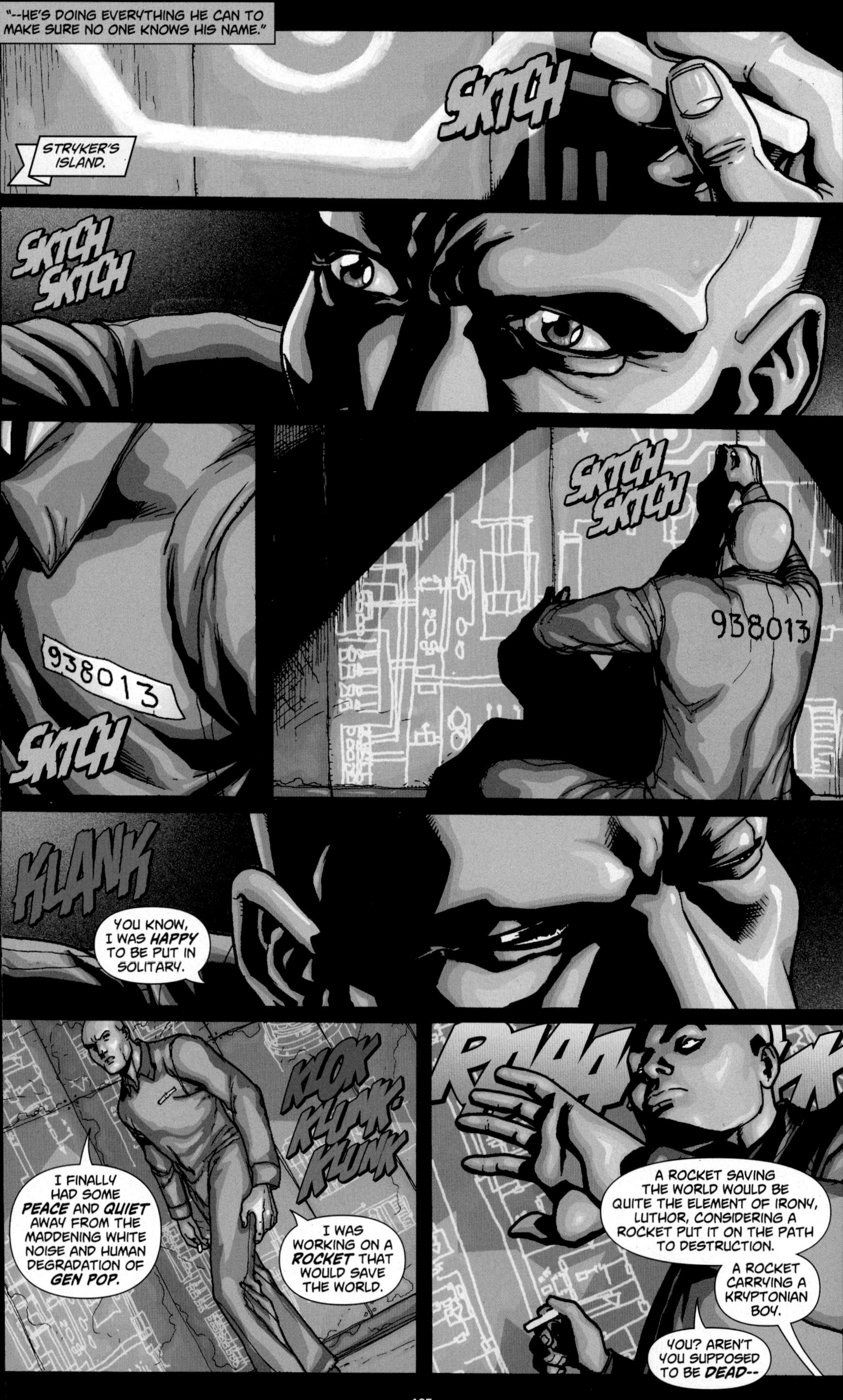

"--HE'S DOING EVERYTHING HE CAN TO MAKE SURE NO ONE KNOWS HIS NAME."
SKTCH
STRYKER'S ISLAND.
SKTCH SKTCH
938013
SKTCH
SKTCH SKTCH
938013
KLANK
YOU KNOW, I WAS HAPPY TO BE PUT IN SOLITARY.
I FINALLY HAD SOME PEACE AND QUIET AWAY FROM THE MADDENING WHITE NOISE AND HUMAN DEGRADATION OF GEN POP.
KLOK KLUNK KLUNK
I WAS WORKING ON A ROCKET THAT WOULD SAVE THE WORLD.
A ROCKET SAVING THE WORLD WOULD BE QUITE THE ELEMENT OF IRONY, LUTHOR, CONSIDERING A ROCKET PUT IT ON THE PATH TO DESTRUCTION.
A ROCKET CARRYING A KRYPTONIAN BOY.
YOU? AREN'T YOU SUPPOSED TO BE DEAD--

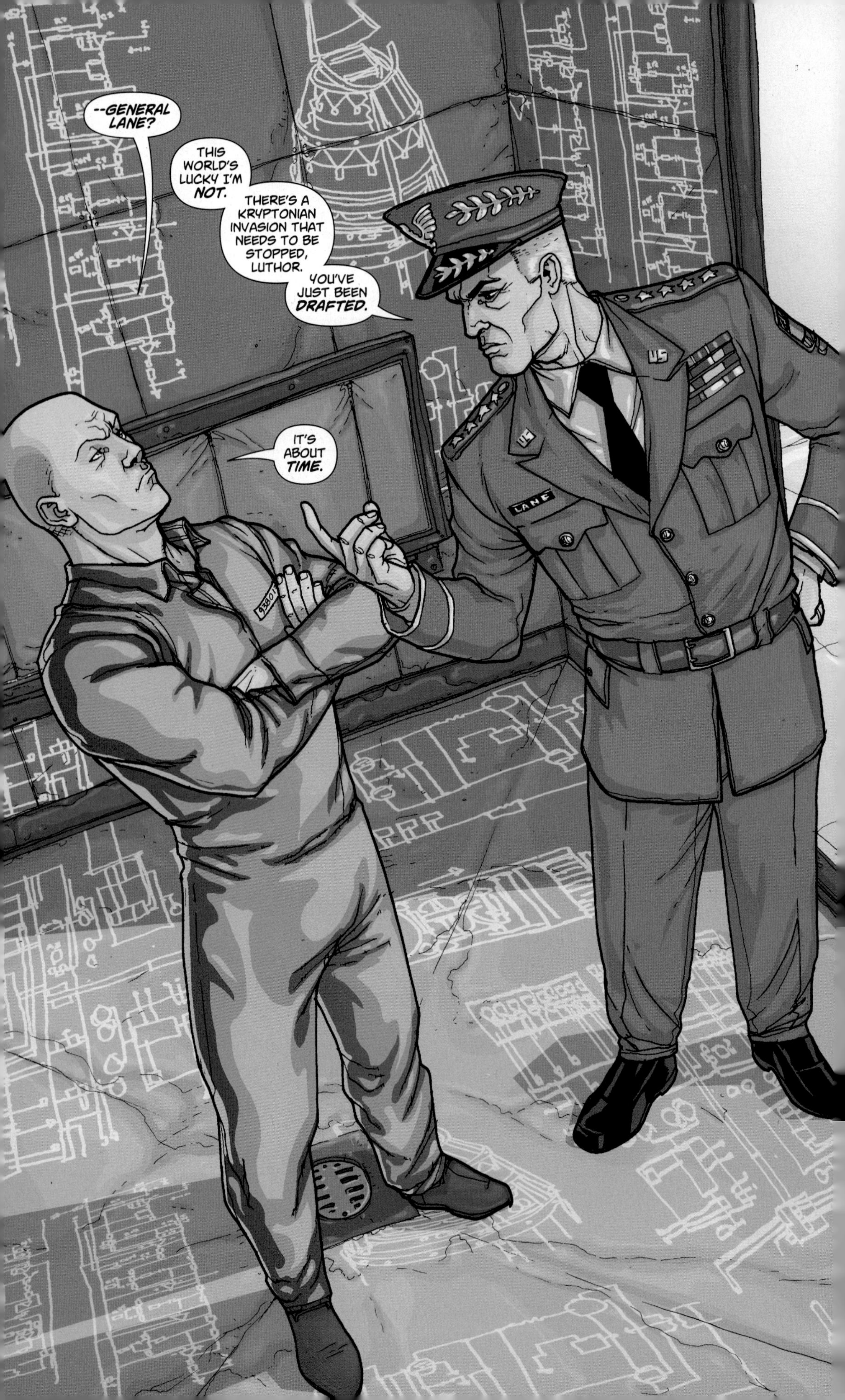
--GENERAL LANE?
THIS WORLD'S LUCKY I'M NOT.
THERE'S A KRYPTONIAN INVASION THAT NEEDS TO BE STOPPED, LUTHOR.
YOU'VE JUST BEEN DRAFTED.
IT'S ABOUT TIME.
LANE

STRANGE MEETINGS AND CHANCE ENCOUNTERS> COVER ART BY **ALEX ROSS**

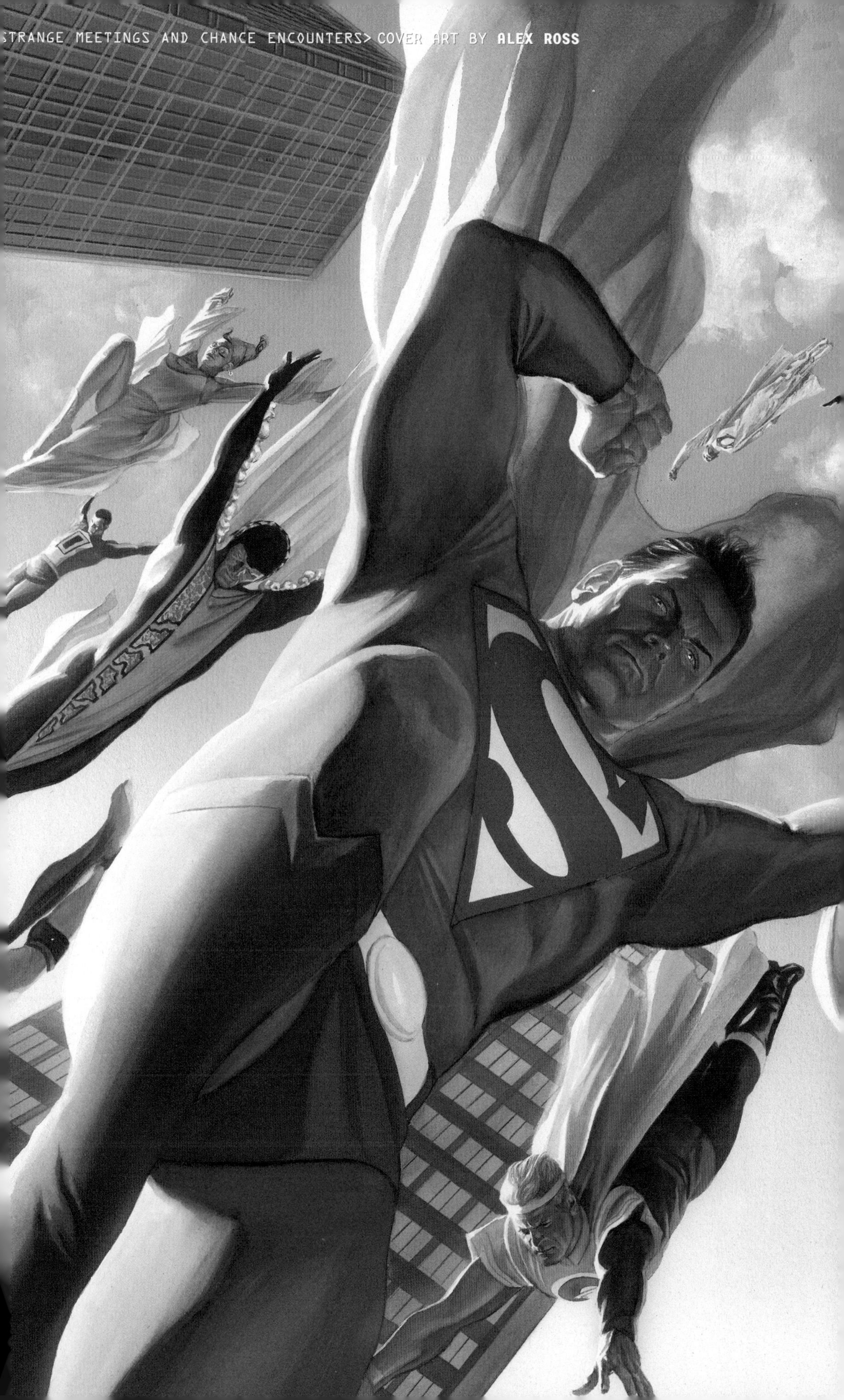

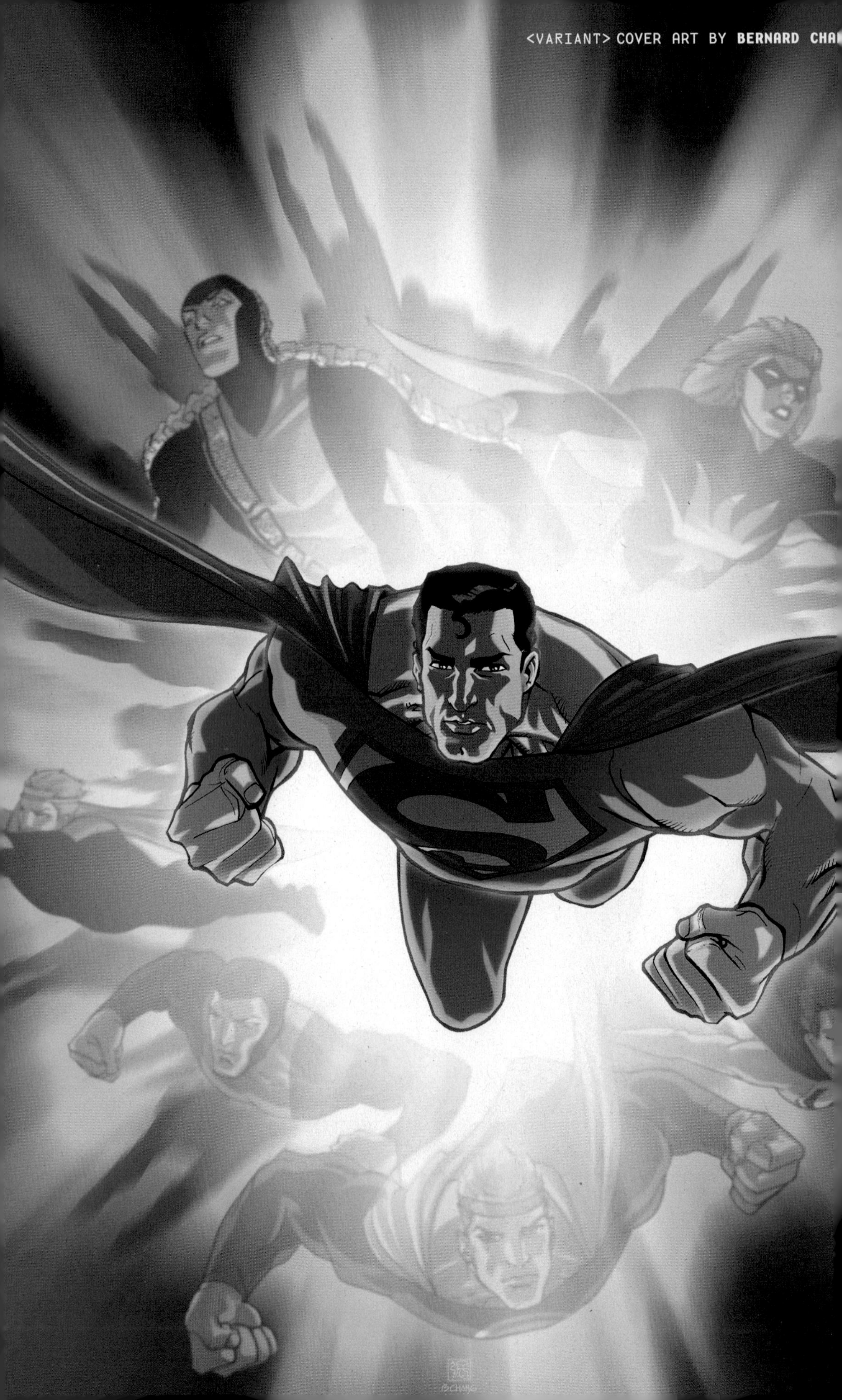

<VARIANT> COVER ART BY **BERNARD CHA**

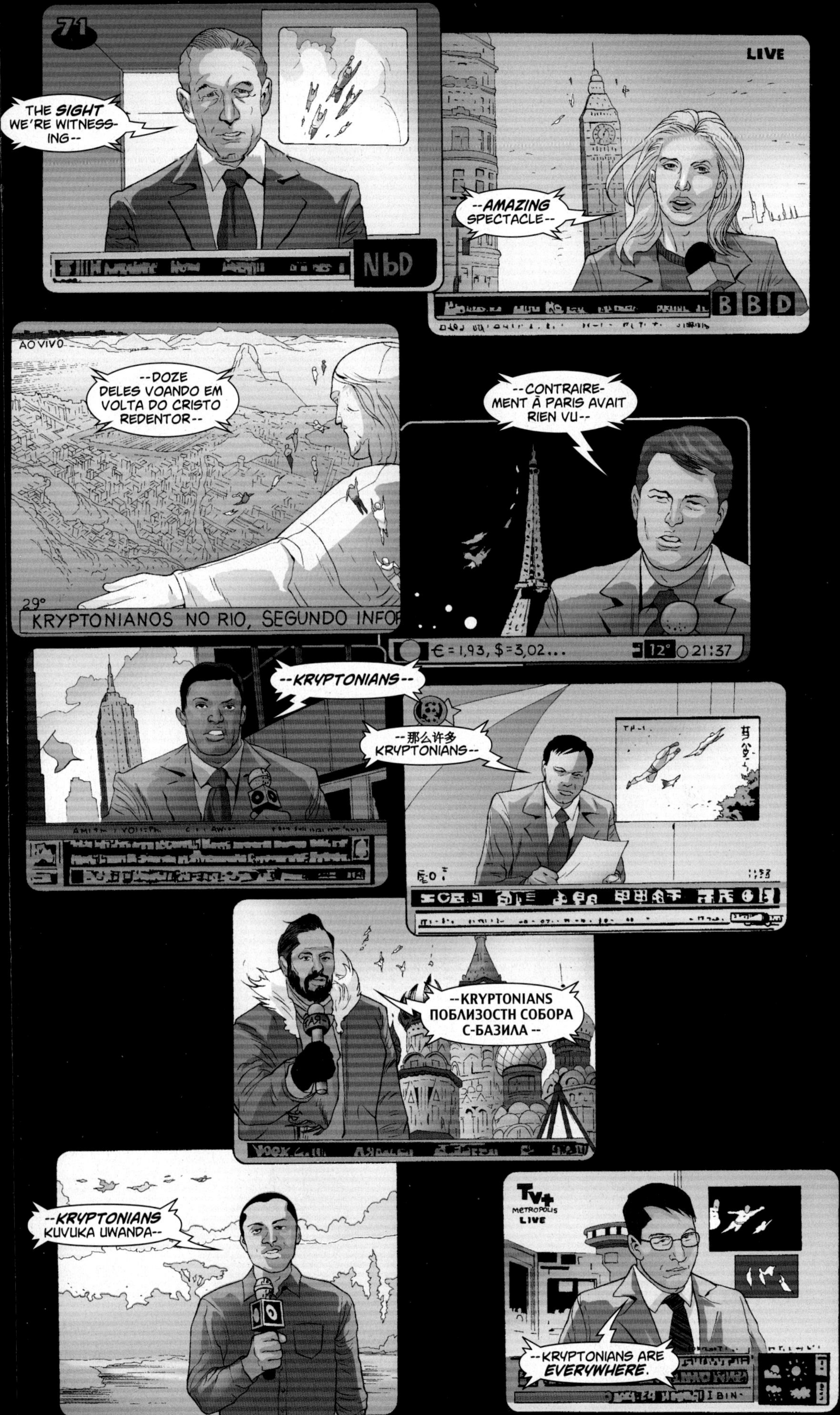
71
THE SIGHT WE'RE WITNESSING--
NbD
LIVE
--AMAZING SPECTACLE--
BBD
AO VIVO
--DOZE DELES VOANDO EM VOLTA DO CRISTO REDENTOR--
29°
KRYPTONIANOS NO RIO, SEGUNDO INFOR
--CONTRAIREMENT À PARIS AVAIT RIEN VU--
€=1,93, $=3,02...
12°
21:37
--KRYPTONIANS--
--那么许多 KRYPTONIANS--
--KRYPTONIANS ПОБЛИЗОСТИ СОБОРА С-БАЗИЛА --
--KRYPTONIANS KUVUKA UWANDA--
Tv+ METROPOLIS LIVE
--KRYPTONIANS ARE EVERYWHERE.

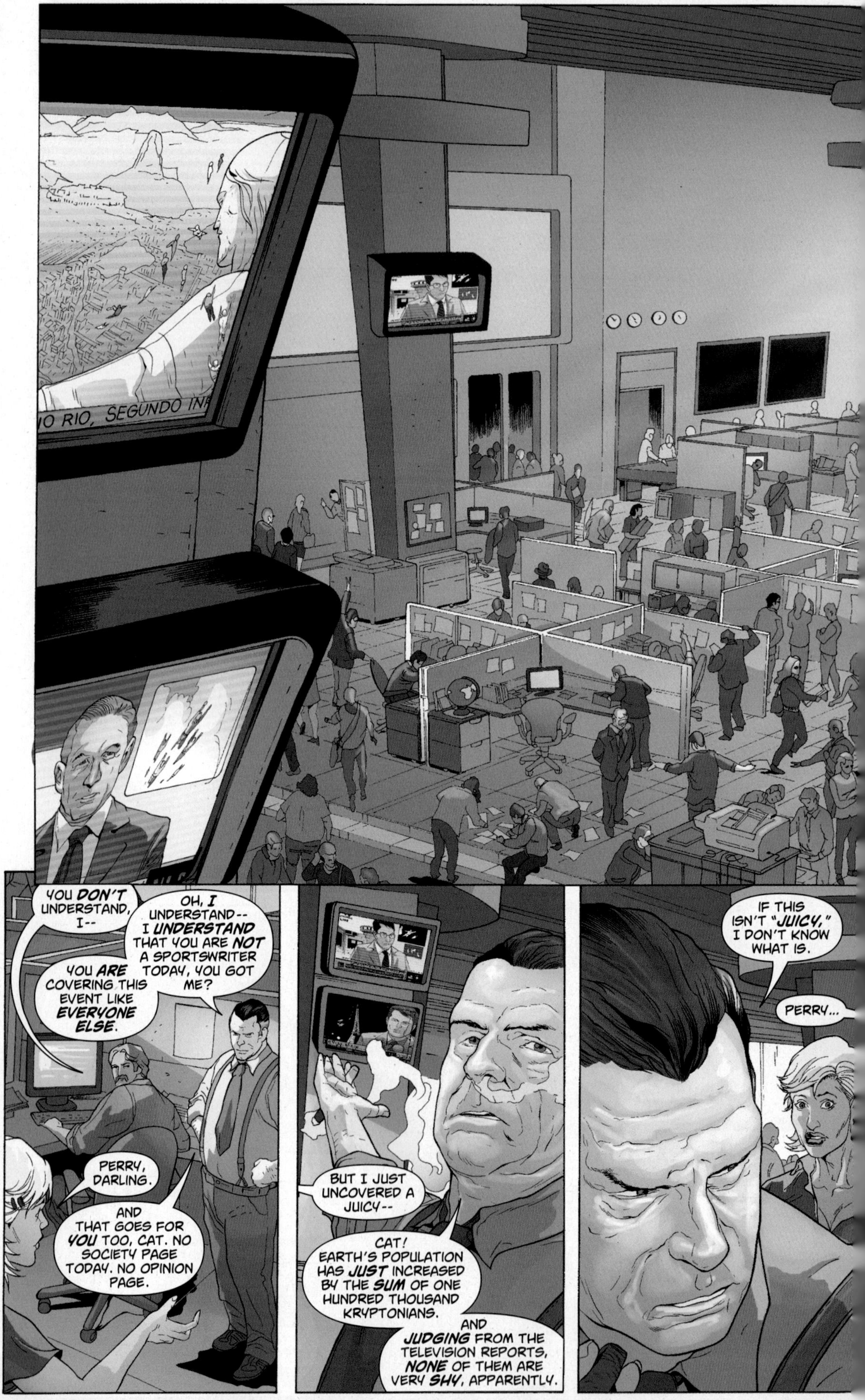
...O RIO, SEGUNDO IN...
YOU DON'T UNDERSTAND, I--
OH, I UNDERSTAND-- I UNDERSTAND THAT YOU ARE NOT A SPORTSWRITER TODAY, YOU GOT ME?
YOU ARE COVERING THIS EVENT LIKE EVERYONE ELSE.
PERRY, DARLING.
AND THAT GOES FOR YOU TOO, CAT. NO SOCIETY PAGE TODAY. NO OPINION PAGE.
BUT I JUST UNCOVERED A JUICY--
CAT! EARTH'S POPULATION HAS JUST INCREASED BY THE SUM OF ONE HUNDRED THOUSAND KRYPTONIANS.
AND JUDGING FROM THE TELEVISION REPORTS, NONE OF THEM ARE VERY SHY, APPARENTLY.
IF THIS ISN'T "JUICY," I DON'T KNOW WHAT IS.
PERRY...

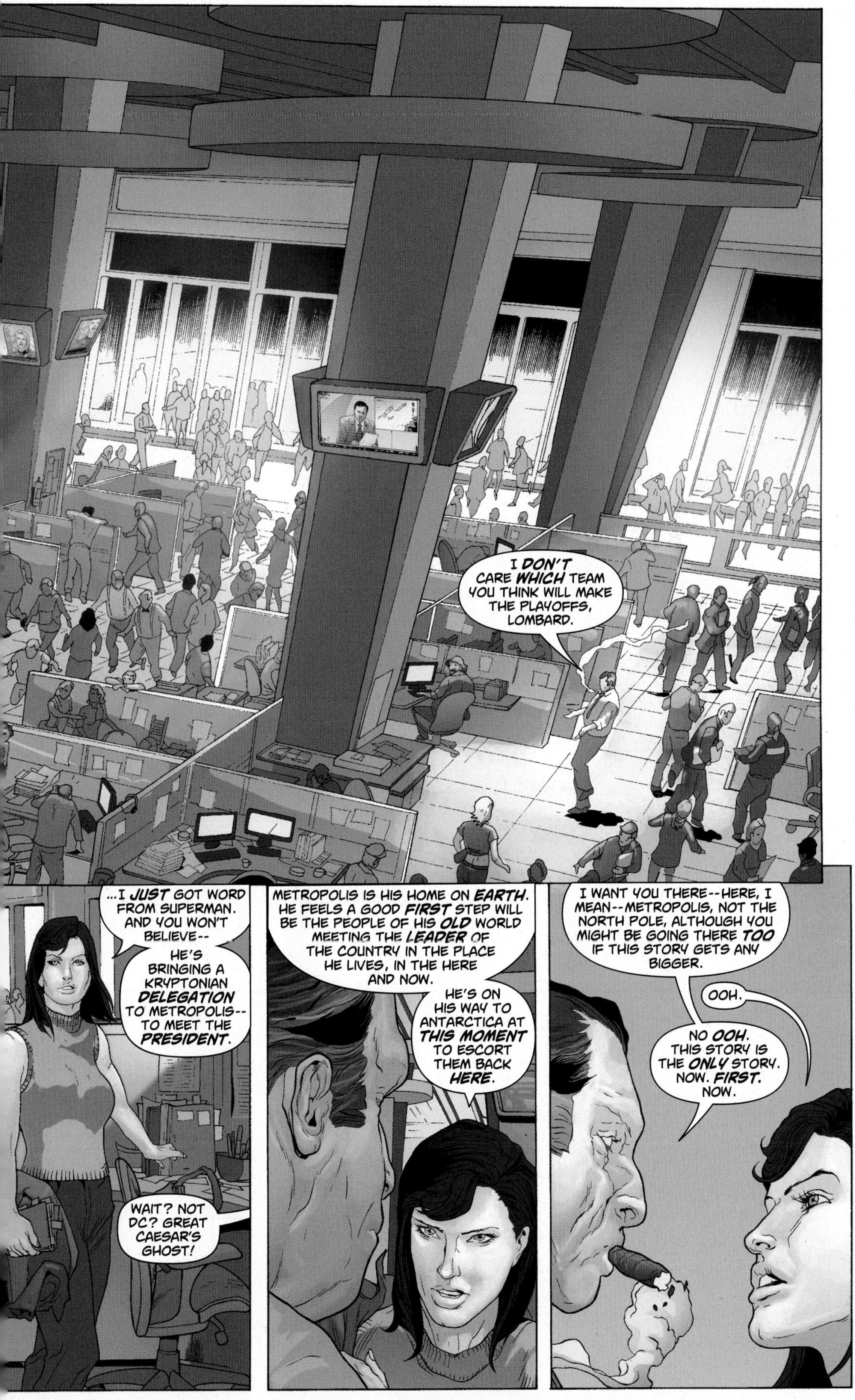
I DON'T CARE WHICH TEAM YOU THINK WILL MAKE THE PLAYOFFS, LOMBARD.
...I JUST GOT WORD FROM SUPERMAN. AND YOU WON'T BELIEVE--
HE'S BRINGING A KRYPTONIAN DELEGATION TO METROPOLIS--TO MEET THE PRESIDENT.
WAIT? NOT DC? GREAT CAESAR'S GHOST!
METROPOLIS IS HIS HOME ON EARTH. HE FEELS A GOOD FIRST STEP WILL BE THE PEOPLE OF HIS OLD WORLD MEETING THE LEADER OF THE COUNTRY IN THE PLACE HE LIVES, IN THE HERE AND NOW.
HE'S ON HIS WAY TO ANTARCTICA AT THIS MOMENT TO ESCORT THEM BACK HERE.
I WANT YOU THERE--HERE, I MEAN--METROPOLIS, NOT THE NORTH POLE, ALTHOUGH YOU MIGHT BE GOING THERE TOO IF THIS STORY GETS ANY BIGGER.
OOH.
NO OOH. THIS STORY IS THE ONLY STORY. NOW. FIRST. NOW.

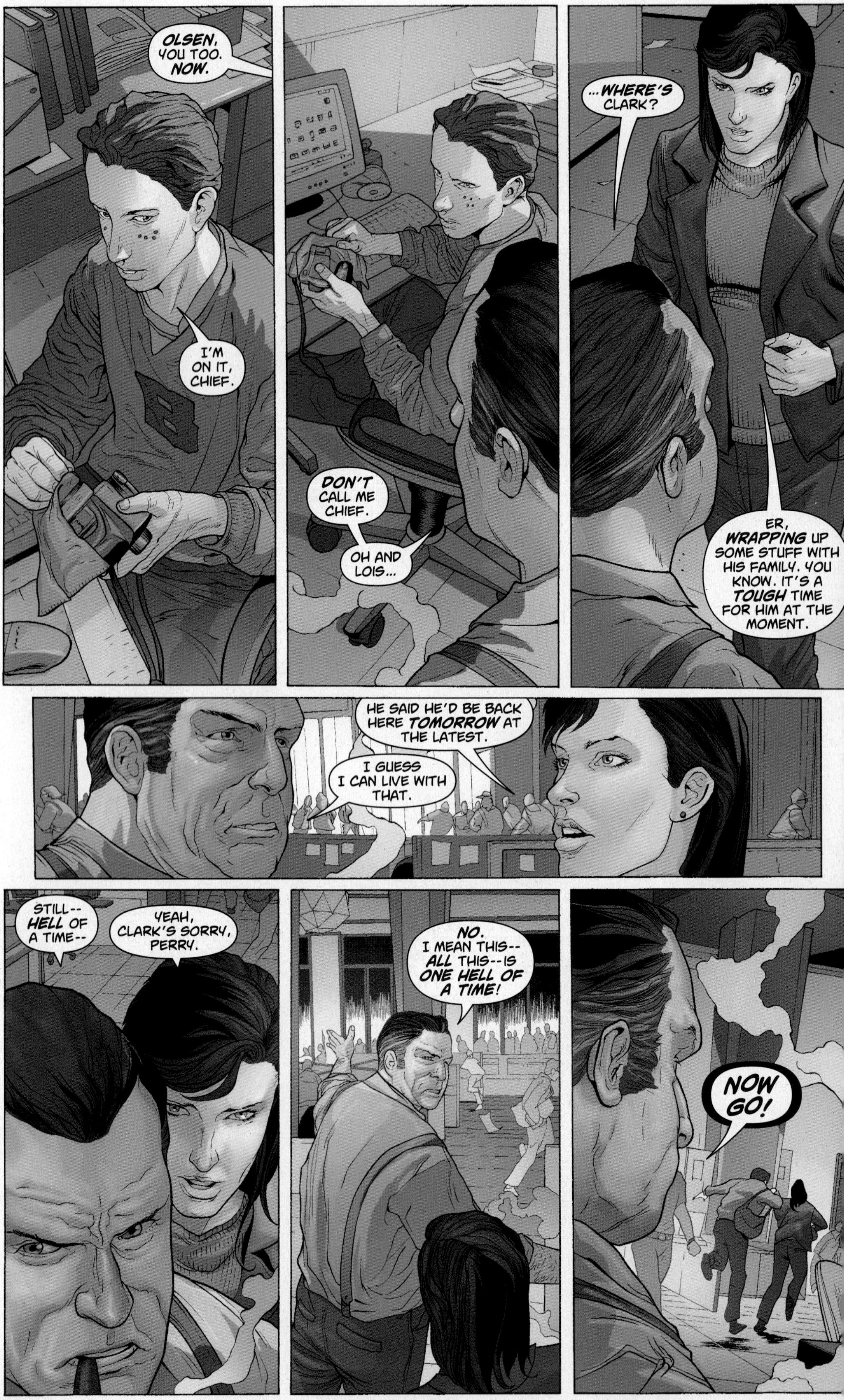

OLSEN, YOU TOO. NOW.
I'M ON IT, CHIEF.
DON'T CALL ME CHIEF.
OH AND LOIS...
...WHERE'S CLARK?
ER, WRAPPING UP SOME STUFF WITH HIS FAMILY. YOU KNOW. IT'S A TOUGH TIME FOR HIM AT THE MOMENT.
HE SAID HE'D BE BACK HERE TOMORROW AT THE LATEST.
I GUESS I CAN LIVE WITH THAT.
STILL-- HELL OF A TIME--
YEAH, CLARK'S SORRY, PERRY.
NO. I MEAN THIS-- ALL THIS--IS ONE HELL OF A TIME!
NOW GO!

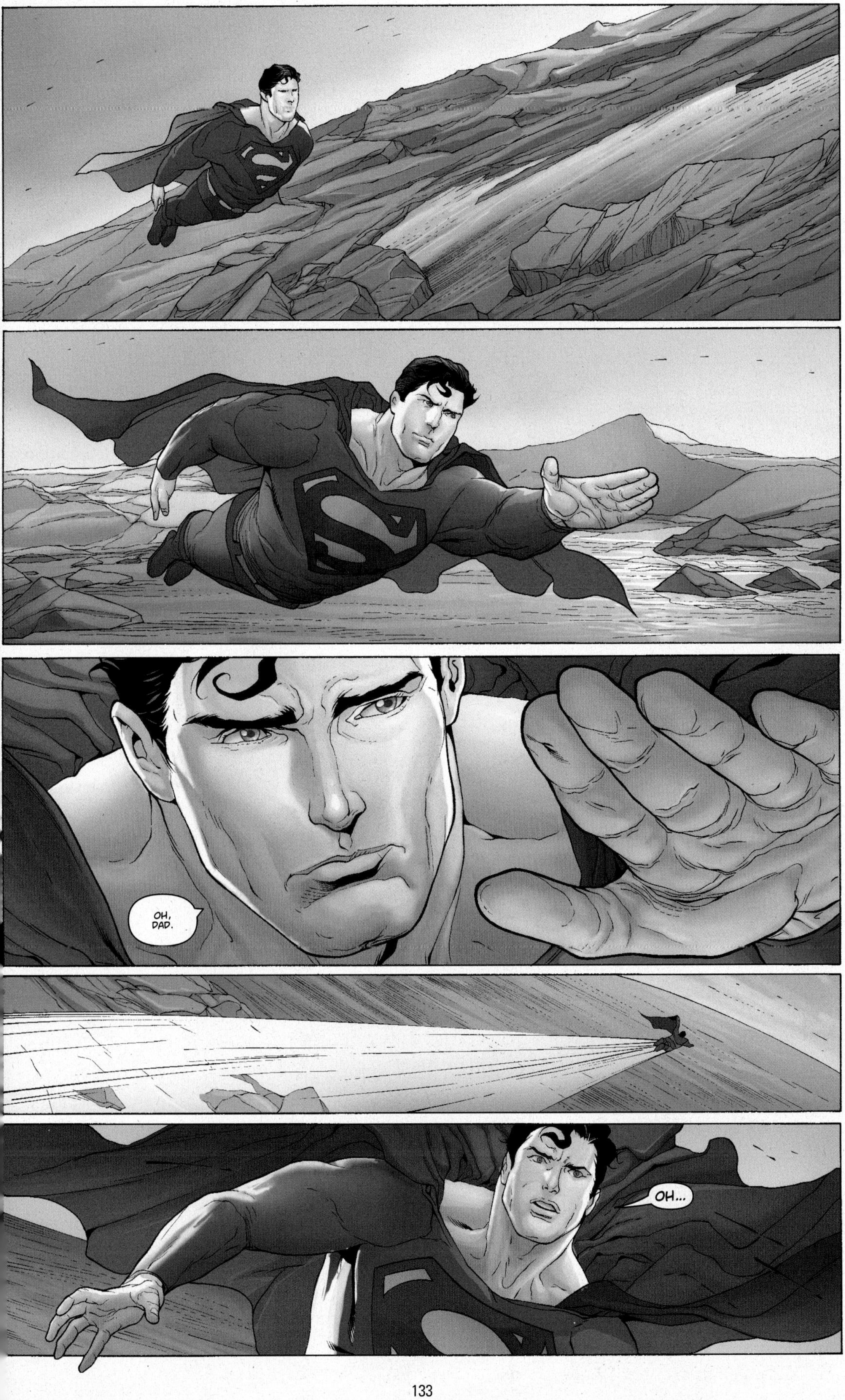
OH, DAD.
OH...

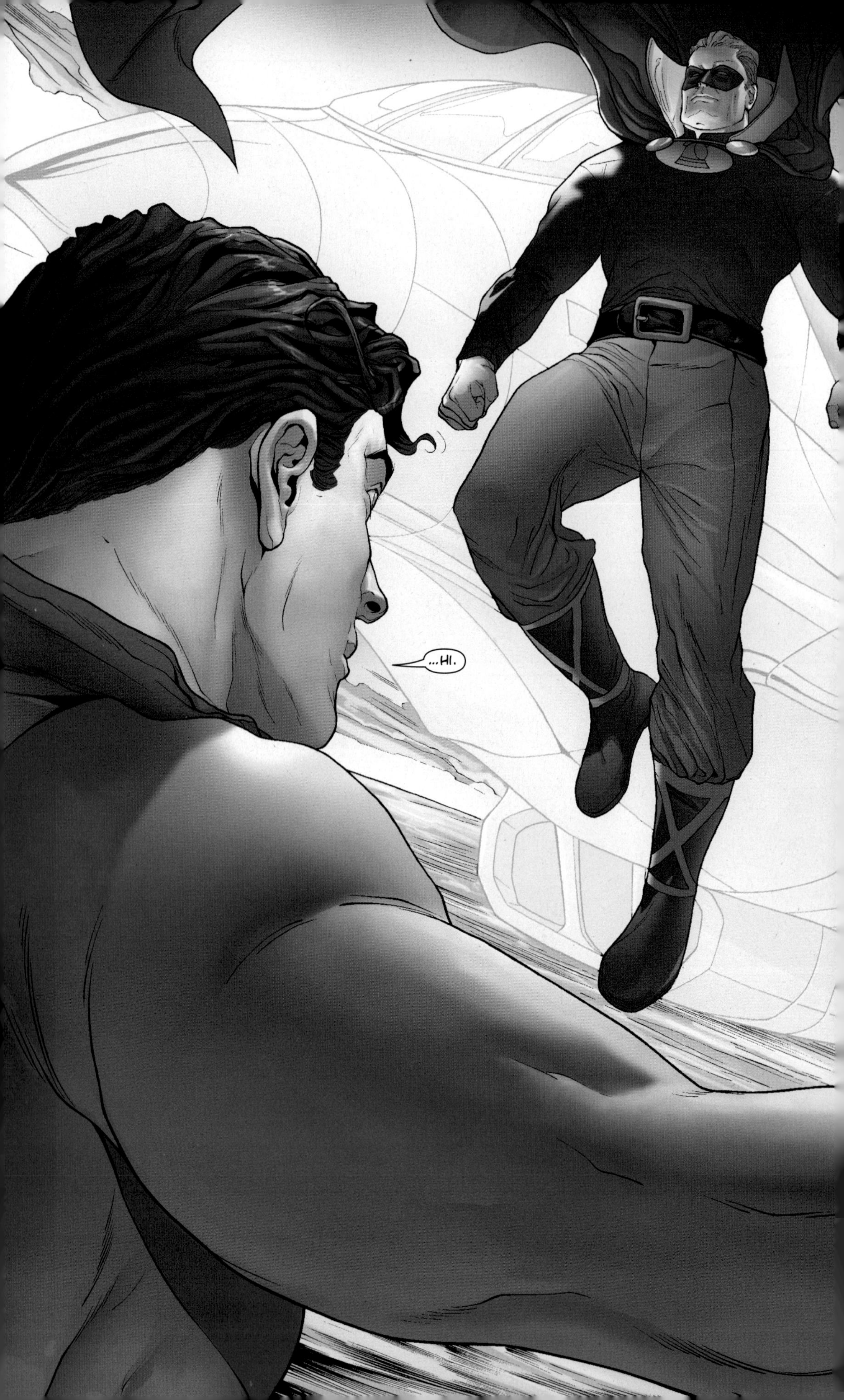
...HI.

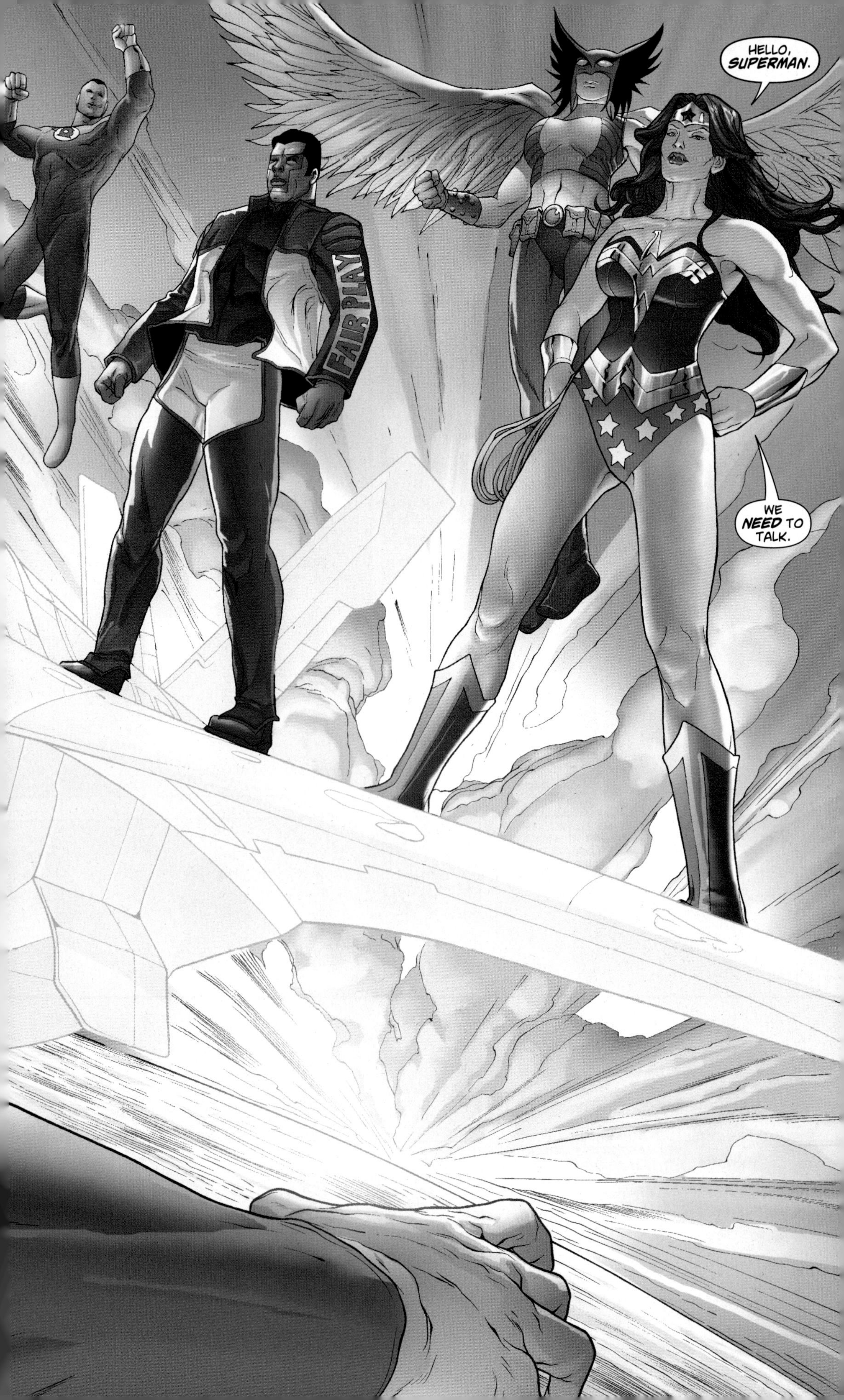
HELLO, SUPERMAN.
WE NEED TO TALK.
FAIR PLAY

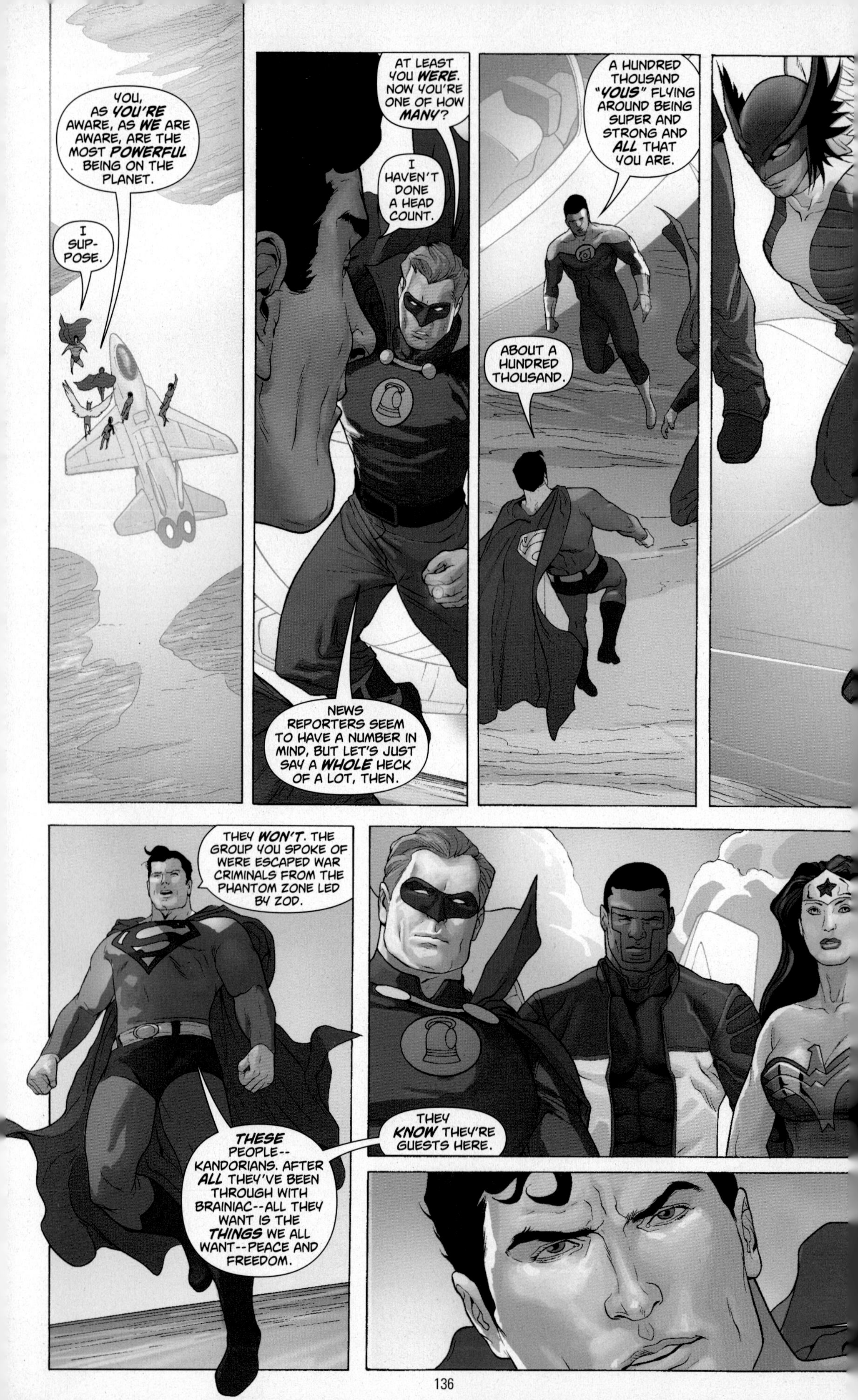
YOU, AS YOU'RE AWARE, AS WE ARE AWARE, ARE THE MOST POWERFUL BEING ON THE PLANET.
I SUP-POSE.
AT LEAST YOU WERE. NOW YOU'RE ONE OF HOW MANY?
I HAVEN'T DONE A HEAD COUNT.
NEWS REPORTERS SEEM TO HAVE A NUMBER IN MIND, BUT LET'S JUST SAY A WHOLE HECK OF A LOT, THEN.
A HUNDRED THOUSAND "YOUS" FLYING AROUND BEING SUPER AND STRONG AND ALL THAT YOU ARE.
ABOUT A HUNDRED THOUSAND.
THEY WON'T. THE GROUP YOU SPOKE OF WERE ESCAPED WAR CRIMINALS FROM THE PHANTOM ZONE LED BY ZOD.
THESE PEOPLE-- KANDORIANS. AFTER ALL THEY'VE BEEN THROUGH WITH BRAINIAC--ALL THEY WANT IS THE THINGS WE ALL WANT--PEACE AND FREEDOM.
THEY KNOW THEY'RE GUESTS HERE.

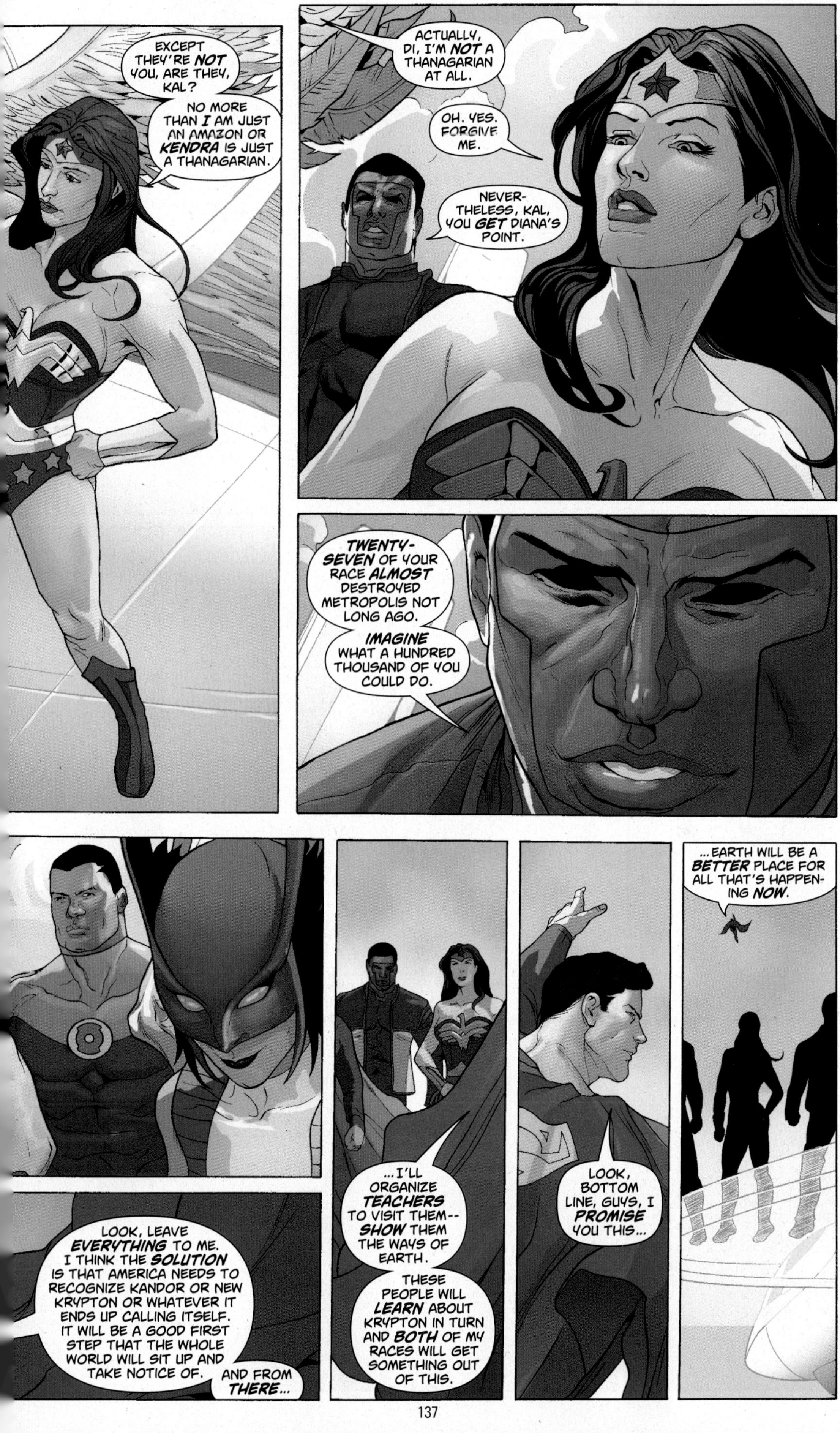
EXCEPT THEY'RE NOT YOU, ARE THEY, KAL?
NO MORE THAN I AM JUST AN AMAZON OR KENDRA IS JUST A THANAGARIAN.
ACTUALLY, DI, I'M NOT A THANAGARIAN AT ALL.
OH. YES. FORGIVE ME.
NEVER-THELESS, KAL, YOU GET DIANA'S POINT.
TWENTY-SEVEN OF YOUR RACE ALMOST DESTROYED METROPOLIS NOT LONG AGO.
IMAGINE WHAT A HUNDRED THOUSAND OF YOU COULD DO.
LOOK, LEAVE EVERYTHING TO ME. I THINK THE SOLUTION IS THAT AMERICA NEEDS TO RECOGNIZE KANDOR OR NEW KRYPTON OR WHATEVER IT ENDS UP CALLING ITSELF. IT WILL BE A GOOD FIRST STEP THAT THE WHOLE WORLD WILL SIT UP AND TAKE NOTICE OF.
AND FROM THERE...
...I'LL ORGANIZE TEACHERS TO VISIT THEM--SHOW THEM THE WAYS OF EARTH.
THESE PEOPLE WILL LEARN ABOUT KRYPTON IN TURN AND BOTH OF MY RACES WILL GET SOMETHING OUT OF THIS.
LOOK, BOTTOM LINE, GUYS, I PROMISE YOU THIS...
...EARTH WILL BE A BETTER PLACE FOR ALL THAT'S HAPPEN-ING NOW.

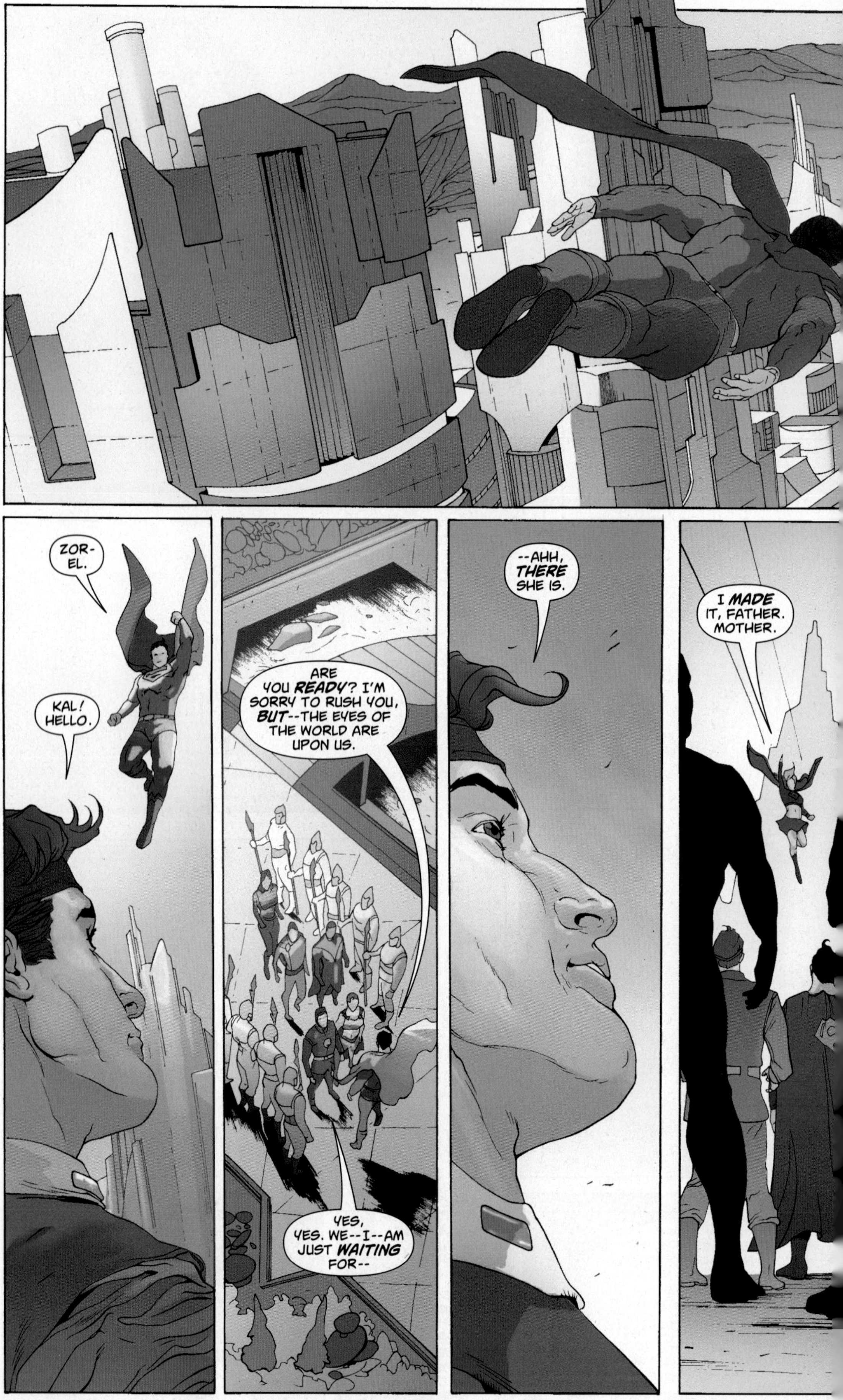
ZOR-EL.
KAL! HELLO.
ARE YOU READY? I'M SORRY TO RUSH YOU, BUT--THE EYES OF THE WORLD ARE UPON US.
YES, YES. WE--I--AM JUST WAITING FOR--
--AHH, THERE SHE IS.
I MADE IT, FATHER. MOTHER.

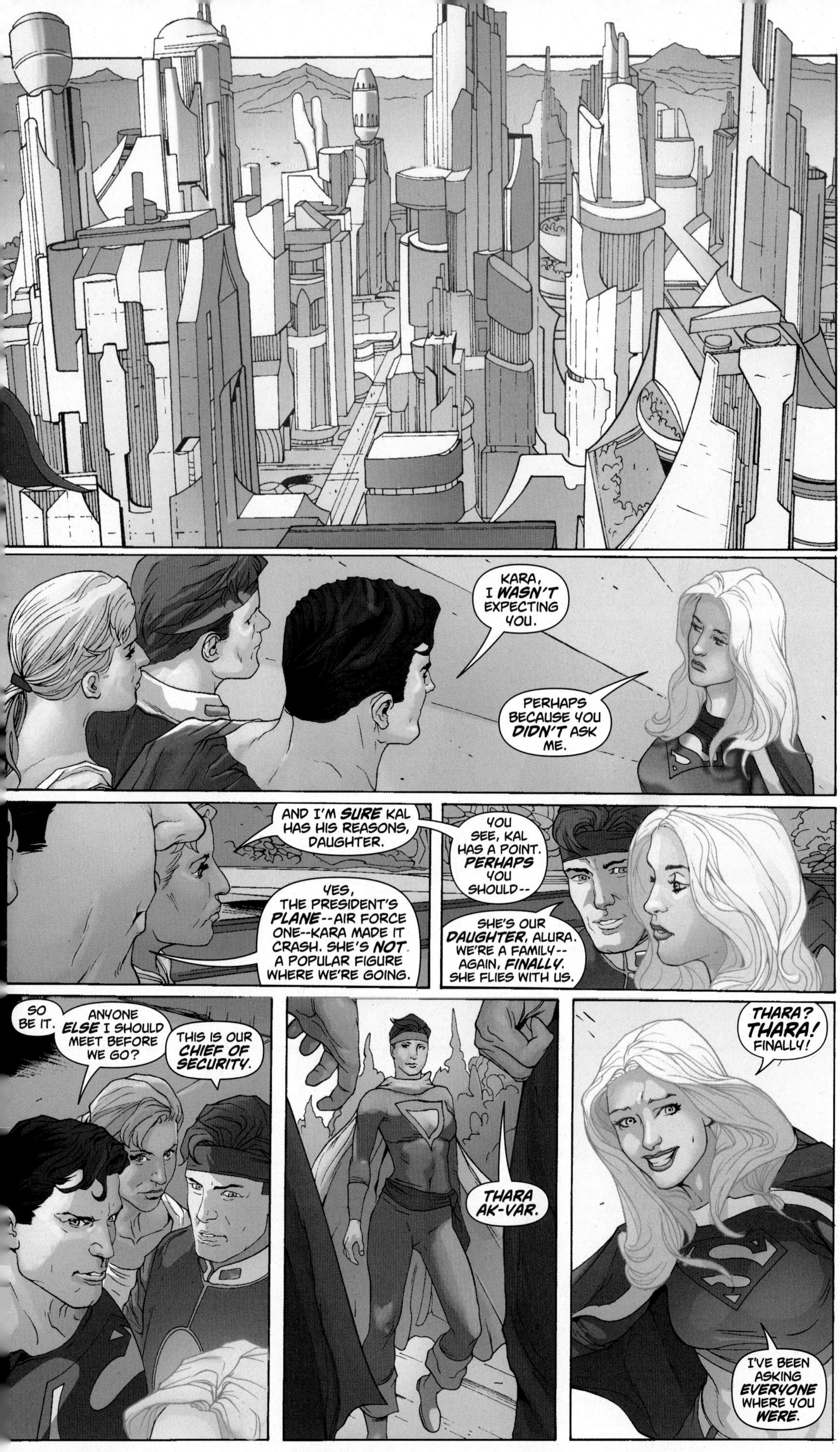
KARA, I WASN'T EXPECTING YOU.
PERHAPS BECAUSE YOU DIDN'T ASK ME.
AND I'M SURE KAL HAS HIS REASONS, DAUGHTER.
YES, THE PRESIDENT'S PLANE--AIR FORCE ONE--KARA MADE IT CRASH. SHE'S NOT A POPULAR FIGURE WHERE WE'RE GOING.
YOU SEE, KAL HAS A POINT. PERHAPS YOU SHOULD--
SHE'S OUR DAUGHTER, ALURA. WE'RE A FAMILY-- AGAIN, FINALLY. SHE FLIES WITH US.
SO BE IT.
ANYONE ELSE I SHOULD MEET BEFORE WE GO?
THIS IS OUR CHIEF OF SECURITY.
THARA AK-VAR.
THARA? THARA! FINALLY!
I'VE BEEN ASKING EVERYONE WHERE YOU WERE.

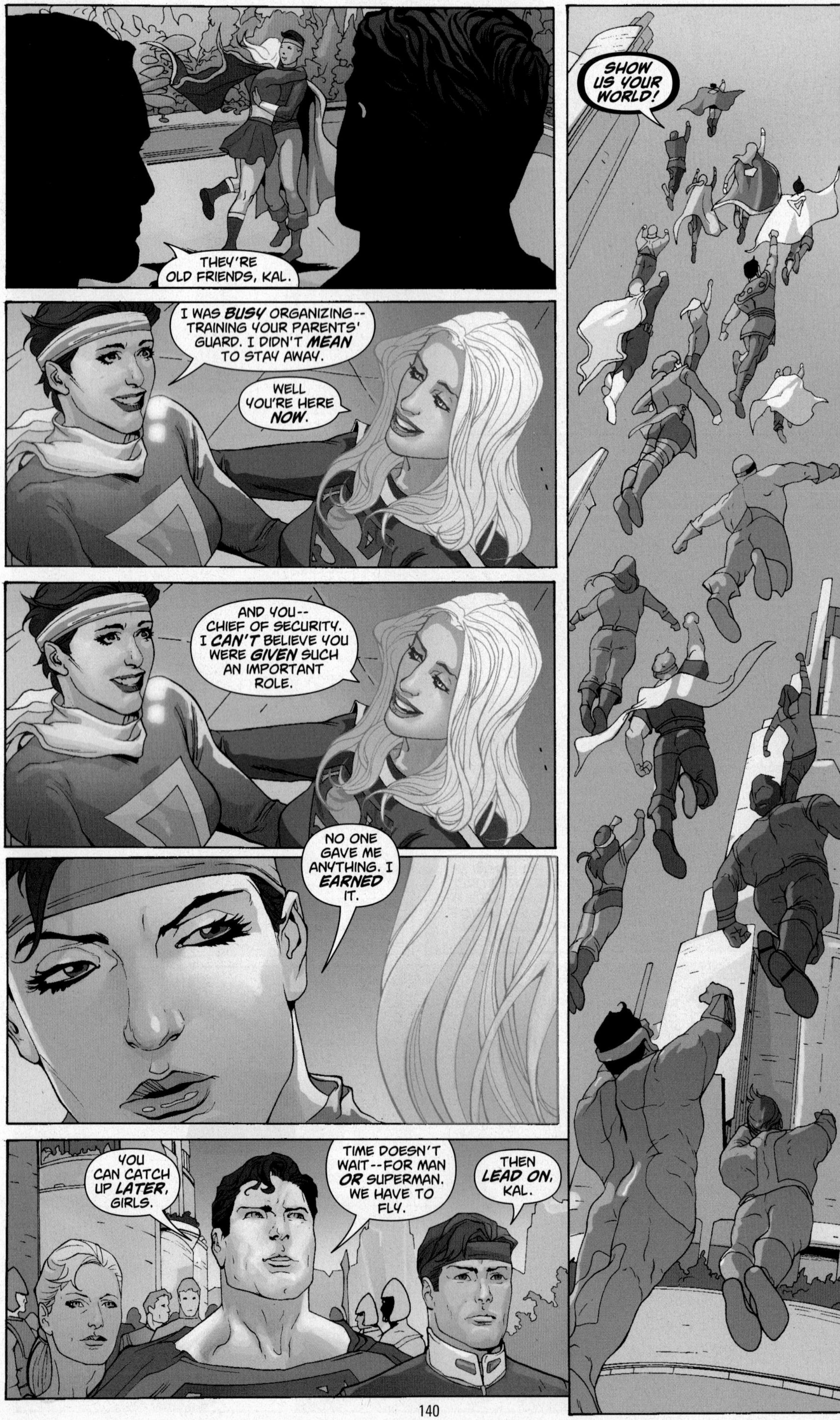
THEY'RE OLD FRIENDS, KAL.
I WAS BUSY ORGANIZING-- TRAINING YOUR PARENTS' GUARD. I DIDN'T MEAN TO STAY AWAY.
WELL YOU'RE HERE NOW.
AND YOU-- CHIEF OF SECURITY. I CAN'T BELIEVE YOU WERE GIVEN SUCH AN IMPORTANT ROLE.
NO ONE GAVE ME ANYTHING. I EARNED IT.
YOU CAN CATCH UP LATER, GIRLS.
TIME DOESN'T WAIT--FOR MAN OR SUPERMAN. WE HAVE TO FLY.
THEN LEAD ON, KAL.
SHOW US YOUR WORLD!

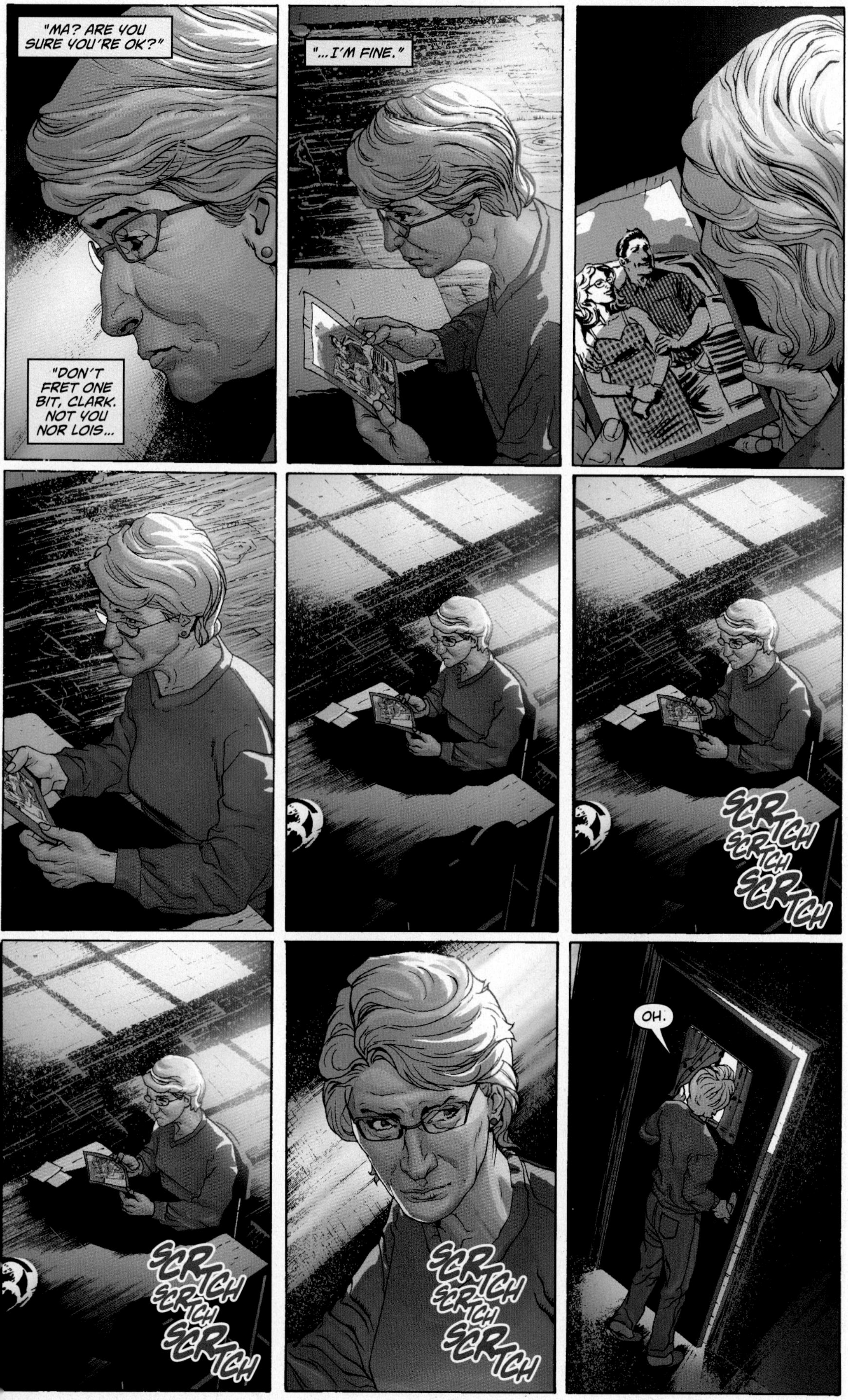

"MA? ARE YOU SURE YOU'RE OK?"
"DON'T FRET ONE BIT, CLARK. NOT YOU NOR LOIS...
"...I'M FINE."
SCRTCH SCRTCH SCRTCH
SCRTCH SCRTCH SCRTCH
SCRTCH SCRTCH SCRTCH
OH.

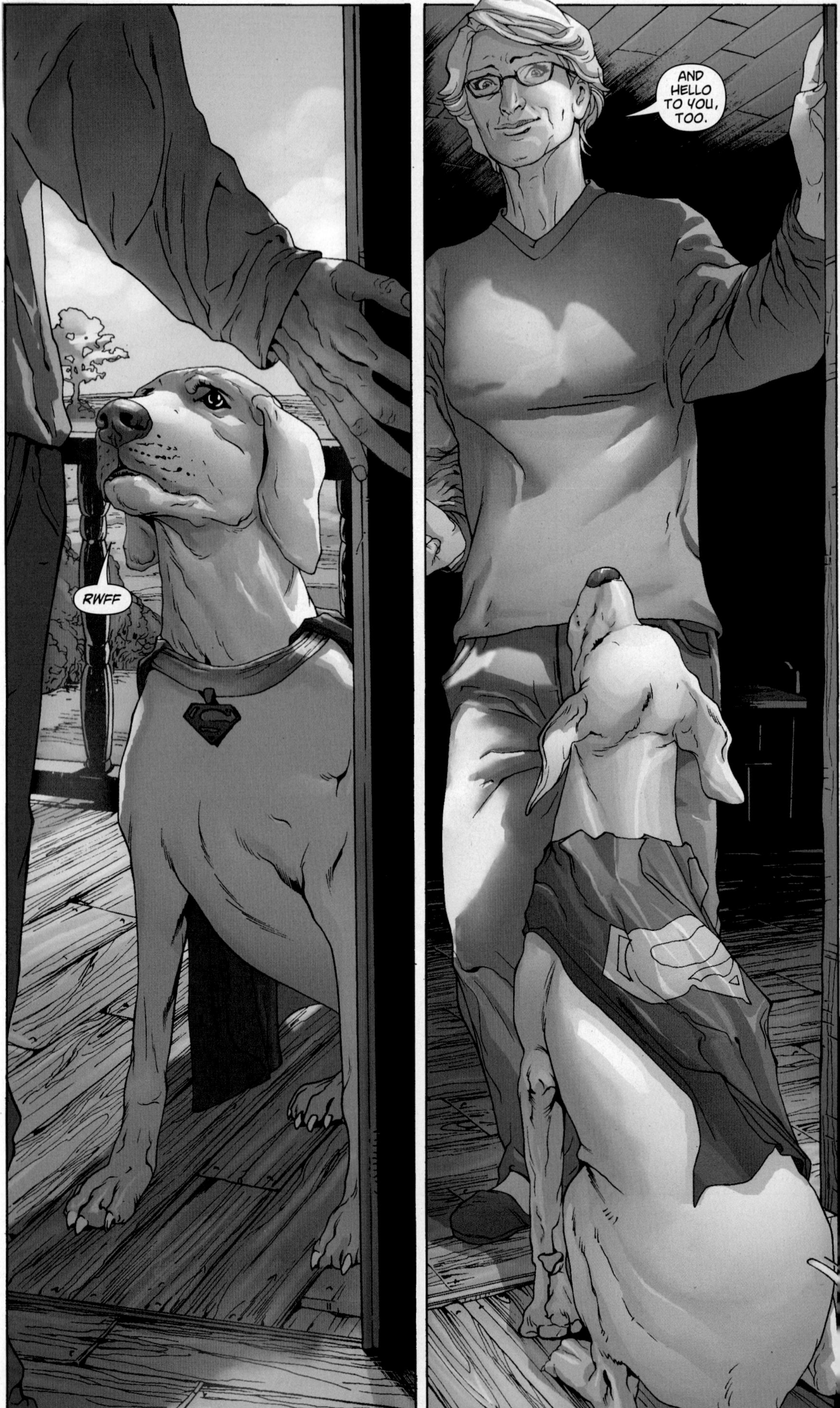
RWFF
AND HELLO TO YOU, TOO.

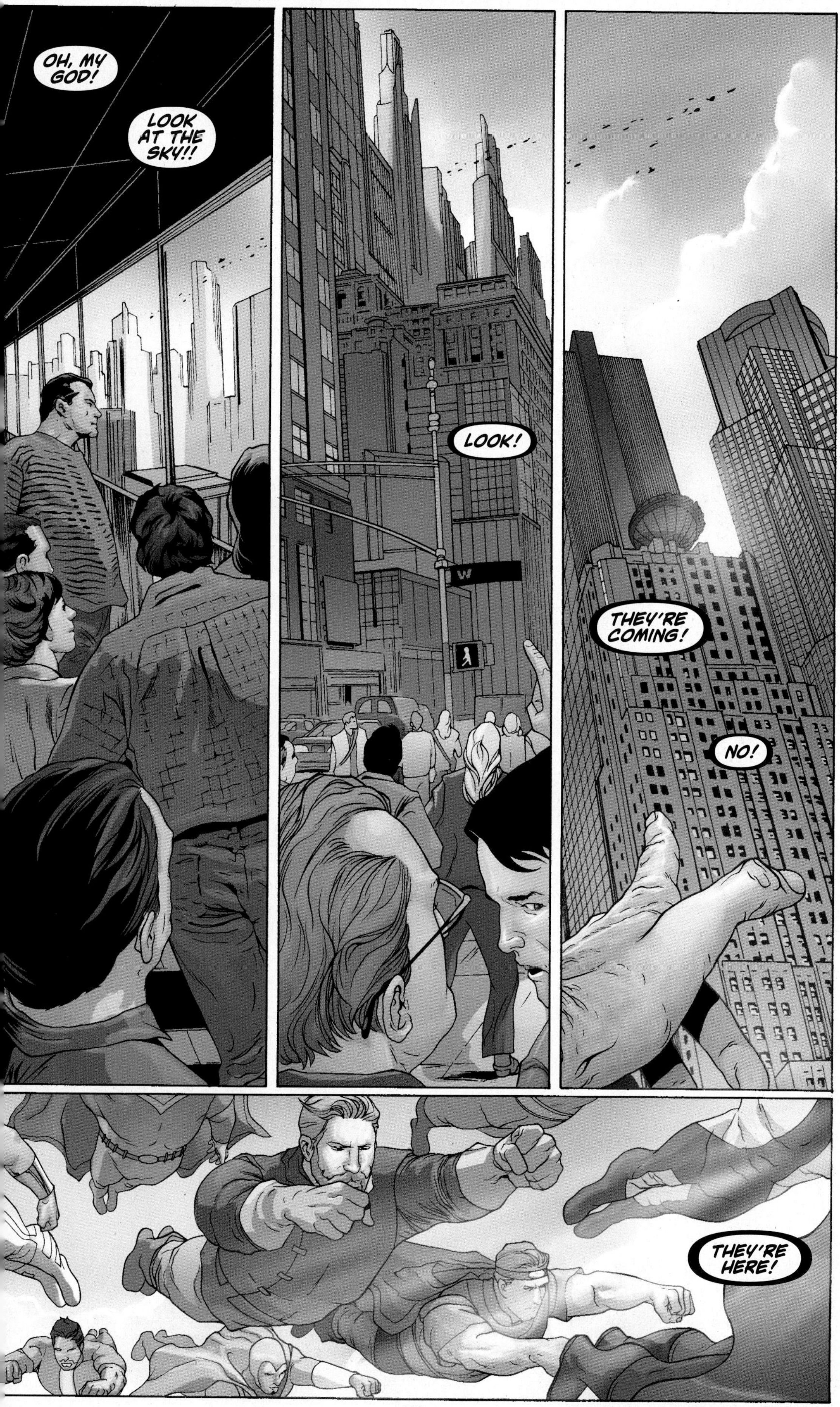
OH, MY GOD!
LOOK AT THE SKY!!
LOOK!
THEY'RE COMING!
NO!
THEY'RE HERE!

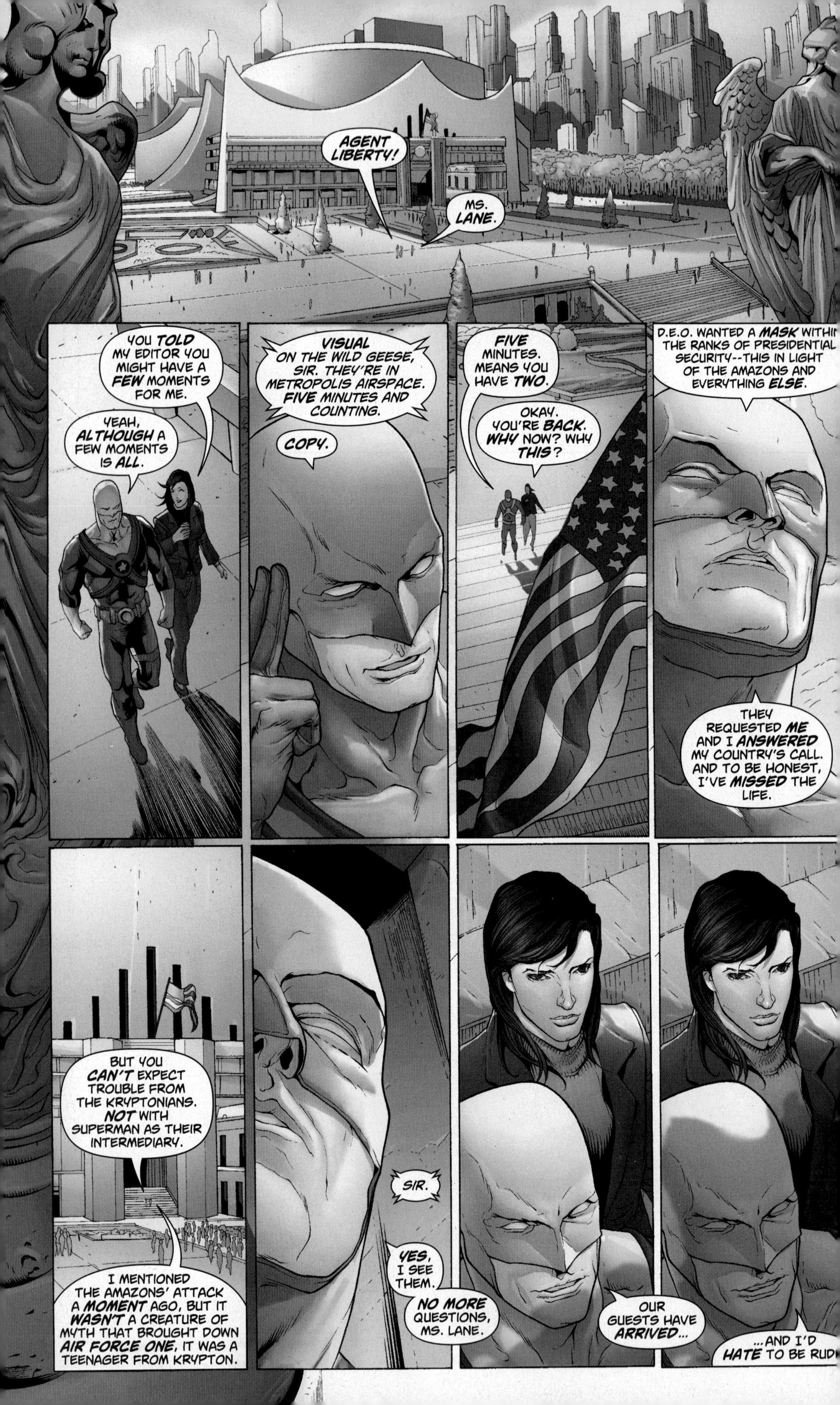

AGENT LIBERTY!
MS. LANE.
YOU **TOLD** MY EDITOR YOU MIGHT HAVE A **FEW** MOMENTS FOR ME.
YEAH, **ALTHOUGH** A FEW MOMENTS IS **ALL**.
VISUAL ON THE WILD GEESE, SIR. THEY'RE IN METROPOLIS AIRSPACE. **FIVE** MINUTES AND COUNTING.
COPY.
FIVE MINUTES. MEANS YOU HAVE **TWO**.
OKAY. YOU'RE **BACK**. **WHY** NOW? WHY **THIS**?
D.E.O. WANTED A **MASK** WITHIN THE RANKS OF PRESIDENTIAL SECURITY--THIS IN LIGHT OF THE AMAZONS AND EVERYTHING **ELSE**.
THEY REQUESTED **ME** AND I **ANSWERED** MY COUNTRY'S CALL. AND TO BE HONEST, I'VE **MISSED** THE LIFE.
BUT YOU **CAN'T** EXPECT TROUBLE FROM THE KRYPTONIANS. **NOT** WITH SUPERMAN AS THEIR INTERMEDIARY.
I MENTIONED THE AMAZONS' ATTACK A **MOMENT** AGO, BUT IT **WASN'T** A CREATURE OF MYTH THAT BROUGHT DOWN **AIR FORCE ONE**, IT WAS A TEENAGER FROM KRYPTON.
SIR.
YES, I SEE THEM.
NO MORE QUESTIONS, MS. LANE.
OUR GUESTS HAVE **ARRIVED**...
...AND I'D **HATE** TO BE RUD

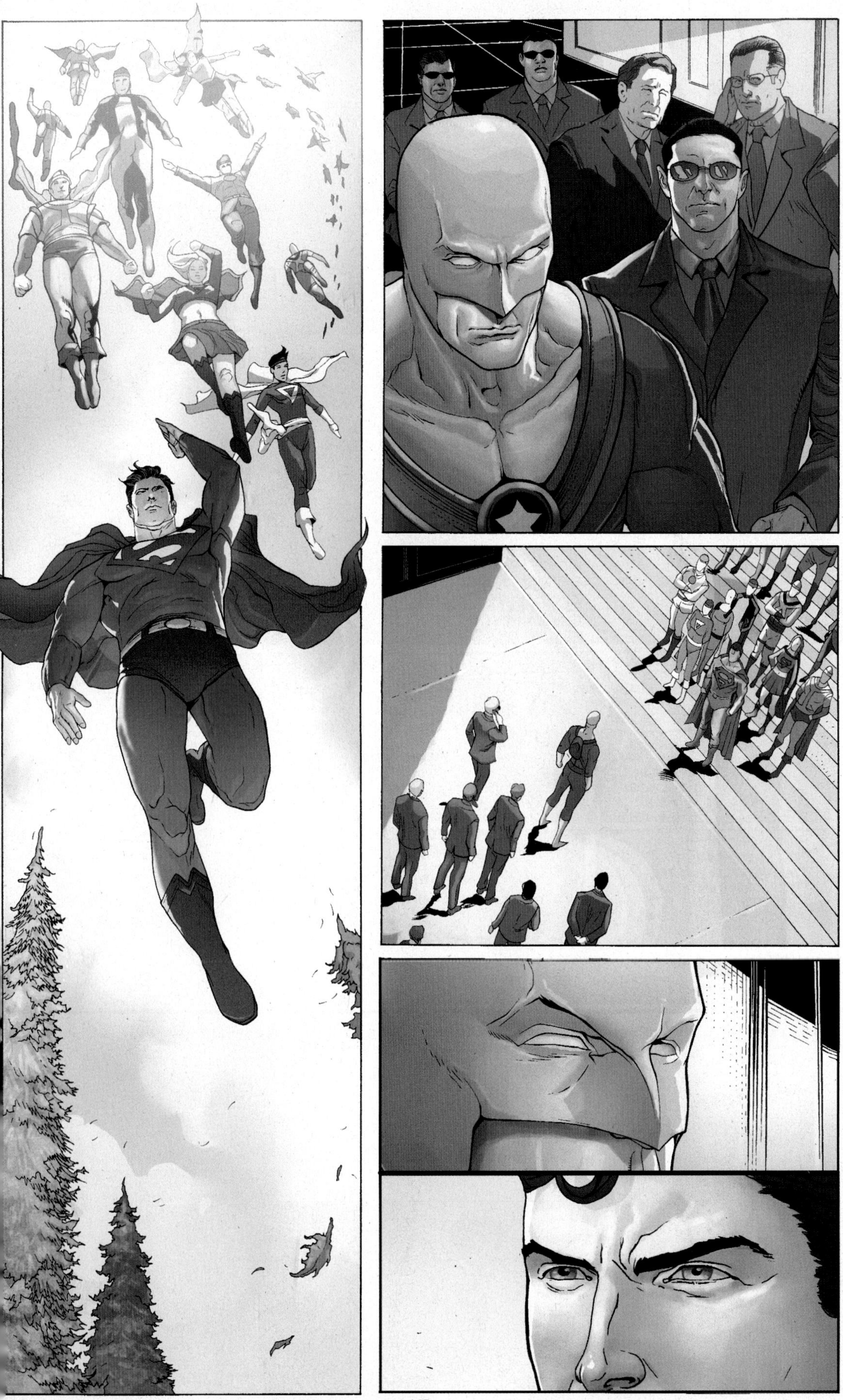

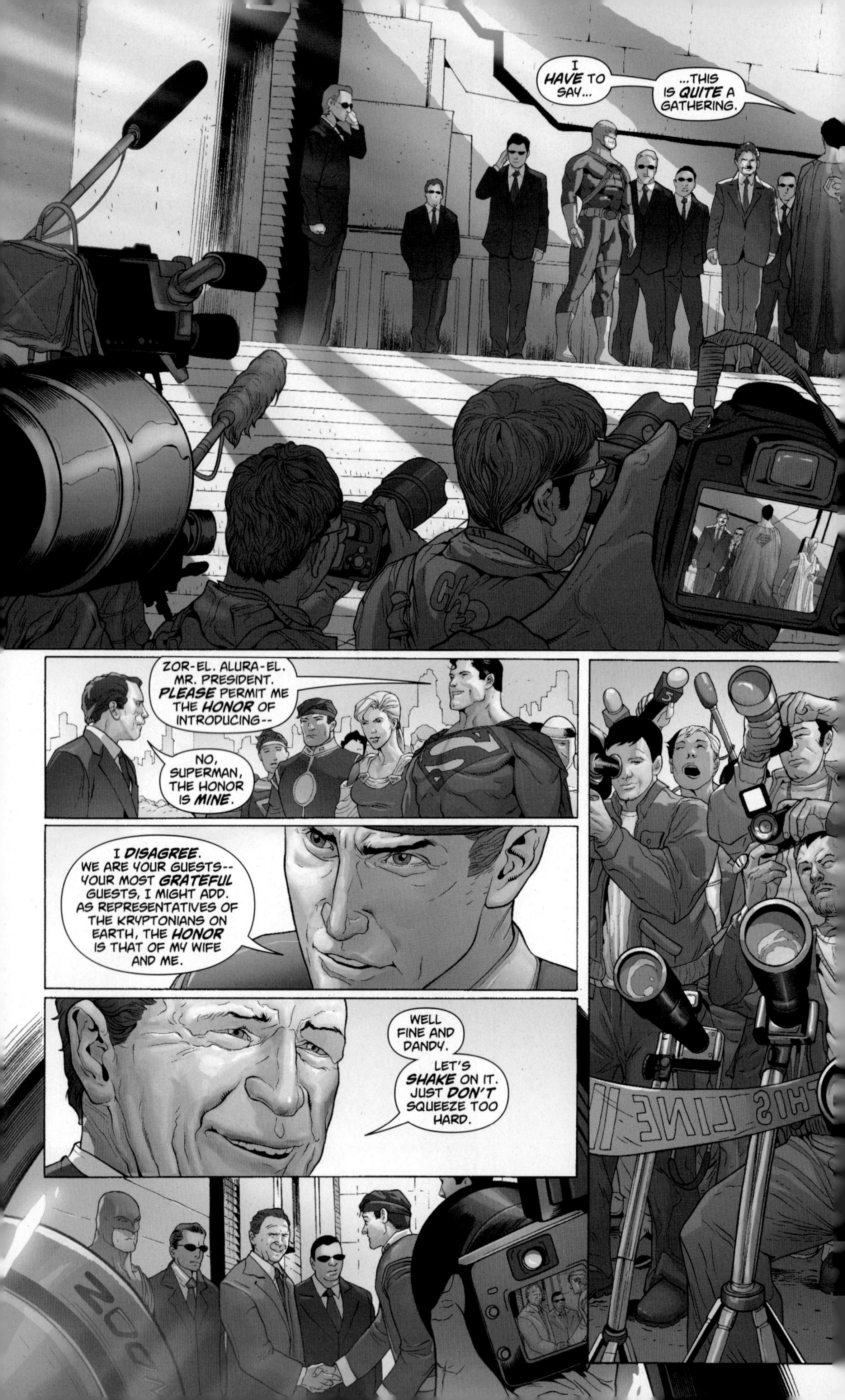
I HAVE TO SAY...
...THIS IS QUITE A GATHERING.
ZOR-EL. ALURA-EL. MR. PRESIDENT. PLEASE PERMIT ME THE HONOR OF INTRODUCING--
NO, SUPERMAN, THE HONOR IS MINE.
I DISAGREE. WE ARE YOUR GUESTS-- YOUR MOST GRATEFUL GUESTS, I MIGHT ADD. AS REPRESENTATIVES OF THE KRYPTONIANS ON EARTH, THE HONOR IS THAT OF MY WIFE AND ME.
WELL FINE AND DANDY.
LET'S SHAKE ON IT. JUST DON'T SQUEEZE TOO HARD.

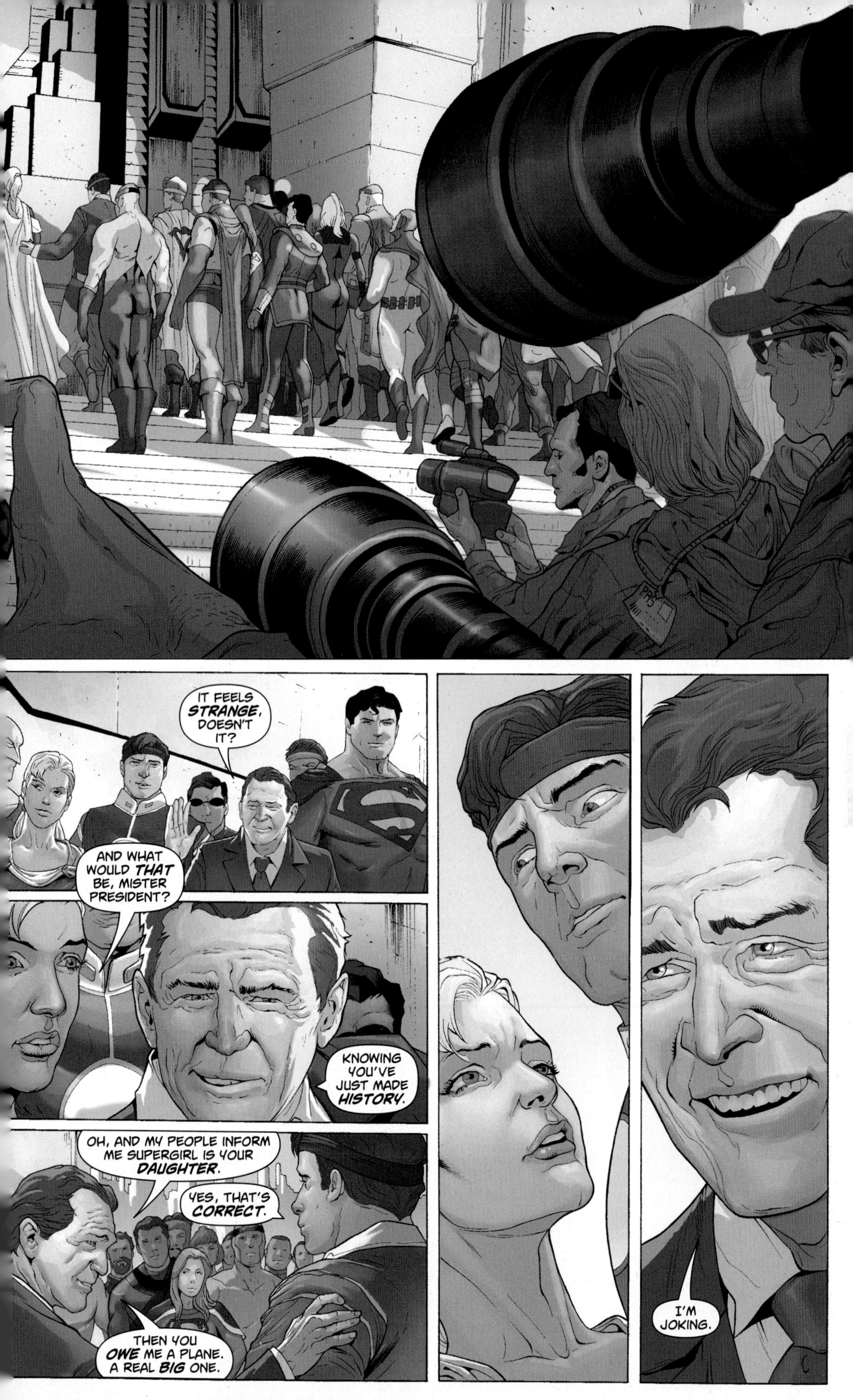
IT FEELS STRANGE, DOESN'T IT?
AND WHAT WOULD THAT BE, MISTER PRESIDENT?
KNOWING YOU'VE JUST MADE HISTORY.
OH, AND MY PEOPLE INFORM ME SUPERGIRL IS YOUR DAUGHTER.
YES, THAT'S CORRECT.
THEN YOU OWE ME A PLANE. A REAL BIG ONE.
I'M JOKING.

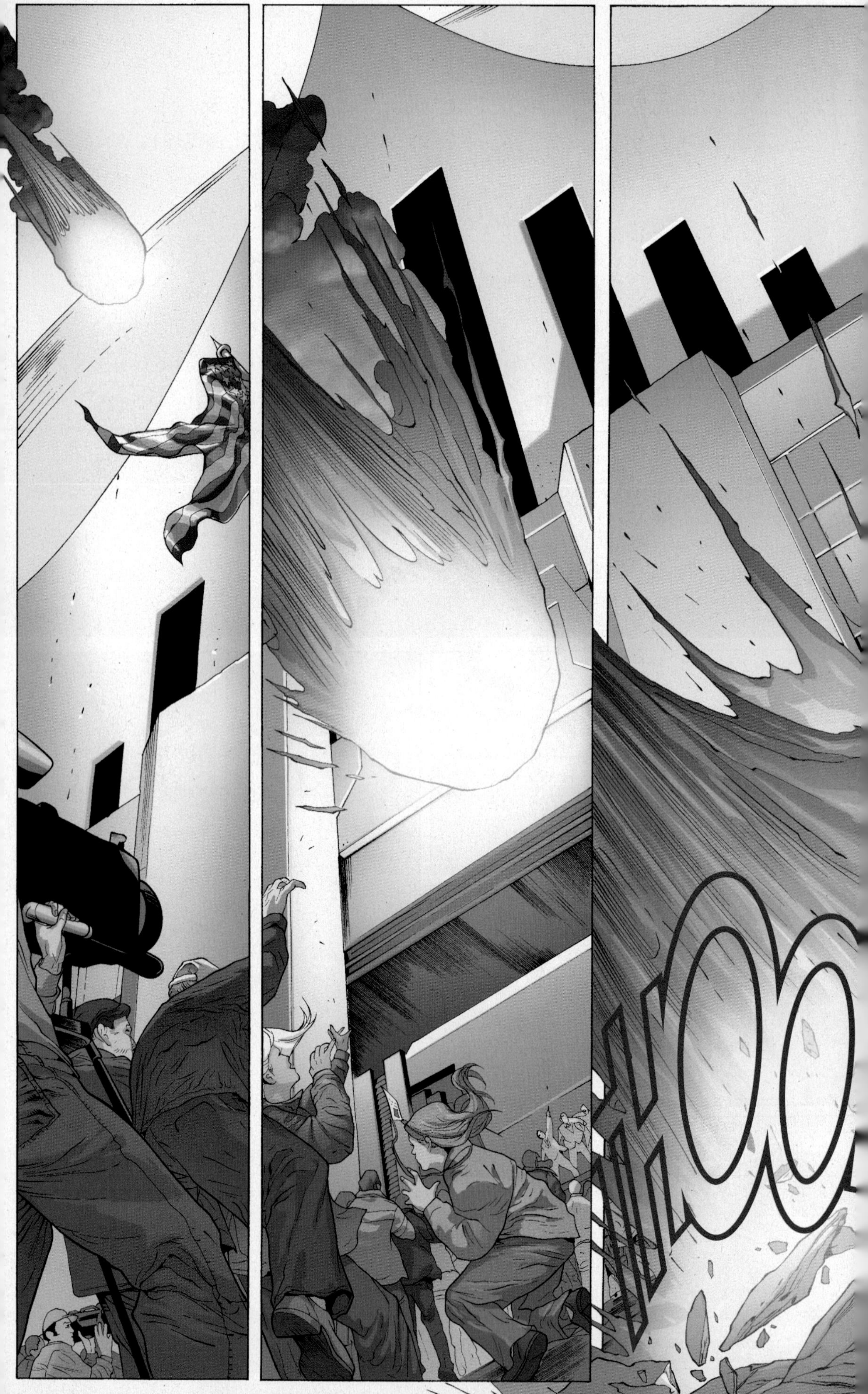
WHOO

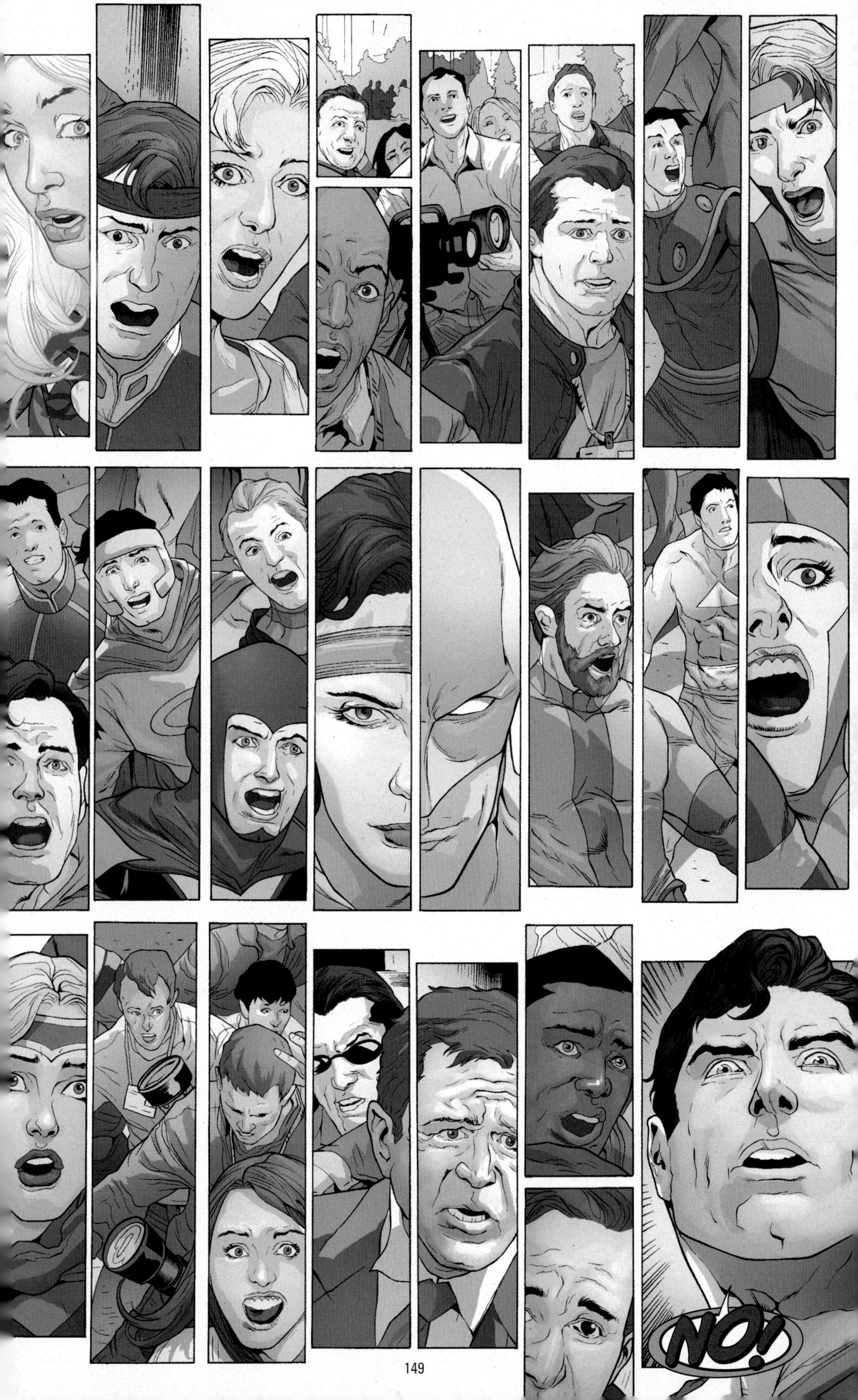
NO!

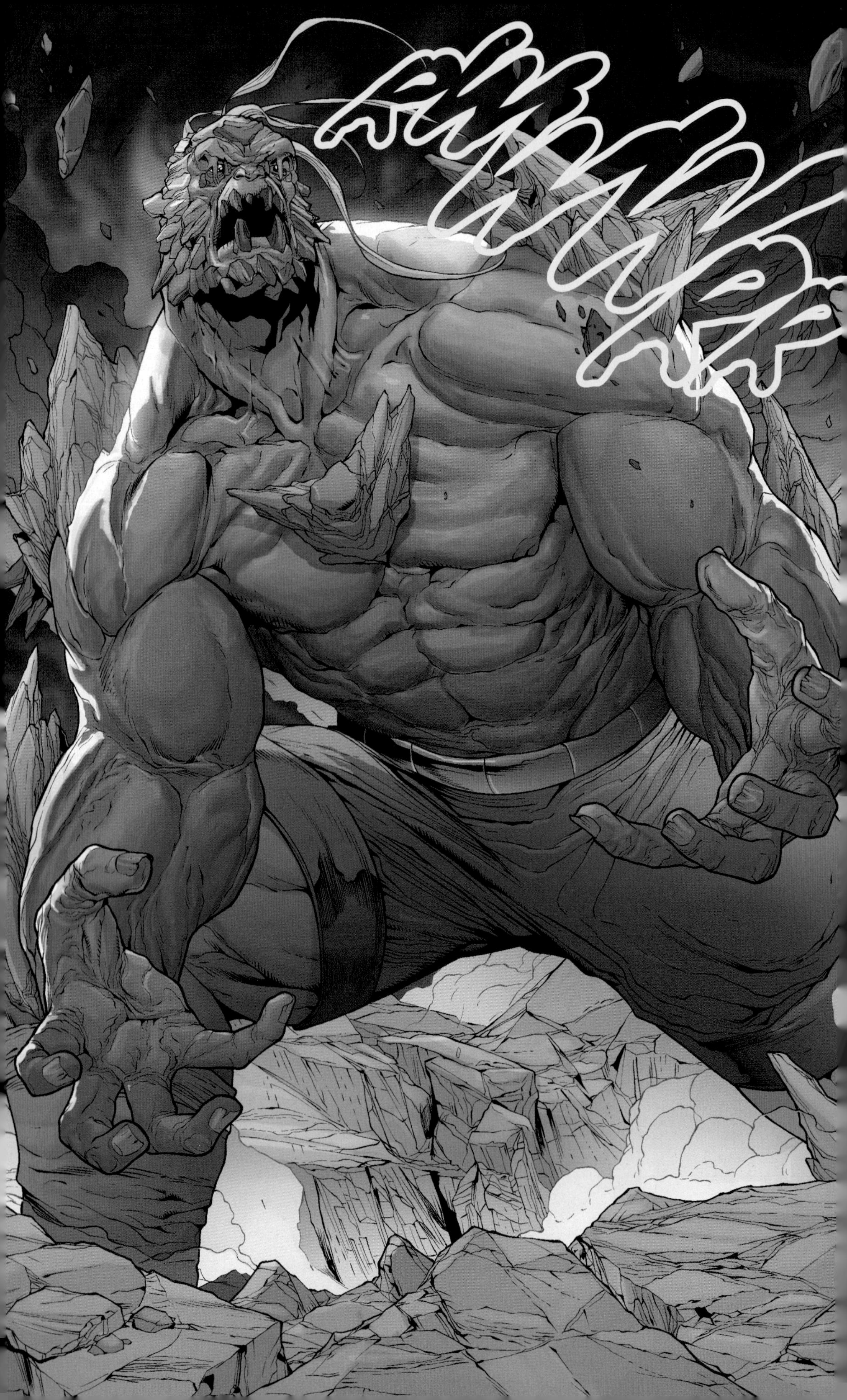

<BEYOND DOOMSDAY> COVER ART BY **ALEX ROSS**

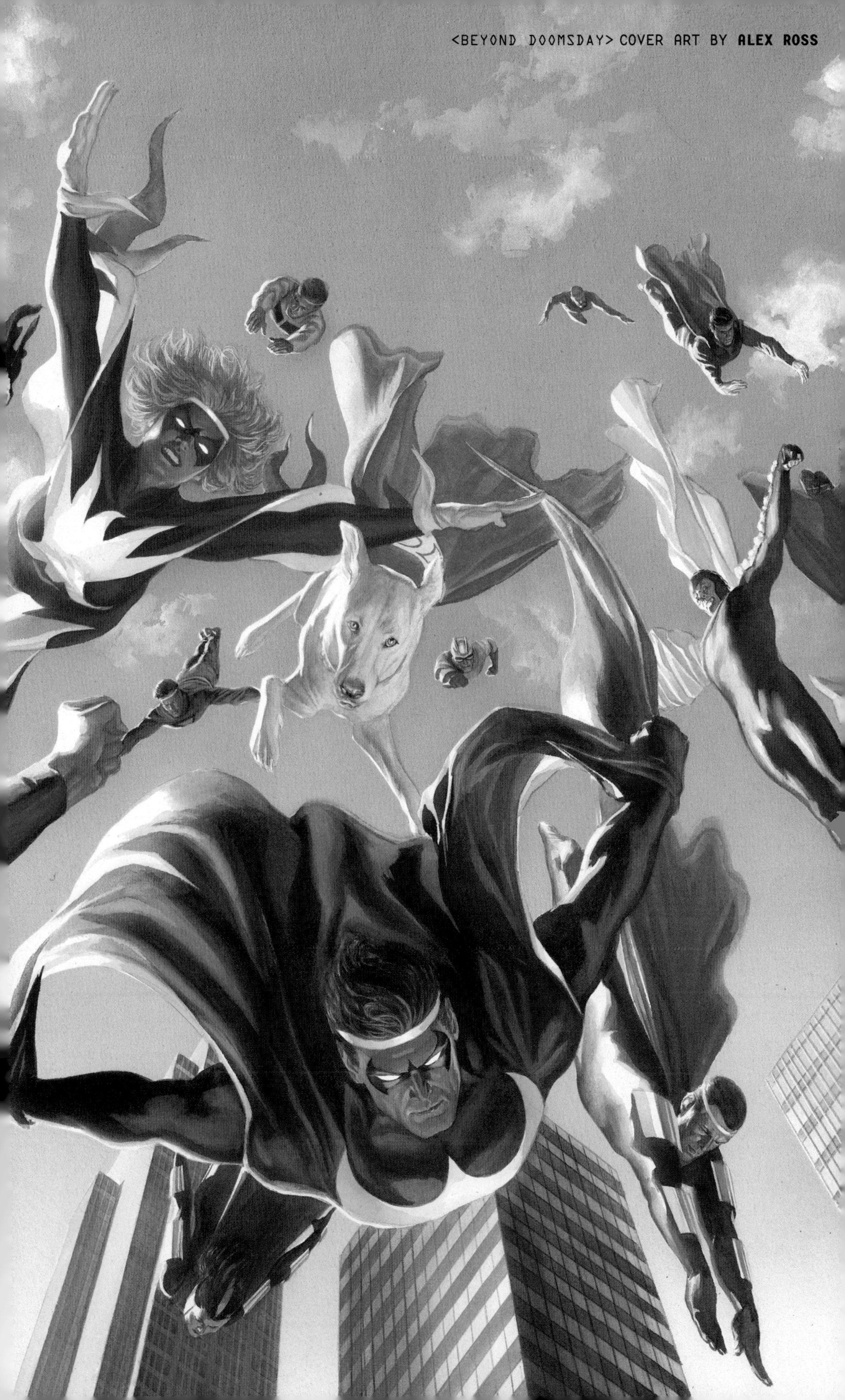

<VARIANT> COVER ART BY **STEPHANE ROU**

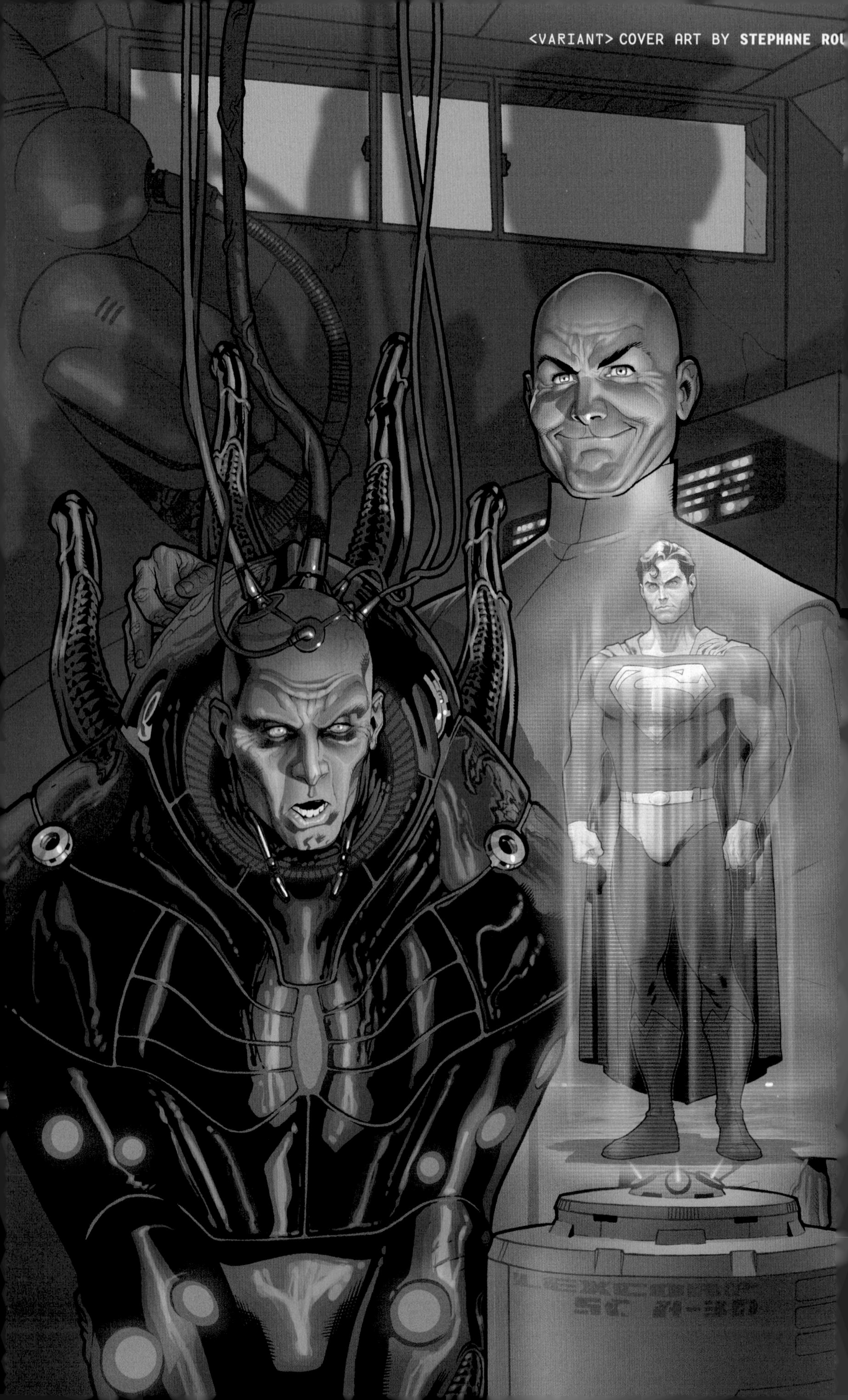

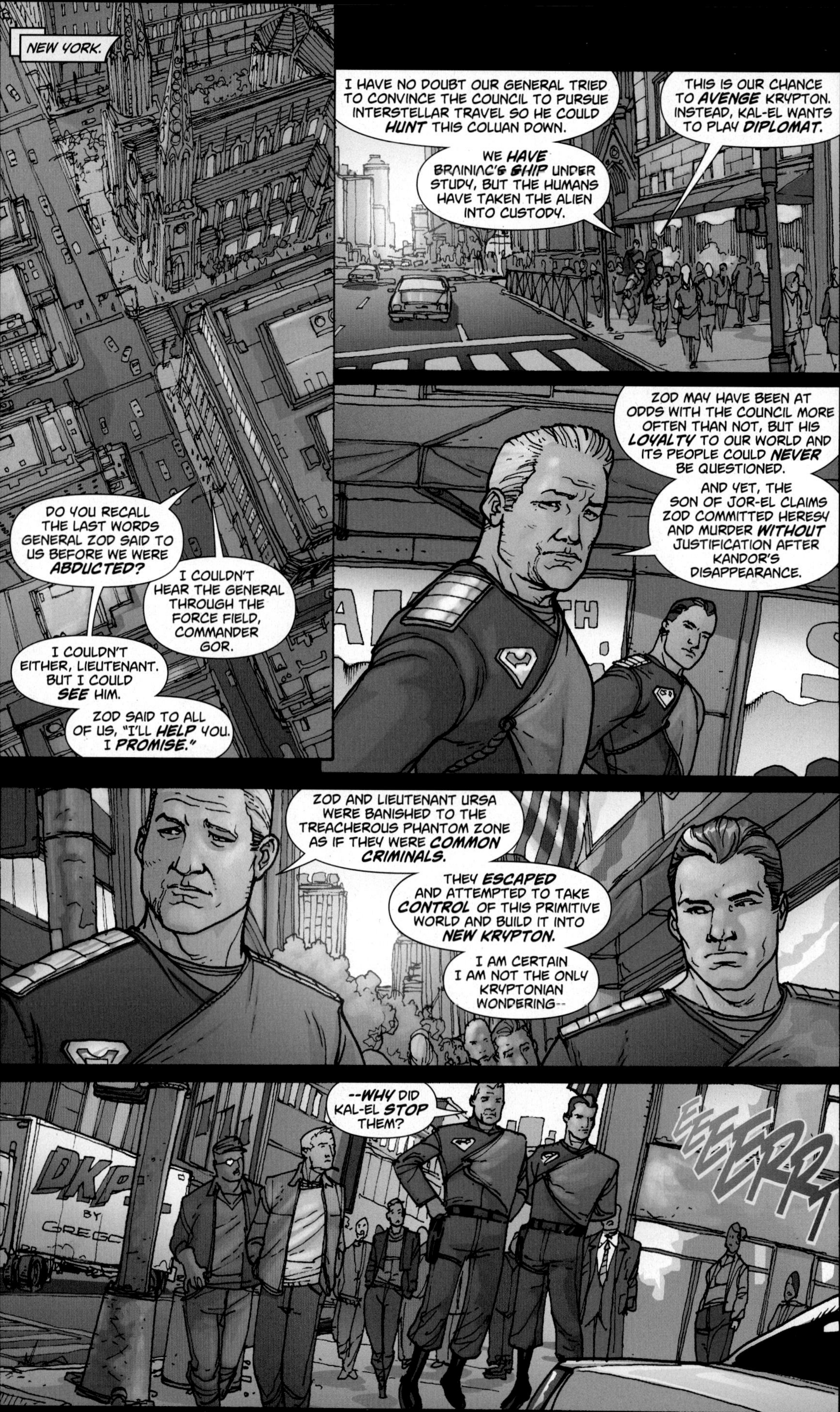
NEW YORK.
DO YOU RECALL THE LAST WORDS GENERAL ZOD SAID TO US BEFORE WE WERE ABDUCTED?
I COULDN'T HEAR THE GENERAL THROUGH THE FORCE FIELD, COMMANDER GOR.
I COULDN'T EITHER, LIEUTENANT. BUT I COULD SEE HIM.
ZOD SAID TO ALL OF US, "I'LL HELP YOU. I PROMISE."
I HAVE NO DOUBT OUR GENERAL TRIED TO CONVINCE THE COUNCIL TO PURSUE INTERSTELLAR TRAVEL SO HE COULD HUNT THIS COLUAN DOWN.
WE HAVE BRAINIAC'S SHIP UNDER STUDY, BUT THE HUMANS HAVE TAKEN THE ALIEN INTO CUSTODY.
THIS IS OUR CHANCE TO AVENGE KRYPTON. INSTEAD, KAL-EL WANTS TO PLAY DIPLOMAT.
ZOD MAY HAVE BEEN AT ODDS WITH THE COUNCIL MORE OFTEN THAN NOT, BUT HIS LOYALTY TO OUR WORLD AND ITS PEOPLE COULD NEVER BE QUESTIONED.
AND YET, THE SON OF JOR-EL CLAIMS ZOD COMMITTED HERESY AND MURDER WITHOUT JUSTIFICATION AFTER KANDOR'S DISAPPEARANCE.
ZOD AND LIEUTENANT URSA WERE BANISHED TO THE TREACHEROUS PHANTOM ZONE AS IF THEY WERE COMMON CRIMINALS.
THEY ESCAPED AND ATTEMPTED TO TAKE CONTROL OF THIS PRIMITIVE WORLD AND BUILD IT INTO NEW KRYPTON.
I AM CERTAIN I AM NOT THE ONLY KRYPTONIAN WONDERING--
--WHY DID KAL-EL STOP THEM?
EEEERRR
DKP
BY
GREG

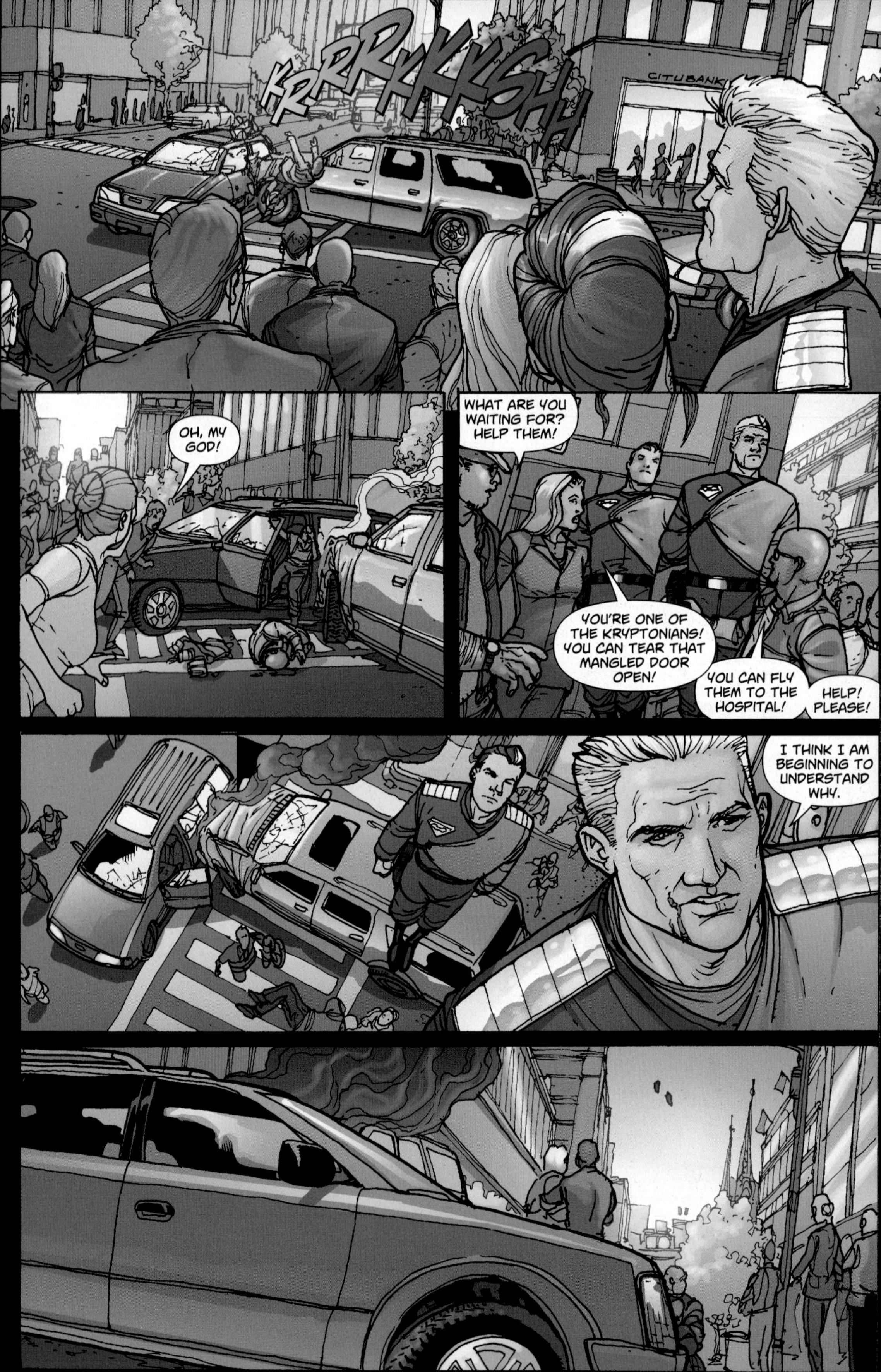
KRRRKKKSHH
CITUBANK
OH, MY GOD!
WHAT ARE YOU WAITING FOR? HELP THEM!
YOU'RE ONE OF THE KRYPTONIANS! YOU CAN TEAR THAT MANGLED DOOR OPEN!
YOU CAN FLY THEM TO THE HOSPITAL!
HELP! PLEASE!
I THINK I AM BEGINNING TO UNDERSTAND WHY.

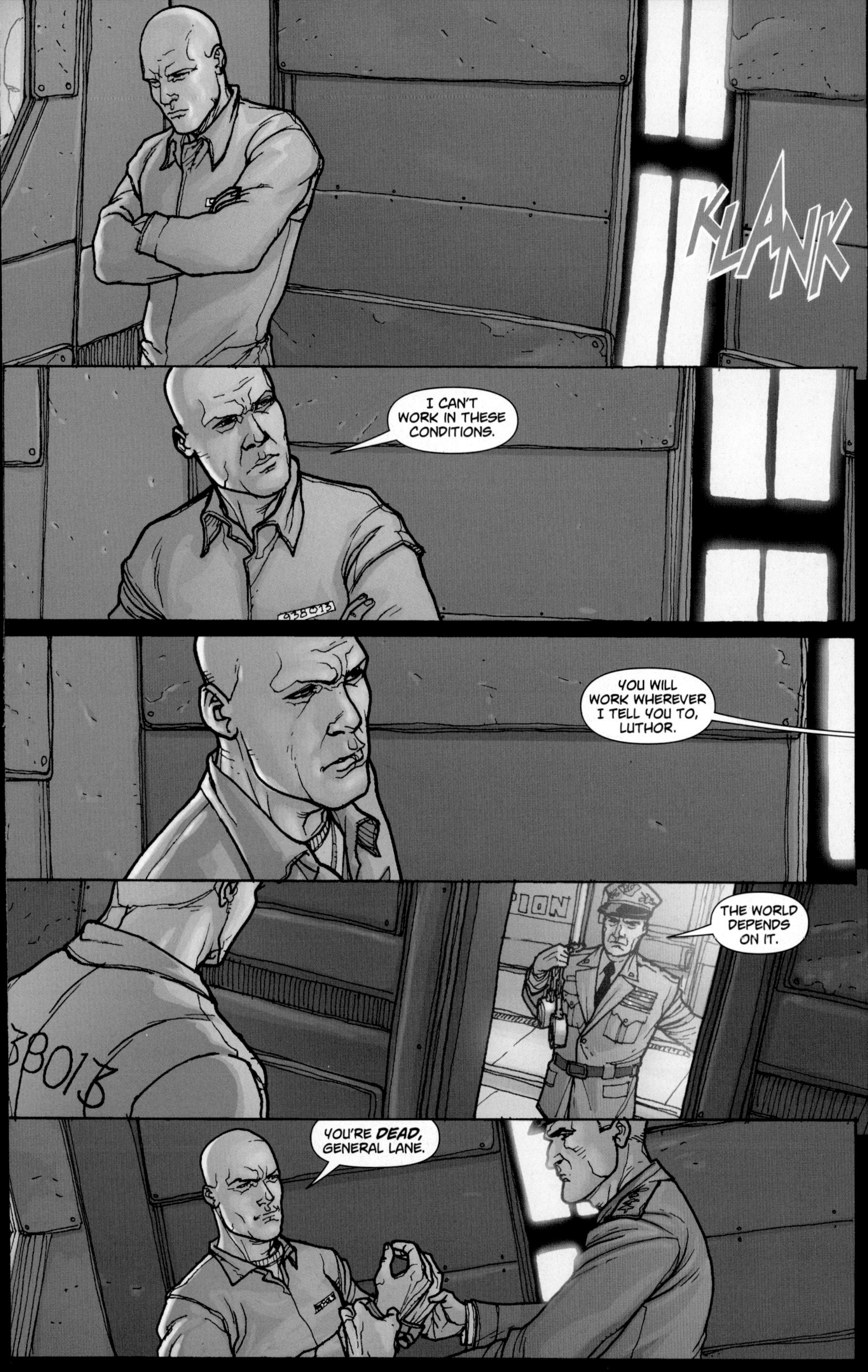
KLANK
I CAN'T WORK IN THESE CONDITIONS.
YOU WILL WORK WHEREVER I TELL YOU TO, LUTHOR.
THE WORLD DEPENDS ON IT.
YOU'RE ***DEAD,*** GENERAL LANE.

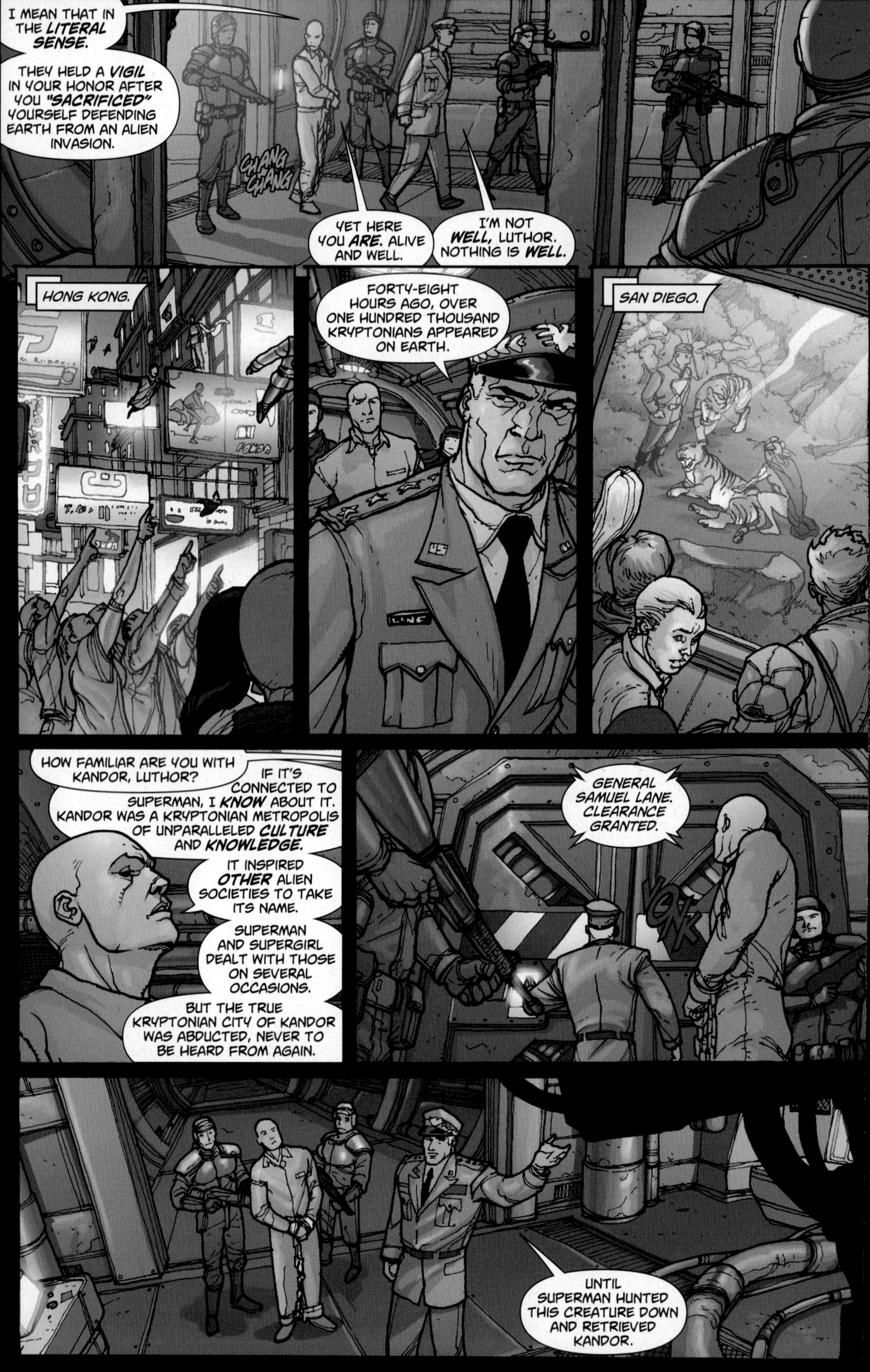
I MEAN THAT IN THE LITERAL SENSE.
THEY HELD A VIGIL IN YOUR HONOR AFTER YOU "SACRIFICED" YOURSELF DEFENDING EARTH FROM AN ALIEN INVASION.
CHANG CHANG
YET HERE YOU ARE. ALIVE AND WELL.
I'M NOT WELL, LUTHOR. NOTHING IS WELL.
HONG KONG.
FORTY-EIGHT HOURS AGO, OVER ONE HUNDRED THOUSAND KRYPTONIANS APPEARED ON EARTH.
SAN DIEGO.
HOW FAMILIAR ARE YOU WITH KANDOR, LUTHOR?
IF IT'S CONNECTED TO SUPERMAN, I KNOW ABOUT IT. KANDOR WAS A KRYPTONIAN METROPOLIS OF UNPARALLELED CULTURE AND KNOWLEDGE.
IT INSPIRED OTHER ALIEN SOCIETIES TO TAKE ITS NAME.
SUPERMAN AND SUPERGIRL DEALT WITH THOSE ON SEVERAL OCCASIONS.
BUT THE TRUE KRYPTONIAN CITY OF KANDOR WAS ABDUCTED, NEVER TO BE HEARD FROM AGAIN.
GENERAL SAMUEL LANE. CLEARANCE GRANTED.
VONK
UNTIL SUPERMAN HUNTED THIS CREATURE DOWN AND RETRIEVED KANDOR.

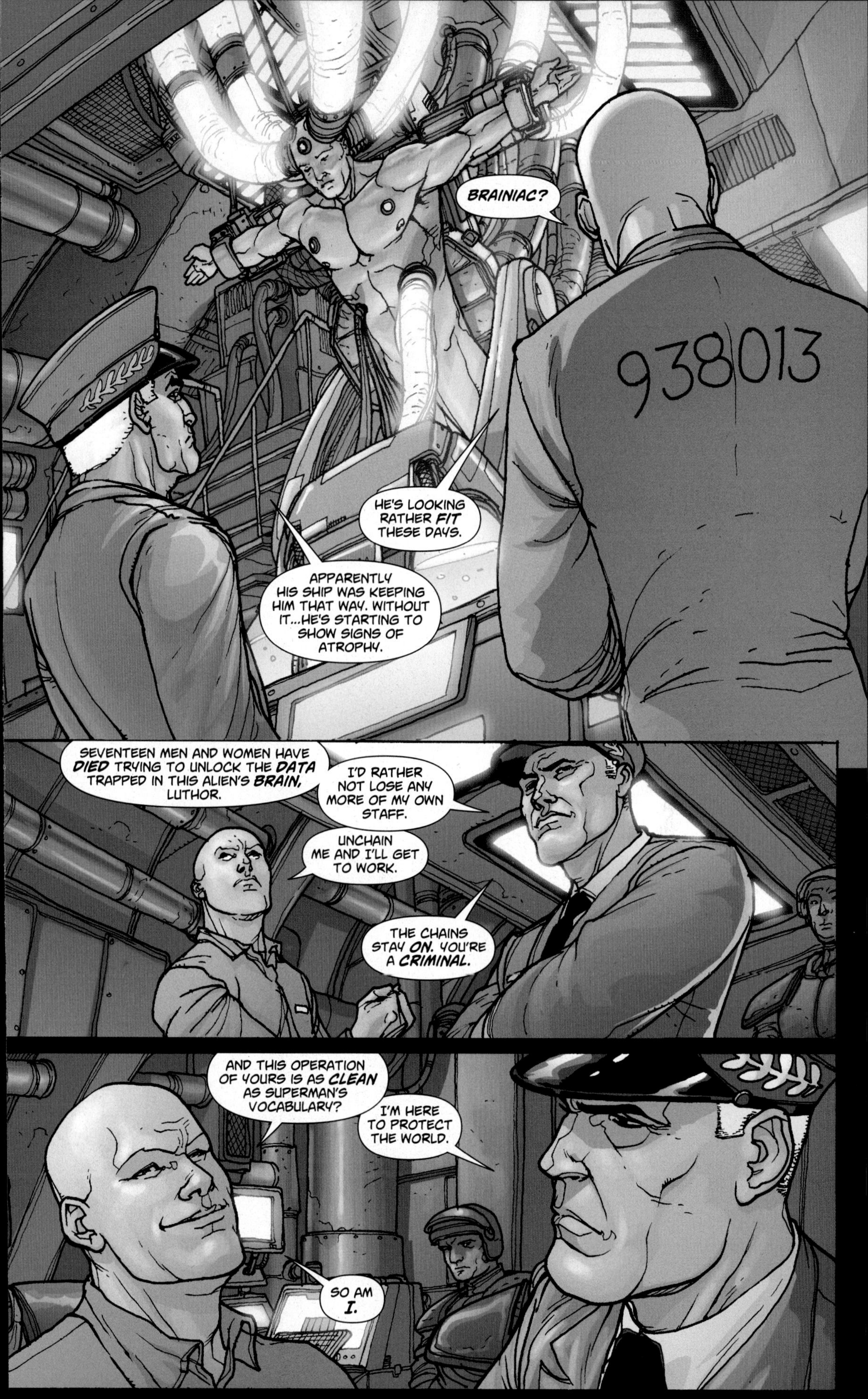
938013
BRAINIAC?
HE'S LOOKING RATHER FIT THESE DAYS.
APPARENTLY HIS SHIP WAS KEEPING HIM THAT WAY. WITHOUT IT...HE'S STARTING TO SHOW SIGNS OF ATROPHY.
SEVENTEEN MEN AND WOMEN HAVE DIED TRYING TO UNLOCK THE DATA TRAPPED IN THIS ALIEN'S BRAIN, LUTHOR.
I'D RATHER NOT LOSE ANY MORE OF MY OWN STAFF.
UNCHAIN ME AND I'LL GET TO WORK.
THE CHAINS STAY ON. YOU'RE A CRIMINAL.
AND THIS OPERATION OF YOURS IS AS CLEAN AS SUPERMAN'S VOCABULARY?
I'M HERE TO PROTECT THE WORLD.
SO AM I.

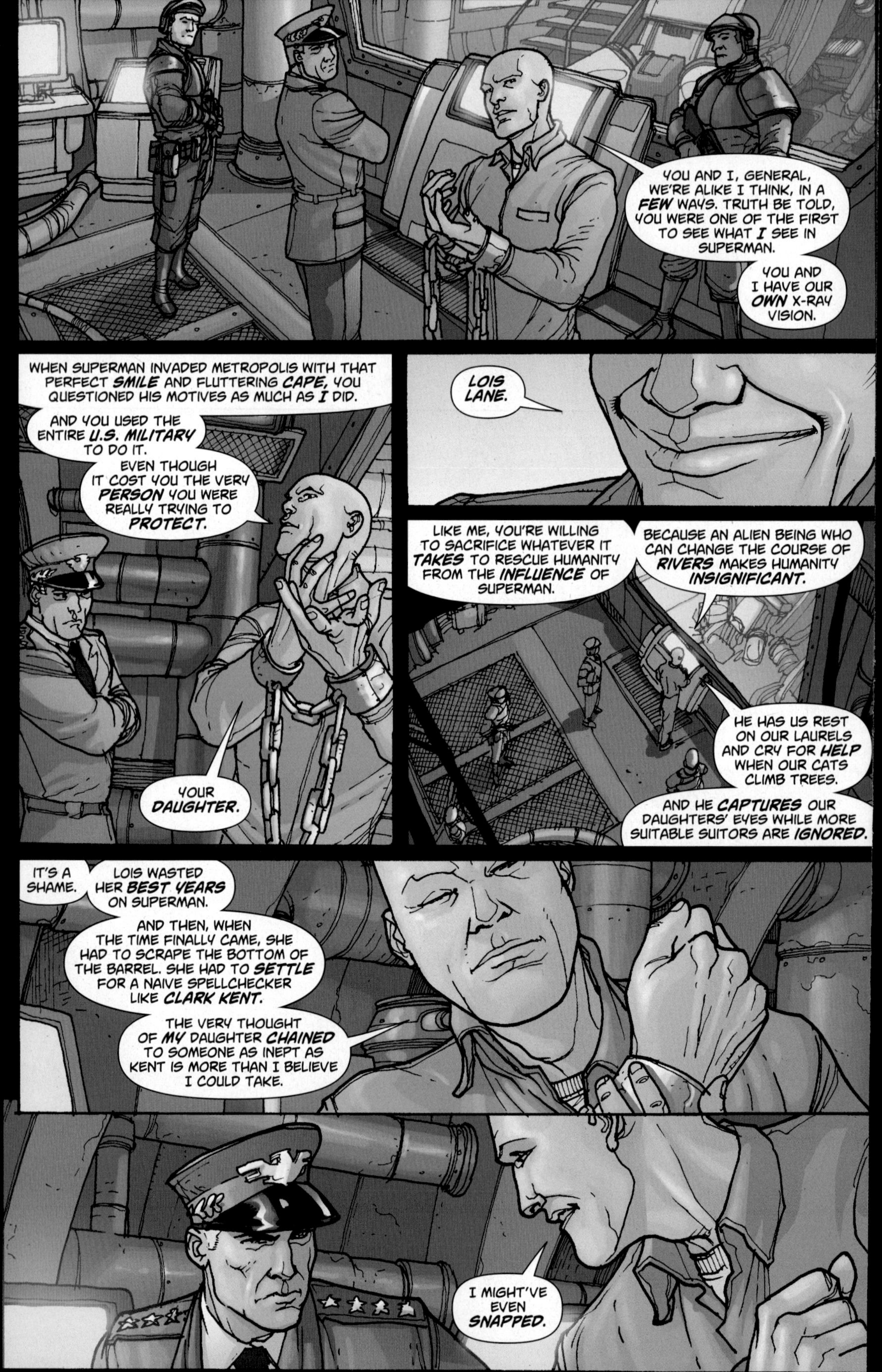
YOU AND I, GENERAL, WE'RE ALIKE I THINK, IN A FEW WAYS. TRUTH BE TOLD, YOU WERE ONE OF THE FIRST TO SEE WHAT I SEE IN SUPERMAN.
YOU AND I HAVE OUR OWN X-RAY VISION.
WHEN SUPERMAN INVADED METROPOLIS WITH THAT PERFECT SMILE AND FLUTTERING CAPE, YOU QUESTIONED HIS MOTIVES AS MUCH AS I DID.
AND YOU USED THE ENTIRE U.S. MILITARY TO DO IT.
EVEN THOUGH IT COST YOU THE VERY PERSON YOU WERE REALLY TRYING TO PROTECT.
YOUR DAUGHTER.
LOIS LANE.
LIKE ME, YOU'RE WILLING TO SACRIFICE WHATEVER IT TAKES TO RESCUE HUMANITY FROM THE INFLUENCE OF SUPERMAN.
BECAUSE AN ALIEN BEING WHO CAN CHANGE THE COURSE OF RIVERS MAKES HUMANITY INSIGNIFICANT.
HE HAS US REST ON OUR LAURELS AND CRY FOR HELP WHEN OUR CATS CLIMB TREES.
AND HE CAPTURES OUR DAUGHTERS' EYES WHILE MORE SUITABLE SUITORS ARE IGNORED.
IT'S A SHAME.
LOIS WASTED HER BEST YEARS ON SUPERMAN.
AND THEN, WHEN THE TIME FINALLY CAME, SHE HAD TO SCRAPE THE BOTTOM OF THE BARREL. SHE HAD TO SETTLE FOR A NAIVE SPELLCHECKER LIKE CLARK KENT.
THE VERY THOUGHT OF MY DAUGHTER CHAINED TO SOMEONE AS INEPT AS KENT IS MORE THAN I BELIEVE I COULD TAKE.
I MIGHT'VE EVEN SNAPPED.

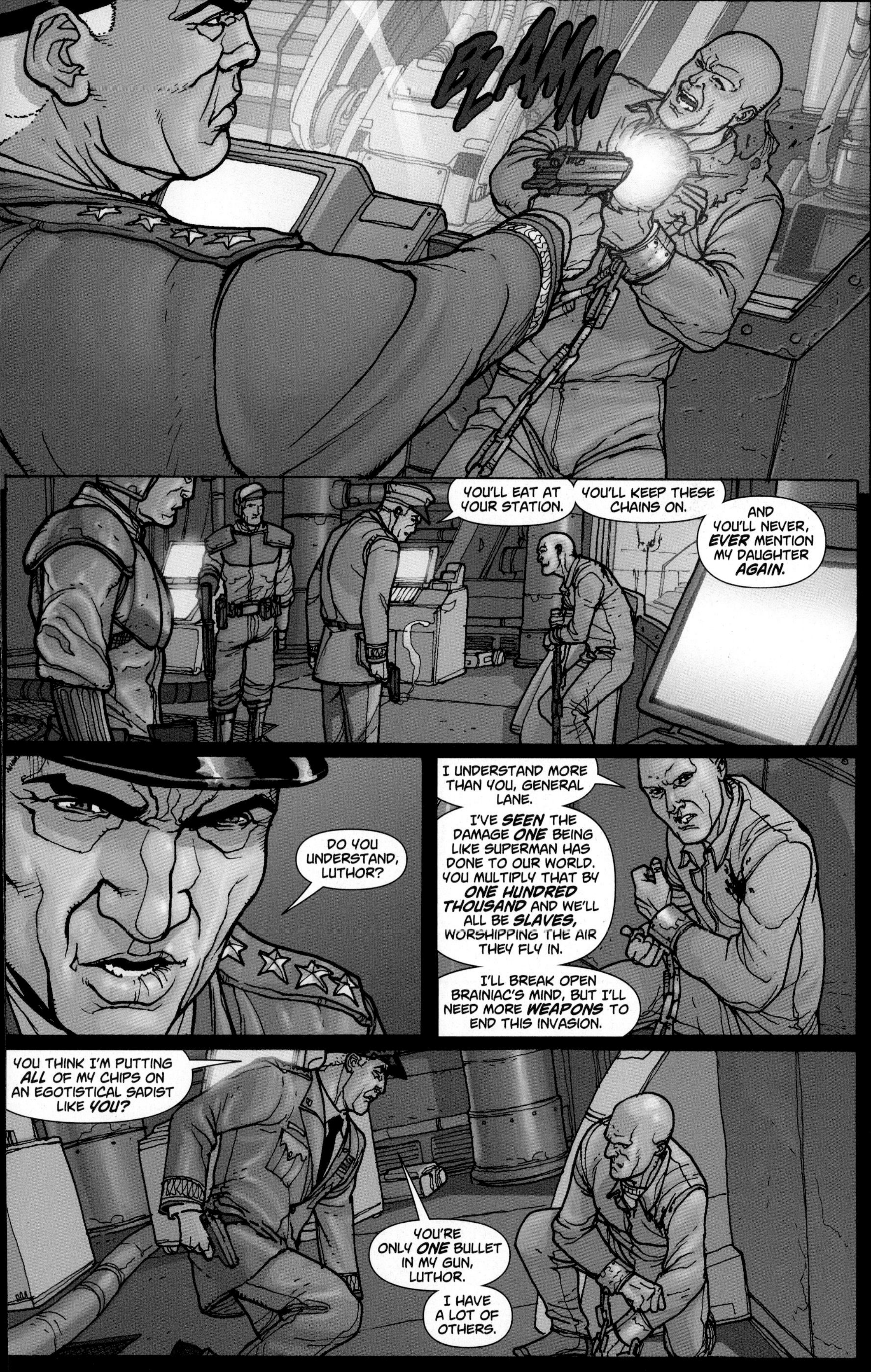
BLAMM
YOU'LL EAT AT YOUR STATION.
YOU'LL KEEP THESE CHAINS ON.
AND YOU'LL NEVER, EVER MENTION MY DAUGHTER AGAIN.
DO YOU UNDERSTAND, LUTHOR?
I UNDERSTAND MORE THAN YOU, GENERAL LANE.
I'VE SEEN THE DAMAGE ONE BEING LIKE SUPERMAN HAS DONE TO OUR WORLD. YOU MULTIPLY THAT BY ONE HUNDRED THOUSAND AND WE'LL ALL BE SLAVES, WORSHIPPING THE AIR THEY FLY IN.
I'LL BREAK OPEN BRAINIAC'S MIND, BUT I'LL NEED MORE WEAPONS TO END THIS INVASION.
YOU THINK I'M PUTTING ALL OF MY CHIPS ON AN EGOTISTICAL SADIST LIKE YOU?
YOU'RE ONLY ONE BULLET IN MY GUN, LUTHOR.
I HAVE A LOT OF OTHERS.

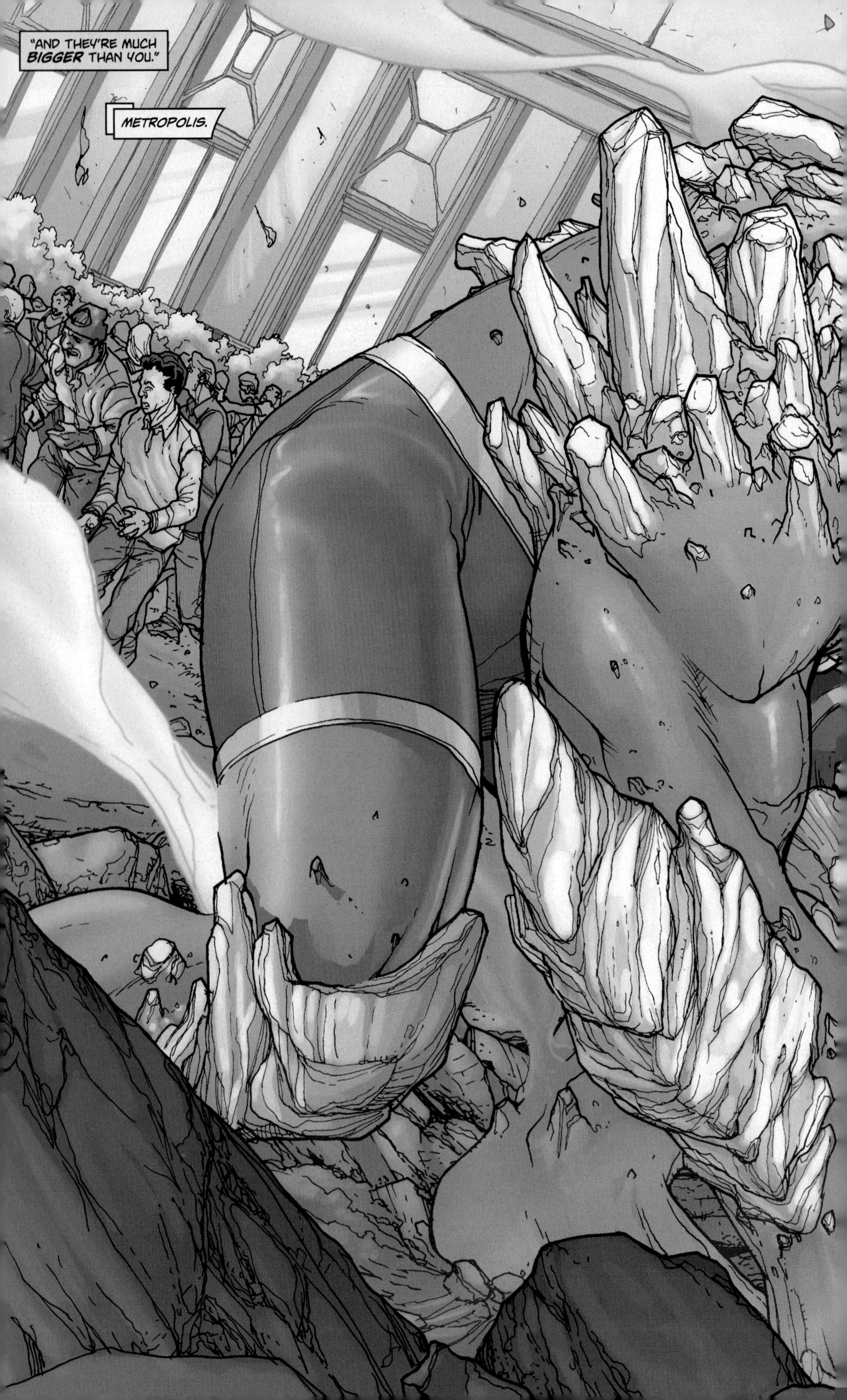
"AND THEY'RE MUCH BIGGER THAN YOU."
METROPOLIS.

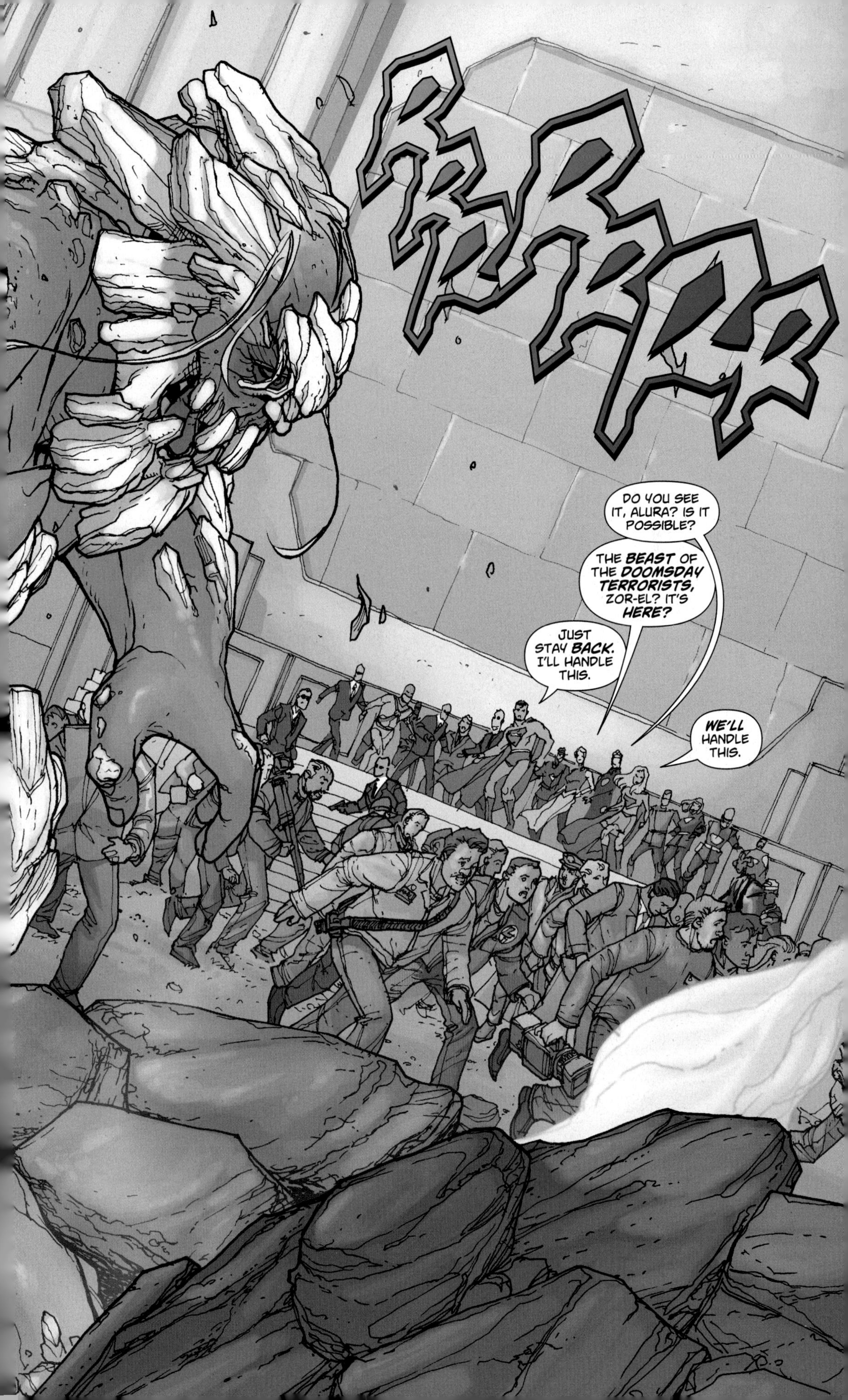
BRRRRR
DO YOU SEE IT, ALURA? IS IT POSSIBLE?
THE BEAST OF THE DOOMSDAY TERRORISTS, ZOR-EL? IT'S HERE?
JUST STAY BACK. I'LL HANDLE THIS.
WE'LL HANDLE THIS.

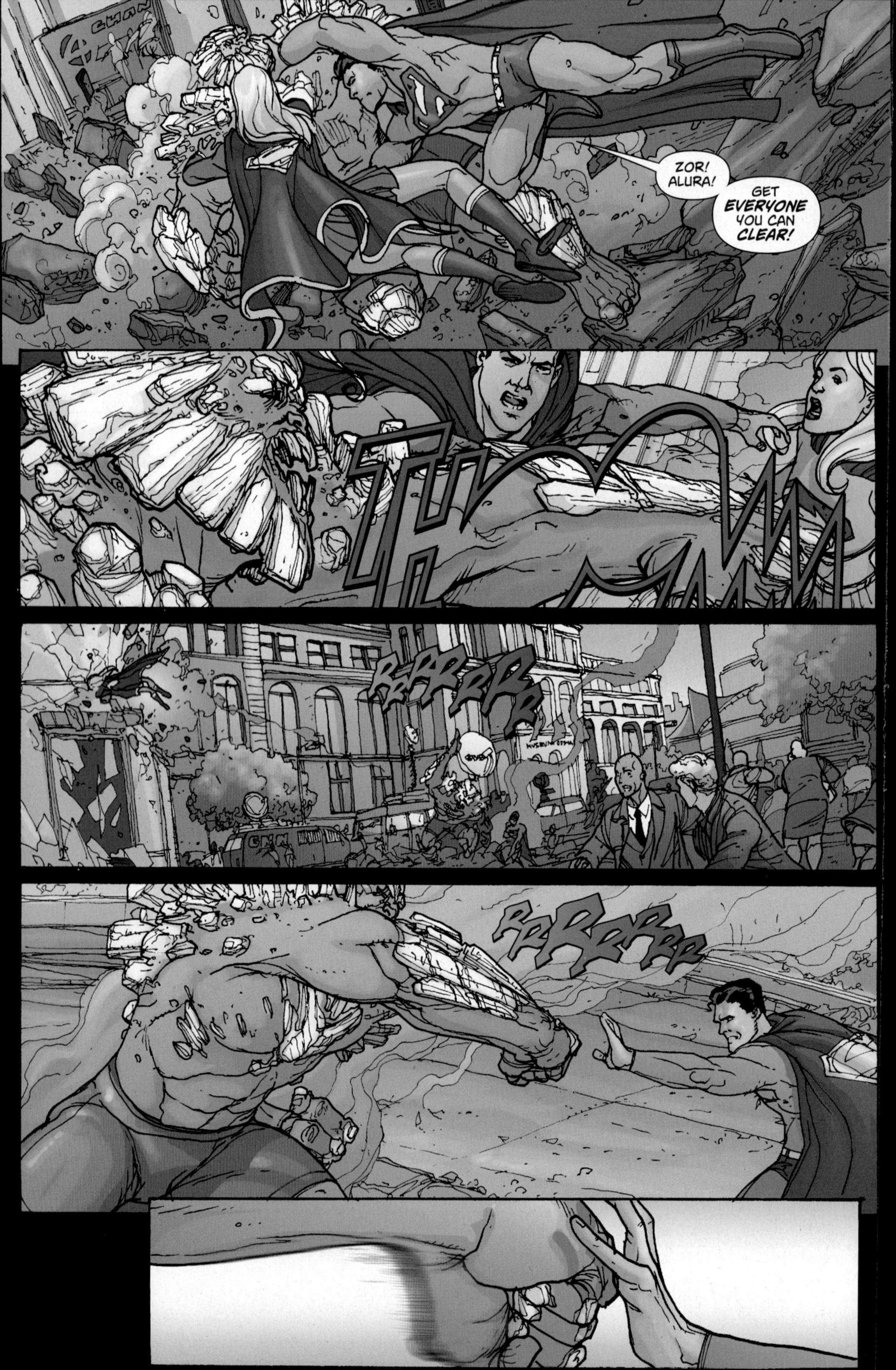
ZOR! ALURA!
GET EVERYONE YOU CAN CLEAR!

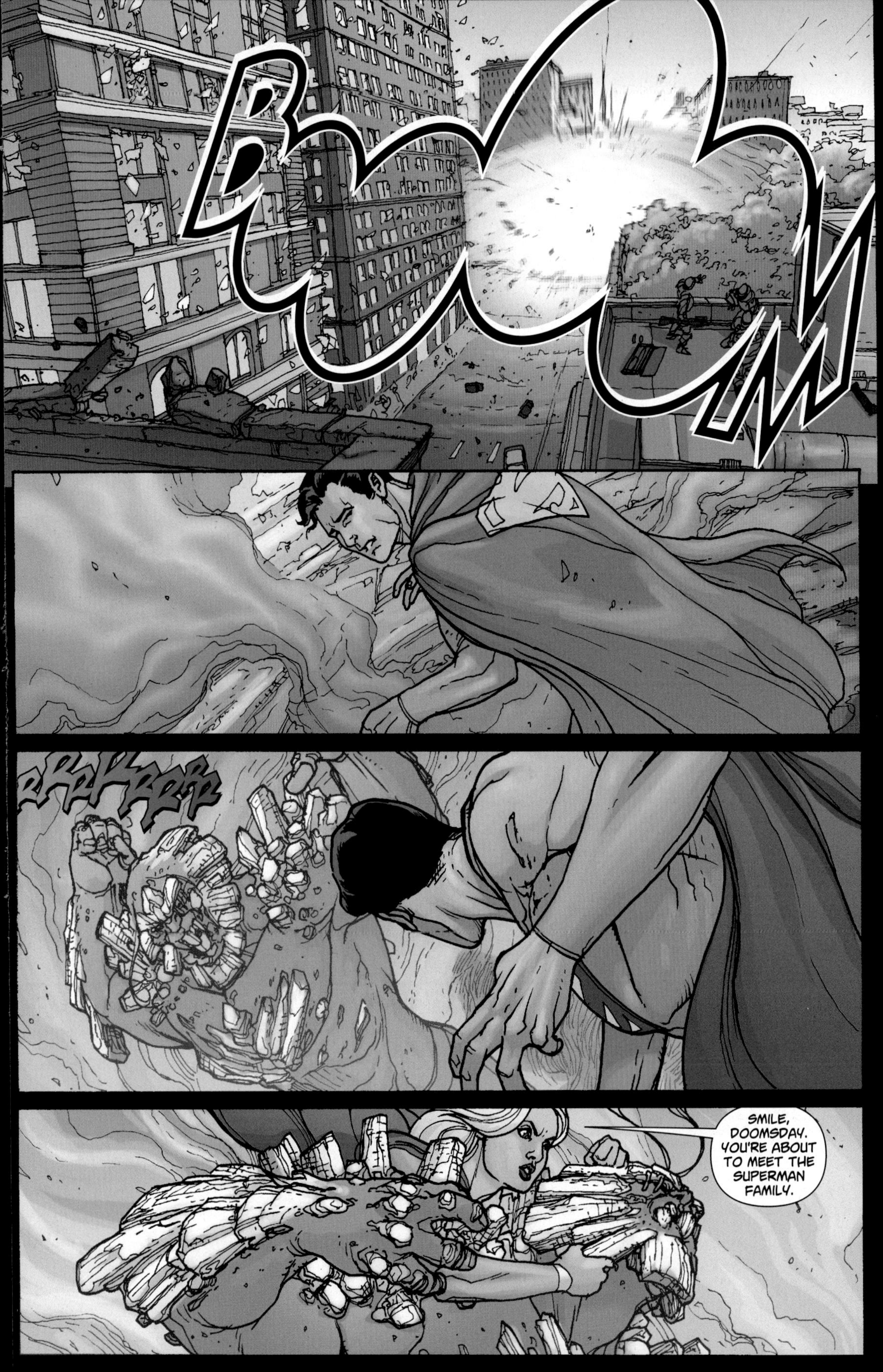
BOOM
SMILE, DOOMSDAY. YOU'RE ABOUT TO MEET THE SUPERMAN FAMILY.

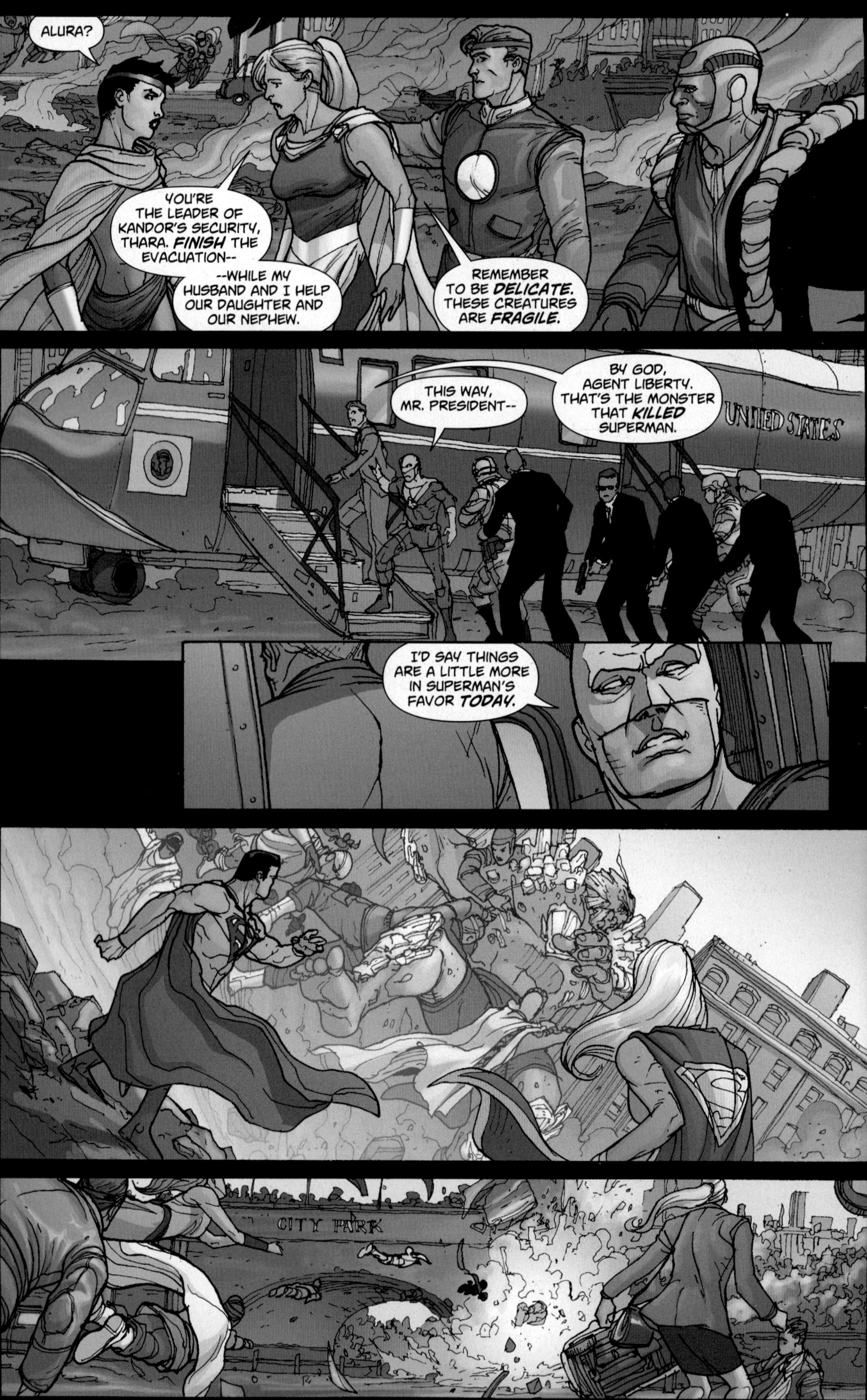
ALURA?
YOU'RE THE LEADER OF KANDOR'S SECURITY, THARA. FINISH THE EVACUATION--
--WHILE MY HUSBAND AND I HELP OUR DAUGHTER AND OUR NEPHEW.
REMEMBER TO BE DELICATE. THESE CREATURES ARE FRAGILE.
THIS WAY, MR. PRESIDENT--
BY GOD, AGENT LIBERTY. THAT'S THE MONSTER THAT KILLED SUPERMAN.
UNITED STATES
I'D SAY THINGS ARE A LITTLE MORE IN SUPERMAN'S FAVOR TODAY.
CITY PARK

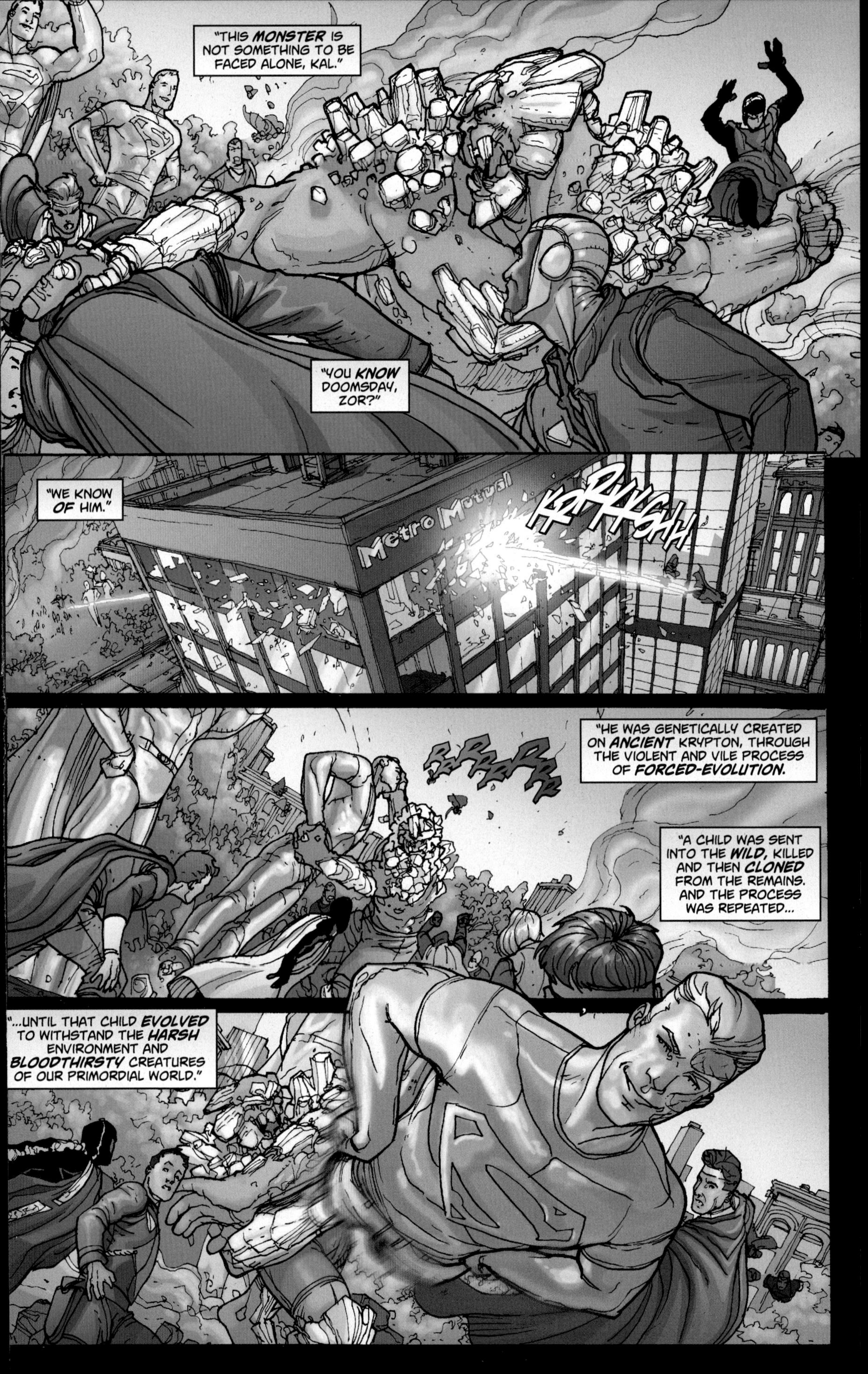
"THIS MONSTER IS NOT SOMETHING TO BE FACED ALONE, KAL."
"YOU KNOW DOOMSDAY, ZOR?"
"WE KNOW OF HIM."
Metro Mutual
KRRKKSHH
"HE WAS GENETICALLY CREATED ON ANCIENT KRYPTON, THROUGH THE VIOLENT AND VILE PROCESS OF FORCED-EVOLUTION.
"A CHILD WAS SENT INTO THE WILD, KILLED AND THEN CLONED FROM THE REMAINS. AND THE PROCESS WAS REPEATED...
"...UNTIL THAT CHILD EVOLVED TO WITHSTAND THE HARSH ENVIRONMENT AND BLOODTHIRSTY CREATURES OF OUR PRIMORDIAL WORLD."

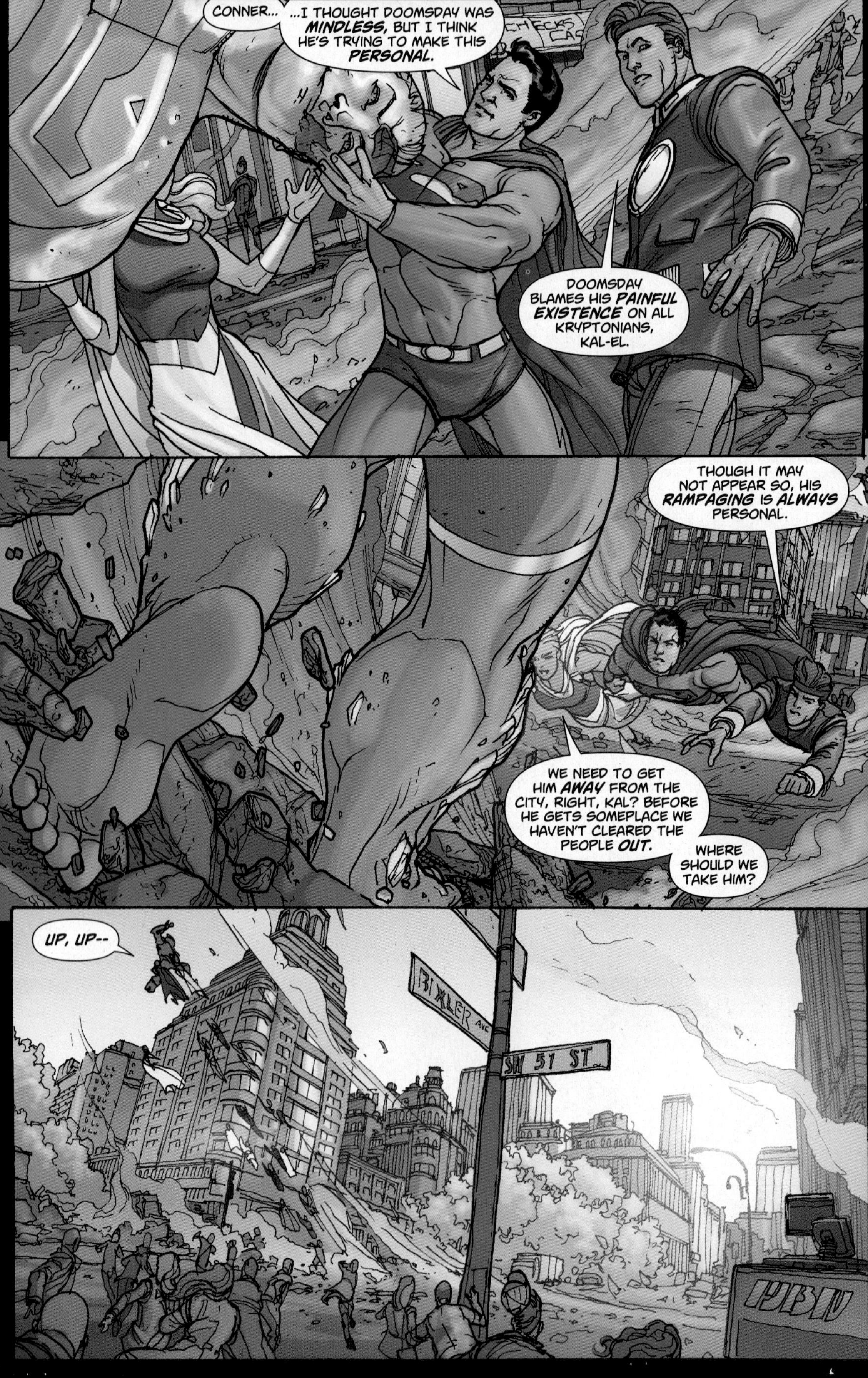
CONNER...
...I THOUGHT DOOMSDAY WAS MINDLESS, BUT I THINK HE'S TRYING TO MAKE THIS PERSONAL.
DOOMSDAY BLAMES HIS PAINFUL EXISTENCE ON ALL KRYPTONIANS, KAL-EL.
THOUGH IT MAY NOT APPEAR SO, HIS RAMPAGING IS ALWAYS PERSONAL.
WE NEED TO GET HIM AWAY FROM THE CITY, RIGHT, KAL? BEFORE HE GETS SOMEPLACE WE HAVEN'T CLEARED THE PEOPLE OUT.
WHERE SHOULD WE TAKE HIM?
UP, UP--
BIXLER AVE
SW 51 ST.
WBN

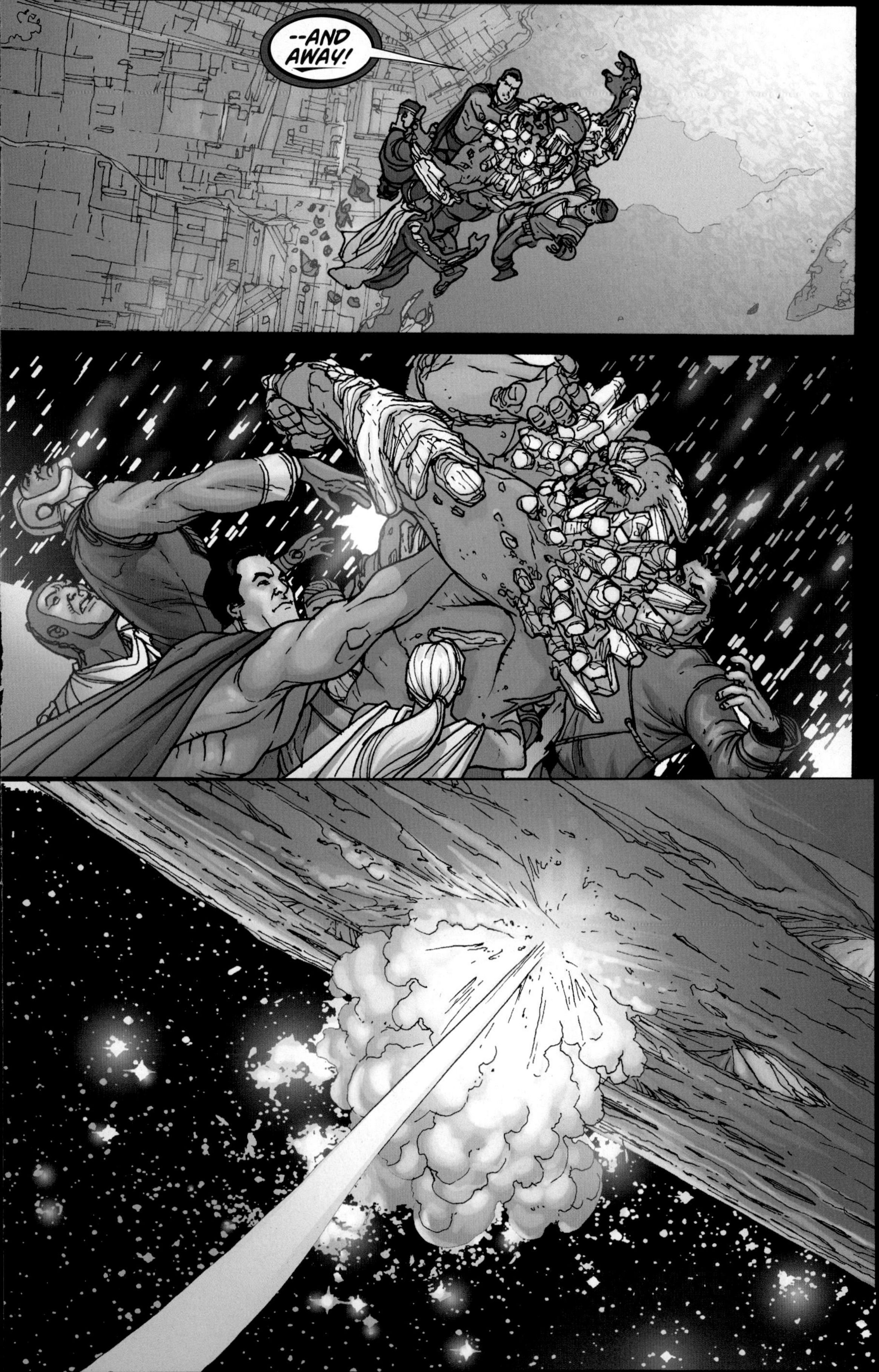
--AND AWAY!

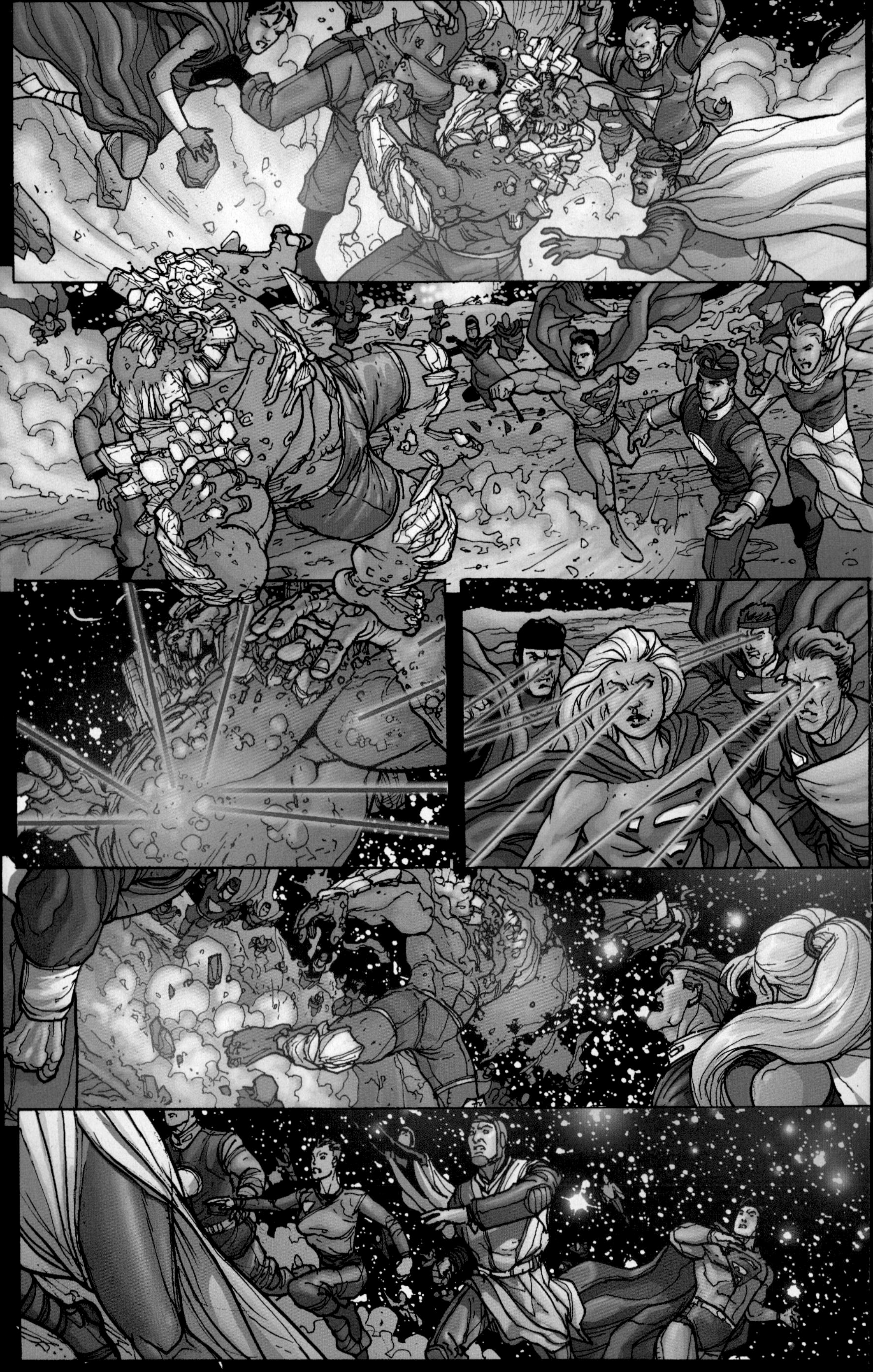

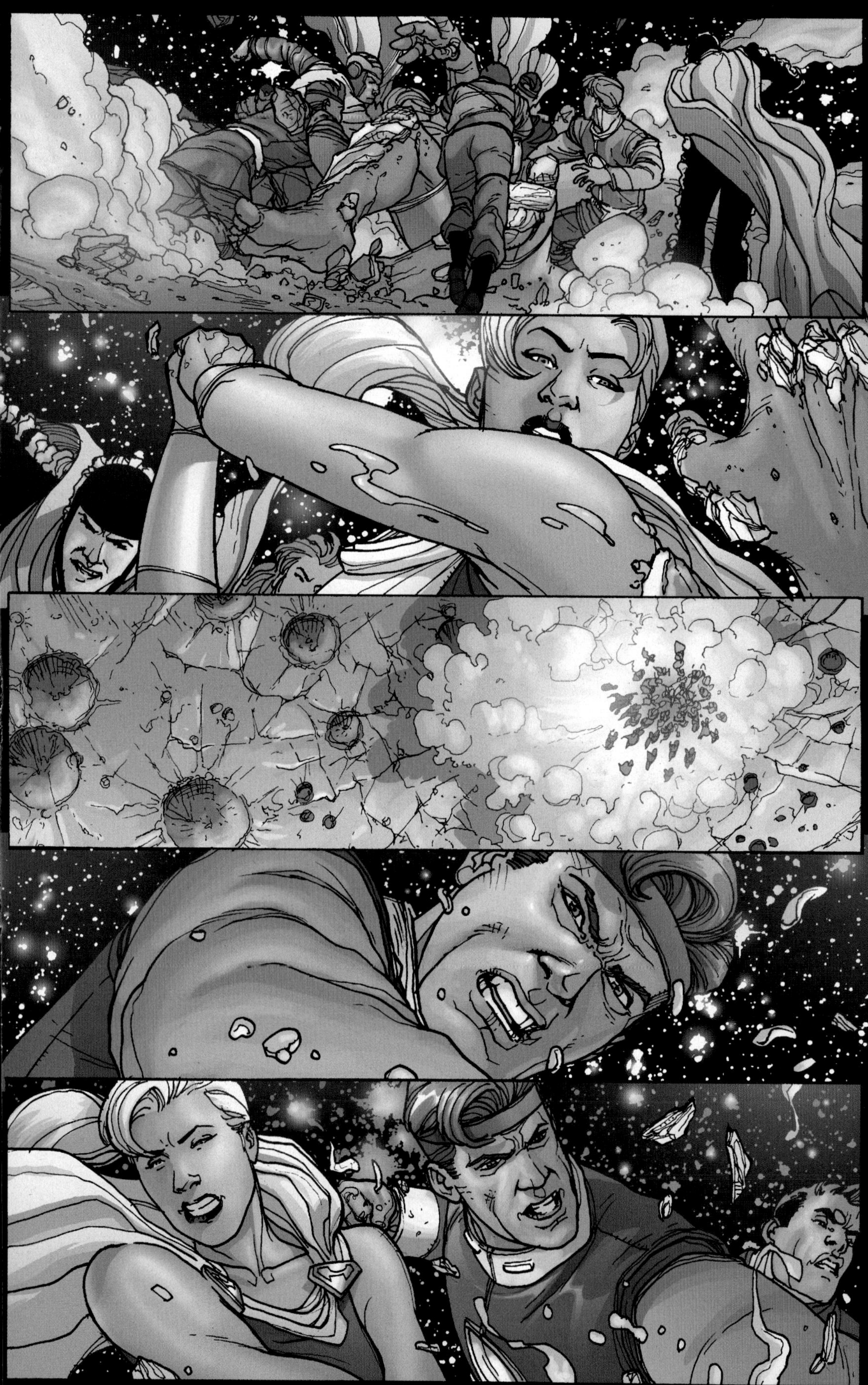

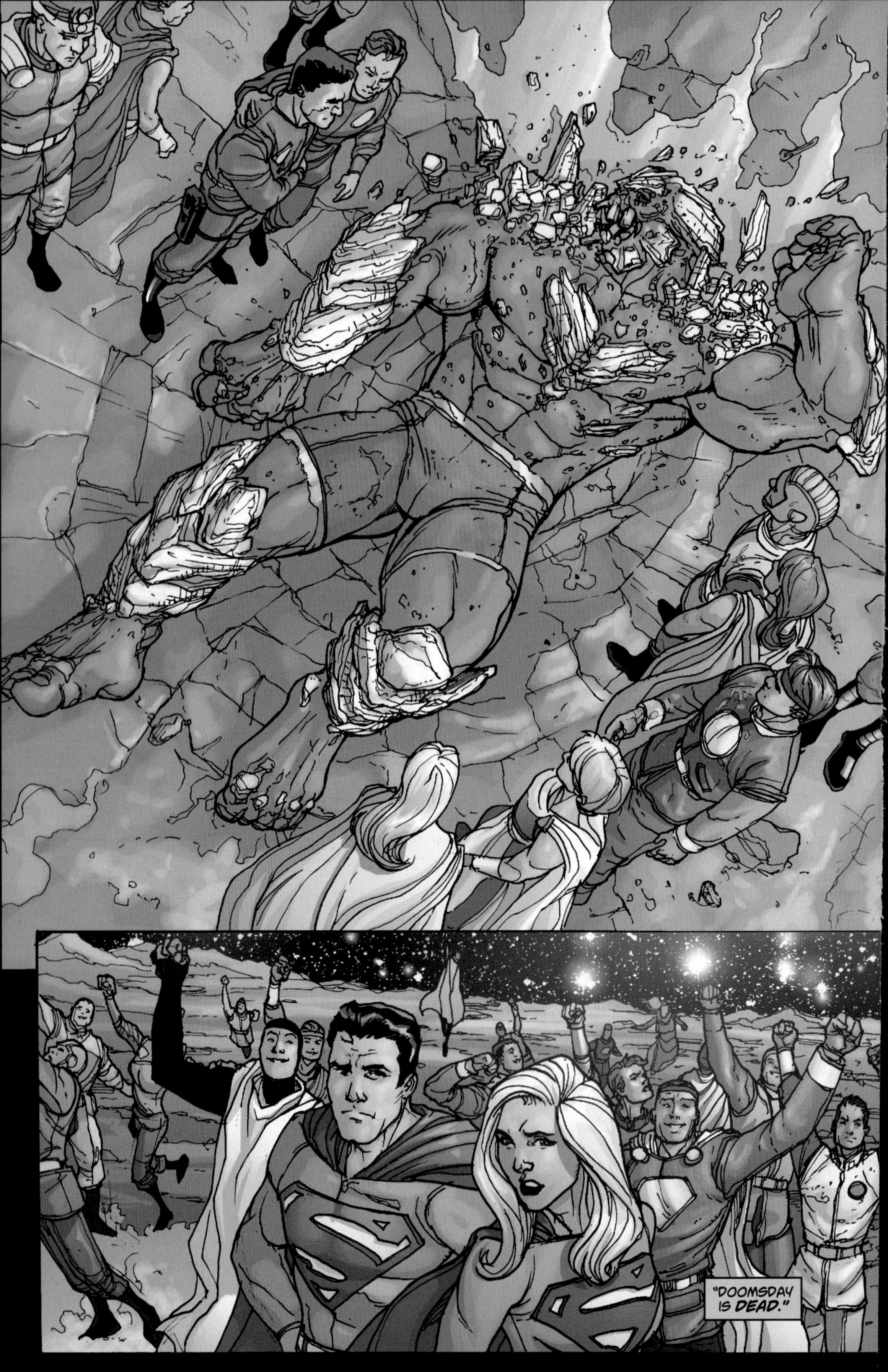
"DOOMSDAY IS DEAD."

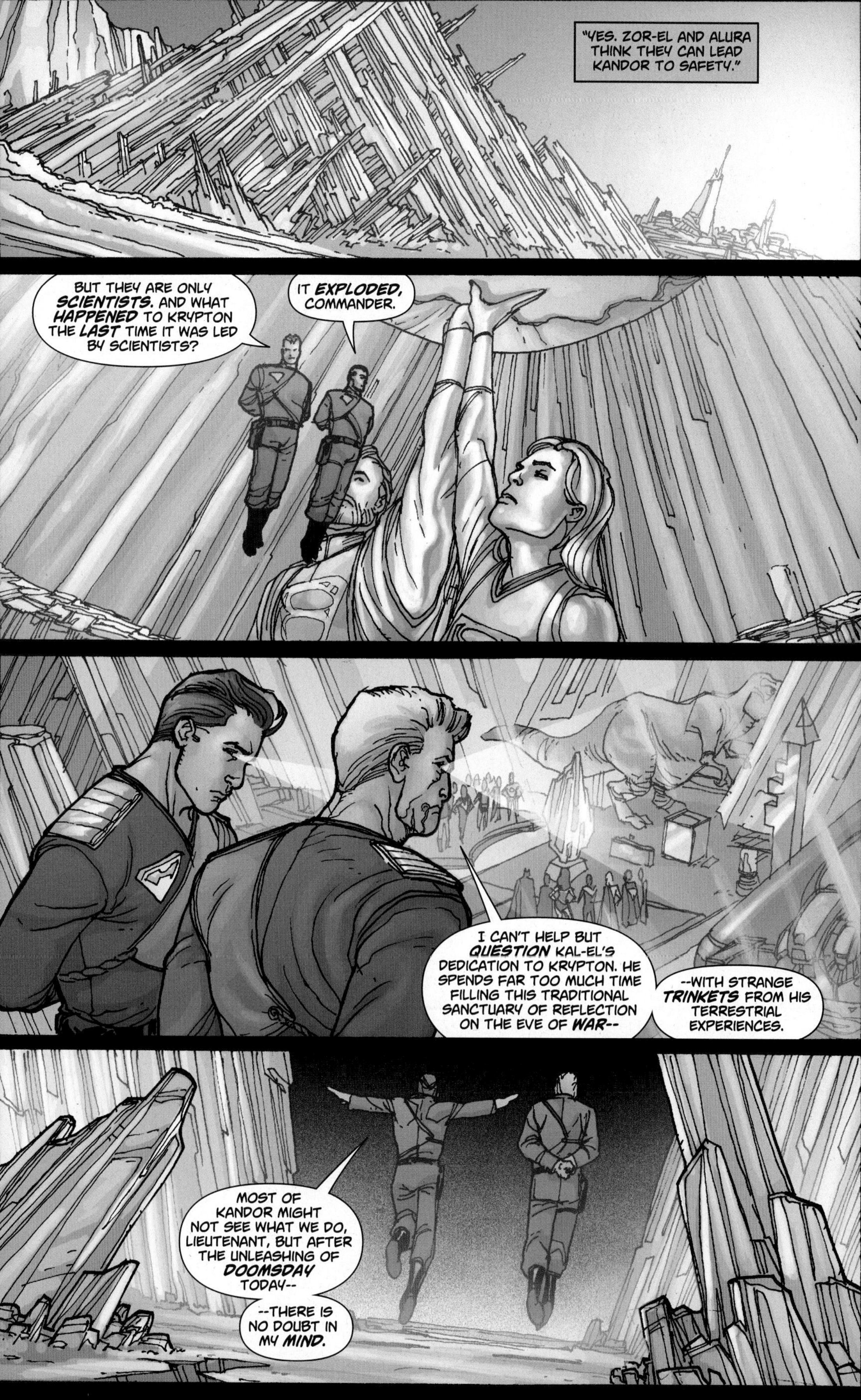
"YES. ZOR-EL AND ALURA THINK THEY CAN LEAD KANDOR TO SAFETY."
BUT THEY ARE ONLY SCIENTISTS. AND WHAT HAPPENED TO KRYPTON THE LAST TIME IT WAS LED BY SCIENTISTS?
IT EXPLODED, COMMANDER.
I CAN'T HELP BUT QUESTION KAL-EL'S DEDICATION TO KRYPTON. HE SPENDS FAR TOO MUCH TIME FILLING THIS TRADITIONAL SANCTUARY OF REFLECTION ON THE EVE OF WAR--
--WITH STRANGE TRINKETS FROM HIS TERRESTRIAL EXPERIENCES.
MOST OF KANDOR MIGHT NOT SEE WHAT WE DO, LIEUTENANT, BUT AFTER THE UNLEASHING OF DOOMSDAY TODAY--
--THERE IS NO DOUBT IN MY MIND.

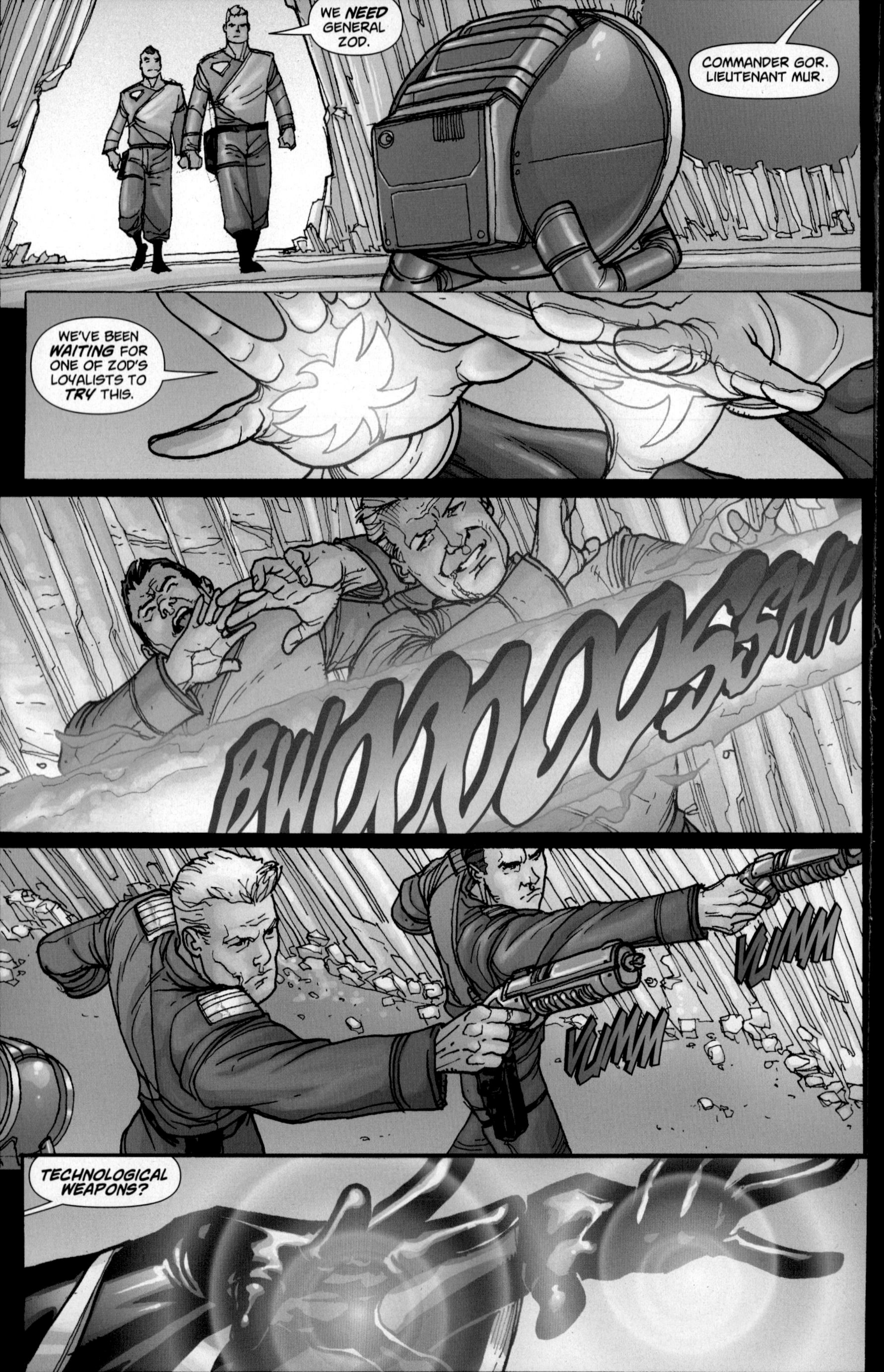

WE NEED GENERAL ZOD.
COMMANDER GOR. LIEUTENANT MUR.
WE'VE BEEN WAITING FOR ONE OF ZOD'S LOYALISTS TO TRY THIS.
BWOOOOOSSHH
VUMM
VUMM
TECHNOLOGICAL WEAPONS?

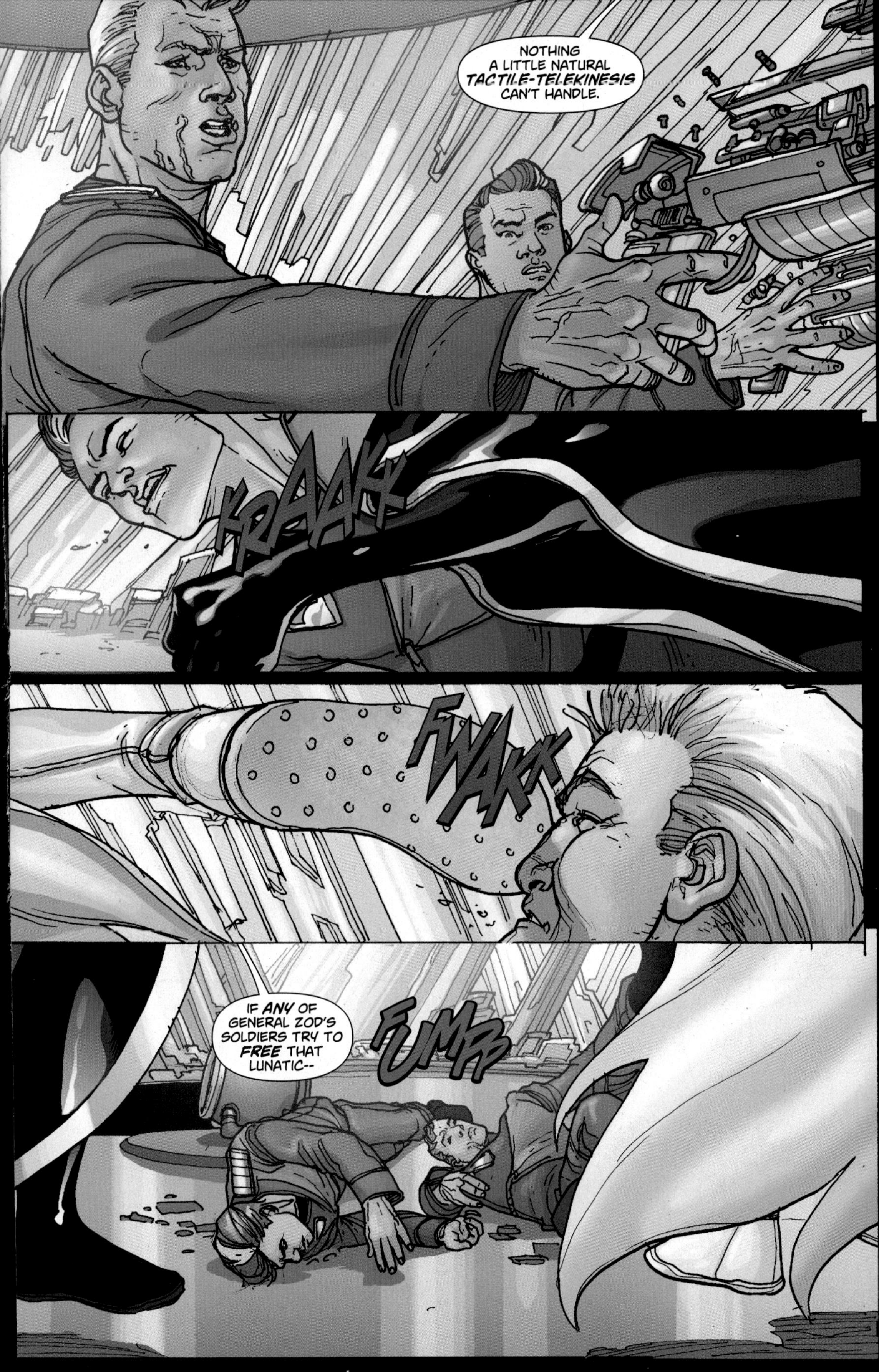
NOTHING A LITTLE NATURAL TACTILE-TELEKINESIS CAN'T HANDLE.
KRAAKK
FWAKK
IF ANY OF GENERAL ZOD'S SOLDIERS TRY TO FREE THAT LUNATIC--
FUMP

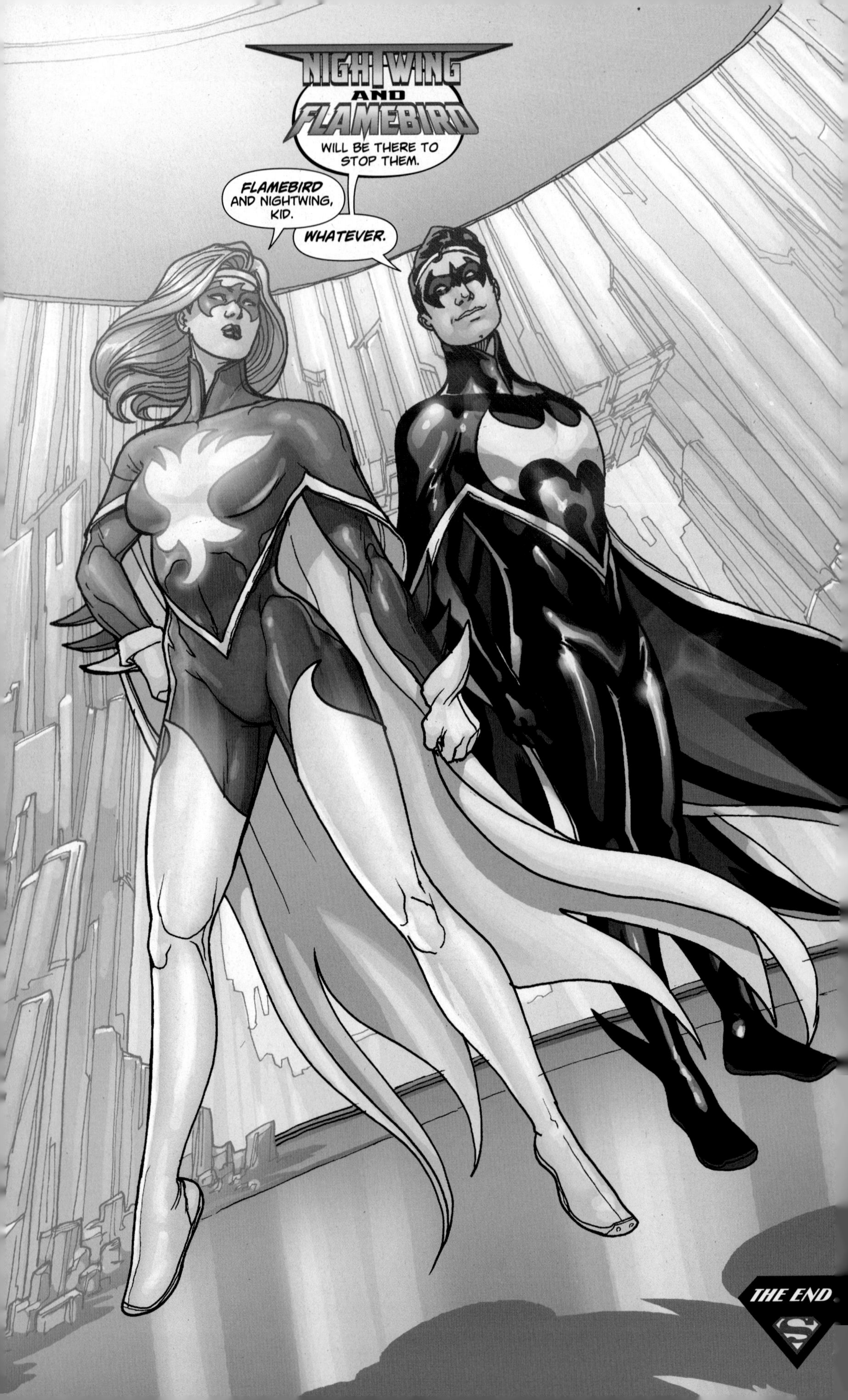
NIGHTWING AND FLAMEBIRD WILL BE THERE TO STOP THEM.
FLAMEBIRD AND NIGHTWING, KID.
WHATEVER.
THE END.

UNUSED COVER FOR <THE WORST NIGHT OF HIS LIFE> COVER ART BY **VICTOR IBÁNÉZ**

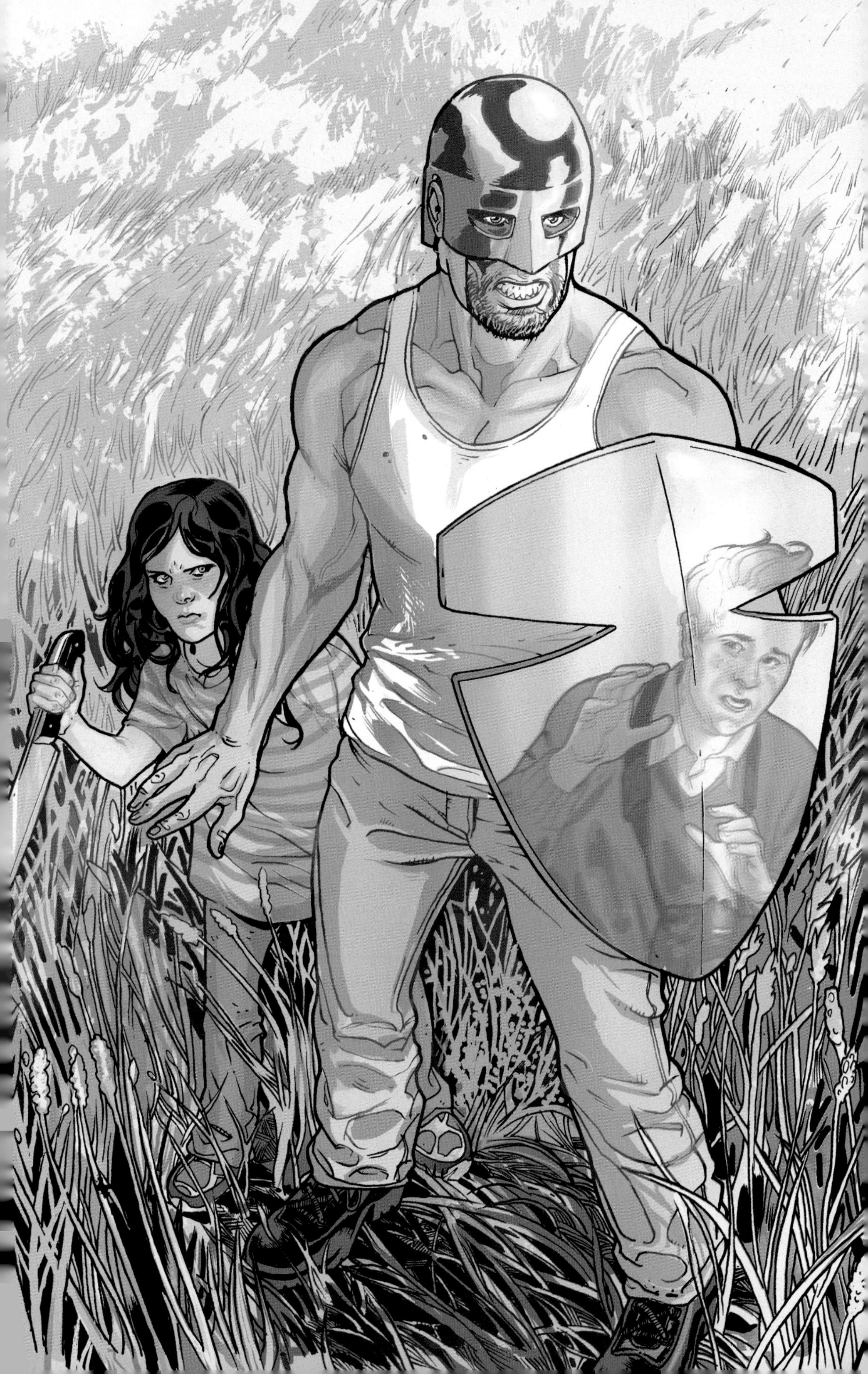

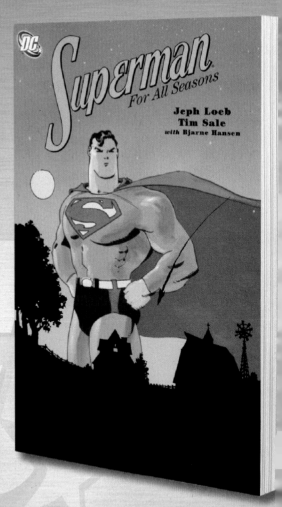